Jackson, Crockett and
Houston on the
American Frontier

Jackson, Crockett and Houston on the American Frontier

*From Fort Mims to
the Alamo, 1813–1836*

PAUL WILLIAMS

McFarland & Company, Inc., Publishers
Jefferson, North Carolina

LIBRARY OF CONGRESS CATALOGUING-IN-PUBLICATION DATA

Names: Williams, Paul, 1946 March 14– author.
Title: Jackson, Crockett and Houston on the American frontier : from
    Fort Mims to the Alamo, 1813–1836 / Paul Williams.
Description: Jefferson, North Carolina : McFarland & Company, Inc.,
    Publishers, 2016. | Includes bibliographical references and index.
Identifiers: LCCN 2016016602 | ISBN 9781476665870
    (softcover : acid free paper) ∞
Subjects: LCSH: Southwest, Old—History—19th century. | Jackson,
    Andrew, 1767–1845. | Crockett, Davy [sic], 1786–1836. | Houston,
    Sam, 1793–1863. | Creek War, 1813–1814—Campaigns. | Alamo
    (San Antonio, Tex.)—Siege, 1836 | Fort Mims (Ala.)—History—
    19th century. | Southwest, Old—Biography.
Classification: LCC F396 .W63 2016 | DDC 976/.03—dc23
LC record available at https://lccn.loc.gov/2016016602

BRITISH LIBRARY CATALOGUING DATA ARE AVAILABLE

ISBN (print) 978-1-4766-6587-0
ISBN (ebook) 978-1-4766-2521-8

Front cover: *insets, top to bottom* Andrew Jackson, David Crockett,
Sam Houston (Library of Congress); *background* Alamo photograph
© 2016 alexeys/iStock

Printed in the United States of America

McFarland & Company, Inc., Publishers
    Box 611, Jefferson, North Carolina 28640
        www.mcfarlandpub.com

Table of Contents

Preface and Acknowledgments

Like most others of my generation, my introduction to the story of the Alamo, came from the popular but fanciful 1950s Disney screen version of Davy Crockett's life. I remember being shocked to learn from a school friend that Davy, swinging ol' Betsy, had died following the final fadeout. I had just assumed he won the battle single handed, somehow.

In later years I saw other screen versions. The best, entertainment wise, was John Wayne's *The Alamo* (1960). Once again, however, liberties were taken with the facts. I still have the colorful brochure handed out at the screening, adorned with Crockett, Bowie and Travis fighting for their lives, surrounded by Mexican troops.

As a teenager, I borrowed a copy of Robert Penn Warren's *Remember the Alamo* and, fascinated with the topic, sat down and wrote a longhand précis of the whole book into a loose-leaf folder. So I guess you could say I started researching this book back in the 1960s.

In the following years, I made copious notes about Custer and the Indian Wars, and the Civil War. Ironically, my school homework suffered as a result—not so good with mathematics and French, but I was great at history. I still have a yellowed newspaper cutting about the CSS *Shenandoah*'s visit to Melbourne in 1865, an early prelude to my book *The Last Confederate Ship at Sea*. The old loose-leaf folder with notes, maps, cuttings, drawings of uniforms and flags is still (more or less) intact.

But what of Fort Mims? What was that place destroyed by an animated flaming arrow plunging into a map at the beginning of the Disney version? The Alamo was famous, but what was Fort Mims about?

Halbert and Ball's *The Creek War of 1813 and 1814*, first published in 1895 and republished in later years, was my introduction to the topic. The story of Crockett's fighting adventures started with a frontier fort surrounded and stormed, and ended with a similar event 23 years later.

This volume follows the careers of three men who came to light as the result of the massacre at Fort Mims. All three have their exponents and detractors today. Andrew Jackson, a major general of Tennessee Volunteers, had a good head start on the two younger men, and ultimately achieved the highest office—president of the United States. Sam Houston, a young officer serving under Jackson also became president, of a less auspicious state, the fledgling Republic of Texas. But the humble David Crockett (that's how he signed his name), enlisted to fight under Jackson as a private, became a folk hero in his own time and, to the general public today, is arguably the best known of the three due to his famous death at the Alamo.

1

Jackson, however, having become president of the U.S.A., has left the most tangible evidence of his illustrious career. Despite some opposition, his image still adorns the 20 dollar bill, and his home, the Hermitage, is a prime Tennessee tourist attraction. The recreated defenses south of New Orleans mark his greatest military triumph, the defeat of the British in 1815. For Crockett and Houston, the shrine of the Alamo and the San Jacinto battlefield are the most visible reminders today.

Andrew Jackson, Davy Crockett and Sam Houston were all famous in their own day and knew each other face to face. Houston, a protégé of Jackson, befriended Crockett despite the bear hunter's abiding hatred of Old Hickory, as Jackson was known. The general had helped Houston rise to become governor of Tennessee, earning his undying devotion along the way. But Houston and Jackson had their differences. Houston had lived with and befriended the Cherokees, while Jackson harbored total contempt for native Americans, whatever the tribe. Crockett too was appalled by Jackson's removal of Indians from ancestral lands, calling it a "wicked, unjust measure." Perhaps this was the bond between the educated and articulate Houston and the bear hunting Crockett, who could only write in a rudimentary style, and spoke in a chatty, backwoods kind of way. Perhaps Crockett charmed Houston with his wit and style, as he did voters who elected him first to the Tennessee Legislature, then as a congressman of the United States.

The three lives were intermeshed and each had his part to play in the fight for Texas. Old Hickory was the first head of state to recognize the new republic, Crockett added his luster to the glorious stand at the Alamo, and Houston, the avenging angel, brought Santa Anna to bay at San Jacinto and won independence for the Republic of Texas.

The author, sword in hand, defends the Alamo against the Mexican hordes, ca. 1956 (author's collection).

I would like to thank a number of helpful organizations, including the United States Information Service, which posted me books on loan back in the 1960s, including *Remember the Alamo*. Those of more recent years include the Library of Congress, Alabama Department of Archives and History, Georgia Department of Archives, University of Texas, Galveston and Texas History Center, San Antonio Public Library, Texas State Library and Archives Commission, San Jacinto Museum of History, and the Daughters of the Republic of Texas Library at the Alamo. Also, I would like to thank those who have paved the way with their own research and separate books about Fort Mims, the Alamo, Davy Crockett, Sam Houston and Andrew Jackson.

Finally, I would like to thank my wife Roz, a fellow history buff, writer and filmmaker who has enjoyed the journey, and watching Alamo movies, despite my historical nit-picking along the way.

Note: The spelling and grammar in quotations from the period are often incorrect but so numerous that the customary "sic" has been excluded. The reader will understand.

Prologue: Burnt Corn Creek

In July of 1813 a large party of Creek, or Muscogee, Indians rode north along the rough Wolf Trail in Spanish West Florida. They had just procured gunpowder and other supplies from the Spanish settlement of Pensacola. Once back over the border into American territory, they splashed their heavily laden packhorses across the ford on Burnt Corn Creek. The shallow stream wound its way through the canebrakes, longleaf pines and swamp cottonwoods in country that would later become part of southern Alabama.

> Fair Alabama's Forest Land,
> In its primeval verdure drest,
> With waving woods, and rivers grand,
> And mountains that like giants stand
> To guard its pictured valley's rest[1]

The party's leader was Peter McQueen, or Talmuches Hadjo, a mixed-blood Creek. White settlers of Mississippi Territory often intermarried with Indians, their numerous offspring either following the native way of life, or that of the American whites. McQueen's party were of the Redstick faction, so-called for their red-daubed war clubs, a primary weapon for hand-to-hand combat. There had been conflict within the Creek nation but, despite being vehemently opposed to expanding American influence, an uneasy peace still existed between the Redsticks and the whites.

Around midday, the travelers stopped to rest and eat. Burnt Corn Creek and a nearby spring provided a suitable place to set up camp. The Indians dismounted, fires were lit and food prepared. They relaxed and chatted in various groups as smoke from cooking fires wafted listlessly into the summer sky.

A cry was heard. A ragged volley of shots rang out. The dismayed Creeks turned to see a force of 180 American militia galloping to the attack. The citizen soldiers had opened fire before dismounting, their aim inaccurate as a result.[2] The Creeks leapt for their muskets, bows and arrows, and returned fire. This briefly stalled the assault, but too disorganized for a proper defense, packhorses and campsite were abandoned as they beat a hasty retreat. Colonel James Caller led the pursuit as the Indians fled in wild confusion. They took refuge in the tall, profuse cane along the stream which, with a haze of gun smoke, provided an effective cover.

Then the lax discipline of the part-time soldiers came into play. Most halted on the captured campsite; much more profitable to seize packhorses laden with valuable munitions and supplies than waste time pursuing a defeated foe.

"Fair Alabama's Forest Land," from Halbert and Ball's *The Creek War of 1813 and 1814*, published 1895.

But the concealed fugitives paused to look back. Seeing the sparse number of militia still confronting them, they quickly regrouped. Moving back, the warriors reloaded, then opened fire. "A portion of them assembled in those reed-brakes," recalled Lieutenant Patrick May, "and opened a brisk fire on each of our flanks, and were annoying us greatly, while from their conceal'd situation, we could do them little or no injury. Our situation you will perceive, was not a pleasant one."[3]

Those militiamen still in the Redstick camp, preoccupied with the captured packhorses, were astonished to see their own men now in retreat. The vengeful Creeks dashed forward with musket, bow and club, uttering wild war whoops as they went. Colonel Caller rode amidst his men vainly calling them to rally but, with no success, ordered a retreat to the base of a nearby hill. Here he hoped to regroup, but in the confusion many assumed there was a full retreat. Still driving the packhorses, most struck out through the woods towards home. Colonel Caller, mixed-blood Captain Dixon Bailey and other officers managed to rally about 80 men to form a firing line in sparse woods at the base of the hill. Here a somewhat disorganized defense was fought.

Dr. Thomas Holmes later recalled first hand accounts: "Towards the Close of the fight Col Callier dispatched Capt Baily to order Col McGrew to come to their relief & him & his men refused to comply.... Col Callier has been blamed for this battle, but he acted bravely and deserved great credit for he was long exposed to fire from the swamp.... McGrew & his party were to blame."[4]

Fighting amidst trees, reeds and canes, confused skirmishes, disjointed charges and retreats by both sides took place. "I discovered an Indian some 50 yds from me in the reeds, with his gun pointed at me," recalled Patrick May, "I raised and cock'd mine, and we fired simultaneously. His ball struck my gun about an inch in front of the lock....

I do not know whether my adversary sustained any injury or not—he fell back at the firing of the guns & I saw him no more."

The firing continued for about an hour amidst gun smoke drifting through the trees. Most bullets missed their targets, but Militiaman Elijah Glass, standing behind a kneeling companion, was struck in the chest. He dropped in the grass and died where he fell.

Captain Samuel Dale felt the thud of a musket ball in his left side. Deflected by a rib, it shot round beneath his skin and lodged near his spine. "I vomited a good deal of blood," he recalled, "and felt easier, and one of my men reloaded my rifle for me."[5]

With most militia having fled the field, those remaining began to fall back. But this quickly turned into a disorderly rout. Many horses had already been taken by those in retreat, and others had fallen into Creek hands. This included the mounts of Colonel Caller and Major Wood. The militiamen grasped any available mount, some riding double, while others fled on foot.

Patrick May recalled, "We had proceeded but a short distance when Lieut. Creagher (who was at my side) was shot down. On falling he exclaimed 'Save me, Lieutenant or I am gone.' ... on casting my eyes around I perceived a horse going at large & I flew with the speed of lightning—got the horse returned & placed the Lieutenant on it, and bore him off in triumph, the Indians firing away all the time."

Private Ballard fought bravely but received a musket ball in the hip. Still able to walk, he staggered back only to see his horse mounted by another man who rode off. Seeing his distress, a few men turned back. They attempted to double mount their wounded companion, but the skittish, rearing horses made this impossible. The Indians closed in and Ballard told his would-be saviors to escape while they could. They rode off as Ballard swung his musket to hold the Redsticks at bay. David Glass looked back to see that Ballard had been knocked down and was being scalped. Glass asked Private Lenoir if his gun was loaded. It has "fourteen buckshots in her," he said. Glass took the weapon, dashed to a nearby tree, then fired. "The warrior with the reeking scalp of Ballard in his hand fell," recalled Sam Dale, "and we made good our retreat."

The beaten command spread out through the trees. They were chased by the triumphant, howling Creeks for the best part of a mile. With no rearguard action being fought, only the speed of flight prevented many more men being cut down. Despite being hampered by the wounded, they kept moving throughout the night.

About 70 men regrouped at Sizemore's Ferry on the Alabama River, but their horses balked at swimming across. David Glass splashed into the stream and managed to cajole the horses to follow, the men then crossing in canoes. They took some small comfort in having captured many of the Creek packhorses and their supplies. This included 200 pounds of gunpowder in addition to musket balls.

Patrick May had procured one packhorse during the retreat. "I regarded my pack as almost invaluable, as I (and all those who saw it) was under the impression that it was powder, as great care had evidently been taken in covering it over ... on returning home I examined my prize; when lo & behold; to my great mortification, my powder turned out to be *Liverpool Salt*."

The Redsticks vanished back into the canebrakes and woods, some returning to Pensacola for replacement supplies while others made for home. Two Americans had been killed: David Glass's twin brother, Elijah, and Private Ballard. There were about 20 wounded, including Sam Dale. There was no reforming of the beaten militia as a fighting force. They made their way home as best they could singly or groups along various routes. No clear tally of Creek casualties is known, but the infuriated survivors were bent on revenge for what they considered a declaration of war.[6]

The recently constructed Fort Mims was commanded by Lieutenant Spruce Osborne of the Mississippi Territorial Volunteers. On July 28, Osborne wrote to his commanding officer, Colonel Joseph Carson, at Fort Stoddert, located about 12 miles to the southwest:

> Dear Colonel, I am sorry to inform you that ten men of the detachment that lately marched against M'Queen have returned, and report that they were yesterday defeated. The battle took place on the eastern side of the Escambia River, near Burnt Corn Creek, about forty miles in a right line from this post, and below it. It commenced at one o'clock and lasted until three P.M. Our men fought in a very disadvantageous position. Colonel Caller and Major Wood are missing, supposed to have been killed; and Captain Sam Dale, Robert Lewis, Alex. Hollinger, Wm. Baldwin. and others wounded; number of killed not reported. This stockade is in good condition, and I am sure will be well defended. We are all in good health and good spirits. God bless you.
> S. M. Osborne, Lt. Comm'g.[7]

Colonel Caller and Major Wood were "supposed to have been killed." But, in fact, "Col Callier himself was lost in the Swamp on the Alabama River for 15 days & suffered great privations and had almost lost his reason when found. Also Major Wood," recalled Doctor Holmes. Colonel Caller, "a very large man" had set out in fine form on a fine mount, but was found on foot wearing nothing but his drawers and shirt. Following the war's end, he managed to retrieve his horse from the Creeks and retain a dignified air despite the recriminations, but Major Wood was another matter. Historian John F. H. Claiborne later wrote:

> No one who knew Caller and Wood intimately doubted their courage; but the disaster of burnt corn brought down on them much scurility. Major Wood, who was as sensitive as brave, had not the fortitude to despise the scorn of the world, and sought forgetfulness, as too many men often do, in habitual intemperance.[8]

No one who served at Burnt Corn boasted of the matter. The fight was seen as a fiasco and disgrace at a time when America was in conflict with a far greater power than the Creek nation—Great Britain. The previous year, American President James Madison had declared war for various reasons including the impressment of American seaman to serve against the French on British warships.

With hindsight, the Burnt Corn debacle achieved nothing but to inflame an already tense situation, and encourage neutral Creeks to take up arms against Americans and their Indian allies. The families and garrison at Fort Mims would pay a heavy price.

1

We Are Perfectly Tranquil Here

The Creeks were a numerous and powerful tribe. They lived on fertile plains amidst groves of walnut, oak and hickory, their towns built on streams with adjacent fields for crops and cattle grazing.[1]

Tukabatchee on the Tallapoosa River was a large, principal town. Two years before the fight at Burnt Corn Creek, the great Shawnee chief Tecumseh had arrived with his entourage from the far north. With a flamboyant show of war songs, dances and prophetic messages, Tecumseh urged a united, vast front to destroy the ever-encroaching whites. A large assemblage of influential Creeks listened to his fiery speech[2]:

> Let the white race perish. They seize your land; they corrupt your women; they trample on the ashes of your dead! Back, whence they came, upon a trail of blood, they must be driven. Back! back, ay, into the great water whose accursed waves brought them to our shores! Burn their dwellings! Destroy their stock! Slay their wives and children! The Red Man owns the country, and the Pale-faces must never enjoy it. War now! War forever! War upon the living! War upon the dead! Dig their very corpses from the grave. Our country must give no rest to a white man's bones. This is the will of the Great Spirit, revealed to my brother, his familiar, the Prophet of the Lakes. He sends me to you. All the tribes of the north are dancing the war-dance. Two mighty warriors [Britain and Spain] across the seas will send us arms. Tecumseh will soon return to his country. My prophets shall tarry with you. They will stand between you and the bullets of your enemies.[3]

Tecumseh claimed to have supernatural powers through Hisagitamisi, the "Master of Breath," the supreme deity of the Creeks.[4] "When the white men approach your towns the yawning earth shall swallow them up. Soon shall you see my arm of fire stretched athwart the sky. You will know that I am on the war-path. I will stamp my foot and the very earth shall shake."[5] Before departing Canada, he had learned from the British that a comet was due to appear. And during 1811 there had been a series of earthquakes throughout the southeast.

Tecumseh departed leaving his influential cousin with the Creeks. Known as Seekaboo, he was an interpreter and gifted linguist, fluent in several languages including Creek and English.[6] His task was to urge the Creeks to join Tecumseh's push to drive the whites into the sea. A few weeks later Tukabatchee was rocked by an earthquake. And then the comet appeared. Seekaboo offered this as proof of Tecumseh's power. Little wonder many believed the great chief's words.

War between the United States and Britain provided an ideal opportunity for discontented Creeks to fulfil Tecumseh's wishes. American military forces were preoccupied fighting elsewhere, including an attempt to invade distant Canada. Americans were fearful that the Creeks would join the conflict supplied with British munitions through the supposedly neutral Spanish who held East and West Florida on the Gulf Coast.

The Redstick Creeks, opposed to the Americans, tended to reside in the upper Creek villages located on the Coosa, Tallapoosa and higher waters of the Alabama rivers. The lower Creeks were seen by the Redsticks, through hostile eyes, as supporters of the recently established Creek National Council. This had evolved from the traditional meeting of headmen from the Indian towns, and was supervised by Colonel Benjamin Hawkins, the American federal Indian agent located in Georgia. Hawkins had encouraged the white man's agricultural way of life and peaceful assimilation. This caused considerable resentment among many Creeks who had no wish to see their traditional culture disappear. The construction of the Federal Road through Creek hunting grounds from Georgia to Fort Stoddert in the Tensaw River region benefited some Indians through increased trade, but the resulting influx of white setters angered many others.[7] Settlements encroaching along the Creek-Georgia border exacerbated the situation.

Prophets, inspired by Seekaboo and Tecumseh's words, urged a revitalization of traditional Creek culture and armed resistance, and assured immunity to American bullets. Far to the north, Tecumseh scored stunning victories, and was called by British General Isaac Brock "the Wellington of the Indians."

On May 16, 1812, Creeks attacked a small settlement at the mouth of the Duck River in Tennessee. A man, a woman and five children were brutally murdered, and Mrs. Martha Crawley taken prisoner. Several weeks later she escaped and was soon rescued by a white trader. She had been subjected to no violence, but newspapers had already printed false stories of her being beaten and stripped in front of dancing warriors.[8] With the frontier in outrage over the killings and kidnapping, Hawkins demanded action from the Creek National Council, and those responsible were tracked down and killed.

These executions were in violation of clans traditionally administering justice to their own.[9] This intensified an increasingly tense situation, and many undecided Creeks felt inclined to join the Redstick cause. In the spring of 1813, Upper Creeks, returning from a journey to confer with Tecumseh, attacked and killed seven white immigrant families near the mouth of the Ohio River. Again Hawkins demanded action by the National Council. A war party tracked down and killed eight of the guilty party, including their leader, Little Warrior.

"Kill the old chiefs, the friends of peace," demanded the Redstick prophets. Leaders in favor of peace were murdered in retribution, and neutral Creeks were pressured to take sides. Tukabatchee, home to peace Chief Big Warrior, was besieged by Redsticks. Creeks from Cusseta township came to the rescue, lifting the siege. American settlers, their mixed-blood and Indian allies, fearing they would be next, fled their homes to hastily built stockades.

Through agents in Pensacola, the American authorities learned of Peter McQueen's trip to procure munitions from the Spanish. These would be used to fulfil Tecumseh's plans to drive white Americans "into the great water." The Redstick leaders may well have reconsidered going on the warpath if their prophets had foreseen Tecumseh's defeat and death only a few months away.

During their trek to Pensacola, McQueen's party had burned the plantation house of Creek mixed-blood James Cornells, and abducted his wife. A blanket offered by a French woman in Pensacola obtained her release. Cornells, absent at the time of the attack, returned to find his home in ashes, his wife gone. He rode through the countryside spreading alarming news of Redsticks on the warpath. More white settlers and their allies headed into stockades for mutual protection.

One girl, age ten, Margaret Eades, watched as her father helped construct a fort at Carney's Bluff on the Tombigbee River:

> It was a busy scene, all hands, negroes and whites ... hard at work chopping and clearing a place for the fort. Women and children crying; no place to sit down, nothing to eat, all confusion and dismay, expecting every moment to be scalped and tomahawked ... with superhuman exertion the Fort was finished in one week. The tents all comfortable, and streets full of soldiers, boys drilling, drums beating, pipes playing, but no Indians yet.... Time passed on with fear and trembling with the grown folks, but we children enjoyed every moment.[10]

General Thomas Flournoy, commander of the Seventh Military District, refused to send regular army troops. His headquarters were in New Orleans, and British warships had been seen off the Gulf Coast. Redcoats were his concern, not Redsticks.

Accordingly, Colonel James Caller and men of the 15th Regiment of Mississippi Territorial Militia rode to intercept McQueen's party on their return from Pensacola. The humiliating debacle at Burnt Corn Creek was the result. This appeared to validate the Creek prophets' predictions of easy victories over the whites. The Americans realized Burnt Corn Creek would inflame the situation, and additional units of the Mississippi Territory Militia were called to arms.

In 1797, Samuel Mims had acquired a land grant of 524 acres near the Boat Yard on Tensaw Lake. He prospered from running slave plantations and operating a ferry across the Alabama River, about one mile to the west of his home.[11] Opulent by frontier standards, this was a large, timber frame structure with attic space in the roof and verandas on either side. With trouble in the air, a timber stockade was built by militia around the Mims home. The walls also enclosed a spinning house, kitchen and smoke house, weaving house, blacksmith shop and two corn houses.[12] As anxious families seeking protection arrived, additional crude cabins and shelters appeared. The stockade is usually quoted as enclosing one acre, based on the writing of historian Albert Pickett. But Pickett's description of the fort's construction using horizontal timbers has been discredited by archaeological surveys which confirm vertical picketing, thus his description is not valid.[13] Considering the number of buildings enclosed, their indicated size on a rough layout drawn after the attack, and the number of people inside, it seems more than likely that the fort was quite a bit larger than one acre, even before an addition was constructed.

Numerous gun portholes were cut through the stockade walls about four feet from the ground. With hindsight, this would receive criticism as inadequate construction but, despite shortcomings, such low gunports were utilized on many frontier stockades. Fort Phil Kearny, Wyoming, professionally built by the United States Army in 1866, would use similar gunports in eight-foot walls. A detachment of 81 men would be wiped out by 2,000 Indians only four miles from the fort, but the post itself would never be stormed.

Once the Fort Mims walls were complete, construction of a timber blockhouse on the southwest corner was commenced. The fort was accessed by two gates; one at the west and another at the east.

Outside, a row of slave cabins in a large potato field lay to the south and stables were located about 80 yards to the southeast. Woods lay between the stockade and the

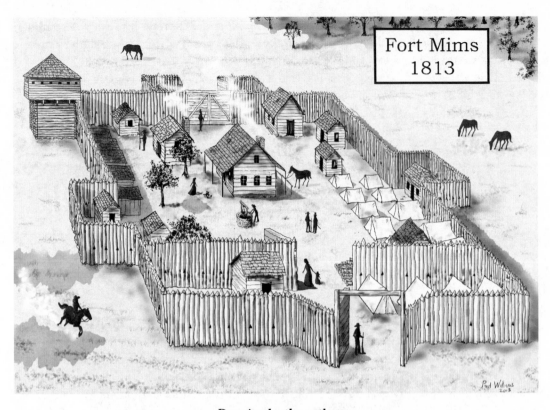

Fort Mims
1813

Drawing by the author.

lake. To the north, swamps with cane growth abounded, and to the east, flat terrain was seen for several miles scattered with cane marshes and ravines.[14]

On August 3, 1813, one week after Burnt Corn Creek, Major Daniel Beasley arrived from Fort Stoddert with 102 infantry and 10 mounted Dragoons of the 1st Regiment, Mississippi Territorial Volunteers. Beasley's task was to protect the settlers gathering at Fort Mims. He was described as "about five foot ten inches high, dark eyes and hair with a very fine looking & determined countenance."[15] Born circa 1766, he had migrated from Virginia to Mississippi Territory, and in 1805 was appointed Jefferson County sheriff. His duties included serving writs, auctioning tax debtors' possessions, apprehending criminals and escaped slaves. In 1807, he was elected captain of the Jefferson County militia, and in 1809 to the territorial legislature. In 1810, he affirmed his reputation as a gentleman of the first order, in the eyes of some, by killing a young attorney, Samuel Frye, in a duel. This took place across the border in Louisiana to bypass Mississippi's anti-duelling laws. Despite the county sheriff being engaged in such an affair, some considered him "brave, chivalrous, frank ... the soul of honor." Beasley's character, however, was apparently also marked by extreme racism, arrogance and a belief in his own invincibility, all of which would lead to tragedy at Fort Mims.

The major assumed command from Lieutenant Osborne, who felt confident of the post's security: "This stockade is in good condition, and I am sure will be well defended."

Three days after his arrival, Daniel Beasley wrote to the commander of Mississippi

Volunteers, Brigadier General Ferdinand Claiborne, at Fort Stoddert, informing him of the enlistment an additional 20 local militiamen from the settlers moving into Fort Mims. Beasley issued orders that the new recruits be permitted to draw rations and elect officers. Dixon Bailey had arrived with various family members, including his wife, two brothers, a sister and children.[16] He was unanimously elected captain.

Lieutenant Patrick May described Bailey as:

> a half-breed Indian—In Stature he was about 5 foot 8, or 10 inches high, Square build inclined to corpulency & would have weighed I suppose 175 or 180 had a dark Complexion was a man of intelligence and noble bearing and of unsurpassed Chivalry and during Burnt Corn battle acted a prominent part, & displayed undaunted bravery.[17]

All of which would make him a prime target for the vengeful Redsticks. They had no time for those with Indian blood who fought alongside the whites, and Bailey was only one of many mixed-bloods who were now with whites and black slaves who had taken shelter in Fort Mims.

Lieutenant Osborne had not only trained at West Point, but studied medicine at the University of North Carolina. Accordingly, he was appointed post surgeon. Feeling, however, that Fort Mims was no place for a fighting soldier, he wrote to General Claiborne requesting transfer to some post where he was more likely to see action. Meanwhile, he prescribed extra rations of whiskey for men on sick call, as was usual in the military at that time. Enlisted men normally received a quarter pint of whiskey per day, and an extra ration if allocated heavy work. The arrival of Beasley's command and the influx of settlers led to overcrowding, thus extra whiskey was requested from Claiborne to cover those working on an extension to the stockade. This was constructed at the east end with another, outer gate in place, the original wall and gate being left intact. At the opposite, west end, an outer bastion with another gate was already in place, thus a double row of gates were at each end of the fort.

Beasley also requested additional muskets from General Claiborne and a drum "to be used by one of the Militia who beats exceedingly well having been in the regular Service for five years."

The general himself arrived for an inspection on August 7. He was not satisfied and recommended a strengthening of "the picketing & to build at least two other blockhouses." He also advised Beasley to "respect" the enemy, prepare for possible attack, and "frequently send out some scouts." Claiborne attached to Beasley eight mounted scouts commanded by a man familiar with the Creek language and customs, Cornet Thomas Rankin. But he also ordered Beasley to detach men to help protect fortified sawmills in the region. Mobile, about 40 miles to the south, had been recently seized from the Spanish by American forces, and a British invasion from the Gulf of Mexico was feared. The mills were supplying timber for a strengthening of Mobile's defences.

Following Claiborne's departure, Beasley wrote him on August 12:

> The men belonging to Capt. Dent's Company here, will be sent on to morrow but it is with regret that I send them as it weakens my command very much and Lieut Bowman having enlisted the most of the men, and also having been at a deal of trouble and pains in disciplining of them, he thinks hard of them being taken from him. One of our soldiers died the night before last and from the report enclosed you will see that we have a good many men on the Sick report; but none of them dangerous. We are perfectly tranquil here, and are progressing in our works as well as can be expected considering the want of tools, we shall probably finish the stockade tomorrow.[18]

His force weakened by this detachment, and the illness that pervaded unsanitary military camps, Beasley enticed more civilians to enlist in Captain Dixon Bailey's militia company, which soon had more than 40 men.

As Beasley's command settled into their routine at Fort Mims, dramatic events were unfolding west of the Mississippi. The Mexican War of Independence from Spanish rule had erupted in 1810, and on August 18, 1813, the Battle of Medina was fought 20 miles from San Antonio de Bexar in the Spanish province of Tejas. After a four-hour battle the rebels broke and fled. All prisoners taken were executed, and of 1,400 rebels only about 100 survived. A young lieutenant fighting with the loyalists named Antonio López de Santa Anna was cited for bravery. He took note of how traitors were dealt with, and rode with the victorious troops when they occupied both San Antonio and the old fortified mission across the river called the Alamo.[19]

Back east, the Redstick warriors drank tea derived from button snakeroot and willow bark. This concoction caused them to throw up which, they believed, had a purifying effect in readiness for war. They also prepared parched corn meal for food to be carried on the war path. Hundreds of warriors from Redstick villages gathered at Flat Creek with the intention of avenging Burnt Corn Creek.

Included in this great council was William Weatherford, or Hoponika Fulsahi. His Anglo name was typical of those with European fathers and Creek mothers. Weatherford's own mother was mixed-blood, thus he was more white than native. Born circa 1781 near the Creek settlement of Coosada, being of the Wind Clan, he was related to many of the most influential Creeks of his time.[20] He distinguished himself in horsemanship, hunting, woodcraft and, according to legend

> He was 6 feet and 2 inches in height and weighed about 175 lbs with a form of perfect mold with the bearing and air of a Knight of the olden times. In activity and muscular power he had no peer amongst his people and as he stood forth in his pride of manhood he looked as though he was born to command "and that there was none to dispute his sway."[21]

Although Weatherford was to play a leading role in hostilities against the Americans, he had adopted the white mans' way of life, running a plantation, owning slaves, growing crops and trading in cattle. He had relatives who, like himself, had embraced white society, and would fight on the American side. Married, he had two children by a previous, deceased wife, and some claim it was because of a threat to their safety he joined the Redstick cause.[22] But Weatherford did more than join, becoming a prominent leader. Others suggest a religious connection with the full-blood Creeks, or the fact his plantation was located in Redstick country on the upper Alabama River. This was 150 miles north of the Tensaw region where his pro–American relatives resided.[23]

Thomas Woodward met Weatherford and stated, 45 years after Fort Mims, that Creek chiefs had taken the "black drink." Weatherford and his brother-in-law, Sam Moniac were told "that they should join or be put to death—Moniac boldly refused, and mounted his horse." Creek prophet Josiah Francis then

> seized his bridle; Moniac snatched a war-club from his hand, gave him a severe blow and put out, with a shower of rifle bullets following him. Weatherford consented to remain. He told them that he disapprobated their course, and that it would be their ruin; but they were his people—he was raised with them, and he would share their fate.[24]

But Weatherford lived a white man's life. Shortly after the war he told Captain Sam Dale: "through the influence of Tecumseh he joined the war party and led the attack on Fort Mims." Tecumseh's words were to drive the whites into the sea and "Slay their wives and children!" Claiming innocence after surrender, however, Weatherford "often deplored to me his inability to arrest the carnage on that occasion. 'My warriors were like famished wolves,' he said, 'and the first taste of blood made their appetites insatiable.'"[25]

But the persuasive Weatherford did not abandon the Redstick cause after Fort Mims. He continued to lead his "famished wolves" in battle.

2

Yelling and Screaming
Like Perfect Demons

"There was an alarm here yesterday," wrote Major Beasley on August 13, "but I believe an entirely false one." A boy had been searching for a lost horse in a swamp near Fort Mims and reported seeing Indians. A subsequent scouting party found nothing—except one abandoned Indian canoe.

One week later Colonel Carson received news from a Choctaw informant of Redstick plans to attack Fort Mims, Easley's Fort and Fort St. Stephens. General Claiborne summoned Beasley to Fort Stoddert, stressed a need for vigilance at Fort Mims, then marched with extra troops to Easley's Fort to the north, considered the most vulnerable post.

At their great council the Redsticks performed a fervent, ceremonial war dance, working themselves into a frenzy for the coming fight. It was decided to divide their warriors, and make simultaneous attacks on two forts. Fort Mims was considered a prime target. Many who had taken part in Burnt Corn Creek were sheltering there, including mixed-bloods, like Dixon Bailey. His scalp was a trophy worth having.

William Weatherford would lead a force of about 700 warriors against Fort Mims, while prominent Prophet Josiah Francis, or Ildas Hadjo, would attack the smaller and weaker Fort Sinquefield with 125 warriors.[1] Francis had gained influence with a variety of "supernatural" deeds supposedly through the Creek supreme deity, the Master of Breath. This included a reputed ability to stay underwater for days while communing with the river gods.[2]

Traveling mainly after dark through sheltering cane and swampy terrain, the Redsticks lived largely off field crops and food from abandoned homes. They captured three slaves sent back from Fort Mims to gather food for the refugees. One managed to escape and made his way back to the fort where he warned Beasley of the approaching menace. The complacent major, however, gave the report little credit.[3]

On August 27 a man ran into the fort and told Beasley of "a great many Indians of mounted and a foot … on the road that led directly to the fort that their number appeared immense as they could only see one end of them in single file."[4] But Beasley remained dismissive. Fort Mims was the most southerly of the three posts thought to be attacked, so it appeared that St. Stephens and Easley's were more likely to feel any Redstick wrath. He did, however, order a resumption of work on the single blockhouse commenced one month before. No hand, however, had been lifted to construct the other two blockhouses ordered by General Claiborne.

On August 29 the blockhouse was completed. On the same day, Weatherford's war party stopped to refresh themselves at a meandering stream. As the warriors gulped cool water and sheltered under trees from the hot summer sun, a scouting patrol of two mounted men from Fort Mims appeared. Paying little attention to the job at hand, the complacent scouts chatted as they rode by to another ford, seeing no sign of the 700 warriors concealed nearby. The Redsticks wisely refrained from taking their first scalps, and allowed the riders to turn back. A missing patrol could have warned even the intransigent Beasley that all was not well—perhaps there were Redsticks closing in after all.

The war party continued towards the unsuspecting fort and camped for the night. It was later claimed by Weatherford's family that he urged the warriors to spare women and children, angering some who accused him of wanting to spare relatives who had sided with the whites. If he did so, it was in contravention of the Master of Breath who, according to the prophets, wanted all whites and mixed-bloods killed.

Whatever the truth, Weatherford decided to scout the fort himself. With two warriors he approached the stockade after dark. Seeing no sentries, he and another brave crept forward to the picket wall. They peered through the low gun portholes, and saw, "a few glimmering lights scattered about," and all "looked obscure and gloomy." Voices could be heard, but there was no talk of an approaching Redstick menace, just the banter of day to day life. Fort Mims was totally unprepared for attack.[5]

As dawn's first light appeared the following day, August 30, the Redsticks prepared for war. Their bodies were daubed in red and black after stripping down to breechclouts, their appearance grotesque; intended to terrify the enemy in the coming fight.

Included in the war party was the Creek prophet Paddy Walsh. He selected four warriors and, assuring them of their immunity to bullets, told them to lead the attack into the fort's interior while others seized the portholes. The four warriors' safety would herald the victory to come. And Walsh himself would run three times around the stockade rendering those inside into "a state of turpitude and paralyzed." War clubs and knives would be used to finish the job.

As these preparations were under way, Beasley wrote to Claiborne:

> [H]aving Scattered my command in so many places that you render me unable, if the Indians should appear in any force, to do anything more than to defend the several forts; that I should be utterly unable to leave the fort, and meet any number of the enemy, more especially when you know that but a few of the volunteer militia can be relied on.[6]

Beasley's command at Fort Mims that morning consisted of 106 Mississippi Territorial Volunteers, and a little over 40 local militia. Six volunteers were absent, being on leave in Mobile. There were also about 300 civilian whites, mixed-bloods, slaves, and a few friendly Creeks, about 400 souls all told.[7]

Only the day before he had been warned by "two negro boys" tending cattle that they had seen "a great number of Indians, Painted, running and hallooing" towards Pierces' Mill, a fortified structure about two miles to the south. Beasley had dispatched a scouting party who found no hostiles, but he had also been warned by another slave of Indians plundering a deserted plantation. He dismissed both reports as fabrications, but "I was much pleased at the appearance of the Soldiers here at the time of the Alarm yesterday. When it was expected every moment that the Indians would appear in Sight, the soldiers very generally appeared anxious to see them."

To discourage any further "false alarms," Beasley ordered that one of the slave boys be given a good whipping, which was readily carried out. While Sheriff of Jefferson County, he had ordered 39 lashes for troublesome slaves as a matter of routine, and this "boy" had caused him unnecessary trouble.

The following day, Monday the 30th, as the Redsticks prepared for the assault, Beasley allowed both stockade gates at the eastern end, and the outer gate at the western end, to be left open. The blockhouse remained unmanned.

Eyewitness accounts following battles are usually erratic and contradictory. Fort Mims was no exception. Based on evidence and logic, however, it appears the following took place:

The whipped boy and another slave owned by Josiah Fletcher were sent out to tend cattle, and again Redsticks were sighted within a mile of the stockade. Not surprisingly, the whipped boy refused to report back to Beasley, instead running to warn those at Pierce's Mill. His companion bravely decided his duty was to Fort Mims, regardless of the consequences, and dashed back with the news. Beasley declined to believe a word, and ordered him to be whipped. But Josiah Fletcher, the boy's owner, disagreed and refused to allow the flogging to proceed. Beasley consulted his officers, then ordered Fletcher and his family to leave the fort by 10 o'clock the following morning. But a dissenting petition did the rounds. Under pressure, Beasley said Fletcher could remain providing he allowed the lashing to take place. With great reluctance, Fletcher complied.

William Weatherford, meanwhile, was concealed along with hundreds of warriors in a verdant ravine about 400 meters to the east. James Cornells, whose wife had been abducted before the Burnt Corn fight, was riding toward the fort. He glanced into the woods and saw a large group of warriors painted and stripped for battle. He galloped through the gates and yelled a warning to Beasley that an attack was imminent. Beasley insisted he had "only seen a gang of red cattle." Cornells yelled back "that gang of red cattle would give him a hell of a kick before midnight." Despite Beasley ordering his arrest, Cornells rode to the gate and warned the sentries. He said would stay and fight if they prepared a defense. Unwilling to defy Beasley, they declined, and Cornells rode out. He would later claim Beasley was drunk.[8]

Weatherford saw Cornells disappear down the road towards Pierce's Mill. A fiddle could be heard playing inside the fort, and no move was made to close the gates. Then the beat of a drum was heard—time for the midday meal.

Stable hand Nehemiah Page had evidently enjoyed the previous evening's frolic, but now paid the price as he slept off the drunken binge. He comfortably reclined amid fodder in a stable loft about 80 yards southeast of the fort. But then he heard the thumping, drumming noise of many running feet. He peered out through a crack in the timber wall to see hundreds of ferociously painted Redsticks rushing towards the open eastern gate. Terrified, he leapt from the loft, then ran to the door. Seeing the savage tide pass, he bolted southeast towards sheltering canebrakes. A small dog running with the Indians saw him, turned and gave chase.

A fort sentry watching others playing cards looked up. He was horrified to see hundreds of Redsticks rushing forward. "Indians!" he shouted as he raised his musket and fired the first shot.

The panic-stricken cry "Indians" echoed throughout the fort. Daniel Beasley, drawing his sword, ran from his cabin and rushed to the open gate. He pushed with all his might, only to be thwarted by a drift of soil. As the Indians rushed through, Beasley was the first to be cut down. Soldiers grasped guns as the warriors' war whoops mingled with the screams of terrified women and children. One survivor recalled that "she saw Billy Weatherford as he came in the gate at full run, at the head of his warriors, jump a pile of logs almost as high as his head ... as he sprang over the logs he saw Captain Dixon Bailey who was a bitter enemy, to whom he shouted, 'Dixon Bailey, to-day one or both of us must die.'"[9]

Dr. Thomas Holmes left a vivid impression of the Redsticks:

> Every Indian was provided with a gun, war club a bow and arrows pointed with iron spikes—With few exceptions they were naked—around the waste was drawn a girdle from which was tied a cows tail running down the back and almost dragging on the ground—it is impossible to imagine people so horribly painted. Some were painted half red and half black.... Some were adorned with feathers their faces were painted so as to show their terible contortions.[10]

At the same time another Redstick detachment struck the open western gate. The guard house inside the bastion was taken, the surprised soldiers cut down by gunshot and club. The warriors were stalled by the closed inner gate, but they scaled the walls of the unmanned blockhouse on the southwest corner. From inside they could fire into the fort. Other warriors took construction tools from the guardhouse and went to work hacking at the closed western gate and wall pickets alongside the blockhouse.

To the east, the four warriors supposedly made bullet proof by Paddy Walsh dashed through the inner gate. Once inside they "got to dancing in defiance of the citizen soldiers, for they had assured their deluded followers, that if they could dance in defiance of American powder or ball for reason if they attempted to shoot them, that their Balls would split." But any split balls were due to shattered bones as three of the four died where they fell. The fourth managed to run back to his compatriots fighting in the outer stockade. These warriors either killed the soldiers there or drove them back through the inner gate. They then blocked the inner eastern wall gunports, or fired through them on those inside. Other warriors, meanwhile, took possession of the gunports on the southern and western walls from the outside.

Captains Middleton and Jack, despite being wounded, rallied an effective defense while Captain Dixon Bailey, with his white and mixed-blood company, ably defended the northern wall and bastion. It took time to reload the single shot muskets, but Bailey had taken this into account. Thomas Holmes recalled, "Capt Bailey very judiciously had supplied with rifles and extra guns most of them double barrels, soon as the first discharge from Bailey's troops was made, the guns were withdrawn from the port holes and the extras put in their place which inflicted such a deadly fire that they past around with out being able to occupy the port holes of which Dixon B had command."

Prophet Paddy Walsh made his promised dash around the stockade to magically disable the defenders. On the third circuit he was hit by a shot from the north wall bastion. Despite the wound, he urged the Redsticks to discard their muskets and "enter the fort with war clubs and scalping knives in hand." The Creek mixed-bloods on the north wall, hearing Walsh's exhortation, dared them "Come and try!" Warriors entering the inner stockade fared little better than the four prophets who had preceded them,

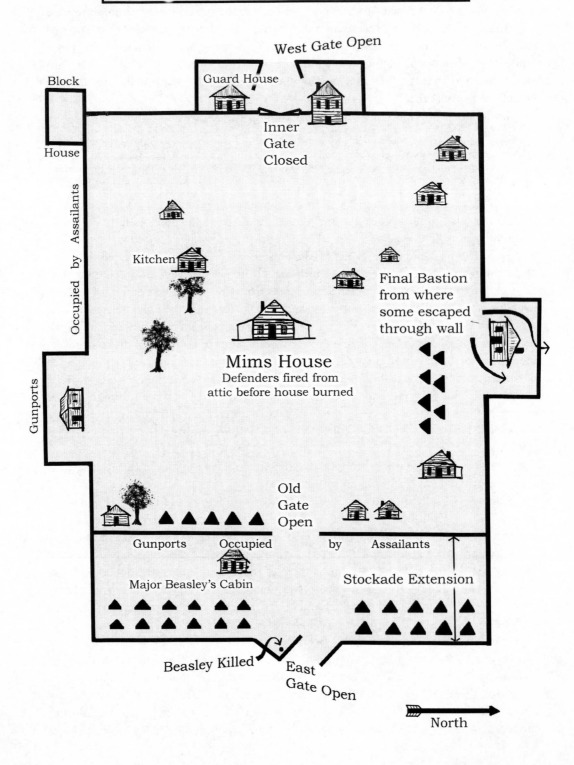

Fort Mims based on rough layout drawn after the battle

West Gate Open

Block

Guard House

Inner
Gate
Closed

House

Occupied   by   Assailants

Kitchen

Final Bastion
from where
some escaped
through wall

Gunports

Mims House
Defenders fired from
attic before house burned

Old
Gate
Open

Gunports   Occupied   by   Assailants

Major Beasley's Cabin

Stockade Extension

Beasley Killed   East
Gate
Open

North

and were shot down or forced back. Captain Jack organized an attack on the Creeks in the blockhouse, and they were driven out. Soldiers, meanwhile, scrambled into the upper attic of the Mims home and, with women helping, removed shingles from the roof. This gave a clear line of fire to Redsticks beyond the stockade. On the north wall "the Indians again made a violent attack upon the bastion commanded by Capt Bailey and were again repulsed with much loss," recalled Thomas Holmes.

After two hours of fighting the Creeks realized all had not gone well. They had captured the outer stockades to the east and west, but any warriors fighting inside had been either killed or driven out. The easy victory promised by prophets had not occurred. As well as dead enemy, their own casualties lay around them. Holmes recalled that the Redsticks

> took a great deal of the baggage out of the additional part of the fort where were encamped the officers and suddenly retreated and went to the House of Mrs O'neal about 300 yds distant and for a short time appeared to be packing up with a disposition to be off. Suddenly a conspicuous indian Warrior supposed to be William Weatherford dashed up on a horse and appeared to be harranging them for about 30 minutes, when their baggage was suddenly laid down...[11]

The hated Captain Dixon Bailey and most of his company were still alive. Escaped black slaves were with the Redsticks, and they, too, urged a renewal of the assault. This was the opportunity to settle old scores for both Creek man and black.

A relative of Weatherford's, J. D. Dreisbach, claimed 61 years after the battle that Weatherford left the fight at this point and went to his half-brother's plantation to hide slaves so the Redsticks would not abduct them. Weatherford had not the heart to witness "the indiscriminate slaughter of the inmates of the fort."[12]

The Redsticks regrouped for a fresh assault—but with different tactics this time. The blockhouse was still occupied by at least one man from Captain Jack's company who could fire along the base of the flanking walls. "they returned with a rush yelling & screaming like perfect Demons," recalled Holmes.

An assault on the blockhouse was successfully made, but at much cost to the Redsticks, according to Holmes. A "brave man" would later be found in the blockhouse with his last cartridge half rammed down his rifle barrel, "his head perforated with a Ball and the brains running [there] from." He appeared to have shot numerous warriors before being killed himself. With the blockhouse back in Redstick hands, the "Indians succeeded in cutting the pickets on the south side of the fort."

Flaming arrows arched through the sky. First the kitchen was set alight, then wind-driven cinders set fire to the Mims house. As other buildings were set alight flames also spread to the pine picket walls. With fire, smoke and chaos inside, the determined Redsticks broke through the militia defense, gaining entry through cut pickets to the inner fort. Those inside the burning buildings had the choice of dying amid flame and smoke or taking their chances outside. As men, women and children fled they were shown no mercy, cut down with musket, arrow, tomahawk and club.

> And now, o'er the buildings, the flames stream away,
> And crackle and gnash in infuriate play;
> And the vanquished who fly from the tomahawk's doom,
> In the flames of their homes find a terrible tomb!
> No spot has a refuge, no corner a path,
> By which to escape from wild Weatherford's wrath.[13]

Lieutenant Osborne ran from the burning Mims house towards Bailey's northern refuge. His desire for action finally fulfilled, he died by a Redstick bullet. Samuel Mims' brother David suffered the same fate as he fled the flames.

Benjamin Hawkins recalled a black survivor's story:

> He said he was in Mims' house, when it was taken and destroyed. An Indian, seeing him in the corner, said, "Come out; the Master of Breath has ordered us not to kill any but white people and half breeds." An Indian woman, who was in the house, was ordered out, and to go home. Dixon Bailey's sister, a half-breed, was asked what family (white or red) she was of? She answered, pointing to her brother [James Bailey], "I am the sister to that great man you have murdered there": upon which they knocked her down, cut her open, strewed her entrails around. They threw several dead bodies into the fire, and some that were wounded.[14]

Another survivor recalled: "One of our Indians, Jahomobtee, in his presence shot three Indians in the act of tomahawking white women."[15] As both soldiers and civilians were cut down, smoke, fire and cinders billowed skywards amid the cries of the wounded, the war whoops of the Redsticks and the crack of musket fire. But still the north bastion held out. Survivors from the slaughter took crowded shelter in and behind the loom house in the bastion center. Most put up a valiant defence, the women desperately reloading muskets as fast as powder and shot could be rammed home.

But the bastion walls, built for defense, were now a death trap for the defenders.

Often considered a one-sided massacre, Fort Mims actually saw a spirited defense. Dixon Bailey's company on the north wall was the last to hold out (drawing by the author).

"Even that brave and worthy soldier Capt Dixon Baily was head to give up—that his large family were all to be butchered by the savages there was no alternative left," recalled Holmes. Their only hope of survival being escape to the outside, Holmes hacked at the picket wall to create an opening.

He recalled:

> Mrs Daniel Bailey loaded guns during the whole engagement for the defence of the Bastion— There was a Sargent Mathews taken with a violent chill, & struck like a man with a third day fever ... his teeth chattering together as though he was freezing. This brave Mrs Bailey urged him from time to time to get up & fight like a man and defend the women and children that were in the fort—he refused to do so, she earnestly assured him that if he did not fight that she would certainly bayonett him which By the way she done some 15 or 20 times in his rump, all to no purpose for he lay like an ox.[16]

Holmes succeeded in breaching the north bastion pickets. A hundred yards to the northwest, woods and swamps provided a possible refuge for anyone who could run the Redstick gauntlet. One of Dixon Bailey's sons, Ralph, had been wounded, and he ordered Tom, a slave, to carry him to the safety of the woods. Tom set out carrying the boy, closely followed by Bailey, Holmes and a black woman named Hester. Redsticks attempted to cut them off, but Bailey shot back, reloading on the run, and Holmes returned fire with his double barrelled musket. Despite Creek arrows and bullets, the five desperate bolters made it into the woods, but Hester had been hit, and Bailey had received a mortal wound. He died where he collapsed alongside a cypress swamp.[17]

Tom decided his best hope of survival was surrender, so he returned to the fort still carrying the wounded Ralph. A Redstick promptly dispatched Ralph with his war club. Slaves not being the target, Tom was spared. He later claimed he regretted Ralph's death, having no idea he would be killed.

Others scrambled from the burning fort through the breached palisade. Ensign Chambliss, already twice wounded, ran for the sheltering woods but two arrows found their mark. He staggered into the trees and collapsed beneath the undergrowth. Despite passing out from loss of blood, he lived through the ordeal to finally escape. Thirteen other men who had made it outside attempted a rally to hold the Indians off while civilians attempted escape. The Redsticks returned fire and Jesse Steadham was hit in the thigh. William Stubblefield had already been wounded by an arrow, and the thirteen continued their dash for the sheltering woods.

An officer's horse had bolted from the fort. Betsy Hoven saved herself when she ran from the stockade, mounted the skittish animal and rode off. Others fled only to be pursued and cut down.

Militiaman Ned Steadham received a ball in the leg as he ran for his life, and Sam Jones had a finger shot off. These two were the last to escape and live, while Josiah Fletcher, previously ordered from the fort by Beasley, survived by hiding in the fort's hog pen.

Some slaves saved themselves by surrendering, and a number of women and children were spared. Creek mixed-blood Susannah Hatterway took in hand one four-year-old white girl, Elizabeth Randon, and one black girl, Lizzie. "Let us go out and be killed together," she said. But their lives were spared when Iffa Tustunaga, (Dog Warrior) claimed all three as prisoners.

Mixed-blood Vicey McGirth saw her son killed, but her five daughters spared, and her niece Polly Jones was taken prisoner along with her three children. Their lives were saved by a grateful Redstick who Vicey had cared for when he was an orphaned child.[18]

The very first to escape, stable hand Nehemiah Page, meanwhile, had made it to the Alabama River with the small Indian dog still in pursuit. Page plunged into the water, but the animal followed. He almost drowned when the dog clambering onto his back. Page scrambled onto the opposite bank, expecting to fight off an attack. But the dog merely panted, wanting to be friends. Page walked off, his new-found pet close behind. They made it to the white settlements and safety, and remained firm friends for life.

3

The Horror of the Scene

"Brave Tennesseans! Your frontier is threatened with invasion of the savage foe! Already they advance towards your frontier with their scalping knives unsheathed, to butcher your wives, your children, and your helpless babes. Time is not to be lost. We must hasten to the frontier, or we will find it drenched in the blood of our fellow citizens."[1]

Major General Andrew Jackson of the Tennessee militia had previously advocated war with the Creeks, and now his time had come. The fiery-tempered, forty-six-year-old planter, a man of dogged determination, was going to avenge the victims of Fort Mims. And this despite recuperating from wounds received in a recent shootout with the Benton brothers in at the City Hotel in Nashville. One pistol ball would not be removed till 1832, and he already carried an inoperable ball from a duel with Charles Dickinson in 1806. Dickinson had fared even worse, dying after Jackson's bullet tore into his chest. Only the brave and foolish crossed swords with Andrew Jackson.

Born March 15, 1767, near the ill-defined border of North and South Carolina, Jackson was the youngest of three brothers. His parents, Andrew and Elizabeth, had arrived from Ireland two years before with sons Hugh and Robert already in tow. Three weeks before his birth, Jackson's father was killed in a logging accident.

The American Revolution erupted in 1775. Brother Hugh went off to war and died at the battle of Stony Ferry in 1779. At age 13, Andrew acted for the rebels as a courier, being captured by the British along with his surviving brother Robert. Andrew famously received a sword slash from an officer after refusing to clean his boots; a hint of the obstinate "Old Hickory" to come. Both brothers contracted smallpox, and Robert died shortly after their release. Jackson's mother then succumbed to cholera while nursing her nephews aboard a British prison ship. An orphan aged 14, both his brothers dead, Jackson blamed the British, and retribution would come.

Raised by his uncles, he studied law, and in 1787 set up a practice in Jonesborough in what was to become the State of Tennessee. The following year he married Rachel Donelson Robards. They did not realize, however, that her divorce from Captain Lewis Robards was not yet complete. Seized on by political opponents, this would cause trouble in years to come.

Despite humble origins, the forceful Jackson made his presence felt and he soon climbed the ladder to success, serving as a congressman, a senator and a supreme court judge. In 1802, he was appointed Major General commanding the Western Tennessee militia, and two years later acquired the Hermitage, a large cotton plantation worked by slaves. The "man of the people" was now one of Tennessee's planter elite.

The *Tennessee Gazette* of October 3, 1804, carried an advertisement he placed which reflected the status quo of the time. "*Stop the Runaway.* FIFTY DOLLARS REWARD." Jackson provided a description of "a Mulatto Man Slave" who had obtained "by some means" certificates of freedom. If returned from interstate, an additional $50 was on offer with "all reasonable expenses paid—and ten dollars extra, for every hundred lashes any person will give him, to the amount of three hundred."[2]

Following the outbreak of the War of 1812, Jackson led a military expedition south from Tennessee to defend New Orleans. When encamped near Natchez, Mississippi Territory, however, he received orders from the war department to end the venture and disband his troops. With no provisions for the homeward trek, Jackson paid for their food himself. He shared the hardship of his men as they marched in frigid conditions across snow-covered terrain, his horse often used to carry sick men. He earned the respect of the troops, being nicknamed "Old Hickory" by the time they reached home.

Then the shocking news of Fort Mims arrived. And 12 more women and children in cabins outside Fort Sinquefield had been killed by Josiah Francis' warriors. They had then attacked the stockade only to be driven off after a lengthy gunfight.[3]

Jackson sent word to Governor Willie Blount advising immediate retaliation. Without authorization from the Federal government, Blount demanded that the Tennessee legislature call out 3,500 militiamen. Howling for revenge, they readily complied.

Mobile, a town with a population of about 500, found itself inundated with thousands as terrified settlers fled south, and General Flournoy was now forced to dispatch regular troops from the Gulf Coast. The Third Regiment U.S. Infantry, under Lieutenant Colonel Gilbert Russell, marched north, and Mississippi Territory Governor David Holmes sent a battalion of mounted volunteers to augment General Claiborne's command. But this was less than one thousand men; nothing like enough to crush the Redstick menace.

Now having little faith in militia-built stockades, Flournoy ordered all troops to congregate at Mobile, St. Stephens and Mt. Vernon. Fort Madison commander, Colonel Carson, informed the 1,000 settlers gathered there that they were to move to a safer post. But many objected to this. Built on old French and Spanish earth fortifications, Fort Madison was considered impregnable, and they felt it unnecessary to abandon homes and crops to the Redsticks.

While Carson departed with some 500 people, Captains Sam Dale and Evan Austill resolved to stay behind and hold the fort. About 80 men joined their militia companies to support the defence. Perhaps Sam Dale was stirred by the humiliation of Burnt Corn Creek. He had been wounded in that fight and was not going to be chased away again. Slanted, sharp pickets were driven into the ground around the fort walls, and during daylight sentinels were posted outside.[4] At night a flaming beacon suspended on a pole 40 feet high illuminated the surrounding terrain. There would be no repeat of Fort Mims here. Dale recalled:

> As a precaution against the Indian torch, I had my block-houses and their roofs well plastered with clay. We displayed ourselves in arms frequently, the women wearing hats and the garments of their husbands, to impress upon the spies that we knew were lurking around an exaggerated notion of our strength.[5]

General Flournoy sent a "very kind note" to Fort Madison advising they move out, but Dale replied that they had women and children under their charge and a "gallant set of boys." If the fort should fall, Flournoy "would find a pile of yellow hides to tan, if he could get his regulars to come and skin them!"

Further south, meanwhile, Major Joseph Kennedy and Captain Uriah Blue had led a detachment of nine men to what remained of Fort Mims. In all, 37 souls had survived the slaughter, either taken prisoner, or by escaping through woods and swamps.[6]

On September 9 the officers reported:

> The place presented an awful spectacle, and the tragical fate of our friends increased the horror of the scene. Our business was to find our friends and number the Dead. An awful and melancholy duty. At the East gate of the stockade lay Indians, Negroes, men, women and children in one promiscuous ruin; within the Gate lay the Brave unfortunate Beasley, he was behind the same, and was killed it was said, in attempting to shut it. On the left within the Stockade we found forty five men, woman and children in one heap, they were all stripped of their clothes without distinction of Age or sex, all were scalped, and the females of every age were most barbarously and Savage like butchered, in a manner which neither decency or language can convey. Women pregnant were cut open and their childrens heads Tomahawked. This was supposed to be the fatal Spot where the few, who escaped the general Massacre, made their last efforts and perished in the attempt.
>
> The large house within the Fort was burnt to ashes, and the ruins Covered with human bones. The number and the persons who there perished could not be ascertained. The plains and the woods around were covered with dead bodies, in some places thinly scattered, in others lying in heaps as the men happened to fall in flight, or in a body resisted to the last.... All the houses within the Fort were consumed by fire—except the Blockhouse and part of the picketts yet unburnt. While employed in the Duty, our hearts were torn with contending passions, by turn oppressed with grief and burning with revenge.[7]

Two weeks later, Kennedy and Blue returned leading 300 soldiers with orders to rebuild the stockade and "bury the bodies of our lamented and very worthy Volunteer Soldiers, Officers and Citizens."

> We collected, and consigned to the earth, Two hundred and forty seven, including men, women and children—The adjacent woods were strictly search'd for our countrymen, and in that pursuit, we discovered at least, one hundred slaughtered Indians,—They were covered with rails, brush &c.,—we could not be mistaken as to their being Indians, as they were inter'd with their war dress, and implements,and although they have massacred a number of our helpless women and children, it is beyond doubt to them, a dear bought victory.[8]

While Old Hickory organized the infantry in Nashville, Colonel John Coffee's 1,300 volunteer cavalry mustered near Huntsville in Mississippi Territory. Choctaw Indian scouts were told to wear white plumes or deer tails in their hair to avoid "friendly fire." The mounted volunteers rode south and established a base camp on the south bank of the Tennessee River.

Despite food shortages, Jackson ordered Coffee to locate and destroy hostile Creek villages to his immediate south. He departed with 650 men on October 15, and several days later burned a few small, abandoned villages before entering a large Creek settlement. A search discovered only a few elderly Indians and 300 bushels of corn, heartily welcomed by the hungry troops. Creek buildings were wooden frames interlaced with strands of cane plastered with clay, and the roofs were covered with grass or bark. They burned fiercely when Coffee's men put them to the torch.

Jackson, meanwhile, marched his command to the southern most point of the Tennessee River where a stockade was erected. This, optimistically, was called Fort Deposit. Here provisions, if they ever arrived, were to be stored for the coming campaign. A lack of supplies would plague Jackson throughout the Creek War.

Cherokee Chief Path Killer arrived and told Jackson of a large enemy force near Ten Islands on the Coosa River. He said the Redsticks planned to attack Creeks who had not joined them in the war. On October 24, Jackson's troops marched out with John Coffee, now promoted to brigadier general, in the advance. Scouts told Coffee of a large Redstick force at the town of Tallushatchee about eight miles from Ten Islands. He set out to attack with the 900 men under his command.

A volunteer named David Crockett rode with Coffee's Mounted Tennessee Gunmen. He recalled, "So we mounted our horses and put out for that town under the direction of two friendly Creeks we had taken for pilots. We also had a Cherokee colonel, Dick Brown, and some of his men with us."

General Coffee's force arrived at Tallushatchee on November 3, 1813. The troops surrounded the township, the Indians oblivious. A small detachment moved into plain view and opened fire. The Redsticks, armed mainly with bows and clubs, streamed whooping from their huts to repel the attack. Coffee's detachment feigned a retreat, drawing the warriors further into the open. Then the woods erupted in fire and smoke. "Remember Fort Mims!" the Tennessee Volunteers cried as musket balls decimated the Indian ranks.

Crockett recalled:

> We began to close in the town by making our files closer and closer, and the Indians soon saw they were our property. So most of them wanted to make themselves prisoners; and their squaws and all would run and take hold of any of us they could, and give themselves up.... We took them all prisoners who came to us in this way; but I saw some warriors run into a house, until I counted forty-six of them. We pursued them till we got near the house, when we saw a squaw sitting in the door, and she placed her feet against the bow she had in her hand, and then took an arrow, and, raising her feet, she drew with all her might, and let fly at us, and she killed a man, whose name, I believe, was Moore. He was a lieutenant, and his death so enraged us all, that she was fired on, and had at least twenty balls blown through her. This was the first man I ever saw killed with a bow and arrow. We now shot them like dogs; and then set the house on fire, and burned it up with the forty-six warriors in it.[9]

Crockett described a 12-year-old boy, wounded, crawling away from the fire "so near the burning house the grease was stewing out of him."

Once the gun smoke cleared, Coffee counted 186 Redstick bodies, including some women and children, while losing only five killed and 41 wounded of his own. Eighty-four women and children were taken prisoner. Crockett described how he and other hungry men returned the following day in search of food. The house with the burned warriors was examined and an underground cellar was discovered.

> We found a fine chance of potatoes in it, and hunger compelled us to eat them, though, I had rather not, if I could have helped it, for the oil of the Indians we had burned the day before had run down on them, and they looked like they had been stewed with fat meat.[10]

Crockett may well have regretted not listening to his wife. She had pleaded with him not to go to war, "but my countrymen had been murdered, and I knew that the next thing would be, that the Indians would be scalping the women and children all about here if I didn't put a stop to it." And his grandparents on his father's side had been killed by Indians in 1777. His parents, John and Rebecca, like those of Andrew Jackson, were typical pioneering stock, struggling to make a subsistence living as the new nation grew. David was born on August 17, 1786, in Greene County, Tennessee, the fifth of nine children.

At age 12 he was sent to school, an unhappy experience. To avoid a thrashing from his father for skipping classes, he ran from home and wandered for three years. He did a variety of jobs, met a lot of people, and generally learned how to survive on the frontier. He returned home in 1802 to a joyous family, who had given him up as a lost soul. Reconciled with his father, he worked as a farmhand to help him out, "for though he was poor, he was an honest man, and always tried mighty hard to pay off his debts."

In 1806, David Crockett married a local girl, Polly Finlay, and in 1811 they moved to the Mulberry Fork of Elk River, then to Bean Creek in Franklin County, Tennessee. A crack shot with a flintlock rifle, Crockett became known for his hunting skills, the meat providing food, and the hides either bartered or sold for cash. But this was subsistence living, and "we had two sons, and I found I was better at increasing my family than my fortune."

Then news of Fort Mims arrived. Crockett, with rifle and horse, set out to protect Polly and sons John and William from the fate of those at Fort Mims.

4

The Doleful Sound from the Treetops

Following the destruction of Tallushatchee, Coffee's victorious but hungry volunteers were soon down to chewing on cow hides as they made their way to Fort Strother, a new stockade under construction about 45 miles south of Fort Deposit. Those Creek women and children taken prisoner were sent north to Tennessee under armed guard. The last thing Jackson wanted was extra mouths to feed.

On November 7, while awaiting reinforcements and supplies, Jackson received word from friendly Creeks that their fortified village of Talladega was surrounded by more than 1,000 hostiles. The Redstick chiefs were demanding they join the Redstick cause. The messenger had escaped by disguising himself in a pigskin and shuffling through the enemy lines after dark.

Leaving his sick and wounded with a small garrison, Jackson marched from Fort Strother to the relief of Talladega with 800 cavalry and 1,200 infantry. The force advanced in three columns and, about six miles from their objective, set up camp. From here scouts moved forward to reconnoitre the Redstick positions. Based on their information, Jackson planned his assault, and on November 9 split his force to encircle the Redsticks in what he hoped would be a vice-like trap.

Crockett recalled how the ploy used at Tallushatchee was used once more, a detachment under Major Russell being sent forward to bring on the battle. "When they got near the fort," Crockett recalled, "the top of it was lined with friendly Indians, crying out as loud as they could roar, 'How-dy-do, brother, how-dy-do?'" The friendlies could see the enemy concealed in a gulch that ran around the fort in a half-moon shape, but they were out of sight to Russell's command. Two Creeks jumped from the stockade and ran to Russell pointing to the concealed warriors, "all painted as red as scarlet, and were just as naked as they were born." The hostiles opened fire, "rushing forth like a cloud of Egyptian locusts," recalled Crockett, "and screaming like all the young devils had been turned loose, with the old devil of all at their head." Russell's men dismounted and bolted through the stockade gate. As their abandoned horses ran back to Jackson's troops, the volunteers delivered a lethal volley and warriors fell amid the musket smoke. They "broke like a gang of steers, and ran across to our other line, where they were again fired on; and so we kept them running from one line to the other, constantly under heavy fire."[1]

But they fought back and "made their escape through a part of our line, which was

30

made up of drafted militia, which broke ranks." The surviving Redsticks bolted through the gap and dispersed through the trees.

Once the battle haze cleared, 299 dead Creeks were counted. Some who escaped would die of their wounds. Jackson lost only 14 men killed and 81 wounded. The Creek prophets' promises of immunity to American bullets was once again proven false.

But William Weatherford was not among the slain. At this time he was with Redstick followers further south. Colonel Carson had been ordered back to regarrison Fort Madison, and had allowed Captain Sam Dale to march out on a Redstick hunting mission with a command of 70 volunteers.[2] Weatherford and his warriors moved to ambush the detachment, and on November 12 both sides witnessed the celebrated Canoe Fight. Sam Dale, Jeremiah Austill, James Smith and a freed African known as Caesar, in a small dugout canoe, confronted nine Creek warriors in a larger craft at the mouth of Randon's Creek on the Alabama River. As Caesar paddled, his three companions attempted to fire on the Redsticks, but only one gun discharged, the priming powder of the other two being damp. The Creek chief recognized Sam Dale

General Jackson earned the title Sharp Knife amongst the Creeks during his savage war against their tribe (Library of Congress).

and shouted, "Now for it, Big Sam!" The canoes came alongside and Astill was knocked down by a swinging musket. Caesar held the Creek canoe as Dale and the other two fought in savage hand to hand combat with swinging muskets, clubs, and thrusting bayonets.

> The combat is brief: the fierce struggle is done,
> And the late foaming waters in red ripples run.
> The conflict is over; but the conquerors who?
> Ah! see the brave three, alone on the view![3]

And for William Weatherford, watching from the shore, it must have been a sobering view.[4] The three whites had killed all nine warriors, with only minor injuries to themselves. The news spread and the three victors became famous throughout the ranks.

From Talladega, Jackson marched back to Fort Strother to find the expected provisions had not arrived, the remaining food almost gone. To head off mutiny by starving troops, he began marching them north to Fort Deposit, leaving a small garrison behind. Twelve miles up the track, however, he encountered a herd of 150 beef cattle and nine wagons of flour coming to their relief. The men ate their fill, but having avenged Fort Mims, they still had home in mind. They shouldered arms and started marching north once more.

But Old Hickory was having none of it. He knew the Redsticks were far from beaten. Weatherford and hundreds of other warriors had not tasted his steel. He rode ahead and, despite a left arm disabled from the recent duel, brandished a musket across his horse's neck. General Coffee and Major John Reid joined him.

"You say you will march," Jackson shouted, "I say by the Eternal God you shall not march while a cartridge can sound fire."[5]

The men murmured and muttered among themselves as Old Hickory stared them

Nine Creek warriors were killed by three militiamen midstream during the celebrated Canoe Fight in 1813 (Wikimedia Commons).

down. Bluffed by his bravado and a gun later found to be defective, they agreed to turn back.

Once returned to the stockade, a bristling Jackson rode north to Fort Deposit to procure more supplies. He returned with provisions on December 10, but his troubles continued as the enlistments of his volunteers began to expire. Most packed their kits and headed for home. Governor Blount advised Jackson to join them, thus abandoning the campaign.

At 12:30 a.m. December 29, Old Hickory penned a response in the dim light of a flickering candle. He reminded Blount that he had "bawled aloud for permission to exterminate the Creeks," and the Tennessee legislature had promised the Madison government that it would keep 3,500 troops in the field till the Creeks were wiped out. Jackson continued:

> And are you my Dear friend sitting with yr. arms folded under the present situation of the campaign recommending me to retrograde to please the whims of the populace and waiting for further orders from the Secy war. Let me tell you it imperiously lies upon both you and me to do our duty regardless of consequences or the opinion of these fireside patriots, those fawning sycophants or cowardly poltroons who after their boasted ardor would rush home or remain at those firesides and let thousands fall victim to my retrograde.... Arouse from yr. lethargy—despise fawning smiles or snarling frowns of such miscreants—with energy exercise yr. functions—the campaign must rapidly progress or you are forever damned and yr. country will be ruined. Call out the full quota authorise—execute the orders of the Secy of War, arrest the officer who omits his duty ... save Mobile—save the Territory—save yr. frontier from becoming drenched in blood.... I will perish first.[6]

On January 14, 1814, a force of 850 fresh recruits arrived at Fort Strother. The campaign would continue. Some troops, including David Crockett, had already returned

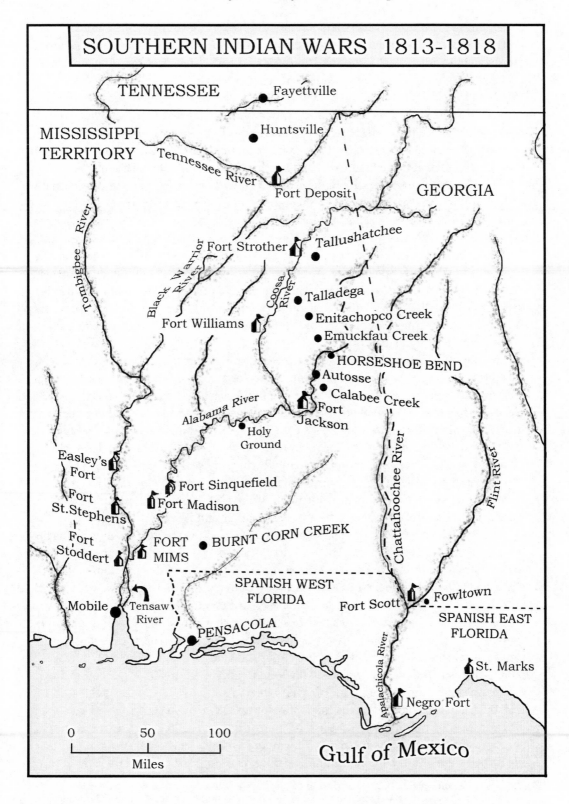

SOUTHERN INDIAN WARS 1813-1818

TENNESSEE

Fayettville

MISSISSIPPI TERRITORY

Huntsville

Tennessee River

Fort Deposit

GEORGIA

Black Warrior River

Fort Strother

Tallushatchee

Coosa River

Talladega

Enitachopco Creek

Fort Williams

Emuckfau Creek

HORSESHOE BEND

Autosse

Calabee Creek

Alabama River

Fort Jackson

Holy Ground

Tombigbee River

Chattahoochee River

Flint River

Easley's Fort

Fort St. Stephens

Fort Madison

Fort Sinquefield

Fort Stoddert

FORT MIMS

BURNT CORN CREEK

Mobile

Tensaw River

SPANISH WEST FLORIDA

Fort Scott

Fowltown

SPANISH EAST FLORIDA

PENSACOLA

Apalachicola River

St. Marks

Negro Fort

0   50   100

Miles

Gulf of Mexico

home, but with other men still on hand, Jackson had a force of over 1,000 men. Determined to destroy the Redsticks, he struck out once more. He would be facing superior numbers, but with Tallushatchee and Talladega under his belt, and knowing most Redsticks had no muskets, he felt confident of success.

Many Creeks resided in a large village, Tohopeka, at Horseshoe Bend on the Tallapoosa River. It was protected by sturdy timber and earth breastworks built across the neck. William Weatherford, Peter McQueen and other Redstick leaders were said to be there. Bent on destruction, Jackson marched confidently south, and on January 21 the troops halted at Emuckfau Creek, about three miles from Horseshoe Bend.

The following morning the undergrowth erupted with a fusillade of musket balls and arrows. Redstick scouts had seen their approach, and a mass of warriors had moved out from Horseshoe Bend bent on doing some destruction of their own. The whites managed to drive them off, and General Coffee's men drove through the woods towards the stronghold. But his men became separated amid the trees and gun smoke as the Redsticks fought back tenaciously. A musket ball hit Coffee in the thigh, and brother-in-law Major Alexander "Sandy" Donelson was shot in the head. The major was carried on horseback to the rear. "Sandy!" cried Old Hickory when he saw the blood covered face of his wife's nephew. But the major was deceased. "Well," said Jackson, with a shake of his head, "it's the fortune of war."[7]

And by the fortune of war, even Tennessee volunteers could not win every fight. Discretion being the better part of valor, Coffee ordered a withdrawal back to camp. Jackson had been taught a lesson. Horseshoe Bend was not going to be an easy victory like Tallushatchee and Talladega. The Indians were prepared to defend their village to the death. "Sharp Knife," as the Creeks called Jackson, had just seen his steel blunted, and he ordered a withdrawal to Fort Strother. The dead were buried, their graves concealed by brush to prevent the bodies being dug up and scalped. They camped for the night behind a makeshift log barricade, sleep broken with frequent false alarms, and resumed the retreat the following morning. Twenty-three wounded, including Coffee, were carried on litters supported by a horse at either end.

At Enitachopco Creek, Jackson's main force crossed the stream in safety, but as his 6-pounder cannon entered the water a flurry of shots were heard in the rear. Jackson looked back and was horrified to see the rearguard "flying in wild confusion." The Redsticks had followed up their success with another attack. Attempting to draw his sword with his crippled arm, he demanded the rearguard stand and fight. The cannon was swung round and hauled to a rise before sending a charge of grapeshot into pursuing Indian ranks a mere 30 paces away. Others rallied to their support, bayonets to the fore. "I never saw such unbending and relentless bravery," recalled John Reid. But Creek bullets and arrows flew and the "Nashville Volunteers" began to fall. Their action, however, gave others time to regroup. A cavalry charge splashed across the creek and the Redsticks fell back, harried by the horsemen for up to two miles. Jackson had saved the day, but was far from happy with the day's performance. His losses vary with different accounts, but some say 20 killed and 75 wounded. When Jackson's army camped that night they were not in a jubilant mood. Artilleryman Richard Call later wrote:

> It was a gloomy night, made so by the sad task of burying our dead, which work we did by
> torches. The flickering and uncertain light of which, added to the funereal gloom of the scene—

increased by the doleful sound from the treetops, as the winter's wind swept over them, making a fit requiem over the graves of the lamentable dead.[8]

The expedition returned to Fort Strother on January 27 with many a hard lesson learned. But Jackson had gained valuable intelligence regarding the approaches to Horseshoe Bend. He claimed the fights as victories, readily endorsed by a Washington administration in want of good news. A wave of new recruits, who believed what they were told, flocked to the banner of the avenger of Fort Mims.

But the truth was Old Hickory had failed in his objective to destroy the enemy stronghold—the campaign was a failure. Redsticks would later state "they whipped Captain Jackson, and run him to the Coosa River."[9]

Someone must be brought to account. Colonels John Stump and Nicholas Perkins were court martialled for disobedience, cowardice, and abandoning their posts. Testimony revealed that Perkins had, in fact, ordered his men to dismount and fight, but they had bolted from the field. He was acquitted, but Stump was sentenced to be cashiered, wear a wooden sword, and be "marched and drummed a half mile from the old line of encampment towards Fort Deposit, at the head of the Artillery Company with their bayonets charged." Jackson, however, took some pity and "upon consideration" ordered that the drumming be dispensed with.[10]

Despite this setback, Major General Thomas Pinckney, commander of the Sixth Military District, was impressed with Jackson's determination to crush the Redstick menace. The hostiles had about 4,000 warriors, but as they lacked muskets, he felt Jackson could defeat them with a well-armed force of 2,000 men.[11] He agreed to place regular infantry under Jackson's command. Old Hickory would no longer be entirely reliant on volunteers who would make for home as soon as their enlistments expired.

Major General John Cocke, commander of the East Tennessee militia, had also campaigned against the Creeks. He had failed to reinforce Jackson at Fort Strother as ordered, and instead sent General White to attack the villages of Hillabee Creeks. These Redsticks, however, had been in contact with Jackson regarding peace. Jackson outranked Cocke due to seniority, and Cocke saw him as a rival. He claimed Jackson's supposed peace with the Hillabees was a hoax, and his own victory over them was more than Jackson's "noble soul" could bear. The Hillabees, not surprisingly, thought Jackson had betrayed them and pressed on with the war.

Under orders from Governor Blount, Cocke assembled a division of six-month men from East Tennessee, then marched south. Cocke addressed his men at Lookout Mountain and claimed that a disproportionate number had been called up from East Tennessee and, according to General John Doherty, stated:

> If the men were taken to Jackson, they would be placed in a situation he did not like to mention, which he could not endure to witness, as it would not be in his power to extract them, that they would suffer from want of provisions on hand, that those who had a desire to serve a 6 month tour, would be compelled to serve it in Mobile, & those whom had not, had better return home now from his camp—that Jackson had the regulars under his command, & would turn his artillery upon them—call to his assistance the Third U.S. Infantry commanded by Colonel Gilbert Russell, making in all 1500, and would compel them to serve 6–9 months and a year if he chose.[12]

With General Pinckney's support, Jackson had Cocke arrested upon his return to Tennessee. He was court-martialled but, having powerful connections, was acquitted of all charges.

Despite having regular troops, Jackson was still reliant on volunteers. General Isaac Roberts wanted a guarantee that his force of 200 men would not have to serve longer than three months. Their request refused by Jackson, they started marching home. Jackson arrested Roberts and declared them deserters, but agreed to a pardon and the three-month enlistment if they returned to camp. Most complied.

One of the "deserters" who returned was 18-year-old John Wood. On sentry duty one cold February morning, he was sent back to camp for warm food and clothing. An officer demanded to know why he had left his post. Wood's insolent response provoked a harsh order to return to duty. Wood refused, and the officer ordered his arrest. When approached by soldiers, Wood kept them at bay with his musket.

As the standoff continued, word reached Old Hickory. "Which is the damned Rascal? Shoot him! Shoot him! Blow ten balls through the damned villain's body."

Wood was persuaded to lay down his musket and promptly placed under arrest. Jackson was determined to set an example and convened a court-martial with instructions to enforce strict military code. Wood, the member of a company with a mutiny-minded reputation, was found guilty and ordered to be shot. Most assumed Jackson would reprieve the sentence, as in the past punishments had not been so severe. On December 4, 1813, nine men had pleaded guilty to charges of desertion. They were sentenced to have one half of their faces blackened, their coats labeled "Deserter," and their hands tied behind them while they were drummed around the camp riding a wooden horse for 15 minutes on three separate days. A lieutenant and ensign were condemned to death the same day, but their sentences were commuted to being cashiered; "dismissed from the service with infamy." Their verdicts were to appear "in all the newspapers published in Tennessee for three months."[13]

But such was not the case for Private Wood. On March 14, 1814, Wood stood in front of a firing squad of the Thirty-ninth regulars for "disobedience of orders, disrespect to your commanding officer, & mutiny." Jackson read aloud:

> The offences of which you have been found guilty cannot be permitted to pass unpunished in an army but at the hazard of its ruin.... An army cannot exist where order and subordination are wholly disregarded.... The disobedience of orders and the contempt of officers speedily lead to a state of disorganization and ruin and mutiny.... This is an important crisis in which if we all act as becomes us, every thing is to be hoped for towards the accomplishment of the objects of our government; if otherwise, every thing to be feared. How it comes us to act, we all know, and what our punishment shall be if we act otherwise, must be known also.[14]

The same day the "damned villain" was shot, Jackson's new expedition set out from Fort Strother leaving a garrison of 450 men. The spectacle of a firing squad had inspired a new respect for authority, and much bad feelings towards Old Hickory. This execution, and others yet to come, would come back to haunt him in future years.

5

Let Every Shot Tell

Flatboats loaded with infantrymen, stores and provisions made their way down the Coosa River. About 60 miles northwest of Horseshoe Bend they established a new post, Fort Williams, whence Jackson could launch a fresh thrust against the Redstick stronghold. The militia traveled by foot and horse to the new post where they were joined by friendly Creeks and Cherokees who provided news of enemy movements. Jackson marched from Fort Williams on March 24, 1814, with a force of about 3,000 regulars, militia and allied Indians—three times the strength of the previous campaign.

"An opportunity is at length offered you of manifesting your zeal to your country and avenging the cruelties committed upon our defenceless fellow citizens," Jackson told his troops. "In the hour of battle you must be cool and collected. When your officers order you to fire, you must execute the command with deliberateness and aim. *Let every shot tell.*" Still licking wounds from the previous campaign, Jackson said he would never order a retreat. "Any officer or soldier who flies before the enemy without being compelled to do so by superior force and actual necessity shall suffer death."

He arrived at Horseshoe Bend on March 27 to be confronted by about 1,000 Redstick warriors behind their impressive, curved fortification. Built of heavy log walls, it was five to eight feet high with gun portholes, and extended about 300 yards across the neck of the river bend. At the far end of a 100-acre peninsula was the village of Tohopeka where women and children sheltered. Jackson observed:

> It is impossible to conceive a situation more eligible for defence than the one they had chosen, and the skill which they manifested in their breast-work was really astonishing. It extended across the point in such a direction as that a force approaching would be exposed to a double fire while they lay entirely safe behind it.[1]

But Sharp Knife had more intricate plans than a suicidal frontal assault. He ordered General Coffee's mounted troops and most Indian allies across the Tallapoosa. Once on the opposite bank, they fanned out and closed in on Tohopeka village from the opposite bank. Jackson, meanwhile, placed his light artillery—one six-pounder and one three-pounder—on a rise about 80 yards from the breastwork's front. At 10:30, both cannon and small arms opened a deafening fusillade. The distant boom of Jackson's cannon was the signal for Coffee's Indians to slip into the water and swim the 120 yards across. They seized Creek canoes along the opposite shore and brought them back to the waiting troops. About 200 Cherokees and Tennesseans piled into the craft and paddled for all their worth back across to the village. With most warriors at the distant breastwork, the few village defenders were driven back.

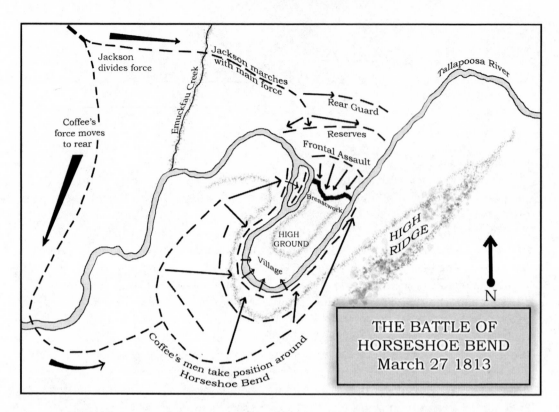

Jackson's cannon fire continued for two hours, doing little damage against the massive logs. Then plumes of smoke billowed skyward as Coffee's men set the village ablaze. Knowing the time had come, Jackson ordered his men to storm the breastworks. The drums rolled and Colonel Williams' Thirty-ninth regulars, flanked by the volunteer brigades of General Doherty and General Johnson, moved forward. Major John Reid recalled:

> I never had such emotions as while the long roll was beating, and the troops in motion. It was not fear, it was not anxiety or concern of the fate of those who were so soon to fall, but it was a kind of enthusiasm that thrilled through every nerve and animated me with the belief that the day was ours without adverting to what it must cost us.[2]

Under fire, the troops rushed across the open space to the breastwork. Some scrambled up the log barricade thrusting at Redsticks with bayonets while others plunged their muskets through gun portholes. Gunfire was exchanged at point-blank range amid screams and smoke as the first soldiers made it over the wooden logs. "At length we mounted the walls and took possession of the other side," recalled Reid. "On every side we heard the groans of the dying and the shouts of the victors."

One young lieutenant of the 39th, Samuel Houston, felt the painful thud of an arrow in his thigh. He was unable to extract the barb and ordered a soldier to pull it out. Failing in the attempt, Houston screamed at him to do it or he'd kill the soldier himself. The arrow was removed, but General Jackson saw the bloody wound and ordered Houston from the fight. The determined Sam Houston, however, disobeyed and rejoined the fray.

The troops fanned out across the peninsula, slaughtering Redsticks as they fell

Old Hickory's troops stormed the Creek breastworks at Horseshoe Bend following Coffee's assault from the rear (Library of Congress).

back to the burning village, but some managed to hold a strong point under a bluff concealed by a barricade. Jackson's demand for surrender was answered with musket fire and a flight of arrows. The two light cannon were brought up and opened fire, but had no success in dislodging warriors, who were determined to fight to the death. Houston attempted to lead a charge, but fell once more with a musket ball to his right arm and left shoulder. He looked back to see no one had followed—it had been a one-man assault. Bleeding and in pain, he staggered to the rear. Old Hickory had taken note of his courage, however. The young Sam Houston was a man to be watched—providing he survived his life-threatening wounds.

Torches were lit by the Tennesseans and thrown down a slope. The undergrowth around the Redstick position burst into flames. Forced out of their refuge by fire and smoke, the warriors were shot down as they attempted to scramble to safe ground.

Redsticks still at large scattered into small groups amid smoke drifting from burning buildings and musket fire. They died where they fought, but not all those slain were warriors; woman and children among the fallen. One small boy was shot because he would have grown into a warrior, so the soldier said. But perhaps stories of dead children at Fort Mims had been the real motivation.

Many Indians fleeing from the burning village attempted to swim across to the opposite shore, "But not one escaped," reported Coffee, "very few ever reached the bank, and those were killed the instant they landed." Major Alexander McCulloch of Coffee's staff recalled, "The Tallapoosa might truly be called the river of blood, for the water was so stained that at ten o'clock at night it was very perceptibly bloody, so much so that it could not be used."

But some did escape, perhaps as many as 200, according to the Creeks. The Redstick commander, Menawa, had received seven wounds during the day's fighting before collapsing and passing out. He regained consciousness during the night and pulled himself from beneath the dead. He staggered to the river where he boarded an abandoned canoe, then set off downstream to eventually reach safe ground.[3]

The fight was over, so the victors thought. But the following morning 16 defiant warriors were discovered in a cave along the riverbank. Called on to come out, they refused to surrender. Unable to direct any effective fire against the stronghold, stakes were driven into the ground above. The loosened earth fell in, burying alive the last of the defiant Creeks.

Dead Creeks were mutilated by the victors, long strips of skin being fashioned into belts and bridle reins for horses. Five hundred fifty-seven dead Redsticks were found across the peninsula, their noses cut off to prevent any mistake in counting the bodies. With those killed in the water, their bodies swept downstream, perhaps 900 Creeks died that day. Only three warriors were taken prisoner along with 350 women and children. The troops, including Jackson, collected souvenirs from amid

Despite numerous wounds, Chief Menewa escaped the slaughter at Horseshoe Bend under cover of dark (Library of Congress).

the dead and debris. He wrote to his wife Rachel telling her to kiss their adopted son Andrew from him and "Tell him I have a warrior's bow and quiver for him."[4] Not found among the dead were William Weatherford, Peter McQueen or Josiah Francis. The men at the top of Jackson's "Wanted" list were still at large.

The American force suffered a disproportionate 49 killed and 153 wounded. But Jackson was grieved at the loss of the first man to die on the breastworks, his friend Major Lemuel Montgomery of the 39th.

Had the Indians been better armed, Old Hickory would have had a much more robust enemy to fight. Less than half the Creeks had been carrying muskets, the rest relying on primitive weapons. And they were outnumbered three to one. But the Creeks were not only crushed by battle. Various American columns had destroyed the Indian crops, so while Jackson returned to Fort Williams for fresh provisions, the Creeks were near starvation. From Fort Williams, Old Hickory marched once more, moving south along the Coosa River, then sweeping down the west bank of the Tallapoosa. The Indians fled before the troops, and their villages were put to the torch. A soldier of Coffee's command recalled a gruesome find in one deserted council house: "High up on the central pole inside were numerous arrows sticking straight out, on which hung the scalps of men, women and children massacred at Fort Mims. These were taken down and decently buried."[5] Communication was established with Colonel Homer Milton's force on the east bank of the Tallapoosa, and together they swept both sides of the river in a futile search for dispersed Redsticks.

Fort Jackson was established at the confluence of the Tallapoosa and Coosa Rivers, the same site as the long abandoned French Fort Toulouse. The various military columns converged here by the end of April 1814, and General Pinckney arrived to take overall command. Troops were dispatched to hunt down hostile bands but, although some would hide in swamps and join Seminole kinsmen in Spanish territory, Horseshoe Bend had crushed any substantial resistance.

This punishing victory would never be surpassed in American territory during four centuries of Indian wars. Following Horseshoe Bend, many starving Creeks surrendered at American posts begging for food. To meet the demand, flatboats carrying provisions were sent upstream from Mobile.

But the "Murderer of Fort Mims" was still at large. Towards the end of April a despondent, lone rider rode into Andrew Jackson's cantonment and requested directions to the general's quarters. The notorious "Billy" Weatherford, a candidate for execution if ever there was one, was shown into Jackson's presence.

The Creek leader had not been at Horseshoe Bend, but his misfortunes had commenced long before that. On November 29, 1813, General John Floyd's Georgia troops had destroyed the Creek town of Autosse, and many Creeks had fled into Spanish territory to avoid further retaliation. Weatherford traveled to Pensacola to procure gunpowder but the Spanish commander had none to spare. Fresh supplies, however, were obtained from British agents and private stores.[6] Weatherford loaded three packhorses and returned north to continue the fight from his village on the Alabama River. Called the Holy Ground, it was magically invulnerable to attack, so said Josiah Francis. But on December 23 General Claiborne's troops arrived.

No hope now, nor mercy!—thy foremen have sworn
Thy life for thy merciless deeds shall atone.
Heard'st not, through the storm of the battle, their cry—
"Revenge for Fort Mimms; let the murderers die!"[7]

Weatherford made his escape by horseback with a huge leap into the Alabama River. Numerous scalps from Fort Mims were discovered on a pole in the town square before the buildings went up in flames.[8]

On January 27, 1814, Redsticks were repulsed after attacking General John Floyd's encampment on Calabee Creek. Weatherford was there, but declined to take part because the Redsticks refused his battle plan. It would appear his influence was on the wane.

Since then, other battles and military operations, including those of Jackson, had seen 60 Upper Creek towns either abandoned or put to the torch. The food, clothing and other belongings of 8,000 Redstick men, women and children had been destroyed.[9] And then there was Horseshoe Bend.

Weatherford now wanted peace. He had come to surrender himself and those Creeks in his immediate band who had taken refuge on a nearby river island. He regretted the massacre of innocents at Fort Mims, he said, and had attempted to prevent the killing that took place. He would fight no longer, and wished for the protection of those Creeks in his care. An officer present, William Carroll, recalled the meeting:

William Weatherford impressed Jackson with eloquent denials of guilt then, changing sides, helped hunt down his former allies (Library of Congress).

He was a little scant of six feet tall, rather slender in build, but sinewy and graceful. His dress was part white and part Indian, like himself. His features were clean-cut and sharp, his nose like a hawk's beak and his complexion almost white. He spoke slowly and deliberately in pretty fair English, but often hesitated for a word as if not much practiced in speaking that language. When he spoke the Muscogee tongue, though, he talked fast and apparently—to judge from the effect of his talk upon the Indians who could understand him—with great force. He was solemn in manner and greatly depressed by the forlorn condition of his people, though he did not seem to care for his own fate, whatever that might be. At first he seemed fearful that the General might doubt his sincerity. But when I fully assured him on that point he displayed the liveliest satisfaction. He said to me "I would be a fool if I tried to deceive now, and I hope the General will think that I am not that!" When he left the fort in the afternoon he said: "I hope we may meet again, General Carroll, when my people are out of their troubles." He was one of nature's great men.[10]

General Jackson thought so too, apparently. He let him go on the promise he would help end hostilities. During May, Weatherford rode with Colonel John Pearson's troops as they searched for Redsticks still at large, inducing them to surrender, and fighting those who would not. Pearson recalled that Weatherford "does not deny that he fought, and that he fought desperately too, but he solemnly avers that he never, knowingly, or intentionally, hurt less killed a woman or child during the War. He says that at Fort Mims he killed, he believes, as many *Men* as any other man there but that he never entered the part of the Fort where the women were."

But Tecumseh had advocated, "Slay their wives and children." Was it possible for Weatherford not to know the outcome when he led the attack? "Actions speak louder than words," as the old saying goes. And the British in Spanish West Florida had news of an American force "headed by Colonel Carson, and joined by Wm Weatherford an Indian Chief, are pursuing the Creek Indians and are killing them wherever they meet them ... they have also attacked a new Indian settlement called Coneta, and Killed all the Indians they could lay hands on, have taken what women and children could be found."[11]

Thus William Weatherford saved himself from the gallows with eloquent denials, and turning on the Creeks he had led in war. Josiah Francis, who stuck to his guns and lacked Weatherford's diplomatic skills, would not fare so well when he finally fell into Sharp Knife's hands. Weatherford, protected by prominent kin who rewrote his role, returned to life as a plantation owner in south Alabama. "I have come to live among gentlemen," he told Sam Dale.[12] He kept a low profile, avoiding tribal affairs, and died in 1824, leaving slaves and land which became the object of a legal battle. In 1855, three years following the Alabama Supreme Court handing down a decision in *Weatherford vs. Weatherford,* he was romantically renamed Red Eagle by the poet Alexander Beaufort Meek. Eulogized, he became a legend despite his track record during the Creek War.

General Pinckney was appointed to negotiate with the Creeks. Following recommendations from the Secretary of War, he offered terms which called for American retention of much conquered Creek lands as compensation for the cost of the war; forts, trading posts and roads could be constructed through Creek lands; the rivers navigated; the war instigators surrendered, and the Creeks must restrict trade with foreign nations (Britain and Spain) as decided by the United States.[13]

Andrew Jackson and his fellow Tennesseans were not pleased. These terms were far too lenient, they felt. Riding high on his success at Horseshoe Bend, Jackson was appointed brigadier general in the regular United States Army, in command of the Seventh Military District. This included most Creek lands. With the resignation of William

Creek chiefs remonstrate with Jackson over the harshness of the treaty terms which punished friend and foe alike (Wikimedia Commons).

Henry Harrison, he was promoted to major general, strings were pulled, and he relieved Pinckney as negotiator with the Creeks. He arrived at Fort Jackson on July 10, 1814, and summoned the Indian chiefs for a meeting on August 1. They were shocked to have Old Hickory abandon the terms proposed by Pinckney and demand relinquishment of lands west of the Coosa River and north of the Alabama River. This would take 22 million acres from both hostile and friendly Creeks alike. Every chief present vented his displeasure and protested the injustice of the terms.

Jackson justified depriving friendly Creeks, saying that they had listened to the words of Tecumseh who considered the United States weak. It stood to reason they had agreed with Tecumseh because

> if they had not thought so, Tecumseh would have had no influence. He would have been sent back to the British, or delivered to the United States as a prisoner, or shot. If my enemy goes to the house of my friend, and tells my friend he means to kill me, my friend becomes my enemy if he does not at least tell me I am to be killed.[14]

"How-dy-do, brother," friendly Creeks had called from the stockade at Talladega. Considering they had been at war with Redsticks before the Americans, then joined forces with Jackson, Old Hickory's argument was spurious to say the least. Not all lands were being taken, however, Jackson claiming the tribe could easily support itself on what remained. He said the Creeks had to be separated from Spanish Florida from where the British still encouraged armed rebellion against the United States. This, Jackson said, would lead to the destruction of the Creek Nation.

> We will run a line between our friends and our enemies. We wish to save our friends, protect them, support them. *We will do these things.* We will destroy our enemies because we love our friends and ourselves. The safety of the United States and your nation requires that enemies must be separated from friends. We wish to know them from each other. We wish to be able to say to our soldiers: Here is one, there is the other.... *Therefore we will run the line.*[15]

Jackson said those who signed the treaty would be provided with clothing and food, and considered friends with the United States. Those who would not would be considered enemies, but they too would receive provisions to help them on their way. "We wish them to join their friends that all may be destroyed together."

Two weeks following Jackson's treaty which punished all Creeks, the British set Washington, D.C., ablaze (Wikimedia Commons).

Jackson wrote to Rachel, his wife: "Could you only see the misery and wretchedness of those creatures perishing from want of food and picking up the grains of corn scattered from the mouths of the horses and trodden in the earth, I know your humanity would feel for them."

It comes as little surprise that the Creek chiefs signed the Treaty of Fort Jackson on August 9. They had no choice. And there were other concerns, as Jackson wrote to a War Department: "They *must* be *fed* and *clothed* or necessity will compel them to embrace the proffered friendship of the British."

Indian Agent Benjamin Hawkins considered the treaty cruel, and a violation of trust but, seeing no alternative, advised them to sign. The 35 chiefs who did so were predominantly "friendlies," and settlements near the confluence of the Chattahoochee and Flint Rivers soon found themselves subject to raids by hostiles who refused the terms. Redsticks sheltering over the border in Spanish territory were joined by neutral Creeks, and even some who had fought on the American side.[16] They were supplied with arms by the British, who could make good use of Indian allies behind American lines once an invasion was launched on the Gulf Coast.

The Creeks must have been delighted to hear that, just two weeks after the Treaty of Fort Jackson, the British put Washington, D.C., to the torch—divine retribution from the Master of Breath.

6

A Rough Sort of Backwoodsman

On July 12, even before his negotiations with the Creeks were under way, Jackson had dispatched Captain John Gordon with a letter to the Spanish commander at Pensacola, Mateo González Manríque:

> I am informed, that the enemies of the United States who have been murdering our unoffending women and children, have sought and obtained an asylum from justice within the territory of Spain, and are fed by order of the governor of Pensacola. Information has also been received, that permission was given to our open enemy, an officer commanding his Britannic Majesty's frigate the *Orpheus,* to land within the territory of Spain 25,000 stands of arms with 300 barrels of ammunition, for the avowed purpose of enabling the vanquished Creeks to renew a sanguinary war with the United States. I trust, sir, that no foundations for these reports exists.... Will you be so good sir as to transmit by the bearer, or through any other medium, immediate information bearing on these subjects; and, should Francis, McQueen, or any other chiefs of the Creek nation hostile to the United States be within the jurisdictional territory of the governor of Pensacola, to cause them to be immediately confined that they may be brought to atone to this government for violations of the rights of humanity and the principles of treaties heretofore existing between the two nations.[1]

Captain Gordon returned on July 29 and reported that Manríque considered "the Generals letter was impertinent and contained demand of two Indian chiefs, namely Peter McQueen and Josiah Francis, which he conceived an insult to the Government, and that the Spaniards would die before they would comply with such a demand"; and Americans, having committed "depredations on the Indians within the Territorial limits of Spain without the consent of the Government, would authorise him to arm the Indians, and furnish them with arms and ammunition." Various British vessels, Gordon stated, had delivered arms to the Indians for a combined attack with British troops "against some of our military posts on the Alabama." The Indians possessed beef cattle stolen from within the United States and "A rumor reached Pensacola the evening before I left it—that there was a Declaration of War by Spain against the United States, but not certain."

His treaty with the Creeks signed, sealed and delivered, Andrew Jackson arrived in Mobile on August 27, 1814. There had been no declaration of war by Spain, but Old Hickory was prepared to risk one if it meant getting his own way. He sent Governor Blount an urgent request that the entire Tennessee militia be dispatched with all due haste. British troop transports carrying 10,000 men were on their way to attack Mobile, so Jackson had heard from Pensacola informants.

Fort Bowyer was located at the end of a sand spit which defended the entrance to Mobile Bay. Commanded by Major James Lawrence with a garrison of 158 men, it was a semicircular earthen structure 400 feet around facing the sea. The rear was protected by a straight wall and central bastion. The landward ground was rough and offered considerable cover to an attacking force. The fort itself fell a long way short of what could be called adequate construction. The inner walls were of flammable pine, and artillerymen serving the eleven cannon would be exposed to enemy fire from the knees upwards. It had no casements to protect ammunition and wounded men.

In mid–September the British helped Jackson substantiate his claim of imminent invasion by attacking Fort Bowyer. Four British warships under Captain William H. Percy arrived, and a force of 60 marines, 180 Indians and one howitzer under marine Captain Robert Henry attacked by land. Henry's men, receiving hot fire from well trained regulars, were driven back under cover with one man killed.

But the naval vessels feared far worse. Despite disabling a number of Fort Bowyer's guns, contrary wind and tide retarded their fire. H.H.S. *Hermes*, raked by American gunfire, her sails and tackle badly damaged, drifted and grounded with her stern to the fort. Marine commander Major Edward Nicholls was blinded in his right eye. Captain Percy had the onerous duty of setting his own ship ablaze as his dead and wounded were taken off in small boats. The flames reached the powder magazine and "I had the melancholy satisfaction of seeing His Majesty's ship blow up in the same place in which I left her,"[2] reported Percy. He would be exonerated at his court-martial, but never command a ship again. The British withdrew to their base at Pensacola with a loss of 24 dead, 44 wounded and one frigate destroyed. The star spangled banner still proudly fluttered above the fort's walls with a loss of only four dead and five wounded.[3]

The British warships, having sailed from Pensacola, provided proof of Spanish connivance, and the secretary of war gave Old Hickory free reign to reinforce the Gulf Coast.[4] The prediction of imminent invasion was premature, but Jackson's build-up of American forces would prove to be a god send for the United States.

Jackson now resolved to remove the British threat at Pensacola whether the "neutral" Spanish, or his own government, liked it or not. He wrote to his wife that should he confront the British, "I trust I shall pay the debt—she is in conjunction with Spain arming the hostile Indians to butcher our women and children."[5] Thus Fort Mims continued to be a justification for Jackson's actions, including war with Spain if need be.

David Crockett, back in Tennessee, again heeded the call to arms. Shortly after Horseshoe Bend, "an army was raised to go to Pensacola, and I determined to go again with them, for I wanted a small taste of British fighting, and I supposed they would be there. Here again the entreaties of my wife were thrown in the way of my going, but all in vain; for I always had a way of just going ahead, at whatever I had a mind to do."[6]

On September 28, Crockett, now a veteran, enlisted with the rank of third sergeant with General Coffee's Tennessee Mounted Gunmen. Food shortages came into play once more and delayed Coffee's march, but the Mounted Gunmen finally moved south in early October, about two days after the main army's departure.

Near Fort Mims, Crockett met a survivor of the carnage who recalled a day he would probably rather forget:

> The fort was built right in the middle of a large old field, and in it the people had been forted so long and so quietly, that they didn't apprehend any danger at all, and had, therefore, become quite careless ... the Indians came in a troop, loaded with rails, with which they stop'd all the port-holes of the fort on one side except the bastion; and then they fell to cutting down the picketing. Those inside the fort had only one bastion to shoot from, as all the other holes were spiked up; and they

shot several of the Indians, while engaged in cutting. But as fast as one would fall, another would seize up the axe and chop away, until they succeeded in cutting down enough of the picketing to admit them to enter. They then began to rush through, and continued until they were all in. They immediately commenced scalping, without regard to age or sex; having forced the inhabitants up to one side of the fort, where they carried on the work of death as a butcher would in a slaughter pen.

The scene was particularly described to me by a young man who was in the fort when it happened, and subsequently went on with us to Pensacola. He said he saw his father, and mother, his four sisters, and the same number of brothers, all butchered in the same shocking manner, and that he made his escape by running over the heads of the crowd, who were against the fort wall, to the top of the fort, and then jumping off, and taking to the woods. He was closely pursued by several Indians, until he came to a small byo, across which there was a log. He knew the log was hollow on the other side, so he slip'd under the log and hid himself. He said he heard the Indians walk over him several times back and forward. He remained, nevertheless, still till night, when he came out, and finished his escape. The name of this young man has entirely escaped my recollection, though his tale greatly excited my feelings.[7]

Crockett was "greatly excited" by this tale, told in fact by Lieutenant Peter Randon. Perhaps the Tennessee Gunman had seen his own destiny flash before his eyes. Fate had decreed that his final day of life would have strong parallels with the soldiers and settlers who had sheltered behind the walls of Fort Mims.

Old Hickory, meanwhile, had ordered Fort Bowyer reinforced and her walls strengthened while he drew his plans against Pensacola. The town itself was defended by a series of blockhouses and a number of forts, but the approaches through swampy terrain were impossible to defend with the small force of 500 regular Spanish soldiers. Additional local militia could double this number, but poorly armed and led, Jackson assumed they would offer no serious threat. He assembled a force of about 4,400 men composed of militia, volunteers, 520 regulars, and 750 Indian allies from the Chickasaw and Choctaw tribes. With no authority from the Madison government, Old Hickory marched his force eastward into Spanish territory. On November 6, he arrived at Pensacola and promptly sent a demand for surrender to Governor Manríque. He required evacuation by all British troops, and the occupation of two key forts by United States soldiers.

Manríque replied that Spain and the United States were not at war, the British used Pensacola without his permission, and "my duty does not permit me" to comply with Jackson's demands.[8] Old Hickory wasted no time. Under cover of darkness, he moved the main force to the east of town, leaving 500 men behind as a decoy. Next morning the surprised Spaniards were horrified to hear the beat of drums and the blare of bugles as four American columns, one Indian and three white, advanced from the east. The British vessels in the bay opened a belated and ineffective fire as the Americans stormed the town. Two Spanish cannon in the central street opened fire, but Pensacola was quickly overrun.

Governor Manríque emerged and ran about frantically waving a white flag, hastily surrendering both town and forts. The commander of Fort Barrancas, however, had other ideas. He had no intention of lowering his colors, and refused a demand for surrender. Jackson held his fire as night came on, but the Spanish garrison and British redcoats were able to evacuate into naval ships under cover of dark. Next morning, as Jackson ordered an assault, "A tremendous explosion was heard, and a column of smoke was seen to ascend it that direction," he reported. "Repetitions of the explosions soon convinced me that the British and Spanish were blowing up the works."[9] Pensacola was taken with light losses on both sides; five Americans killed and 10 wounded, and 14 Spanish killed and six wounded.[10]

Crockett and his fellow Mounted Tennessee Gunmen arrived shortly after the surrender—but without their mounts. They had "trudged merrily on" the last 80 miles on foot, their horses left under guard, the terrain between Fort Mims and Pensacola lacking adequate forage.

Once on the outskirts of Pensacola, the dismounted Gunmen set up camp. "That evening we went down into the town, and could see the British fleet lying in sight of the place," recalled Crockett. "We got some liquor, and took a 'horn' or so, and went back to the camp."

Jackson learned from informants that the British had both troops and naval vessels at Jamaica with plans for the expected invasion. Mobile was no longer the target, however. New Orleans, the gateway to the Mississippi, was where they would strike. Jackson ordered a withdrawal back to Mobile where he would draw up fresh plans.

General John Coffee wrote to his wife: "Like the rest of the boys, I am tired of thrashing redskins.... My men are so used to killing Indians they are almost sorry for them. But they have no pity for the redcoats, who, they declare, are to be held responsible for all the devilment the Indians have done. Every one of my boys wants to get within fair buckrange of a redcoat."[11]

But not all would get a chance to shoot redcoats. Redsticks sheltering in Pensacola had fled when "Sharp Knife" arrived. Major Uriah Blue had been one of those to bury the dead after Fort Mims. Perhaps Jackson thought he would rather fight Creeks than the British. Blue was ordered to take the Tennessee Mounted Gunmen and hunt the Redsticks down. He was to do a northern sweep through Creek lands in American territory, then head south to attack a British fort on the Apalachicola River in Spanish East Florida; a haven for fleeing Redsticks and escaped slaves.

A few days after Jackson's withdrawal from Pensacola, Blue's command marched back to Fort Montgomery, just a few miles from Fort Mims. Here the Tennessee Gunman retrieved their horses. Sergeant Crockett recalled, "we supplied ourselves pretty well with beef, by killing wild cattle which had formerly belonged to the people who perished in the fort, but had gone wild after the massacre."

The regiment of Tennessee Gunmen, along with 168 Chickasaw, Choctaw and Creeks allies, moved out from Fort Montgomery on December 8. Major Blue was forced to dismount many men to allow packs to be carried instead. Heavy rains had made the roads quagmires that could never support lumbering, heavy supply wagons.[12] The troops camped near the Escambia River where they received supplies sent up by boat from Pensacola. This included not only basic rations like coffee and sugar but also "liquors of all kinds" to satisfy the thirsty volunteers.

The allied Indian leaders suggested taking their braves to hunt Redsticks along the opposite side of the river. Major Blue agreed, and dispatched Major Russell with the Indians and 16 white soldiers, including Sergeant Crockett. The detachment camped that night on the opposite bank, then set out to hunt Redsticks believed to be lurking nearby. They struck a vast area of swampy terrain which looked like an inland sea. "We didn't stop for this," recalled Crockett, "but just put in like so many spaniels, and waded on, sometimes up to out armpits, until we reached the pine hills, which made our distance through the water about a mile and a half."[13] Badly chilled, they built warming fires before pushing on. Six miles later, "our spies on the left came leaping the brush like so many old bucks, and informed us that they had discovered a camp of Creek Indians, and that we must kill them." Major Russell found himself being daubed with war paint by his Indian allies as they prepared themselves for battle.

The command pressed on with two Choctaw scouts well in advance. A war whoop and shots were heard. "With that we all broke like quarter horses, for the firing." They arrived to find their scouts in possession of two freshly decapitated Creeks. The Choctaws had gained their confidence by claiming in the Shawnee tongue that they were escaping from Jackson's attack on Pensacola. Where could they get something to eat? The Creeks told them of their encampment on an island nearby, and a village further on, then "struck up a fire, and smoked together, and shook hands, and parted." The Choctaws turned, shot one Creek who possessed a musket, then, their other flintlock misfiring, took after the remaining warrior on foot. The Choctaws proved faster and brought him down with a blow to the head, then killed him with a musket butt. They returned to the other dead Creek and discharged his captured musket. Russell, Crockett and the others soon arrived.

The Indians walked up to the severed heads and struck one or the other with their war clubs. "This was done by every one of them," recalled Crockett, "and when they had got done, I took one of their clubs, and walked up as they had done, and struck it on the head also. At this they all gathered round me, and patting me on the shoulder, would call me 'Warrior—warrior.'"[14]

The Indians scalped the victims, and the party continued on through the woods. They soon stumbled across the dead bodies of a Spaniard, a woman and four children. Any sympathy felt for the two trusting Creeks would have been lost with this reminder of Fort Mims. Warfare in the American wilderness was a savage and bitter affair. "I began to feel mighty ticklish along about this time," recalled Crockett, "for I knowed if there was no danger then, there had been; and I felt exactly like there still was."

Towards evening, the party discovered the Creek encampment on the opposite side of the river. Crockett and his comrades took cover behind trees and logs while some of their Creek allies hailed the village in their native tongue. They conversed with a woman until dark came on. She said there was a canoe on their side of the river, taken by two warriors to hunt for horses. It came as no surprise to Crockett and his companions that they had not returned.

Under cover of darkness, 40 of Russell's Indians used the canoe to cross to the woods on the other side. They rushed the village to see one man escaping into the trees "and they took two squaws, and ten children, but killed none of them, of course."

The detachment was nearly out of provisions, but there was another village nearby. Russell wanted to push on and strike it if possible. Crockett and two others were sent out in the captured canoe to report to base camp, then return with provisions. After a perilous trip through fast flowing, flooded waters, Crockett arrived at Major Blue's camp at about 10 p.m. But "It would be bad times for him" said Blue, if Russell was not back the following day. A man from Crockett's company was sent to fetch the wayward Russell back.

Following Russell's return, Blue's regiment moved towards Pensacola where Redsticks had fled across the bay following Jackson's capture of the town. Two companies with scouts in advance moved through the woods to flush them out. They had "a little skirmish with the Indians. They killed some, and took all the balance prisoners, though I don't remember the numbers," recalled Crockett. The detachment rejoined the rest of the regiment, and the prisoners were sent to Fort Montgomery under the guard of Indian allies. "I did hear, that after they left us, the Indians killed and scalped all the prisoners, and I never heard the report contradicted. I cannot say the report is positively true, but I think it entirely probable, for it is very much like the Indian character."

Hunger and fatigue set in as the regiment moved towards the Chattahoochee River. "At the start we had taken only twenty days' rations of flour, and eight days' rations of beef; and it was now thirty-four days before we reached that place," recalled Crockett. His main subsistence was now his diminishing supply of coffee.

A scout brought news of a Creek village on the Chattahoochee, and the troops immediately set out on an overnight forced march. This village could provide vital food supplies. Crockett recalled:

> We arrived about sunrise, and near the place prepared for battle. We were all so furious that even the certainty of a pretty hard fight could not have restrained us. We made a furious charge on the town, but to our great mortification and surprise, there wasn't a human being in it. The Indians had all run off and left it. We burned the town, however; but, melancholy to tell, we found no provisions whatever. We then turned about, and went back to the camp we had left the night before, as nearly starved as any set of poor fellows in the world.[15]

Any thought of striking the British fort in Spanish East Florida disappeared, merely surviving becoming the aim. The regiment divided, Major Childs' battalion setting off to Baton Rouge while Russell's men, including Crockett, struck for Fort Decatur on the Tallapoosa River. They hunted any "hawk, bird and squirrel" as they marched, the proceeds being equally divided at camp each night. To bag game, Crockett and a few companions decided to "come up missing." By going absent without leave, they figured they had nothing to lose because they were going to starve to death anyway. They set out, finding nine dead Creeks in one camp and three in another, the victims of Indian scouts moving in advance. "We continued on for three days," recalled Crockett, "killing little or nothing to eat; till, at last, we all began to get nearly ready to give up the ghost, and lie down and die." But then their luck changed. Following animal trails across grasslands, they shot some squirrels. Crockett had to scale 30 feet up a branchless tree to retrieve one from a hole. "I shouldn't relate such small matters, only to show what lengths a hungry man will go to, to get something to eat." Some large wild turkeys were also brought down—substantial food at last. They returned to camp. The Indian scouts returned with some flour, and bee trees had been found with honey for the taking, "though we had been starving so long that we feared to eat much at a time, till ... we got used to it again."

Some deer were shot before the main army came up. The food was shared out and they tramped on to Fort Decatur where they hoped to find ample provisions, but only one ration of meat per man could be spared. Crockett set out in a canoe and traded gunpowder and bullets for corn with local Indians. Subsisting on parched corn, the command made it to Fort Williams where one ration of pork and one of flour was all that could be issued. Crockett managed to retain his horse despite others being abandoned, and the hungry troops trudged on towards Fort Strother.

It was thirty-nine miles to Fort Strother, and we had to pass directly by Fort Talledego, where we first had the big Indian battle with the eleven hundred painted warriors. We went through the old battle ground, and it looked like a great gourd patch; the skulls of the Indians who were killed still lay scattered all about, and many of their frames were still perfect, as the bones had not separated. But about five miles before we got to this battle ground, I struck a trail, which I followed till it led me to one of their towns. Here I swap'd some more of my powder and bullets for a little corn.[16]

The following morning they encountered East Tennessee troops on their way to Mobile. Not only did they have plenty of provisions to share, but David Crockett was reunited with his younger brother John. That night Crockett's company crossed the Coosa River while he stayed behind swapping yarns with John and other Tennessee friends. He was a good raconteur, something that would be a great benefit in later life. He crossed the Coosa himself the following morning, and rejoined his comrades at Fort Strother where ample food was on hand.

"Nothing more, worthy of the readers attention, transpired till I was safely landed at home once more with my wife and children," Crockett recalled. "I found them all well and doing well; and though I was only a rough sort of backwoodsman, they seemed mighty glad to see me, however little the quality folks might suppose it. For I do reckon we love as hard in the backwood country, as any people in the whole creation."[17]

7

Rattling Peals of Thunder

Andrew Jackson arrived with a small staff in New Orleans on December 1, 1814. Located on the Mississippi, much of the terrain surrounding the city was swampy marshland, and large lakes in the area opened to the Gulf of Mexico. This invited the landing of invading troops, and the shadowy trails threading through the swamps did not exist on maps. Amid this maze, Jackson was tasked with organizing a defence with little idea of where the enemy may land.

After a reconnaissance on horseback, he sent parties of local militia to construct defences with fallen trees along the numerous paths and small streams. Choctaw Indians and free blacks commanded by white officers from local militia were sent to guard the Chef Menteur Road, and militia reinforced Fort St. John standing guard over the approach from Lake Pontchartrain. Navy gunboats were sent to patrol Lake Borgne, another likely landing place.

A key problem was the existing defence arrangements, a hodge podge of various committees. And the populace cared little for the United States. Louisiana had been Spanish territory from 1763 till 1800 when it passed to the French, who sold it to the Americans in 1803. Most citizens were not American, but Spanish and French. Jackson's predecessor General Flournoy had written to the secretary of war complaining that the inhabitants were only interested in commerce, including dealing with the enemy if need be. "I do believe," he wrote, that there was "not one person in twenty throughout this State, that is friendly towards the United States, or would take up arms in its defence."[1]

Prior to Jackson's arrival some actually hoped for a British victory, believing it would see Louisiana returned to Spanish rule, while others, appalled at the prospect, felt that American militia would never stand against seasoned redcoats.

On December 15, Jackson issued a proclamation to the citizens of New Orleans: "The major-general commanding, has, with astonishment and regret, learned that great consternation and alarm pervade your city. It is true that the enemy is on our coast and threatens an invasion of our territory, but it is equally true, with union, energy, and the approbation of Heaven, we will beat him at every point his temerity may induce him to set foot upon our soil." Jackson went on to repudiate "such incredible tales" as the country being returned to Spain, and called Britain "the common enemy of mankind, the highway robber of the world.... Then look to your liberties, your property, the chastity of your wives and daughters."

Old Hickory warned that the articles of war proscribed death for those who dealt with the enemy and he would "execute the martial law in all such cases which may come within his province." The safety of the country was entrusted to the general and "will be maintained with the best blood of the country; and he is confident all good citizens will be found at their posts, with their arms in their hands, determined to dispute every inch of ground with the enemy: that unanimity will pervade the country generally: but should the general be disappointed in these expectations, he will separate our enemies from our friends—those who are not for us are against us, and will be dealt with accordingly."[2]

Then a courier arrived with startling news. The enemy had arrived on Lake Borgne, the American gunboats captured after a determined fight.

This report, along with Jackson's compelling presence, galvanized a wave of anti–British sentiment. Declaring martial law, he took control of the local militia as the Creek War veterans came marching into New Orleans. Every available firearm was seized from attics, shops and arsenals. The local naval depot contained a host of essential weapons, including 32-pounder cannon, the largest available at the time. The previous July, the secretary of the navy had ordered 100 tons of shot and 200 barrels of gunpowder to be delivered; a timely arrival for those about to defend New Orleans.

Jackson was concerned with the capture of the gunboats. They had been his eyes and ears for British movements from the east. The enemy, once landed, could now infiltrate the numerous canals and bayous that provided access to the city.

On December 23 Jackson received word that British troops had landed on the shores of Lake Borgne. They were establishing themselves at the Villere plantation alongside the Mississippi about eight miles southeast of the city. The enemy strength was estimated at about 1,700 men; merely the advance guard of regiments yet to arrive.

Jackson had about 3,500 men in and around New Orleans, the number growing due to the constant arrival of troops.

"I lost no time in making preparations to attack him that night," Jackson recalled, ""I was not ignorant of the inferiority of my force, nor of the hazard of making night attacks with inexperienced troops. But the fears to be entertained from these sources were overbalanced by the greater evils to be apprehended from delay." About 1,800 men were mustered; 800 volunteers under General Coffee, 400 militia, and 600 regulars of the Seventh and 44th regiments. It was possible the Lake Borgne landing was merely a diversion, so Jackson ordered his remaining troops to defend the north of the city. Perhaps the real attack would come from Lake Pontchartrain.

Naval support was requested from Commodore Daniel Patterson, and the only available vessel, the *Carolina*, set sail. She carried one long barreled 12-pounder, and a number of carronades.[3]

At about 7:30 that evening, the British became aware that they were not alone. American troops were seen advancing towards their encampment, but it was assumed there would be no hostilities till the following day. As the redcoats huddled around their cooking fires a schooner moved up the Mississippi. She dropped anchor a short distance offshore as her canvas was furled. They assumed she was British and hailed her. "Give them this for the honor of America" was the reply. The *Carolina*'s guns flashed in the twilight and grapeshot ripped through the British camp. The redcoats dashed for cover and replied with muskets and rockets to no effect as the American artillery on land opened fire. Then the ranks of Jackson's army dashed to the attack. George Gleig, a young Scots ensign with the British, recalled:

> Now began a battle of which no language were competent to convey any distinct idea, because it was one to which the annals of modern warfare furnish no parallel. All order, all discipline were lost. Each officer, as he succeeded in collecting twenty or thirty men about him, plunged into the midst of the enemy's ranks, where it was fought hand to hand, bayonet to bayonet, and sabre to sabre.[4]

Each side inflicted casualties and took prisoners as the British line was pushed back about 300 yards. A redcoat counterattack nearly captured Jackson's artillery, but Old Hickory ordered a company of the Seventh Infantry to the defense. His guns were saved as the redcoats were driven back with a bayonet charge. The firing eased off as a heavy fog rolled in, and silence reined by about 9 p.m.

Despite the British having held their ground, "The result equalled my expectations," Jackson claimed. "From every point on which we assailed him, he was repulsed.... The enemy, taken by surprise and thrown into confusion, was unable to penetrate our designs and feared to prosecute his own." The Americans lost 24 killed, 115 wounded and 74 captured. The British lost 46 killed, 167 wounded and 64 captured. Many more casualties were yet to come.

Before dawn the following morning Jackson ordered a withdrawal of two miles to the Rodriguez Canal which ran between the Mississippi and a cypress swamp. Located about four miles southeast of New Orleans, it was ideal for defense, and work commenced on digging a trench and earthen rampart.

The audacity of the prompt American night attack convinced the British advance guard commander, General John Keane, that he was facing a far larger force than Jackson actually commanded. Keane lost his best chance of seizing New Orleans as he awaited the arrival of more troops over the next few days allowing Jackson to reinforce and strengthen his defences. This included receiving muskets, gunpowder and men from Jean Lafitte's pirates of Barataria Island. Jackson had once described them as "hellish banditti," but now accepted support from any quarter.[5] Lafitte had rejected British overtures to assist in their attack and offered his services to Jackson, despite his base having been ravaged a few months before by the American navy. The forgiving Lafitte would now work with Commodore Patterson, the man who had directed the attack.

Mississippi and Louisiana dragoons were left at the Laronde plantation to keep an eye on British movements and reinforcements, and the *Carolina* was joined by another vessel hastily fitted out, the *Louisiana.* Lafitte's pirates provided seasoned gunners and crews, and the two vessels opened fire on the British camp, keeping up a constant bombardment. Levees on either side of the camp gave some protection but, along with sniping from riflemen, including Choctaws, British morale was dealt a decided blow. They considered this conduct inconsistent with the way gentlemen waged war: "to us at least it appeared an ungenerous return to barbarity," complained Ensign Gleig.

Christmas Day saw the arrival of a large reinforcement under British commander-in-chief Major General Sir Edward Pakenham, brother-in-law of the Duke of Wellington. He had taken command shortly after the burning of Washington, General Robert Ross having been killed in a skirmish with American troops. Pakenham studied the field, and expressed his dissatisfaction with the way the army was deployed. He wished to withdraw and renew the attack from another quarter. Admiral Alexander Cochrane of the British fleet, however, felt the hodge podge force of enemy regulars, volunteers, militiamen, pirates, free blacks and Indians, speaking various languages, would flee when faced with veterans who had defeated Napoleon. He convinced Pakenham to persevere.

With considerable difficulty, heavy guns were brought across boggy ground from the British ships, and on December 27, loaded with glowing hot shot, they opened fire on the American vessels in the Mississippi. The *Carolina* caught fire forcing her crew to abandon ship before she blew up. But the *Louisiana* continued to fight, at one time being pulled by mooring lines from the shore to keep her guns within range of British positions.

Despite the stalled enemy advance, Jackson heard that the legislature wished to surrender the city to avoid its destruction. Governor William Claiborne, the brother of General Claiborne, received instructions to "blow up" the legislature if need be. He promptly locked the administration doors and posted guards to prevent them from meeting. Once assured there was no serious talk of surrender, Jackson relented and posed no further interference to the civil authority. The American soldiers, meanwhile, dug furiously along the Rodriguez Canal. Picks and shovels did their work as the defensive ditch grew ever deeper, the soil flung onto an earthwork that grew ever higher. Cannon were wrestled forward and mounted along "Jackson's Line," about three-quarters of a mile long, one-third in the cypress swamp.

On December 28, the redcoats attacked, but those nearest the river were hit with gunfire from both the *Louisiana*'s guns and Old Hickory's artillery along the canal. They were forced to seek cover while their comrades in the cypress swamp fared much better. They could have carried the American line but received orders to retire. Pakenham could only see his assault stalled near the river, and assumed the worse for the troops in the cypress swamp.

The American defense was strengthened as additional artillery arrived, and a redoubt was established on the opposite, west river bank. From there guns could fire on the flank of any British advance against Jackson's line. But Pakenham also strengthened his artillery, teams of seamen offloading big guns from the ships and positioning them in various redoubts along the British line.

On the first day of the year 1815, fog shrouded the field separating the opposing forces. Major Arsene Latour, a French officer with Jackson's army, recalled:

> As soon as the horizon began to clear up, the enemy opened a very brisk fire from his batteries.... A cloud of Congreve rockets accompanied the balls, and for fifteen minutes the fire was kept up with unexampled celerity. The first discharges of the two batteries nearest the river, were principally directed against Mercer's house, where the headquarters were established. In less than ten minutes, upwards a one hundred balls, rockets and shells struck the house, and rendered it impossible to remain there. The general-in-chief and all his staff were in the apartments when the firing began; but though bricks, splinters of wood and furniture, rockets and balls were flying in all directions, not a single person was wounded.[6]

The Americans found the British fire well maintained and well directed. The redcoat soldiers were poised and ready for a general assault should the American defences be breached. Three American cannon sustained damage and

> the rockets blew up two artillery caissons, in one of which was a hundred rounds. When the enemy perceived this accident, he suspended his fire for some seconds, and their troops ranged in the ditches, and those at the batteries, gave three cheers which were instantly answered by all the artillery of our lines.[7]

The Americans smashed several enemy cannon, the earth-filled barrels supposedly protecting them having shattered when hit. The soft American earthworks, on the other hand, simply absorbed the enemy cannon balls. Cotton bales did not fair so well, "made fly in all directions," some catching fire, and three cannon were damaged. A redcoat infantry regiment advanced once more through the cypress swamp against the American left, commanded by the redoubtable John Coffee. A cloud of gun smoke erupted as the lethal rifles of the backwoodsmen spoke. "Wellington's heroes discovered they were ill qualified to contend with us in woods," recalled Latour, "where they must fight knee deep in water and mud, and that the various kinds of laurel which abound in Louisiana, in the cypress swamps and prairies, were not intended to grace their brows."[8] The colorful redcoats made excellent targets amid the foliage, and soldiers fell as others splashed a hasty retreat. The British fire slackened off as the afternoon came on, then fell to silence as their ammunition ran out.

"Too much praise cannot be bestowed on those who managed my artillery," recalled Jackson, "Our loss was inconsiderable, and certainly much less than that which the enemy must have sustained." The Americans did not suffer from a lack of firepower, as recalled by Ensign Gleig: "For two whole days and nights not a man had closed an eye, except as were cool enough to sleep amidst showers of cannon-balls." But Jackson was still not happy with Claiborne's delivery of munitions. "By the almighty God," he told him, "if you do not send me balls and powder instantly, I shall chop off your head, and have it rammed into one of those field-pieces." Little wonder the governor was "so frightened he could barely speak."[9]

More American militiamen arrived and, in want of clothing and supplies, additional money was raised by subscription from the people of New Orleans. Still greatly outnumbered, Jackson could risk no major attack, and Pakenham dug in to await reinforcements while the navy planned an operation to capture the American guns on the opposite river bank. On January 6, Pakenham and his senior officers met to plan their next move. Having been reinforced with 2,000 extra troops, a massive frontal assault on Jackson's entrenchment was proposed.

With Pakenham were Josiah Francis and other Creek chiefs. They watched the massive British build-up with approval, hoping to witness revenge on old Sharp Knife for Horseshoe Bend, the Treaty of Fort Jackson, and various other calamities to the Creek Nation.[10]

Under cover of dark on January 7-8 Pakenham established an advance battery, and bundles of thick cane, called fascines, were prepared for filling Jackson's long, defensive ditch. Once troops crossed, scaling ladders would be used for climbing the earthworks. These preparations were seen through telescopes from the American lines so they knew a full-scale assault was being planned.

British morale was low. Many doubted the success of a frontal charge against heavy earthworks their artillery had been unable to breach. The weather had been cold and wet since arrival, and provisions sparse. The 44th regiment was to lead the attack carrying the fascines and ladders. Their commander, Lieutenant Colonel Thomas Mullins was not happy. "It is a forlorn hope," he complained to another officer, "and the regiment must be sacrificed."[11]

Approximately 5,300 men were to take part in the frontal assault, and another 1,400 were to cross by boat to capture the entrenched American battery on the opposite bank. Under cover of dark, the boats launched off only to become mired in Mississippi mud, stalling their attack till after sunrise.

And then the reluctant Colonel Mullins made a blunder of epic proportions. He had misunderstood at which redoubt his men were to procure the fascines and ladders. As planned, his regiment moved forward before the main assault was due to be launched, but passed the appointed redoubt. They halted for half an hour without the required goods until ordered back. Mullins was later cashiered because

> the 44th Regiment on being sent back to the redoubt, and returning hurriedly with the Fascines, &c. &c. was thrown into confusion, and moved off to the attack in an irregular and unconnected manner leading to the fire and disorder which ensued in the attacking Column, and the disasters attending it.[12]

Old Hickory's artillery opened fire when the advancing columns were 500 yards to their front. The muskets and rifles of the infantry opened fire at 300 yards. They had orders to aim a little above the white cross belt, an admirable target. Gaps appeared in the British ranks, but on they marched to the rattle of drums with the admirable discipline expected of British troops.

Jackson had about 4,500 men manning his line or held in reserve. Most defenders were concentrated between the river and cypress swamp, where the trees prevented a full-scale assault. All along the line, the redcoats faced a withering fire of grapeshot and ball from Jackson's large naval guns. Muskets fired buckshot and rifles fired balls with deadly effect. At the outset, the Americans stood in four ranks, the first firing a volley, stepping back and reloading as the second took their place. With this repeated through four ranks, they could pour a steady torrent of lead into the redcoat targets to their front. Latour recalled:

> Batteries Nos. 6, 7 and 8, now opened an incessant fire on the column, which continued to advance in pretty good order, until, in a few minutes, the musketry of the troops of Tennessee and Kentucky, joining their fire with that of the artillery, began to make an impression on it, which soon threw them into confusion. It was at that moment that was heard that constant rolling fire, whose tremendous noise resembled rattling peals of thunder. For some time the British officers succeeded in animating the courage of their troops, and making them advance, obliquing to the left, to avoid the fire of battery No. 7, from which every discharge opened the column, and mowed down whole files, which were almost instantly replaced by new troops coming up close after the first; but these also shared the same fate.[13]

Smoke from battery number 7 obscured the aim of the riflemen, and it was ordered to cease fire. The grey swirl cleared and the Americans delivered a devastating fire into the redcoats at about 150 yards. The men around them cut down, the survivors returned fire, and a redoubt a little foreword of Jackson's line was overrun. Further to the rear, many of the missing ladders and fascines were thrown to the ground so those who held them could also fire on the American line, thus catching their own troops in a cross-fire.

The four ranks of American riflemen lost cohesion as the fight continued, firing as individuals rather than in volleys, but with few losses and the advantage of cover, a

Old Hickory at New Orleans. His defeat of the British Army with a mixed force of militia, volunteers, regulars, Indians, and pirates earned him everlasting fame (drawing by the author).

steady, deadly fire was maintained. Those redcoats making it to the earthwork had no way to cross, as Gleig recalled: "to scale the parapet without ladders was a work of no slight difficulty. Some few, indeed, by mounting one upon another's shoulders, succeeded in entering the works, but these were speedily overpowered, most of them killed, and the rest taken; whilst as many as stood without were exposed to a sweeping fire, which cut them down by whole companies."[14]

The attack stalled as red coats fell back, and the captured American redoubt was retaken. Pakenham attempted to rally his men but was wounded by grapeshot that killed his horse. Helped to another horse, he was hit again and died as he was being carried by stretcher from the field.

General Keane ordered the elite 93rd Highlanders into action. Bagpipes playing, they led another assault but were cut down by the hail of lead. Their commander, Colonel Robert Dale, was one of many to fall amid the carnage. The British fell back, their morale broken, as some officers cursed and struck at them with the flats of their swords. Major Thomas Wilkinson of the 21st North Britain Fusiliers led 100 men in a futile charge. He scrambled up the earthen bank only to fall with a mortal wound. Troops under Colonel Robert Rennie advanced through lingering fog along the riverbank. They scrambled up the earthen bank only to be repulsed, Rennie killed in the assault.

Pakenham was dead and his two senior officers mortally wounded. General John Lambert assumed command. Surveying the carnage amid a haze of battle smoke, he could see the day was lost. Bugles sounded the wrenching order to withdraw. The redcoats stumbled back across a blood soaked carpet of fallen comrades, as others surrendered to the Americans behind them. According to Ensign Gleig, "Making a foreword motion, the 7th and 43rd presented the appearance of a renewed attack, by which the enemy were so much awed that they did not venture beyond their lines in pursuit of the fugitives." On the west bank the British had finally achieved their aim, the capture of the American battery. But this was far too late. Advised it would take 2,000 additional men to hold that position, General Lambert ordered the only British victors of the day to withdraw.

The day's battle had cost the British 2,037 casualties; 291 killed, 1,262 wounded and 484 captured. The Americans suffered six killed and seven wounded.[15]

Old Hickory may well have been awed as suggested by Gleig, but by his resounding victory rather than the appearance of reserves. America's first "Stonewall Jackson" had emerged long before the Civil War.

8

Unlawful and Improper

Amid the groans of the wounded of Horseshoe Bend, an army surgeon extracted the musket ball from Sam Houston's upper right arm, and dressed his wounded thigh. But, having lost much blood, it was felt he would join the list of dead before sunrise. The ball in his left shoulder was not removed, and the surgeons busied themselves with those who had more hope of survival.

But this robust young officer's time had not come. For him fate had decreed important things in life. Next day, despite the bleak prognosis, Houston's minders found he was still breathing. He was placed on a litter for the jolting, painful trip over rugged terrain back to the sheltering walls of Fort Williams. From there he was again moved by a litter, the pain only relieved by blackouts and doses of medicinal whiskey.[1]

Houston's arrival back in Tennessee was recalled by family friend Colonel Willoughby Williams: "he was greatly emaciated, suffering at the same time from wounds and the measles. We took him to the house of his relative, Squire John McEwen … where he remained for some time, and from there he went to the house of his mother in Blount County."[2] Once home, Houston's return as a wounded hero from a triumphant battle helped mend a somewhat awkward relationship with his brothers.

Born March 2, 1793, on a plantation on Timber Ridge, Virginia, Sam Houston came from a background more promising than that of either David Crockett or Andrew Jackson. His father, Major Samuel Houston, had fought in Morgan's Rifle Brigade during the American Revolution. The father died in 1807, when Sam, his fifth child, was 13. Sam attended the local school for no more than six months, but his lack of formal learning was overcome by a sharp, inquisitive mind. Following her husband's death, Elizabeth Houston moved her five sons and three daughters to eastern Tennessee where they established a farm on Baker's Creek near Maryville. Houston furthered his education at a nearby academy where classical literature caught his eye. He was especially taken by Homer's *Iliad*, the epic poem of the siege of ancient Troy by the Greeks.[3]

His elder brothers decided a store keepers' lot in the family business would suit young Sam. But the restless, free spirit had other ideas. Like David Crockett, he bolted from home. In 1809, the 16-year-old crossed the Tennessee River into Cherokee country. Here he was welcomed and adopted by the tribe. His brothers followed and sought his return, but Sam, ensconced with new Cherokee friends, let it be known he now had a new home. Sam considered Chief Oolooteka, known to the whites as John Jolly, as his Indian father. The chief called him Ka'lanu, meaning "the Raven," a symbol of good luck. It would seem fate had played a hand here, as a raven appeared on the Houston family crest.[4] Sam learned the Cherokee language and ways, and felt a great empathy for his adopted people.

He borrowed money, however, and purchased gifts for his Cherokee friends on credit. He also found alcohol to his liking. On one return visit, Houston incurred a fine of $5 for his activities with militia compatriots outside the Blount County Courthouse: "disorderly, riotously, wantonly, with an assembly of militia annoying the court with the noise of a Drum ... and with force and arms disturbing the Good order of said Court and abusing their Sherriff and demeaning themselves against the peace and dignity of the State."[5] These charges would seem a mild portent of events yet to come.

To repay debts Houston returned from Cherokee country to Maryville, set up a school house, and enrolled local children. Each pupil was charged $8 per term, payable one-third each in cash, cotton and corn. When not teaching he supplemented his income by clerking at Sheffy's store in Kingston.

In 1812, President Madison declared war on the British. In March of 1813, Houston's friend Willoughby Williams recalled seeing him "take his dollar from the drum and enlist as a private." Apparently the recruiters were impressed with their find. A robust six feet two inches tall, with a deep, imposing voice, his eyes a striking blue, Sam was hard to miss. He "was taken immediately to the barracks, dressed as a soldier, and appointed the same day as a sergeant."[6] But some of Houston's associates were not impressed. Being the son of Major Houston of Morgan's Rifle Brigade, they felt he should have applied for a commission.

"And what have your craven souls to say about the ranks? I would much sooner honor the ranks, than disgrace an appointment. You don't know me now, but you shall hear of me," so Sam later wrote.[7] But, having just turned 20, he was below the legal age of enlistment of 21, and needed his mother's permission. She gave it, said Houston, saying this:

> Here my son, take this musket and never disgrace it; for remember, I had rather all my sons fill one honorable grave, than that one of them should turn his back to save his life. Go, and remember, too that while the door of my cottage is always open to brave men, it is eternally shut against cowards.[8]

Elizabeth Houston placed a gold ring on her son's finger with the word "Honor" engraved on the inner surface. Houston wore this ring till removed by his widow the day he died.

Houston's regiment, the 7th Infantry, was merged into the 39th. Lieutenant Colonel Thomas Hart Benton, the man who wounded Old Hickory in the Nashville tavern gunfight, noticed Sam's "soldierly and gentlemanly qualities," and the sergeant quickly found himself promoted to ensign, then to third lieutenant. News of Fort Mims had rocked the frontier, the Creek War was under way, and the 39th marched into Fort Strother on February 13, 1814. Here Houston came under Andrew Jackson's command and fought at Horseshoe Bend.

Once home the wounded Houston traveled to Washington for expert medical care but, the ball in his shoulder not removed, his wound refused to heal. By March of 1815, Sam was back in Maryville when he heard of Old Hickory's triumph at New Orleans. And then news of the war's end arrived. The treaty had been signed in Ghent, Belgium, on December 23, 1814, before the bloodshed at New Orleans. But peace meant the demobilization of the volunteer troops, and Houston would soon be unemployed. He wrote to Secretary of War James Monroe, applying for a commission in the regular army, and Congressman John Rhea of East Tennessee received a plea for assistance:

> I have fought and bled for my country in consequence of which I am in some measure rendered unfit for other business. You are not a stranger to the manner in which I enter'd the army at a time I had not friends to patronize me & by my own merits and good fortune have been promoted & I think it consistent with a virtuous government to reward bravery & merit both of which I claim. You will be so good as to use your influence to have me continued in the army. I would not have intruded on you had you not assured me when I saw you last that you would be happy to serve me if it was in your power.... P.S. My wound is nearly healed and my health is entirely recovered.[9]

But the P.S. was not true. A short time later he wrote to a friend, Captain Alexander Campbell: "I will not court any of the Dear Girles before I make a fortune and if I come no better speed than I have done heretofore it will take some time ... my wounds are not near well." The legacy of Horseshoe Bend would give Sam Houston trouble for years to come.

His desired commission, however, came through on April 20, 1815. He was transferred from the 39th to the 1st Infantry, who were stationed in New Orleans where better medical treatment was on hand. After arrival, the ball in his shoulder was removed during an awkward procedure, profuse bleeding almost finishing the job begun by the Redsticks at Horseshoe Bend. Despite recurring medical attention, this and his other wounds were slow to heal.

Houston received orders on January 1, 1817, to report to the army's headquarters in Nashville, Tennessee. From here Andrew Jackson commanded the military Southern Division. Houston's bravery had received no mention in his report on Horseshoe Bend, but Old Hickory had kept the young officer very much in mind. They became friends and Jackson became Houston's mentor in the following years.

The following March, Houston was promoted to first lieutenant. With light duties to perform, he had time to socialize and, despite having written he would not be courting any ladies before making his fortune, he became entangled with a "Miss M—," referred to by a friend as the "Princess of E.T.—East Tennessee." Sam may have been a lion on the battlefield, but when it came to awkward moments with ladies his courage was wanting, it would appear. Miss M. was not his heart's desire, he decided, and asked his friend Jesse Beene to speak to her on his behalf, ending the courtship.

But Jesse wrote back: "You know J. Beene is your friend & if I were to advise you it would be to speedily marry M—by moonshine or any other way most handy." There had been a rival for the young lady's affections, wrote Beene, but she had thrown him "sky high" and was "ready to leave mother home friends and every thing dear to her ... and go with you to earth's remotest bounds."[10] Sam must have winced when he read this. Now what to do? But then Andrew Jackson inadvertently saved Houston from further entanglement with the Princess of East Tennessee.

Several chiefs of the Cherokee nation had signed a treaty with the United States ceding their lands in Tennessee in exchange for alternative territory west of the Mississippi. But as was a common problem with Indian treaties, the signatories did not speak for all their tribe. Chief John Jolly, Houston's adopted Cherokee father, was one who had not signed. Despite having been a good friend to the whites, he was now expected to move from his home.

To many Cherokee, the land of the west, where night consumed the day, was seen as a place of evil—as well it might. The resident Osage tribe had proven hostile to Cherokees who had arrived from the east in earlier days. And John Jolly's brother had returned with a depressing report, the land quality inferior to what had been signed away.

Indian affairs were administered by the War Department, and the Cherokee agent was Colonel Return J. Meigs. A hero of the Revolution, Meigs had been presented with a sword from Congress for burning 12 British ships and taking 90 prisoners without losing a man. Meigs had the welfare of the Cherokee at heart, and his death, aged 83, would be attributed to catching pneumonia while sleeping in a tent while his own quarters were occupied by a visiting Cherokee chief.

Who better to help implement government policy than a bright young officer who knew the Cherokee as friends and spoke their language? The colonel asked Andrew Jackson for Lieutenant Sam Houston. But this would be a difficult task for one who had the Indians' welfare at heart. On one hand Houston was obliged to follow orders, but on the other hand had no desire to see his Cherokee friends lose their homeland. If he resigned in protest, who would take his place? Quite possibly someone with as little regard for Indian rights as Andrew Jackson himself. Sam, being an admirer and protégé of Old Hickory, conveniently turned a blind eye to his attitude towards native peoples.

Houston's appointment as sub-agent to the Cherokees was handed to him by Andrew Jackson personally on October 21, 1817. Meigs, aware of Houston's distaste for the job at hand, wrote to him that the Cherokees who agreed to move "will have in every sense the most liberal patronage, countenance & support of the Government— the emigrants are not from home on the contrary they are going home in the best sense of the word." Not surprisingly, many Cherokee would disagree with the colonel's interpretation.

And when Houston arrived at the subagency of the Hiwassee Cherokee he was astonished to find an entrenched system of corruption—a sobering lesson in life. In order to do his job effectively, Houston knew he was going to make enemies with powerful connections, and wrote to Andrew Jackson: "of 2000$ only 884$ could be produced, and the notes not current." But there were other problems as well: "Mr. Smith A.A.A. has a store at the garrison, and also keeps spirits, & (from Good authority I have learned), sells them.... You know General Jackson? how difficult it is to keep the Indians sober? and also how difficult it is to transact business with them when intoxicated?"[11] Especially if Houston is intoxicated himself, as could be the case.

But he closed Smith's store and removed the subagency from the army post to Cherokee land where he could prevent the arrival of alcohol. To protect himself from the inevitable counter-attack by Smith and his cohorts, Houston wrote directly to Secretary of War George Graham explaining his actions. Others, meanwhile, also felt the arrival of the 24-year-old subagent. Smugglers attempting to illegally bring slaves through Cherokee lands into the United States found their efforts thwarted by the vigilant Sam Houston.

He met with John Jolly and other Cherokees not happy with their imminent removal. While sympathizing with their plight, he was now representing United States government policy. No doubt the recent fate of the Creeks came to mind when he warned them not to resist by force of arms. What chance had they against the might of the American army? Houston assured them that the government's pledges would be honored, and a dejected John Jolly agreed to the move.

> You must not think that by removing we will return to the savage way of life. You have taught us to be Herdsmen and cultivators.... Our women will raise the cotton and the Indigo and spin and weave cloth to cloath our children. Numbers of our young people can read and write, they can read what we call the preachers book.... By intermarriages with our white brethren we are gradually becoming one people.[12]

To dispel any doubts of the government's good intentions, a delegation of chiefs, including John Jolly's older brother, Tahlontusky, "a king among his people," was asked to visit the Great Father, the newly elected President James Monroe in Washington. Houston was to shepherd the delegation, and included in his instructions from Governor Joseph McMinn were the following words: "I have a particular dislike to the intemperate use of Spirits among men on business, particularly in the elevated character in which you and the Delegation stand ... and no mortification could wound my feeling, with equal depths to that of hearing of a single case of intemperance (much less drunkenness) charged to any one of the company." "in which *you* and the Delegation stand," wrote McMinn. This would appear to be a warning for the shepherd as well as the flock.

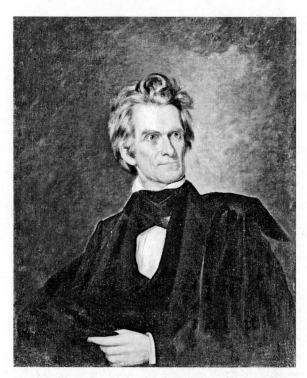

Secretary of War John Calhoun was shocked when Houston arrived in Washington garbed as a Cherokee. He had no time for army officers who "went injun," no matter what the reason (Wikimedia Commons).

The Delegation arrived in Washington on February 5, 1818. "One great bottle" of whiskey had been allowed to ward off the chills of harsh winter travel. Secretary of War John C. Calhoun received his guests in a most cordial fashion, then ushered the chiefs to an adjoining room where President Monroe awaited them. But Houston was asked to stay behind. Calhoun then lashed into the young lieutenant with a vicious tongue. The sub-agent had chosen to attend dressed as a Cherokee. How did an officer on the United States Army dare to appear in such garb? Houston replied that as the Cherokee agent he felt obliged to do so out of respect for the Delegation. But Calhoun was not impressed. Sam was dismissed with a reprimand never to repeat the outrageous transgression. The line in the sand was drawn between Sam Houston and John C. Calhoun.

And then Houston was summoned back to Calhoun's office.

Charges had been laid of his involvement in slave running. Congressional cohorts of the slave smugglers, closed down by Houston's actions, now accused him of their own crimes. But Houston was smart enough to anticipate retribution, and had a well prepared account of his agency activities at the tip of his tongue. Calhoun knew the truth when he heard it, and quickly backed down. President Monroe agreed to an inquiry which exonerated Houston in short order. The attempted revenge on Houston backfired completely, merely demonstrating his effective and honest tenure as subagent to the Cherokee. Calhoun admitted Sam's conduct had been "approbated and very proper" and the charges "unlawful and improper." Calhoun refused, however, to place any exoneration in writing, saying the charges were verbal, not written. But Houston knew mud, once thrown, tends to stick. He now felt betrayed as well as humiliated by the tongue lashing for dressing as a Cherokee:

Washington City
March 1st 1818

Sir
You will please accept this as my resignation to take effect from this date.

I have the honor to be
Your Most Obt. Servt
/s/ Sam Houston
1st Lieut 1st Infy

Genl D. Parker
A & Ins Genl.
W. City[13]

So ended the career of Sam Houston as an officer in the United States Army. No doubt he was mortified by the whole unpleasant business. But Calhoun had done him a favor. As is so often the case, people with a great future must be shaken from their comfort zone before they can move on to bigger and better things.

9

Rapine and Plunder

Sam Houston may well have felt vexed by his treatment for those he sought to serve, but Major General Andrew Jackson had faired little better himself. Astonishingly, just a few months after the battle smoke cleared, the Hero of New Orleans was on the wrong side of the bench in a U.S. Federal Court. Louis Louailler, a member of the Louisiana Legislature, had published an article alleging "abuse of authority" on Jackson's part and, martial law still being in force, had found himself placed under arrest. Federal Court Judge Dominick Hall, unhappy with these proceedings, issued a writ of habeas corpus for Louailler's release. Old Hickory had not only ignored the writ, but seized the judge as well:

> I have thought it proper to send you beyond the limits of my encampment, to prevent you from a repetition of the improper conduct for which you have been charged. You will remain without the line of my sentinels until the ratification of peace is regularly announced, or until the British shall have left the southern coast.[1]

The following day, March 13, 1815, a special courier arrived at Jackson's headquarters, and a new proclamation was issued:

> The commanding general, with the most lively emotions of joy and of gratitude to heaven, announces to the troops under his command that a treaty of peace between the United States and Great Britain was ratified and exchanged in Washington on the 17th of February ... he loses not an instant in revoking and annulling the general order issued on the 15th day of December last, proclaiming martial law ... the commanding general proclaims and orders a pardon for all military offences heretofore committed in this district, and orders all persons in confinement under such charges be immediately discharged.[2]

The indignant Judge Hall lost "not an instant" in resuming his judicial seat. He ordered Jackson to appear and explain why he should not be held in contempt of court for ignoring the writ of habeas corpus.

Jackson made an explanation to his "fellow soldiers" justifying his actions. Writs of habeas corpus had to be ignored during martial law, he said. "Let the sentry be removed by subpoena from his post, let writs of habeas corpus carry away the officers from the lines, and the enemy may conquer your country by only employing lawyers." He refused to apologize for his actions: "I am not insensible to the good opinion of my fellow citizens. I would do much to obtain it. But I cannot, for this purpose, sacrifice my own conscience or what I conceive to be the interests of my country."[3]

The general agreed to appear in Hall's court, but declined to answer questions put by the prosecution, a defence of his actions having previously been submitted in writing. Judge Hall, however, refused to accept this. "Under these circumstances," Jackson said,

"I appear before you to receive the sentence of the court, and have nothing further to add."

But Judge Hall had something to subtract—a massive $1,000 from Jackson's purse.

Old Hickory was greeted outside the courtroom by a shouting throng of admirers who had little time for Hall and his verdict. The general had arrived on foot, but moved away in a fine carriage drawn by people who jostled for the honor. Having calmed his devotees against any form of violence, Jackson withdrew to his quarters, wrote out a bank draft for $1,000, and dispatched it to the Federal Court.

Jackson's wife Rachel had arrived in New Orleans, and a great ball was held in the French Exchange to celebrate the victory. Local merchant Vincent Nolte recollected:

> The upper part of the exchange was arranged for dancing, and the under part for supper, with flowers, colored lamps, and transparencies with inscriptions. Before supper, Jackson desired to look at the arrangements unaccompanied, and I was appointed to conduct him. One of the transparencies between the arcades bore the inscription, "Jackson and Victory: they are but one." The general looked at it, and turned about to me in a hail-fellow sort of way, saying, "Why did you not write 'Hickory and Victory: they are but one.'" After supper we were treated to most delicious *pas de deux* by the conqueror and his spouse, an emigrant of the lower classes, whom he had from a Georgian planter, and who explained by her enormous corpulence that French saying, "She shows how far the skin can be stretched." To see these two figures, the general a long, haggard man, with limbs like a skeleton, and Madame la Generale, a short, fat dumpling, bobbing opposite each other like half-drunken Indians, to the wild melody of *Possum up de Gum Tree*, and endeavoring to make a spring in the air, was very remarkable, and far more edifying a spectacle than any European ballet could possibly have furnished.[4]

Rachel Jackson was the apple of the general's eye, regardless of what others thought.

Finding himself the greatest American hero since George Washington, Old Hickory sat for portraits and advised artists who portrayed the magnificent victory with canvas, brush and paint. He was flocked by journalists, and cooperated with his aide-de-camp, Major John Reid, in writing an account of his life. Reid started work, but died the following year. Based on his notes, Jackson's young friend John Henry Eaton, a future Secretary of War, resumed the task. In 1817, *The Life of Andrew Jackson*, his first biography, appeared.

The portraits and images of the gallant Jackson, however, did not reveal all. Beneath the heroic veneer, he suffered abundant health problems. A man in pain is not a happy man—a violent temper is the result. He still carried lead balls from both the Dickinson and Benton affairs. Routine actions such as mounting a horse were painful. He also suffered from internal maladies. While being wined and dined in New Orleans he wrote to a friend, "I have had a serious attack of dysentery that reduced me very much. I have not been clear of it for four months, except ten days after I first arrived at this place."

Jackson's pain and resulting temper may have influenced a contentious decision shortly after the Battle of New Orleans. In September of 1814, 200 militiamen had been charged with desertion after marching from Fort Jackson. Their three-month enlistment was up, they said. Their commanding officer, however, insisted a six-month enlistment was correct. Jackson, in Mobile at the time, ordered the offenders' arrest and court martial. Most were fined and dishonorably discharged at the end of the six-month term, but six ringleaders were sentenced to death. Jackson received this news in January of 1815 as the redcoats were advancing on New Orleans. Once the smoke had cleared, the victory won, the executions went ahead. Had he known the war over, a peace treaty signed, it seems unlikely this would have occurred. The execution of these six men, and that of John Wood, would be put to use by political opponents more than a decade later.[5]

General and Mrs. Jackson, along with their entourage, departed New Orleans in early April 1815. It was a slow progress back towards Tennessee, the general lionized by all along the way. "He is every where hailed as the saviour of his country," John Reid reported, "He has been feasted, caressed, and I may say idolized. They look upon him as a strange prodigy; and women, children, and old men line the road to look at him as they would the Elephant."

Once back in Nashville, Governor Willie Blount gave the finest celebratory dinner in the history of Tennessee. Outside the Hermitage, Jackson delivered a prophetic speech to an admiring crowd:

> The sons of America, during a most eventful and perilous conflict, have approved themselves worthy of the precious inheritance bequeathed them by their fathers. They have given a new proof how impossible it is to conquer free men fighting in defense of all that is dear to them. Henceforth we shall be respected by nations who, mistaking our character, had treated us with the utmost contumely and outrage. Years will continue to develop our inherent qualities until, from the youngest and the weakest, we shall become the most powerful nation in the universe.[6]

President Madison invited Jackson to Washington for advice on a reorganization of the American Army. To have Jackson now on side in a very public role would help erase the tarnish of the capitol having been being burned by the enemy. But after two years away the general was in no hurry to travel east. Rachel wished to see more of her husband, and there was Andrew Jr., to consider, along with other relatives and wards in residence at the Hermitage. This included Lyncoya, an orphan Creek boy taken from the ruins of Tallushatchee.[7] Given Jackson's general disregard for Indians and his punitive peace treaty, this benevolent gesture seems out of character. Perhaps the general, hearing how the Creeks were shot down "like dogs," as described by Crockett, had taken pause. Whites were supposed to be more civilized than those who killed the defenceless at Fort Mims. Jackson, once an orphan himself, had written to Rachel that he had an "unusual sympathy" for the child. For Old Hickory, such sympathy was certainly unusual.

Needless to say, the $1,000 fine affair had been followed with considerable interest in Washington's corridors of power, rather cramped for the moment as a result of Washington's burning, the administration meeting in makeshift quarters. The debacle of Jackson being fined had created a precedent, and new rules regarding martial law were required. Acting Secretary of War Alexander Dallas informed President Madison that he would "manifest a just respect for the Constitution and laws without wounding the feelings of General Jackson." Old Hickory received a curious letter from Dallas that seemed to condone his actions, but then went on to vindicate Judge Hall; a fence-sitting compromise. Jackson penned a brief defence of his conduct, and made plans to travel to Washington. The rest could be said in person.[8]

Following another triumphal journey of dinners and speeches, Jackson arrived in Washington on November 16, 1815. He met with the president and "all the great men at the city" in a capitol under reconstruction.

Jackson was informed of plans to divide the United States into two military districts, North and South. To Madison's relief, he accepted command of the southern division. The president had feared the famous general may wish to run for president himself, scuttling plans for James Monroe to be his successor. An appreciative Madison assured Old Hickory of support should any political opponents wish to attack him regarding his dispute with the federal court and Judge Hall.

Jackson's aide John Reid was appalled at the cost of living in the capital: "Have our horses attended to and fattened; my expenses can't be less than forty dollars a week! Most monstrous! What must the General's be? Our stay can't be long."[9]

Jackson returned to Nashville in January 1816. Unfinished business required the general's attention. Major Blue's expedition to destroy the British fort in Spanish East Florida had been abandoned due to hunger and fatigue, Crockett and the other volunteers returning home. Although no longer in British hands, the fort was still a thorn in the side of the United States. The solid walls protected blacks who had served in the British Army, along with Indians and escaped slaves. About 800 men and women resided in and around what was dubbed "Negro Fort," cultivating plantations and fields for miles along the river.

They were "well armed, clothed, and disciplined," wrote Secretary of War William Crawford to Jackson. "This is a state of things which cannot fail to produce much injury to the neighbouring settlements and excite irritations which may ultimately endanger the peace of the nation." Jackson was to give notice to the Spaniards at Pensacola to destroy Negro Fort or not interfere with American troops who would do the job for them. The killing of two Americans near Fort Claiborne in Mississippi Territory was conveniently attributed to occupants of Negro Fort.

"The conduct of this banditti," Jackson wrote to Governor Mauricio de Zúñiga, "is such as will not be tolerated by our government, and if not put down by Spanish authority will compel us in self-defence to destroy them." Jackson knew well the weak Spanish garrison had no means to destroy Negro Fort. Zúñiga, no doubt well remembering Jackson's occupation of Pensacola, replied that he would be "proud to be commanded" by General Jackson. Old Hickory did not feel Negro Fort needed his personal attention, however. General Edmund P. Gaines had taken command of the troops remaining in New Orleans, and Jackson wrote to him:

> I have little doubt of the fact, that this fort has been established by some villains for rapine and plunder, and that it ought to be blown up, regardless of the land on which it stands; and if your mind shall have formed the same conclusion, destroy it and return the stolen Negroes and property to their rightful owners.[10]

It comes as no surprise that Gaines did not form a different conclusion to that of Andrew Jackson, believing the fort would "produce much evil among the blacks of Georgia, and the eastern part of Mississippi territory." Preparations were initiated for a campaign into Spanish East Florida.

Jackson's relationship with Secretary of War Crawford, meanwhile, took a turn for the worse. American settlers had been encroaching on Cherokee lands and Crawford, no doubt wishing to avoid another Indian war, ordered them out. If they did not comply, Jackson was to remove "with military force all persons who shall be found upon the public lands within your command, and destroy their habitations and improvements."

Old Hickory was aghast at such a proposition. White Americans would fight for flag and country if war erupted once more, but the Indians may well side with the British or Spanish, he claimed. The fact Indian allies had just helped defeat the Creeks and British did not seem to matter. In any case, Jackson stated that American militia would simply refuse to carry out the orders. "Their feelings are the same with the settlers." And if regular army troops did obey such orders, the settlers would simply move back in as the troops marched out. "When this is attempted I fear it will lead to scenes that will make human nature shudder. I might not be mistaken if I was to say it may lead to the destruction of the whole Cherokee nation, and of course civil war."[11]

Jackson did not move against the settlers. And firing the Hero of New Orleans was out of the question. No doubt the Madison administration wondered who exactly was running the country.

In preparation for the destruction of Negro Fort, Gaines instructed Lieutenant Colonel Duncan Clinch to establish a new post, Camp Crawford, just north of the Florida border where the Flint and Chattahoochee Rivers merged to form the Apalachicola River.[12] This flowed south for about 65 miles through Spanish territory into the Gulf of Mexico. The post was basic, consisting of a powder magazine protected by a rough stockade.

A supply convoy of two schooners and two gunboats under the command of Sailing Master Jairus Loomis arrived at the Apalachicola River mouth from New Orleans on July 10, 1816.[13] Negro Fort, several miles upstream, overlooked the river from Prospect Bluff. This formidable bastion and its menacing guns provided an impediment to the convoy reaching Camp Crawford. Loomis received a dispatch with orders to wait while escort troops under Clinch moved downstream by boat.

Loomis ordered a midshipman and four sailors ashore in a small boat for fresh water. A black man appeared and signaled for them to row in. As the boat party approached, the undergrowth erupted in a burst of gunfire, killing three men while another fell overboard. He swam back to the convoy while the remaining seaman was taken prisoner.

Clinch's troops, meanwhile, moved south from Camp Crawford. The 116 soldiers were joined by Seminole Indians, who shared a similar language and culture with the Creeks. Their scouts captured a black man from Negro Fort who was carrying the fresh scalp of a white man as a trophy for an allied Indian chief. From the captive, Colonel Clinch learned of the attack on the water party, and sent word for Loomis to proceed up river for a combined attack on Negro Fort. Clinch's command arrived first and surveyed the enemy position, located on the east side of the river:

> The parapet was about fifteen feet high and eighteen thick, and defended by one thirty-two, three twenty-fours, two nines, two sixes, [and] an elegant five and a half-inch howitzer. It was situated on a beautiful and commanding bluff, with the river in front, a large creek just below, a swamp in the rear, and a small creek just above, which rendered it difficult to be approached by artillery.[14]

Clinch sent a surrender demand to the commander, a black known as Garcon. He refused, saying he "had been left in command of the fort by the British government, and that he would sink any American vessels should they attempt to pass it; and he would blow up the fort if he could not defend it." Garcon raised a Union Jack and below that a red flag, signifying no quarter.

Gunfire was exchanged without any real effect. Then, at 5 o'clock on the morning of July 27, Loomis' gunboats arrived. Cannon fire from the fort proved to be ineffective, but the Americans fared no better. The stout, earth-backed pickets of the fort walls proved too tough for the light guns mounted on the boats. Different tactics were required. The following morning, the elevation was increased, round shot were heated, and the first, glowing ball soared up and over the wall. In the next instant, a massive fiery explosion shook the ground as splintered timber, earth, bodies, arms and legs went flying. The shot had smashed right into 700 barrels of gunpowder stored in the fort's magazine.[15] A young officer, Marcus Buck, wrote to his father:

> The explosion was awful, and the scene horrible beyond description. You cannot conceive, nor I describe the horrors of the scene. In an instant lifeless bodies were stretched upon the plain, buried in sand and rubbish, or suspended from the tops of the surrounding pines. Here lay an innocent babe, there a helpless mother; on the one side a sturdy warrior, on the other a bleeding squaw. Piles of bodies, large heaps of sand, broken guns, accoutrements, etc, covered the site of the fort. The brave soldier was disarmed of his resentment and checked his victorious career, to drop a tear on the distressing scene.[16]

The flames were hastily doused before reaching a second magazine containing another 163 barrels of gunpowder. The blast had killed 270 men, women and children outright; others died shortly afterwards. Of about 300 residents, only a handful survived. From them it was learned that the American seaman captured from the water party had been tarred and feathered before execution. Buck recalled that among the survivors "were the Negro and Indian Chiefs; but they enjoyed but a short respite from the Indians. The Indian Chief was scalped alive, and stabbed, the Negro Chief was shot." Once the smoke had cleared, the victors tended the wounded and rummaged through the remains for anything of value. For their assistance, gunpowder and hundreds of firearms were given to the Seminoles; much appreciated by warriors who would soon be at war with the United States.[17]

10

A Whapper of a Lie

"Death, that cruel leveller of all distinctions—to whom the prayers and tears of husbands, and of even helpless infancy, are addressed in vain—entered my humble cottage, and tore from my children an affectionate good mother, and from me a tender and loving wife."

David Crockett had seen a good deal of death since the fall of Fort Mims, but a few months after his return from fighting Creeks the cruel leveller really hit home. Polly Crockett, only 26 years old, passed on from one of the lethal maladies that pervaded a frontier where medical treatment was rudimentary at best. The precise cause of her death is unknown. "I met with the hardest trial that which ever falls to the lot of man," Crockett recalled. "It was the doing of the Almighty, whose ways are always right, though we sometimes think they fall heavily on us; and as painful as it is even yet the remembrance of her sufferings, and the loss sustained by my little children and myself, yet I have no wish to lift up the voice of complaint."[1]

Polly was buried in a grave not far from home, and a cairn was erected to mark the spot.[2] For 141 years, those affectionately placed stones were the only physical reminder of Polly Crockett. But in 1956, following the renewal of Crockett's fame, a granite headstone arose[3]:

> Polly Finlay Crockett
> Born 1788 in Hamden County
> Married to
> David Crockett
> Aug. 12, 1806
> Mother of
> John Wesley Crockett—1807
> William Crockett—1809
> Margaret Finlay Crockett—1812
> Died 1815
>
> Tennessee Historical Commission

With Polly gone, how was Crockett to eke out a living from his small farm with three youngsters on his hands, one only three years old? There were fields to tend and game to hunt. "I couldn't bear the thought of scattering my children," he recalled. Younger brother John and his family moved into his log cabin to help out. "They took as good care of my children as they well could, but yet it wasn't all like the care of a mother." And a young man, naturally, yearned for a woman of his own.

Elizabeth Patton and her two children, George and Ann, lived in relative comfort on a 250-acre farm on Bean Creek, not far from Crockett's home. The same age as Polly, Elizabeth was a robust frontier woman by all accounts, and had a fine brain for business. It was said she had $800 in gold, a handsome sum at the time. Her husband had fought with Crockett and the Tennessee Volunteers at the Battle of Talladega in 1813, but had not lived to tell the tale.

> I soon began to pay my respects to her in real good earnest; but I was as sly about it as a fox when he is going to rob a hen roost. I found that my company wasn't at all disagreeable to her; and I thought I could treat her children with so much friendship as to make her a good stepmother to mine, and in this I wasn't mistaken, as we soon bargained, and got married, and then went ahead.[4]

Things were looking up for David Crockett. His friends and neighbors were impressed with this personable young man who had a tendency to "go ahead," no matter what. He was a popular raconteur at social events with his stories of Indian fighting and tracking bears and other game through the Tennessee woods. A few "horns" downed by himself and others no doubt added to the festivity. The drinking horn, dating back to ancient cultures, was ideal for such informal gatherings, as it could not be put down until drained.[5]

As the Creek War wound down, Crockett had declined to ride with the troops once more, and hired another to take his place; not unusual at the time. He was given an honorable discharge on March 27, 1815, with a commendation for "good conduct, subordination and valor." "This closes my career as a warrior, and I am glad of it," he recalled, unaware of events to come. "I am glad all over that I lived to see these times, which I should not have done if I had kept fooling along in war, and got used up in it."

Yet, less than two months after discharge, he was elected a lieutenant in the 32nd Regiment of the Tennessee Militia of Franklin County.[6] During the war, one of the "hateful ways of the world" had been John Coffee ignoring a report of Redsticks he brought in, "because I was no officer; I was no great man, but just a poor soldier." Crockett kept his fury to himself despite "burning inside like a tarkiln, and I wonder that the smoke hadn't been pouring out of me at all points." But when the same information was brought in by Major Gibson "why, then, it was all as true as preaching, and the colonel believed every word."[7]

But, despite now having a secure and comfortable future at hand, new lands, taken from the Creeks, had opened for settlement in what would later become central Alabama. Crockett had crossed this country during the war, and with restless eyes cast towards the horizon, rode south with three companions. "Their names were Robinson, Frazier and Rich," he recalled. They crossed the Tennessee River and a day's ride further on stopped for the night at the home of an old acquaintance who had recently settled on former Creek land.

But Frazier, the next day, found himself in considerable pain, the result of snake bite while out hunting. He was in no fit state to travel, and stayed behind.

The three remaining explorers passed through a "large rich valley, called Jones's valley where several families had settled, and continued our course till we came to the place where Tuscaloosa now stands."[8] This was the former Black Warrior's Town, put to the torch by Coffee's troops during the war.

That night the trio hobbled their horses and lay down to sleep near the charred remains. But it seems that even experienced frontiersmen could make mistakes worthy of a tenderfoot from the east. "About two hours before day, we heard the bells on our horses going back the way we had come, as they had started to leave us," recalled Crockett. At the crack of dawn, leaving his companions in camp, he set out on foot, rifle in hand. Wading across creeks and splashing through swamps, the pursuit lasted all day. Settlers had heard the tinkling animals pass, luring him on; so near and yet so far, always seeming just within reach. Finally, overcome with exhaustion, he gave up the futile chase and turned back.

The last settler's cabin provided refuge for the night. Crockett awoke the next morning "so sore and fatigued, that I felt I couldn't walk any more." But, having little choice, the ailing woodsman plodded on, the heavy rifle still in hand. A little after midday, overcome with sickness and headache, he virtually collapsed, alone in the wilderness and miles from help. Malaria had struck. The mosquito-borne disease would trouble Crockett for the rest of his life.

Then some "good Samaritans" came along. Crockett did not identify the tribe, but they could have been warriors who would have lifted his scalp a few years before. The Indians offered ripe melon to the ailing man, but he was so sick he could not eat. One Indian signalled that he was going to die, and be buried where he lay. Perhaps that was what was needed to get the woodsman to his feet. "I got up to go; but when I rose, I reeled about like a cow with the blind staggers, or a fellow who had taken too many 'horns.'" The Indians knew of a house a mile and a half down the road, and one offered to help him walk there. Crockett gratefully accepted the offer and, handing over half a dollar in gratitude, made it to the cabin "pretty far gone."

He was kindly received and cared for, but out of his senses with a high fever. Two days later some Tennessee neighbors looking for new land arrived. Sharing their horses with the still ailing Crockett, they made it back to the camp where Robinson and Rich still awaited his return. Crockett was taken to the cabin of Jesse Jones and family who took him in while the others moved on. The patient remained delirious for two weeks and, convinced he was about to die, Mrs. Jones made a pre-emptive strike. A full bottle of Bateman's Drops, usually taken in small doses, would settle the sick guest one way or the other. The main ingredients were camphor, aniseed and opium.[9] "She gave me the whole bottle," the patient recalled, "which throwed me into a sweat that continued on me all night; when at last I seemed to make up, and spoke, and asked her for a drink of water." Mrs. Jones was startled to have the almost dead man revive. Perhaps the potentially lethal dose was intended to put Crockett out of his misery, like an ailing horse that needed to be put down.

He continued to mend, despite "looking like a ghost." The feeble patient hailed a passing wagon driver who said he was heading for home, only 20 miles from Crockett's own abode. Virtually next door by frontier standards, the still recovering Crockett hitched a lift, the kindness of Jesse Jones and his family forever in his heart. From the wagoner's home, Crockett hired a horse and rode back to his family. "When I got there, it was to the utter astonishment of my wife; for she supposed I was dead."[10] Crockett's traveling companions had made it back to Tennessee, and reported meeting men who had seen her husband take his last breath, then helped bury him. "I know'd this was a whapper of a lie, as soon as I heard it," the supposedly dead man recalled.

Mark Twain would undoubtedly have read Crockett's autobiography, and would later say "the reports of my death have been grossly exaggerated," quite possibly inspired by the "whapper" line.[11]

Upon hearing of her husband's death, the ever-practical Elizabeth had hired a man to find out what had become of the money and other possessions he carried. The seeker had traveled far and wide, eventually arriving at the Jones home to learn that Crockett "was still in the land of the living and a-kicking." The man arrived back in Tennessee with the good news, but not till some time after the deceased's live return.

Crockett regained his health and vigor, the result being the birth of Robert Patton Crockett on September 16, 1816. This was the first of a second brood of children Crockett fathered to help populate the Tennessee frontier.[12]

At this time Andrew Jackson and two other Indian treaty commissioners, David Meriwether and Jesse Franklin, were using threats and bribes to acquired huge tracts of land from the Cherokees and Chickasaws. The Cherokees begged for less land to be taken, but old Sharp Knife insisted that if they wished to remain friends with the United States, they must agree. In return for a series of payments, the Cherokees ceded millions of acres on the understanding that the United States would forever be their friend. The treaty was signed at Turkey Creek on September 14, 1816.

One year later, Jackson wrote to President Monroe, "I have long viewed treaties with the Indians an absurdity not to be reconciled to the principle's of our government."[13] Although future generations of whites would benefit, during the War of 1812 and years following, immigration from the old world to the new was low. There was, in fact, no pressing need for room to expand at this time.

But, regardless of necessity, Crockett's wanderlust got the better of him and: "I therefore set out the next fall to look at the country which had been purchased of the Chickasaw tribe of Indians." He rode about 80 miles to Shoal Creek, but then an old haunt returned: "I took the ague and fever, which I supposed was brought on me by camping out. I remained there for some time, as I was unable to go farther; and in that time, I became so well pleased with the country about there, that I resolved to settle in it."[14] Well, for the time being at least.

Crockett, having recovered from the dreaded malaria once more, spent the winter of 1816–1817 with kinfolk a little south of Kentucky border. His Uncle Jim lived with Conrad Pile and his family of 12 children. Affectionately known around Sand Springs as "Coonrod," the old settler's daughter Delila was married to David's uncle, William Crockett. Coonrod had settled there in 1791 after riding off on a camping expedition. He came across a stretch of fertile ground with a stream fed by clear spring water, the basis for making a good living from the land. He stayed there for some time living in a cave, hunting game, and drinking from a tortoise shell. A fire was kept alight at the cave entrance, day and night, to prevent wild varmints from sharing his humble dwelling place.[15]

Coonrod's sharp-shooting blood flowed to a famous descendant, his great-great grandson Sergeant Alvin York. During World War I, York won the Medal of Honor for killing 28 German soldiers and capturing 132 others, virtually single handed. In 1918, he wrote in his diary: "I think we had just about the best shots that ever squinted down a barrel. Daniel Boone and Davy Crockett used to shoot at these matches long ago. And Andrew Jackson used to recruit his Tennessee sharpshooters from among our mountain shooters."[16]

Polly's lonely grave in Franklin County was left behind when the Crockett family moved to 160 acres at the head of Shoal Creek, part of recently purchased Indian lands. They were early settlers in what would become Lawrence County, Tennessee. The fertile soil yielded excellent crops including tobacco, cotton, corn and wheat. And the woods and waterways teemed with fish, waterfowl, wild turkey, deer and bears. It was probably just as well that Indians had sold their land for, as was usual on the frontier, white settlers had arrived before the deal was done—often the cause of Indian wars. Crockett's own grandparents had been killed by Indians after settling on their land.

It was while residing in this area that big changes began to shape in Crockett's life. Now 30, it was time for the simple backwoodsman to begin a political career that would see him either befriend or alienate those who controlled the nation. He would even be talked of as a future president of the United States—but all while remaining, or appearing to remain, a simple backwoodsman.

Having either sold off or leased the farm in Franklin County, the Crocketts had money to keep them afloat while establishing themselves in their new home. Crockett impressed his new neighbors, and was asked to be one of five land commissioners responsible for establishing the new county boundaries.[17] The name Lawrence County was decided upon, named after Captain James Lawrence, a naval commander of the War of 1812. Despite losing his life, battle and frigate to the British, his dying words, "Don't Give up the Ship," had become the battle cry of the American Navy as "Remember Fort Mims" had been to troops fighting the Redsticks.

The boundaries procedure went smoothly enough, and Crockett was one of five selected to choose the township site for the Lawrence County seat of government. He and his friend Enoch Tucker, however, had a difference of opinion to the other three. Then, amid heated debate, the foundations for the County court house appeared right where the opposition had staked their claim. The Builder was Joseph Irvine, and it was no coincidence that he happened to be one of the three in favor of that particular site. It seems somewhat ironic that Irvine, noted for his frontier fist fighting, should be the one to build the county's first bastion of law and order. Crockett and Tucker, outfoxed, lost the battle and Lawrenceburg rose around the new county court house.

But adversity can lead to better things in life, and the public wrangle brought Crockett to the attention of people as a man of note. Despite the new court house, Lawrence county was "without any law at all," recalled Crockett, "and so many bad characters began to flock in upon us, that we found it necessary to set up a sort of temporary government of our own…. I was appointed one of the magistrates; and when a man owed a debt, and wouldn't pay it, I and my constable ordered out our warrant, and then he would take the man, and bring him in before me for trial." Crockett, knowing nothing of the law, had his own way of extracting the sum due: "an order of an execution would easily scare the debt out of him."

The locals apparently approved of Crockett's quirky sense of law and order, and the state legislature formalized his appointment as magistrate on November 25, 1817.[18] "I gave my decisions on the principles of common justice and honesty between man and man, and relied on natural born sense, and not on law learning to guide me; for I had never read a page in a law book in my life."

Captain Daniel Matthews of the Tennessee Militia approached Magistrate Crockett with a request. Would he support his run for election as lieutenant colonel of the 57th? Matthews was a notable member of the local establishment, having been one of the earliest settlers, and since then a very successful farmer. Crockett agreed, but Matthews then suggested that the former militia lieutenant run alongside him for major. "I objected to this, telling him that I thought I had done my share of fighting, and I wanted nothing to do with military appointments." But the persuasive Matthews kept at him "until at last I agreed."[19]

Matthews arranged "a great frolic" and "a general treat" at his prosperous farm where he and Crockett would announce their joint candidature. The crowd would be well fed at Matthews' expense, and "horns" aplenty brimming with liquid refreshment would be on hand. Crockett duly arrived with his family, but then things turned sour. A friend tipped off the potential major that Matthews was actually going to have his son run against him, Crockett having the rug pulled from under him by the man he had helped. Not surprisingly, this got Crockett's "dander up" and he took the "old gentleman" to one side for an explanation. Matthews admitted that the rumor was true; his son was going to stand. Crockett informed the captain if that was the case there'd been a change of plans; he would now run against Matthews for colonel instead. They walked in front of the crowd and the captain gave a speech which also announced that David Crockett would be running against him. Crockett then had his turn: "I told the people the cause of my opposing him, remarking that as I had the whole family to run against anyway, I was determined to levy on the head of the whole mess."

Crockett won the election, and Matthews' son lost his race for major against a new candidate. The reluctant warrior was commissioned lieutenant colonel of the 57th Regiment of Tennessee Militia on March 27, 1818.[20] Colonel Crockett, land commissioner, justice of the peace, Indian fighter and noted bear hunter—someone to look up to, a man with a future. Yet still humble in his own backwoods way, a man of the people.

11

I Will Be Governor of Tennessee

Just a few weeks before Crockett's election as lieutenant colonel, Sam Houston tendered his resignation from the United States Army. The affray with Secretary of War John C. Calhoun would never be forgiven nor forgotten. Houston had seen firsthand the fragile grip on justice in the corridors of power in the Land of the Free. The honest could be framed by the corrupt and selfish if it could be arranged. And the subagent had learned that treaties with Indians were scarcely worth the paper on which they were written. It must have been hard to have the man he admired so very much, Andrew Jackson, so whole-heartedly opposed to his own views on Indian rights.

Although no longer a military officer, Houston was still subagent to the Cherokees, reporting to Governor Joseph McKimm of Tennessee. McMinn was in favor of Indian removal, but would become Cherokee agent himself in 1823, and cause much friction by burning out whites who had illegally settled on Indian land.[1]

On April 22, 1818, Houston received instructions from McMinn to visit Indian villages and explain the arrangements regarding their removal. The governor had secured 1,500 bushels of corn to assist with food supplies, and the Cherokees were pleased to learn that their Arkansas agent would be Dick Taylor, one of their own tribe.[2] Flatboats took the Cherokees, supplied with new muskets and blankets, down the Tennessee River towards their new home, "corrupt as it may appear," wrote McMinn to Calhoun "to have purchased" the cooperation of those chiefs who signed the agreement. This did not include John Jolly, who was removed along with the rest.

Houston had done his best for his Cherokee friends, but now that the dark deed was done, had no desire to continue with his current position. He handed in his resignation, and found more cooperation from McMinn than Calhoun when it came to vindication in writing: "you have in every instance which has come under my view acted with Integrity and Firmness, as Sub agent for the Cherokee Nation," the governor wrote.[3] Houston sent this note to Andrew Jackson to ensure his knowledge of the climate surrounding his departure from the Indian service.

Judge James Trimble of Nashville, an old Houston family friend, agreed to take Sam Houston on as his apprentice to learn the law. This was the usual route to becoming a law practitioner at that time, despite Magistrate Crockett having "never read a page in a law book." Trimble was not disappointed in Sam Houston, who covered in six months the work which typically took others a year and a half. Before the end of 1818, Houston was admitted to the Tennessee bar.

But even his intense study had allowed for activities of a more genial nature. Andrew Jackson was an honory member of Dramatic Club of Nashville, and Houston appeared in several plays. He loved the limelight and did particularly well in comedy roles. Club mentor Noah Ludlow recalled, "he never met a man who had a keener sense of the ridiculous."[4] In later years Houston's political enemies would tend to agree.

Presumably, however, Houston suppressed this sense when he opened his own law office in Ludlow, about 30 miles from Nashville. Merchant Isaac Golladay must have seen in Sam Houston a man with a bright future. He clothed him on credit, rented him office space for one dollar a month, and recommended his services to the business establishment in town. And no doubt Sam's known friendship with the great Andrew Jackson did little harm. The young lawyer did well, and his appointment as adjutant general to the Tennessee Militia with the rank of colonel by Governor McMinn added to his prestige.

But Houston's stay in Lebanon was short-lived. Appointed by McMinn as Tennessee solicitor general, he packed his bags to head back to Nashville. Before leaving he delivered a farewell speech to friends and associates which brought tears to the eyes of some: "I shall ever remember with emotions of gratitude the kindness which I have received at your hands," he said. "I came among you poor and a stranger, and you extended the hand of welcome, and received me kindly. I was naked, and ye clothed me; I was hungry and ye fed me."

But Houston, despite having sought the post, found being solicitor general did not clothe and feed him well enough. Having joined the Freemasons and established other helpful contacts, he resigned less than two years later to set up a lucrative private law practice in Market St. His advertisement in the Nashville *Whig* on December 26, 1821, read: "Sam Houston attorney at Law. Having removed to an office second below A. Kingsley's Esq. on Market Street, can be found at all times where he ought to be."[5] Perhaps those last words were to assure potential clients he would not necessarily be found in the Nashville Tavern, his fondness for liquid refreshment well known.

Despite still having health problems, courtesy of Horseshoe Bend, the successful lawyer was a commanding presence. He stood six feet two inches, with a robust, muscled build, striking eyes of blue and chestnut hair. In 1821 his fellow militia officers elected him major general of the Tennessee Militia's southern command. Secretary of War Calhoun must have been vexed to find himself in correspondence with Major General Sam Houston, the young Lieutenant he had upbraided for dressing as Cherokee only four years before. But it would appear that Calhoun had not finished with the upstart yet. Shortly after Sam's election a government auditor found a supposed discrepancy of $67.52 from Houston's time as subagent to the Cherokees. Houston had been scrupulously honest in his financial dealings, even reporting at one point possibly having been overpaid.

The alleged shortfall led to a protracted dispute with Calhoun, the government withholding $237.61 owed to Houston for expenses while subagent. These proceedings did not "meet our Backwoods notion of Justice," Houston complained to Calhoun. The dispute continued, and in July of 1822 Houston wrote:

I can see no reason for the course of conduct pursued by you, unless it be that I am the same man against whom you conceived so strong a prejudice in 1818, when I was assist. Indian Agent.... Sir I would have forgotten the unprovoked injuries inflicted upon me, if you were not disposed to continue them. But your reiteration shall not be unregarded. I will remember your personal bad treatment.... As a citizen of Tennessee I will mark your treaty of 1819 with the Cherokees ... replete with mischief to our state.[6]

Before the year was out, Houston received the funds due him, less $30 for the hire of a horse. But he wanted that $30. Calhoun had not heard the last of this matter yet.

In February of 1823, Sam Houston announced his candidacy for congress. Andrew Jackson and Joseph McMinn went to work on Sam's behalf and pulled influential strings to see that he ran unopposed.

On September 13, 1823, Houston was duly elected as representative for the Ninth District of Tennessee. He packed his bags once more and headed east for Washington armed with a letter of introduction to Thomas Jefferson:

Hermitage October 4th 1823

Dear Sir,
    This letter will be handed you by Genl Saml Houston, a representative to Congress from this State, and a particular friend of mine to whom I beg leave to introduce to you.... He has attained his present standing without the extrinsic advantages of fortune & education, and has sustained in his various promotions from the common soldier to the Major General the character of the high minded and honorable man—as such I present him to you...
    With a sincere wish that good health and happy days are still yours, I remain your friend and very obliged servant.

Andrew Jackson[7]

Thomas Jefferson, author of the Declaration of Independence and third president of the United States, at 80, was a living idol who received selected visitors at Monticello, his splendid home. No doubt Houston was entertained in Jefferson's impressive entrance hall adorned with treasures accumulated over the years. This included paintings and maps, and even artefacts from the Lewis and Clark Expedition.

Shortly after Houston's arrival in Washington, the Tennessee Legislature sent Andrew Jackson to the U.S. Senate, thus the two friends, both still suffering from old wounds, saw much of each other. Houston rated Jackson as one of the greatest Americans who lived, eclipsed only by the likes of Thomas Jefferson, and even noted Old Hickory's decorum: "He makes as fine a bow as any man I have seen at court."

When shown over the House chamber by Mr. E. G. M. Butler, once Jackson's ward, Houston remarked, "Now, Butler, I am a member of Congress, and I will show Mr. Calhoun that I have not forgotten his insult to me when a poor lieutenant."[8]

Secretary of War Calhoun must have winced when he received from Congressman Houston a demand for the $30 transportation cost not previously paid. It could hardly be ignored that this eccentric, who had presented himself as a Cherokee, was now a member of the Military Affairs Committee overseeing the Secretary's budget. To make things worse, Andrew Jackson, Houston's friend and mentor, was chairman of that same Committee. "Gen Houston not being bound to furnish a horse to perform the journey, the charge for the use of the horse is allowed. J.C.C."[9]

Houston watched and learned from the political luminaries of the day—the likes of Daniel Webster and Henry Clay—and on January 22 made his first important speech. It was an appropriate topic for someone who had committed Homer's *Iliad* to memory: American recognition of Greek independence.

Houston had said he would not get involved with the "dear Girles before I make a fortune." But being a member of Congress, even without the fortune, was certainly impressive enough for many southern belles. In early 1825, Sam expected to marry a certain Miss M—, but not the same of his previous acquaintance. The new lady was probably Mariah Campbell of Lancaster, South Carolina. But the blossoming romance soon faded, possibly due to Houston putting his time and political ambitions before "dear Girles"—no matter how attractive.

Houston was re-elected for a second term in Congress, and in January of 1826 wrote his friend William Worth: "I am making myself less frequent in the Lady World than I have been. I must keep up my Dignity, or rather I must attend more to politics and

Sam Houston, praised by some and vilified by others. But in the end there is no substitute for success (Library of Congress).

less to love."[10] But Sam still found time to pursue a certain Mary Parke Custis, a blue-blood descendent of George Washington. Sam, however, was crestfallen when he wrote his doubts about "the good taste and discernment of Mary Custis who preferred to tie herself by long engagement to that shy underclassman at West Point when she might have been Houston's bride and the belle of Washington society."[11] So Mary Custis married that shy underclassman, a gentleman of the old South named Robert E. Lee.

Sam Houston had not seen a shot fired in anger since Horseshoe Bend, but southern gents often resolved differences, where honor was at stake, to the smell of gunpowder. According to Judge Guild of Nashville, his friend General William White was, "one of the most gallant men I ever knew, and was the very sole of honor. He never gave or submitted to an insult." Events came to pass, however, where White felt Houston had insulted him.

This unfortunate business was the result of a dispute regarding the position of postmaster in Nashville. With the resignation of the incumbent, the post was awarded to one John Patton Erwin, a relative of Elizabeth Crockett. Sam and the others felt the former postmaster's assistant was far better qualified for the position. Erwin heard of Houston protesting in strong terms to the administration, and dispatched John T. Smith of Missouri, with White as his witness, to deliver a written challenge to Houston at the Nashville Inn. Smith delivered the note, but in the process harsh words passed between Houston and White. Then, according to White:

Erwin then advertised Houston as a coward and calumniator. Houston, in the next paper, denounced Erwin as a rogue, and procured a certificate from Erwin's rival candidates to prove that he had taken a newspaper belonging to another person before Erwin became Postmaster. To this publication Houston attached the certificates of two persons, in which the altercation betwixt him and myself was very much misrepresented, thereby placing himself in a defensive, and me in an offensive attitude. Houston, who was somewhat popular, hoped, in this manner, to escape public censure himself and at my expense, and that, too, without subjecting himself to the necessity of a combat with anyone, for he was fully aware of the inequality of our situations.[12]

White was not known for proficiency with firearms, but "a coward cannot live except in disgrace and obscurity," he wrote, and felt obliged to challenge Houston to a duel. Sam practised shooting in the grounds of the Hermitage, and Jackson gave him some pointers, one being to bite on a bullet when firing to steady his aim.

Early on September 22, 1826, White and Houston confronted each other at Linkumpitch, just across the border in Kentucky. After walking 15 paces, they turned and fired. Houston remained unscathed while White fell with a bullet wound to the groin. Houston walked across and knelt beside his fallen foe. Honor satisfied, they supposedly resolved their differences with a few quietly spoken words, and White soon made the best of a bad situation:

I did not hesitate as to my course, nor shall I have cause ever to regret it, for I find that, although I fell in the combat, I conquered even in my fall. Yes, I conquered the prejudices and extorted the admiration of my foes themselves, whilst I am established in the esteem and approbation of my friends. And now it affords me pleasure to add further that, although I was very severely wounded, I have entirely recovered from it.[13]

In 1827, Houston declined to run for a third term in Congress. He had set his sights on bigger game, and at age 34 ran for governor of Tennessee. Perhaps Calhoun being elevated to vice-president with the election of the Adams administration in 1825 had influenced his decision to quit Federal politics for the time being. Whatever the reason, he had enjoyed an astonishing rise in the world during the previous decade, the result of his own determination, intelligence, and being the protégé of Andrew Jackson.

But during the run-up to the election, the White duel came back to haunt him. The governor of Kentucky sent a warrant to William Carroll, governor of Tennessee, for Sam's arrest. Carroll had fought alongside Jackson at Horseshoe Bend and New Orleans, and was no stranger to duelling himself, having lost part of a thumb in an exchange with Jesse Benton. Carroll ignored the warrant, but with Houston running against him, it was in his interest to have the matter known. At a dinner in Tellico, Houston gave his side of the White affair. He expressed his basic conviction against duelling, and relief that White had recovered from the wound. The *Niles Register* paraphrased Houston's words:

But here the matter, it seems, was not to rest. [I] shall not be governor, is the decree of those in power and their minions. A *witness is sent from Tennessee to Kentucky*, an indictment is there framed and a grand jury procured to find a true bill, and I am proclaimed a felon. Yes! A *felon*, under a belief no freeman will agree to have a felon for his governor, and with a view to its being generally known it is published in their favorite prints *The Focus* and the *Whig and Banner*. If my fellow citizens think of me in the light of a horse-thief, a felon, they ought not to vote for me; but if they view me as acting involuntarily, from a necessity imposed by others, I hope they will vote for me, and should I be favored with a majority, I will be Governor of Tennessee.[14]

Election day arrived, and so did Sam Houston mounted on a fine grey steed. He appeared at Nashville polling booths sporting a handsome black beaver hat, ruffled blouse beneath an Indian hunting shirt and black satin waistcoat. A splendid red, beaded sash completed the candidate's flamboyant ensemble. "He was the observed of all the observers,"[15] according to one spectator. Houston beat William Carroll comfortably by 12,000 votes with fewer than 75,000 cast. The inauguration took place on October 7, 1827, at the First Baptist Church in Nashville where he gave his first speech as governor of Tennessee:

> To me it is a source of grateful pleasure, and manly pride, that Tennessee is my adopted country. At an early age I came here within her limits unattended by those adventitious aids, so necessary in pointing out the path of usefulness, and sustaining youth under the pressure of inexperience and misfortune; and, however wayward and devious my course may have been in youth, her citizens have magnanimously upheld me.[16]

He went on to say that the Constitution of the United States must be upheld, but at the same time "guard with firmness our own sovereignty" and whenever an infraction is attempted by the general government "preserve the rights of the state." These innate "states rights" beliefs held by many who lived in the South would come into play in Texas eight years later, and help split the United States 26 years after that.

12

Scalping Knives and Tomahawks

In July of 1816, eleven years before Houston's election as governor of Tennessee, the Negro Fort at Prospect Bluff lay a shattered ruin—a long-standing thorn removed from Andrew Jackson's side. The forests and bayous of Florida however—in addition to alligators, frogs, toads, turtles and herons—would continue to harbor hostile Indians, escaped slaves, smugglers and pirates. Unless, of course, the whole area was removed from what Old Hickory considered lax Spanish control.

The Seminoles had helped remove Negro Fort, but this southernmost branch of the Creek Indians, according to Jackson, carried out raids north of the border. Under Jackson's direction, General Gaines spoke to King Hatchy: "Your Seminoles are very bad people: I don't say whom. You have murdered many of my people, and stolen my cattle and many good horses, that cost me money; and many good houses that cost me money you have burned." Gaines accused Hatchy of still conniving with the British, and threatened to visit him with "good strong warriors, with scalping knives and toma-hawks," unless he gave up the murderers and ceased harboring hostile blacks. "If you give me leave to go by you against them, I shall not hurt any thing belonging to you."

Hatchy hotly replied that he was the one who had cause to complain. "While one American has been justly killed, while in the act of stealing cattle, more than four Indians while hunting have been murdered by these lawless freebooters. I harbor no negroes." He denied any knowledge of Englishmen and "I shall use force to stop any armed Americans from passing my town or my lands."[1]

Camp Crawford, renamed Fort Scott, was reinforced and strengthened. In late November 1817, a force of 250 soldiers marched to Fowltown, a Seminole village within territory taken from the Creeks in the Treaty of Fort Jackson. Their influential chief, Neamathia, was to be placed under arrest. Considered a troublemaker, he refused to recognize a treaty he had not signed, and insisted his tribe was Seminole, not Creek.

The Indians saw the troops surrounding their village and, convinced they were about to be attacked, opened fire. The soldiers delivered a return volley which killed four warriors and one woman as the Indians fled into the surrounding swamps. The soldiers marched in, and during the following search a British uniform and letter of support from Marine Major Edward Nicholls was found. Nicholls had commanded the fort at Prospect Bluff before the British withdrawal.

The troops returned to Fort Scott without Naemathia, and General Gaines dispatched another force of 300 men under Lieutenant Colonel Matthew Arbuckle to finish the job. They arrived to find the village deserted, and were loading corn into a wagon when about 60 warriors opened fire from the swamps. Shots were exchanged for about 20 minutes before the outnumbered Indians pulled back and disappeared into the smoke-shrouded foliage. The troops finished ransacking the village, set the buildings ablaze, then marched out. They halted on a nearby bluff and built a small blockhouse called Fort Hughes, named for the only soldier killed in the fight, three others having been wounded.[2]

Creek Indian agent, ex–Governor David Mitchell of Georgia, would attribute this attack to the start of the Seminole war, and regarding Indian depredations: "truth compels me to say, that, before the attack on Fowltown, aggressions of this kind were as frequent on the part of whites as on the part of the Indians, the evidence of which can be furnished from the files of the Executive of Georgia."[3] Mitchell resigned his post as Indian agent after fending off false accusations of slave smuggling, something he and Sam Houston had in common.

One week after the burning of Fowltown, a flatboat was taking supplies up the Apalachicola River to Fort Scott. On board were 40 men, seven women and four children under the command of Lieutenant Richard Scott of the 7th Infantry. Half the men were unarmed, being on the sick list. The lieutenant, warned of possible attack, had sent this news ahead by courier to General Gaines. At a point where the current sent the sluggish vessel close to shore, 300 Indians concealed along the riverbank opened fire. Scott and most of the men were killed with the first volley, then the Indians swarmed into the river and clambered into the boat. Six men, five of them wounded, jumped from the boat and swam to the opposite bank. They made their escape while the Indians killed and scalped those left behind in a frenzied attack. One woman was taken prisoner while the other females and children died.[4]

Fowltown and Burnt Corn Creek had much in common; both starting an Indian war. Jackson wrote to Secretary of War Calhoun:

> I have deemed it both prudent and advisable to call from the west end of the state of Tennessee, for one thousand volunteer mounted gun men, to serve during the campaign. With this force, in conjunction with the regular troops, I can act promptly, and with the smiles of Heaven, successfully, against any force that can be concentrated by the Seminoles and their auxiliaries.[5]

Old Hickory, however, had learned his lesson fighting the Creeks. Not wanting to see his men "risked in a contest with savages, with the odds of two to one" had written to the governor of Georgia requesting 1,000 of his militia be kept in the field. Jackson realized mounted troops meant extra expense, but "mounted gun-men, as auxiliaries, in such a campaign as the one contemplated, will be found to save both blood and treasure to the U. States."[6]

Andrew Jackson marched from Nashville at the head of his mounted gunmen, who were joined by nearly 2,000 Creek allies under the command of William McIntosh, a mixed-blood brigadier general. But the wet, winter weather combined with the same food shortages suffered in the early days of the Creek War returned to plague the beleaguered Jackson. "How these failures have happened, under the superintendence of regular officers, I cannot imagine, but blame must rest some where, and it shall be strictly investigated as soon as circumstances will permit."[7]

The hungry and damp troops arrived at Fort Scott in March 1818. Despite his supply problems, Jackson continued south down the Apalachicola by boat into Spanish territory. Fortunately for the hungry troops, they encountered an army flatboat carrying flour upstream. The command reached the remnants of Negro Fort and, Prospect Bluff being ideal for defence, Jackson ordered a new structure built alongside the ruins; Fort Gadsden, named after the chief engineer.

But then General Gaines staggered into Jackson's camp on foot. He and others had been wandering through the woods after being wrecked upstream. Vital food and clothing had been lost along with the lives of several men. It was fortunate for Gaines they had not encountered hostiles who would have relished scalping the perpetrator of Fowltown. It seems ironic that Gaines, lost in the woods, had repeated Colonel Caller going astray after perpetrating Burnt Corn Creek.

Jackson ordered McIntosh and his Creeks to march east and they pursued "Couchatee Micco, or Red Ground Chief."[8] This was none other than the elusive Peter McQueen, still on the run. But the pursuing Creeks encountered a swamp about six miles wide, and were forced to discard their clothes and provisions while they waded in. The water being too deep, McIntosh and his warrior swam half the distance to the opposite shore. The Creeks closed in on the enemy camp, but McQueen escaped on horseback "We have taken 53 men and about 180 women and children prisoners, without the fire of a gun," reported McIntosh, "and we killed ten men that broke and tried to make their escape."[9]

Old Hickory received word that a party of Seminoles and escaped slaves were fleeing towards the Spanish garrison at Fort St. Marks at the head of Apalachee Bay on the Gulf Coast. Included was another old adversary from the Creek War, Josiah Francis. The prophet had recently returned from London where he had sailed with Major Nicholls in an attempt to gain support for restitution of Creek Lands. Many presents, however, were all he received. The War of 1812 was over, and the need for Creek collaboration had expired. A disgruntled Francis sailed back to Florida and rejoined Redsticks who were still prepared to fight. "It is all important that these men should be captured and made examples of," Jackson said.[10]

The troops marched from Fort Gadsden and made contact with McIntosh and his Creeks on April 1. Jackson's advance companies came under fire from Seminoles on an island surrounded by a marshy swamp. A brisk skirmish ensued until flanking companies closed in on the outnumbered hos-

Mixed-race Brigadier General William McIntosh fought with Jackson against the Seminoles in Florida. He would be killed by Creeks in 1825 for ceding more Indian land to the whites (Wikimedia Commons).

tiles. Seeing further resistance suicidal, the Indians fled and dispersed amid the cane-brakes. Jackson sent detachments out in all directions who, to his "satisfaction," burned nearly 300 Seminole houses. His men pillaged corn and rounded up cattle to feed the hungry troops. In one town, "More than fifty fresh scalps were found," Jackson reported to Secretary of War Calhoun, "and in the center of the public square, the old red Stick's standard, *a red pole*, was erected, crowned with scalps recognised by the hair, as torn from the heads of the unfortunate companions of Scott."[11]

Old Hickory continued on and planted his colors before the walls of Fort St. Marks. He penned a letter to the commandant: "To chastise a Savage Foe, who, combined with a lawless band of Negro Brigands, have for some time past, been carrying on a cruel and unprovoked war against the Citizens of the United States, has compelled the President to direct me to march my Army into Florida. I have penetrated the Mickasky Towns, and reduced them to ashes."[12] Jackson went on to say he had arrived as "the friend of Spain" but claimed the fortress harbored hostiles, and would therefore be occupied by American troops.

The commandant, Caso y Luengo, replied he had no authority to surrender the post and would need instructions from the governor at Pensacola. Jackson's troops promptly marched in without opposition, and Luengo protested about being "threatened by your Aid-de-Camp and other officers ... so large a body of Troops entered, without awaiting my permission, and taken possession of all the Stores and Posts, lowering the Spanish Flag, and hoisting the American."[13]

Duncan McCrimmon, a young American private was found inside the walls. He had wandered from Old Hickory's camp at the ruins of Negro Fort, and now had an amazing tale to tell. Captured by Josiah Francis' band, he had been interrogated, then told he would be executed. But Francis' 15 year-old old daughter, Milly, pleaded with her father for McCrimmon's life. Francis, however, said this could only be decided by the warrior who had captured the soldier. Two of his sisters had been killed by American troops, so Francis thought his mercy most unlikely. Milly pleaded with the warrior; killing McCrimmon would not bring his sisters back to life. Moved by her words, he spared the soldier and handed him to the Spanish at Fort St. Marks. Thus the true story of the "Creek Pocahontas" was born. McCrimmon would not have believed his luck to have his life saved, and see the troops march in to raise the American flag.

Caso y Luengo requested boats to convey himself and other Spaniards to Pensacola, which Jackson graciously granted. But Josiah Francis and another chief, Homathlemico, did not receive the same consideration. An armed schooner arrived in port showing British colors, a chance for the Indians to escape. The two chiefs seized a canoe and paddled out to be welcomed aboard by smiling faces.

The following day Milly Francis' younger sister and a companion paddled out towards the schooner. As they approached, however, no sign of the prophet was seen on deck. There was something about that craft that did not seem right. They turned their canoe and commenced paddling back. A hail of lead erupted from the "British" schooner. The two girls paddled furiously as bullets splashed about, and made it to shore before fleeing into the marshes.

But there would be no escape for Josiah Francis and Homathlemico.[14] Jackson ordered them brought ashore from the vessel, the USS *Thomas Shields*, in fact, sailing in support of his campaign. Without trial, the two chiefs were promptly hanged by the neck till dead outside the fort gates.[15]

Indians having escaped to the east, Jackson marched for the Suwannee River to strike the stronghold of Chief Bowlegs. But 100 miles of soggy terrain; bayous and cane-brakes lay between St. Mark's and his prey. McIntosh, in advance with his Creek warriors and Tennessee Gunmen, heard of "Peter McQueen being near the road we were trav-elling, and I took my warriors there and fought him." They fired at each other "in a bad swamp" for about an hour, then the hostiles broke. During a three-mile pursuit across soggy terrain 37 warriors were killed and six captured, along with 98 woman and children. Amid the prisoners was one white woman, Elizabeth Stewart, captured when Scott's party had been killed on the Apalachicola River.[16] McIntosh's losses were three killed and five wounded. To Old Hickory's ire, the elusive Peter McQueen had escaped yet again.

McIntosh rejoined Jackson's command, and seven days out from St. Marks they neared Bowlegs' camp. Orders were issued for the coming attack, which should, accord-ing to Jackson, end the campaign:

> The general however expects that in their execution of this plan, no man will so far lose sight of the boasted character of the soldier, as to wilfully destroy the women and children, but to recol-lect we war with savages who have without mercy torn the locks from the head of the aged matron down to the infant babe. These are the wretches who should feel the avenging rod.[17]

On April 16, Jackson forged ahead during the morning hoping to surprise the Semi-noles with an attack in the early afternoon. But the advance stalled when his troops found themselves on the shore of "a remarkable pond." He planned to halt and resume marching the following morning, but six mounted enemy scouts were seen to gallop away. Old Hickory was counting on capturing Indian food supplies for his own troops, and gave immediate orders to move out. The command marched at the double and struck the Seminole camp at sunset. Warned by the scouts, the Indians were already crossing the river, and managed to avoid a repeat of Horseshoe Bend despite a hail of fire. "Nine negroes & two Indians were found dead & two negro men made prisoners on the 17th," recalled Jackson.

Corn and cattle were gathered, and a detachment under General Gaines crossed the river in captured canoes. They pursued the fugitives through the swamps, the trail easily followed by abandoned food and goods. Some prisoners were taken, but catching the main party proved impossible. Gaines contended himself with gathering 30 head of cattle, but due to "the disobedience of his orders by the Indians, not one pound was brought into camp." It can only be assumed Jackson's Creek allies ate heartily that night.

Having scattered the enemy, Old Hickory felt his actions "will end the Indian War for the present, & should it be renewed, the position taken, which ought to be held, will enable a small party to put it down promptly." These words meant American occu-pation of Spanish East Florida. Jackson had won again, but the elusive Peter McQueen had escaped the hangman's noose. Rumors were later heard of his death on an island off the Florida coast in 1820.[18] This may well have been true; or perhaps a ruse to shake old Sharp Knife from the relentless pursuit.

Seminoles and blacks were not the only prisoners taken during this campaign. Two British citizens had also been caught in Old Hickory's net. Robert Ambrister had been a marine officer serving under Major Nicholls during the War of 1812. After discharge in 1815, he had returned to Spanish Florida where he continued to aid the Indians. Alexander Arbuthnot was a Scots trader who been had lived in Florida since 1803. He worked with the Seminoles and acted as a diplomatic go-between and translator.

Old Hickory had them charged with assisting enemies of the United States. Unlike the Indian leaders, these white British nationals were granted the privilege of a court-martial, presided over by General Gaines, where the defendants were permitted a defence. After sitting from April 26 to 28, the court delivered to Jackson their recommendations; For Ambrister, a former marine officer, death by firing squad. For the civilian Arbuthnot, hanging was deemed appropriate.

But was shooting a fellow officer really correct? Fifty lashes and 12 months at hard labor "with a ball and chain" was thought more fitting for Ambrister, and the verdict was amended accordingly. But Old Hickory, in camp four miles north of St. Marks, had other ideas. Upon receiving news of the verdicts, he replied:

> The Commanding General orders that Brevet Major A. C. W. Fanning, of the corps of artillery, will have, between the hours of eight and nine o'clock, A.M., A. Arbuthnot suspended by the neck, with a rope, until he is *dead*, and Robert C. Ambrister to be shot to *death*, agreeably to the sentence of the court.[19]

Jackson had dismissed the second recommendation, and wrote justifying his actions to Secretary of War Calhoun. He felt "the execution of these two unprincipled villains" would set an "awful example" to the world that "retribution awaits those unchristian wretches who, by false promises, delude and excite an Indian tribe to all the horrid deeds of savage war."[20]

At least one compassionate deed during this savage war would gain ultimate recognition. In 1844 Congress belatedly voted Milly Francis a special medal of honor, and a pension, for having saved Duncan McCrimmon. Living with her tribe in Indian Territory (Oklahoma), however, she only heard of this four years after the vote. She was dying from tuberculosis at the time and never received the pension and medal.

13

Possessed with the Furies

Defeating the Seminoles and executing the "two unprincipled villains" did not end Andrew Jackson's operations in Florida. The capital, Pensacola, still lay in Spanish hands, and Old Hickory had little regard for international law. He had occupied the town before the Battle of New Orleans, and a return visit now seemed appropriate, with or without his own government's approval.

But Jackson had more than Spaniards to worry about. The fractious military organization on the American frontier had many drawbacks. News arrived of an attack by Georgian militia on an undefended Creek town whose warriors were fighting alongside Old Hickory against the Seminoles. Governor William Rabun received a letter from Jackson referring to the perpetrator, Captain Obed Wright, as

> a cowardly monster in human Shape.... Such base cowardice and murderous conduct as this transaction affords, has not its parallel in history and should meet with its merited punishment.... You Sir as Governor of a State within my military Division have no right to give a military order when I am in the field.... This act will do to the last ages fix a Stain upon the character of Georgia.
>
> I have the honor to be with due Respect Yr. Mot. Obt Sert—
> Andrew Jackson
> Major Genl. Comg[1]

Rabun's respectful and "most obedient servant" had Captain Wright placed under arrest. A civil writ of habeas corpus, however, saw Wright gain temporary release. With a court martial pending, he fled into the Florida everglades to disappear from sight, and no individual was ever put on trial for the attack.

Old Hickory led his troops to Pensacola, and on May 23 wrote to Governor José Masot accusing the Spanish of aiding enemies of the United States. His actions were necessary for the protection of American citizens, Jackson claimed, and demanded the surrender of both Pensacola and Fort Barrancas, rebuilt since being blown up by the British during Jackson's last occupation. "If the peaceful surrender is refused, I shall enter Pensacola by violence, and assume the Government until the transaction can be amicably adjusted by the two Governments. The military in this case must be treated as prisoners of war." Masot withdrew from the town to the fortress leaving Lieutenant Colonel Don Lui Piemas with the dishonorable task of surrendering the town, which was promptly occupied by American troops.

The following day Governor Masot wrote to Jackson. He denied Spanish support for hostiles, and, "Finally, if, contrary to my hopes, your excellency should persist in your functions to occupy this fortress, which I am resolved to defend to the last extremity, I shall repel force by force; and he who resists aggression can never be considered an aggressor."

"You cannot expect to defend yourself, successfully" Jackson replied, "and the first shot from your fort must draw upon you the vengeance of an irritated soldiery."

The governor, however, felt obliged for honor's sake to take his chances with the irritated soldiery, Old Hickory the most irritated of all. An American battery of one nine-pounder and one 8/10 howitzer took position 385 yards from the heavier artillery of the Spanish fort, and the guns spoke. Shells flew back and forth, and Jackson commended his officers for bravery, which "cannot be surpassed by any military act recorded in history." The Americans held their ground until the garrison "struck with a panic," surrendered, wrote Jackson. He felt that Masot's "boasted threat of opposing force by force in case I advanced, deserved a severer chastisement than he recd., but the humiliation he experienced after his boast of desperate resistance ... was a severe punishment to military feelings."[2] The smoke cleared on the last shots of Old Hickory's stormy military career.

It comes as little surprise that Spanish national feeling was severely punished as well. And the British were none too pleased with the execution of two citizens after what they considered an unfair trial. And Jackson's critics were also found at home, Secretary of War John Calhoun among them. Many saw the emergence of a man with too much power who could well become a military dictator in his own right. But Jackson's Florida campaign won admiration from his devotees and, once again, the applause of the masses. It seemed to them the hero of New Orleans could do no wrong.

The Spanish minister to the U.S., Luis de Onis, demanded to know if President Monroe had ordered the invasion of Spanish territory, a country at peace with the United States. Monroe found himself with a dilemma. If he approved Jackson's acts, he was in violation of international law. If he disapproved, it showed he had no control over generals who violated the law. Taking the middle ground, he refused to censure Jackson, but did order the American troops from the Spanish forts.

What emerged, however, was final proof that Spain had no real hold on power along the Gulf Coast. The Spanish empire was fighting rebellion on various fronts, including Mexico, and had neither the money nor troops to hold Florida. The time had come, in fact, for the United States to relieve Spain of the Florida burden—for a price. Secretary of State John Quincy Adams negotiated the Florida Treaty with Minister Onis. This also settled a long standing border dispute regarding Texas. The Americans had claimed the Louisiana Purchase from France included Texas to the Rio Grand, but the Spanish insisted the Sabine River was the correct border. The Americans now relinquished their claim to Texas, and paid Spain $5 million for Florida. This agreement was signed on February 22, 1819, but the Spanish government seemed in no hurry to ratify the deal.

Old Hickory, his troops having been withdrawn, offered to reconquer Florida in three months. And why stop there? "If Congress should will it, with the regulars alone and the necessary equipment and naval aid, Cuba in six months."[3]

The treaty was finally proclaimed on February 22, 1821. And who best to haul down the Spanish flag and raise the American? Andrew Jackson, of course. But was an autocrat hated by the Spanish really the ideal man to become governor of the conquered territory?

Following his occupation of Pensacola, Jackson, suffering from fatigue and his other ailments, had been happy to return home to his loving wife. The country was in a depressed economic state, but Old Hickory decided the Hermitage house was due for an improvement or two—total replacement, in fact. The old wooden structure came down to be rebuilt into slave quarters, and was replaced with a fine, two-story brick dwelling typical of those found on thriving plantations. It had four large, high ceilinged rooms upstairs and down, warmed by nine fireplaces, and a basement kitchen. Fine French wallpaper lined the walls. Further alterations and additions would occur during the following years including a portico with tall, Doric columns.

Early in 1821, that revolutionizing invention, the steam engine, propelled the incoming governor of Florida and his wife down the "Big Muddy" to New Orleans. Ten years had passed since a steam boat first plied the Mississippi. From the Crescent City the Jacksons sailed to Pensacola. Jackson, however, declined to live within the town until after the official transfer of power from the governor, Colonel José María Callava. This soldier was a distinguished veteran of the Peninsula War who had been knighted into the Military Order of St. Hermenegildo in 1811.

On July 23, Rachel Jackson wrote home describing events in Pensacola to her friend Elizabeth Kingsley:

> At length, last Tuesday was the day. At seven o'clock, at the precise moment, they hove in view under the American flag and a full band of music.... They marched up to the government house, where the two Generals met in the manner prescribed, then his Catholic majesty's flag was lowered, and the American hoisted high in the air, not less than one hundred feet.... O how they burst into tears to see the last ray of hope departed of their devoted city and country.... How did the city sit solitary and mourn. Never did my heart feel more for a people.[4]

Rachel's heart, however, did not feel for the inhabitants' activities of a Sunday: "The Sabbath profanely kept; a great deal of noise and swearing in the streets; shops kept open; trade going on, I think, more than on any other day." It seems, however, Andrew Jackson was not the only one to wield power. His wife issued her own orders to Major Stanton, and the following Sunday: "Great order was observed; the doors kept shut; the gambling houses demolished; fiddling and dancing not heard any more on the Lord's day; cursing not to be heard." All of which, no doubt, gave the city even more reason to "sit solitary and mourn." She continued her observations:

> Pensacola is a perfect plain: the land nearly as white as flour, yet productive of fine peaches, oranges in abundance, grapes, figs, pomegranates, etc. flowers grow spontaneously, for they have neglected the gardens, expecting a change of government. The town is immediately on the bay, the most beautiful water prospect I ever saw; and from 10 o'clock in the morning until 10 at night we have the finest sea-breeze. There is something in it so exhilarating, so pure, so wholesome, it enlivens the whole system. All the houses look in ruins, old as time. Many squares of the town appear grown over with the thickest shrubs, weeping willows, and the Pride of China: all look neglected. The inhabitants all speak Spanish and French. Some speak four or five languages. Such a mixed multitude you nor any of us ever had an idea of. There are fewer white people far than any other, mixed with all nations under the canopy of heaven, almost in nature's darkness.[5]

Old Hickory hoped to relieve nature's darkness, writing to John Coffee of "Passing such ordinances, for its Government as I find absolutely necessary for its peace and good order," and the flag being raised with the full band playing "long may it wave o'er the land of the free & the home of the brave."

But even with the American flag in place, there was much official paperwork to be done. The changing governors not speaking each other's language, combined with mutual distrust, did nothing to assist a smooth transfer of power. Interpreters were required, and Jackson's temper was not sweetened by the recurring pain and ailments that dogged him through life.

Any *modus vivendi* went out the window when Jackson attempted to obtain paperwork from Callava relating to a lawsuit by a local resident. Details differ from the two sides involved, but the scenario appeared as thus: On August 22, 1821, Callava's assistant, Domingo Sousa, declined to furnish the papers on the grounds that he only took instructions from Callava. Jackson promptly, and characteristically, ordered Sousa's arrest, and the documents seized. But, one step ahead, Sousa had already handed the papers to Callava's steward, Antoine Fullarat. Colonel Robert Butler and *alcalde* Henry Brackenridge were dispatched by Jackson to Callava's residence to either obtain the papers, or bring Callava in for interview. They found Callava dining with both American and Spanish officials and their ladies. The papers were requested, and Callava declined to hand them over. When told he would be taken before Jackson, he said he would supply the documents once he had their requirements in writing. This supplied, Butler returned two hours later with a party of soldiers only to find Callava's door unanswered. The soldiers moved in through an unlocked rear door. "Lights were procured and the rooms searched," Butler reported, "when Colonel Callava was found in his bed divested of his coat." The papers were demanded, but to Butler's "astonishment they were still refused," despite the fact "his refusal would be viewed as an act of open mutiny to the civil authority exercised in the Floridas, and that he must expect the consequences." Callava insisted he would never be taken from his house alive "but he seemed to act without much difficulty when the guard was ordered to prime and load."[6] Callava later complained: "the commissioners entered my apartment; they surrounded my bed with soldiers with drawn bayonets in their hands, they removed the mosquito net, they made me sit up, and demanded *the papers, or they would use the arms against my person*." Despite being sick, said the colonel, he was forced from bed and "I dressed in my uniform, was going to put on my sword, but, upon reflection, thought it better to deliver it to the officer. I did so, and one of the three took it from his hand and threw it upon the chimney, and in this manner I was conducted through the streets among the troops."

Callava appeared before Jackson, who was in no mood for small talk, apparently. A Spanish officer present at the time stated: "The Governor, Don Andrew Jackson, with turbulent and violent actions, with disjointed reasonings, blows on the table, his mouth foaming, and possessed with the furies, told the Spanish commissary to deliver the papers."[7] It comes as little surprise that Callava found himself locked up. The papers were found in the colonel's bedroom and duly delivered to Jackson. But then a writ of habeas corpus for Callava's release arrived, sworn out by Judge Eligius Fromentin. A heated disagreement between Jackson and Fromentin ensued regarding the Judge's right to interfere with the governor's duties. Old Hickory wrote to Fromentin "you will be treated and punished as you may deserve, regardless of your boasts of bloodflowing &c &c which pass by me as the fleeting breeze."[8]

The papers having been obtained, Callava was released. The disgruntled colonel soon sailed for Washington, and on October 6 Spanish chargé d'affaires Rivas y Salmon wrote to Secretary of State John Quincy Adams "with complaints" directed against "an Officer of The United States, a conspicuous Citizen of the Union, and a highly distinguished General, the Hero of New Orleans." Adams declined to comment till all the facts were before him, and a diplomatic skirmish followed which stirred up other matters including the removal of other documents to Havana. Finally, on April 5, 1822, Adams closed the business by stating that Callava's refusal to produce the documents "was a high and aggravated outrage upon his (Jackson's) lawful authority; that the imprisonment of Colonel Callava was a necessary, though by the President deeply regretted consequence, of his obstinate perseverance in refusing to deliver the Papers."[9]

By this time the disagreement was of no great consequence, Andrew Jackson no longer the governor of Florida. Six months earlier, November 13, 1821, he had written his letter of resignation nine days after returning to the Hermitage. "My duties have been laborious and my situation exposed me to heavy expense, which makes it more necessary that I should retire to resuscitate my declining fortune to enable it to support me in my declining years."[10] Old Hickory stepped back from the public limelight to run his business concerns.

This included plantations other than the Hermitage, and during 1822 Jackson received word from Egbert Harris, who managed his Big Spring Farm in Alabama, of a slave named Gilbert having run off. Jackson wrote to Harris, that should he be recaptured:

> I wish him well secured with irons, until an opportunity may offer to send him down the river, as I will not keep a negro in the habit of running away ... although you may find some of my negroes at first hard to manage—still I hope you will be able to govern them without much difficulty. I have only to say, you know my disposition, and as far as lenity can be extended to these unfortunate creatures, I wish you to do so; subordination must be obtained first, and then good treatment.[11]

Gilbert was recaptured, but not sent "down the river," He escaped twice more, however, in 1824 and 1827. Moved to the Hermitage, Jackson ordered that he be given corporal punishment, "moderately with small rods." The overseer, Ira Walton, marched Gilbert away to administer the sentence in front of other slaves as an example, but all did not go as planned. Walton claimed Gilbert slipped out of his bonds and attacked him, and he was forced to defend himself with a knife.

Jackson arrived on the scene and summoned a doctor, but Gilbert died shortly afterwards. Jackson sacked Walton and wrote to the prosecuting attorney Andrew Hays: "I have no wish to prosecute Mr. Walton should you think justice does not demand it, but being the guardian of my slave, it is my duty to prosecute the case so far as justice to him may require it." Despite a slave boy having testified that Walton's version was correct, Hay replied: "the place of the wound in Gilbert's back, afford a strong presumption that he was stabbed in the back while running, and not in the first scuffle ... it is not a case of justifiable homicide, is, that his hands were tied; and I do not believe they were ever untied." Hays recommended Jackson have Walton brought before the circuit court "to answer a bill of indictment for the death of Gilbert." Jackson signed a bill to indict Walton for murder, but a grand jury returned a verdict of "not a true bill." Walton walked free and no further action was taken.[12] This matter, awkward to begin with, was complicated by Jackson's owing Walton $500, the result of a loan. It comes as little surprise that the accused demanded his money back. Jackson was forced to request partial repayment of a loan he had made to Major William Lewis, in order to balance the books.

Upon resigning his governorship, Jackson had written that he was "truly wearied of public life." But wearied or not, his public life, at the age of 55, had barely begun.

The year following his return to the Hermitage, the Tennessee Legislature nominated Jackson as their candidate to run for president of the United States. His protégé Sam Houston, now a prominent name in Tennessee politics, wrote to him in August of 1822:

> The canker worms have been (already too long) gnawing at the very core and vitals of our government, and corruption stalks abroad, without obstruction or reprehension.... You are now before the eyes of the nation. You have nothing to fear, but everything to expect. The hopes of men in Washington will be *frost bitten* by the bare mention of your name! ... You have been your country's Great Sentinel, at a time when her watchmen had been caught slumbering on post, her capital had been reduced to ashes. You have been her faithful guardian, her well-tried servant! ... Will not the nation look to you again?[13]

In preparation, Jackson reluctantly allowed himself to be elected to the Senate once more, having served over two decades earlier. "Thus you see me a Senator, contrary to my wishes, my feelings, and my interests," he informed John Calhoun. The recycled senator traveled to Washington, mobbed by admirers who finally forced him to ride by stagecoach rather than horseback to maintain obscurity. Once settled down to his senatorial duties, the old soldier found the shuffle of paperwork tedious work after the excitement of battle. But he soothed relationships with old adversaries who now wished to count the most famous living American in their circle. This included Missouri Senator Thomas Hart Benton, whose 1813 bullet Jackson still carried. "I have become friendly with all here," he wrote to Rachel, "This has destroyed the stronghold of my enemies who denounced me as a man of vengeful temper and of great rashness. I am told the opinion of those whose minds were prepared to see me with a tomahawk in one hand and a scalping knife in the other has greatly changed."[14]

Time came for the 1824 presidential election. The dysfunctional Federalist Party had dissolved, thus the Democratic-Republican Party was going to send their uncontested candidate to the White House. Andrew Jackson, the hero of New Orleans, seemed the man for the time. "The office of Chief Magistrate of the Union is one of great responsibility. As it should not be sought by any individual of the Republic, so it cannot with propriety be declined when offered by those who have the power of selection," he said.

But Old Hickory, despite polling the most votes, did not win the 1824 election. John Quincy Adams "stole" the election, according to Jackson, who retained an outward calm while seething within. Jackson received 154,000 popular votes to Adams' 109,000 and 99 Electoral College votes to Adams' 84. Neither Jackson or Adams, however, or the other three candidates, received the 131 Electoral College votes required to win. The president now had to be elected by the House of Representatives. House Speaker Henry Clay, no lover of Jackson, used his considerable influence to secure Adams' victory. Once president, Adams appointed Clay his secretary of state. This was denounced by Jackson's supporters as a premeditated "corrupt bargain." Democracy and the will of the people had been thwarted, they cried. "The Judas of the West has closed the contract and will receive the thirty pieces of silver," said Jackson. "His end will be the same." Adams and Clay would have "corrupt bargain" allegations hanging over them till the next federal election.

Old Hickory probably felt much the same way as he did when retreating from Enitachopco Creek, the Redsticks having "whipped Captain Jackson, and run him to the Coosa River." But now, as then. Jackson withdrew in good order and regrouped for the next assault. And the fight would be as savage with words as Horseshoe Bend had been with musket and bayonet.

14

I Had Come for Their Votes

Colonel Crockett found little time for leisure on the 1818 Tennessee frontier. As a justice of the peace he took depositions, settled property disputes, paid bounties for wolf scalps, issued warrants for the arrest of debtors and thieves, and sat in judgment on the miscreants once brought in. As regards the militia, one observer noted that:

> The general muster was the grand event of the year, and brought together more of all classes of people than any other meeting. The officers were dressed in the gayest trappings; plumed and belted warriors, who vied in all that related to their military equipment and tactics, were these primitive soldiers, and they won for Tennessee the appellation, "Volunteer State." Their hardy looks, their athletic forms, their marching with the light and noiseless step peculiar to their pursuit of woodland game, and their picturesque costume, made them the observed of all the observers, and awoke in them an honest pride in the hearty plaudits they won from admiring spectators.[1]

It must be assumed Colonel Crockett bought, borrowed or stole "gayest trappings" for such occasions. No doubt he felt more at home when it came to shooting matches, the observer noting:

> They were not only cool and determined, brave as men dare be, but were among the most splendid marksmen the country has produced, and their death-dealing aim made them a terror to the enemy on every battle-field where the yell peculiar to the Tennessee volunteer was heard. From youth they were accustomed to the use of the rifle, which made them experts. At stated times they had shooting matches, and with their flint locks they acquitted themselves admirably and won the plaudits of friends.[2]

No doubt the "yell peculiar to the Tennessee volunteers" was an early version of the famous "Rebel Yell" of the Civil War.

But David Crockett needed to spend less time with the militia and dispensing justice, and more time securing financial security for his family. On land he owned at Lawrenceburg, he made a huge investment in money and time which, in late 1819, required his resignation from both militia and judiciary. Although no longer a militia officer, however, once a colonel always a colonel in the old south, and "Colonel Crockett" became the way he was known.

At a cost of $3,000, the grassy banks of Shoal Creek saw the foliage hacked away. Hammers banged and saws hacked as a whiskey distillery, gunpowder plant and gristmill took shape. The money, mostly borrowed, was "more than I was worth in the world." But on paper this was a sound investment that would yield good returns for the Crocketts over time. He had, however, also purchased two parcels of land totaling 380 acres, and such wheeling and dealing took its toll. In October of 1820 he wrote to one creditor, John McLemore:

I have been detained longer than expected my powder factory have not been pushed as it ought and I will not be able to meet my contract with you but if you send me a three-hundred acre warrant by the male I will pay you interest for the money until paid. I do not wish to disappoint you— I don't expect I can pay you the hole amount until next spring.[3]

John Christmas McLemore was married to Elizabeth, the daughter of John Donelson, a lifelong friend of Old Hickory and related to his wife. With two other partners, Jackson and McLemore had recently founded the settlement of Memphis, Tennessee.[4]

Despite financial difficulties, "I just now began to take a rise," recalled Crockett, "as in a little time I was asked to offer for the Legislature in the counties of Lawrence and Heckman (Hickman)."[5] So in February of 1821, Crockett put himself up for election. He still had a need to make money, however, and rode out with a herd of horses to be sold in Buncombe County, North Carolina, where his wife's parents lived. Being gone for three months, with the election looming in August, left little time to drum up support in the two counties he hoped to represent. He left his family once more, his wife expecting another child in two months.

He decided to canvass the good folk of Hickman County first, but he had a big disadvantage to overcome:

It now became necessary that I should tell the people something about the government, and an eternal sight of other things that I knowed nothing about more than I did about Latin, and Law, and such things as that. I have said before that in those days none of us called Gen'l Jackson the government ... but I knowed so little about it, that if any one had told me he was "the government," I should have believed it, for I had never read even a newspaper in my life, or anything else, on the subject.[6]

It can be well believed that Crockett was noncommittal when some citizens said they wanted their town moved closer to the center of the county. "There's no devil if I knowed what this meant, or how the town was going to be moved."

During the election campaign a squirrel hunt was organized at Duck River. Perhaps Crockett recalled scaling that tall tree during the Creek War to fetch down the shot squirrel for his cooking pot. Two teams were to compete, the losing side to pay for "a big barbeque, and what might be called a tip-top country frolic." The shooters spent two days decimating the local squirrel population with powder and ball, and "when we counted scalps, my party was victorious."

There was to be a dance, but first there was the serious business of politics. The candidates were called on to make a speech. Crockett's opponent was not at all worried, so Crockett said, because he "didn't think for a moment, that he was in any danger from an ignorant back-woods bear hunter." But Crockett rose, telling them "I had come for their votes, and if they didn't watch mighty close, I'd get them too." He tried talking about government, but choked up "as bad as if my mouth had been jam'd and cram'd chock full of dry mush." If this candidate was to get a single vote, a very different tack was required. So he launched into a story about a man who was: "beating on the head of an empty barrel near the roadside, when a traveler who was passing along, asked him what he was doing that for? The fellow replied that there was some cider in that barrel a few days before, and he was trying to see if there was any then, but if there was he couldn't get at it. I told them there had been a little bit of a speech in me a while ago, but I believed I couldn't get it out." The crowd roared with laughter, and Crockett, encouraged by his success, continued with other amusing tales tall and true.

It seemed backwoods humor was the key to success. He finished his speech saying he was "dry as a powder horn, and I thought it was time to wet our whistles a little; and so I put off to the liquor stand, and was followed by the greater part of the crowd."[7] This left the facts and figures speech of the opposition candidate with very few listeners.

This established the pattern of Crockett's appeal: don't talk policies and politics, give the crowd what they want—entertainment and a horn or two after the event. He created a rapport with the backwoods folk no educated gent could hope to match. As Crockett spun yarns from town to town, his daughter Matilda was born on August 2, 1821. There were now eight children under the Crockett roof.[8]

His folksy, backwoods way of chasing votes paid off and "I was elected, doubling my competitor, with nine votes over." So commenced a public career of defending the underdog; poor people whose land claims came under threat. He would also defend, to his detriment, the rights of the redmen who had occupied the fertile forests and plains of America before the first white settlers arrived.

Legislator David Crockett was in the Tennessee state capital, Murfreesboro, on September 17, 1821, for the first session of the Fourteenth General Assembly, "and before I had been there long, I could have told what the judiciary was, and what the government was too; and many other things that I had known nothing about before."

He was appointed as a member of the Standing Committee of Propositions and Grievances, which seems appropriate as, if the story is true, he soon had a grievance of his own. Feeling ill at ease amid learned and well-heeled gentleman who knew "what the government was" even before the election, Crockett rose to his feet and spoke in support of a bill he had proposed. He took his seat, and lawyer John C. Mitchell rose to speak in opposition. As the articulate Mitchell put his case, he mentioned Crockett as "the gentleman from the *cane*," in rather disparaging terms, apparently.

"Answer him, Crockett, answer him," the assembly shouted. Crockett, feeling derided, stood lost for words. Gathering his wits, however: "I told him he had got hold of the wrong man; that he didn't know who he was fooling with; that he reminded me of the meanest thing on God's earth, an old coon dog, barking up the wrong tree."

The House adjourned shortly afterwards, and Crockett approached Mitchell outside, proposing they take a walk. Mitchell agreed, but when they stopped Crockett informed him, "I brought you here for the express purpose of whipping you, and I mean to do it." To avoid a thrashing, Mitchell apologized profusely until he got Crockett "into a good humour." They walked back together, but the backwoods bear hunter felt Mitchell's apology was insincere. He still held a grudge.

Mitchell, according to Crockett, had more than one enemy, and soon exchanged blows in the street with a member of the Senate. The following day the House erupted into gales of laughter when Crockett "strutted in." On his "coarse cotton shirt" was the lawyer's very own cambric ruffle, "as conspicuous as possible." Crockett had retrieved the foppish accessory from the dust, where it was torn from Mitchell during the scuffle. Mitchell, embarrassed and displeased, strutted from the House in anger. He later approached Crockett for the ruffle's return. Crockett said he regarded it as a flag won in battle, but handed it back just the same.[9]

"The gentleman from the cane," ultimately worked to Crockett's advantage. These words symbolized the member from West Tennessee, an uneducated man who, with wit and humor, could hold his own. He stood out from the usual gray crowd who held, and often misused, the reigns of power.

But as Crockett sat in the Legislative Assembly, mother nature failed to back him up. "I was born for luck, though it would be hard for any one to guess what sort."[10] Torrential rain swamped the woods and streams of Lawrence County, and the placid waters of Shoal Creek swelled to a raging torrent. The tools and timbers of Crockett's gristmill and gunpowder factory were swept downstream, washed away along with his family's hopes for a secure future. The millrace and distillery were still intact, but with the grindstone damaged beyond repair, the distillery was useless.

Elizabeth Crockett, however, proved a rock of support. "Just pay up," she said, "as long as you have a bit's worth in the world; and then every body will be satisfied, and we will scuffle for more." Crockett saw the sense of her words. "This was just such talk as I wanted to hear, for a man's wife can hold him devilish uneasy, if she begins to scold, and fret, and perplex him at a time, when he has a full load for a rail-road car on his mind already."[11]

Resolved to pay back his debts any way he could, Crockett returned to the Legislative Assembly for the remainder of the session. The farmers of Lawrence and Hickman counties produced wheat, corn, cotton and oats along with other crops, and he introduced bills to assist them in any way he could. A revised state constitution was being discussed that would alter property taxes to assist poorer farmers at the expense of the wealthy. This received Crockett's hearty support. He voted to abolish gambling and, considering his own financial situation, it comes as little surprise that he voted against the state having the right to hire out debtors as labor.[12] But there was no doubt that Crockett was a *genuine* "man of the people" unlike Andrew Jackson who would be presented as such to voters. Despite modest beginnings, Old Hickory had become one of the planter elite; a large landholder with myriad business interests and the owner of many slaves.

On November 17, 1821 the first session of the Fourteenth General Assembly concluded, and the legislators headed for home. Carroll County had just been established in West Tennessee, named after new governor William Carroll, friend and comrade-in-arms of Andrew Jackson. Crockett, his 14-year-old son John, and hired hand Abram Henry, loaded their saddle bags and rode west. Elizabeth's father had transferred 800 acres to them in the new county, on the understanding $1,600 would be paid in future.[13]

The area had been rocked by violent earthquakes a decade earlier, leaving terrain described as "peculiarly weird and uncanny." Witness Eliza Bryan described the ground being "torn to pieces" with fissures opening and closing which threw up "a substance somewhat resembling coal." There was "a complete saturation of the atmosphere with sulphurous vapor causing total darkness." Terrified people had run aimlessly about, their screams intermingled with "the cries of the fowls and the beasts of every species; the cracking of trees falling, and the roaring of the Mississippi," the flow of which actually reversed for a short while.[14] Reelfoot Lake had been created by the cataclysm:

> Far out in the lake, beyond the sight of shore, one gets the impression of being in a vast ruined temple. On every side rise endless spires of decaying cypresses, branchless, leafless, shorn of their beauty, gleaming in the still air like gaunt, mysterious monuments of destruction and death.[15]

When Crockett arrived, cracks and fissures scarred the ground, but with time nature was reclaiming its own. Fresh growth of hickory, oak and cypress softened the ravaged landscape. The woods abounded with wildlife that would have gladdened any hunter's heart: "Bears, deer, wolves, panthers, wildcats, wild turkeys, and all sorts of lesser game abound in the forest on the borders of the lake." Crockett liked what he saw: "I got there, where I determined to settle.... It was a compete wilderness, and full of Indians who were hunting. Game was plenty of almost every kind, which suited me exactly as I was always fond of hunting."[16]

But he was not the first white man to settle this neck of the Tennessee woods. Crockett decided to visit his nearest neighbors, the Owens family, seven miles away on the opposite side of the Obion River. The Crocketts set out on foot leading one horse to carry provisions. This was hobbled once they reached the river which had "overflowed all the bottoms and low country near it." They waded in, Crockett leading with a pole in hand, feeling the way through icy water to avoid deep holes. When they reached the river's central, deep channel, he downed a tree with his tomahawk. The long trunk provided a bridge to another fallen tree on the opposite side. They made their way across, then waded on for another mile before reaching dry land where Owens' welcoming cabin came into view.

Owens and some visiting boatmen, standing outside, were astonished to see the wet and bedraggled pioneers emerge from the undergrowth. Young John Crockett was shivering with the cold, but they were shown inside "where I found Mrs. Owens, a fine friendly old woman; and her kindness to my little boy did ten times as much good as any thing should have done for me, if she had tried her best." Her husband provided what the men needed most, setting "out his bottle to us, and I concluded that if a horn wasn't good then, there was no use for its invention." Such was hospitality on the Tennessee frontier.

The boatmen had brought a load of "whiskey, flour, sugar, coffee, salt, castings, and other articles suitable for the country" and a few days later they agreed to move the boat along the river to Crockett's acreage. "We slap'd up a cabin in little or no time. I got from the boat four barrels of meal, and one of salt, and about ten gallons of whiskey." To pay for this Crockett agreed to work for the boatmen till the craft reached their destination. Leaving young John and Abram Henry with provisions, the boat cast off, Crockett expecting to return in about a week.

The voyage was delayed that night when they encountered fallen trees across the river, blown down by a recent hurricane. Next morning Crockett took his rifle and powder horn, and went ashore in a quest for fresh meat. He bagged six bucks in the course of the day, but upon returning found the boat nowhere in sight. His companions had found a way through, and moved beyond the fallen trees to avoid being stranded as the flood water fell. Crockett fired his rifle to attract attention, which was answered by a shot about two miles away. "It was now dark, and I had to crawl through the fallen timber the best way I could; and if the reader don't know it was bad enough, I am sure I do. For the vines and briers had grown all through it, and so thick, that a good fat coon couldn't much more than get along." Signal shots were exchanged, but when nearing the boat more flood waters barred the way. "I halted and hollered till they came to me with a skiff." Scratched and sore, he was rowed back to the boat where, "I took a pretty stiff horn, which soon made me feel much better; but I was so tired I could hardly work my jaws to eat."[17]

Next morning, most of the freshly killed game was dragged on board, then the journey resumed once more. After eleven days of slow progress on the river, the boatmen arrived at their destination, McLemore's Bluff. Crockett had forged a friendship with one of the boatmen, Flavius Harris, and together they returned in a skiff. Over the next few months the new settlers saw few white faces, "Indians though, there were still plenty enough."[18] Having planted corn, and shot ten bears to provide food for Henry and Harris, Crockett and his son saddled their horses and rode back east.

But his wife and children were not the only ones awaiting his return. He arrived at Lawrenceburg in late April 1822 to learn of court action for outstanding debts, and Justice of the Peace Mansil Crisp had been given power of attorney to sort out his financial situation.

The Legislative Assembly held a special sitting in Murfreesboro, and Crockett was, no doubt, glad to have this financially helpful diversion once more. Although he did own a few slaves in the course of life, usual in Tennessee at the time, one of his bills sought relief for a "Mathias, a free man of color."[19] It was proposed by his opponents that redemption laws, which allowed for slaves to be purchased and set free, be repealed. The Southern slaveocracy did not like to see blacks escaping, legally or not. Crockett opposed the repeal and another bill which advocated the restoration of certain "out-of-doors" fees to justices of the peace, a source of corruption. "There is no evil so great in society," he said, "among the poor people—as the management and intrigue of meddling justices and dirty constables. I have seen more peace and harmony among my constituents since the repeal of the fees, than I had seen for several years before."[20] The fees were not restored, and he also opposed the repeal of laws providing assistance for widows and orphans.

Once the Legislature rose, Crockett returned to Lawrenceburg to consult with Mansil Crisp. Settling various debts, he sold off most of the 800 acres in Carroll County for the $1,600 owed to his father-in-law, but retained enough land for a farm. The family packed their belongings and headed 150 miles west. Here they were joined by three of Elizabeth's sisters and their families who fancied a fresh start themselves.

"I gathered my corn, and then set out for my Fall's hunt," he recalled. "This was the last of October 1822. I found bear very plenty, and, indeed, all sorts of game and wild varments, except buffalo."[21] But success with his long rifle led to a gunpowder shortage. "I had a brother-in-law who had moved out and settled about six miles west of me, on the opposite side of Rutherford's fork of the Obion river, and he had brought me a keg of powder, but I had never gotten it home." Winter had set in, the flooding river a mile wide and ice cold but, necessity being the mother of invention, "I determined to go over in some way or other, so as to get my powder." Despite objections "with all her might" from his wife, he went ahead with a bundle of dry clothes across the snowy landscape. At this time of year, he was probably wearing a fur jacket over a home-dyed butternut linsey-woolsey hunting shirt, made from cotton and wool, produced for the masses, including slaves. His trousers would have tight leggings to prevent entanglement with vegetation. A tomahawk and knife would have graced his belt, while a powder horn and bullet pouch swung from shoulder straps.

He waded, sloshed and scrambled onto logs, the dry clothes kept above water. "I didn't know before how much any body could suffer and not die." Once having made it to the opposite bank, the freezing woodsman dressed himself in the dry clothes and plodded on another five miles to his brother-in-law's home. "I got there late in the evening, and he was much astonished at seeing me at such a time." Crockett thawed out for a few days, but the weather turning even colder meant the freezing waters were now covered with ice. With gunpowder and rifle, he retraced his steps using the same logs, and sometimes walking on ice till falling through. "By this time I was nearly frozen to death." He saw what he thought was ice broken by a bear, and a trail leading through the snow away from the shore. "I, therefore, fresh primed my gun, and, cold as I was, I was determined to make war on him." Crockett tramped on through the snow, but was surprised to see this "b'ar" was headed straight for his log cabin. Elizabeth had sent out one of the hands to see if there was any sign of her husband, who she thought probably had frozen or drowned. "When I got home I was'nt quite dead, but mighty nigh it; but I had my powder, and that was what I went for."

Crockett went out the following day on a bear hunt. He followed a fresh bear trail and came across "about the biggest bear that was ever seen in America." It took three shots to bring the 600-pound animal down. "I continued through the winter to supply my family abundantly with bear-meat and venison from the woods."

In February of 1822, Crockett and son John rode to the small settlement of Jackson, about 40 miles from home. There they sold animal skins and purchased provisions including coffee, sugar and salt, and an abundant supply of lead and gunpowder to avoid further icy crossings of freezing rivers.

He shared a few drinks with veterans of the Creek War, and one suggested he run for the Tennessee Legislature again. He laughed it off, saying he now lived too far from any hint of civilization. A few weeks after returning home, however, a visitor showed him a newspaper that carried news of his intention to run. "I told my wife this was all burlesque to me." But it seemed fate had taken a hand to place the humble backwoodsman on center stage once more. He hired a man to work the farm while he went out "electioneering." He hadn't been on the road long before "I found the people began to talk about the bear hunter, the man from the cane." He found himself in competition with one of those he had met in Jackson township: Dr. William Edward Butler. The doctor was wealthy, educated, and married to Old Hickory's niece. In the campaign's early days the candidates made a chance encounter in the street. "Crockett, damn it, is that you?" said Butler.

"Be sure it is," replied Crockett. "But I don't want it understood that I have come out electioneering. I have just crept out of the cane, to see what discoveries I could make among the white folks."[22]

Butler invited Crockett to his opulent home, possibly a ploy to keep the gentleman from the cane in his place. How can a mere backwoodsman win against such wealth and resources; why compete? The government would later take western Indian chiefs to Washington, D.C., for the same reason. But, if so, Butler's ruse backfired badly.

"Fellow citizens," said Crockett when on the election trail, "my aristocratic competitor has a fine carpet, and every day he *walks* on truck finer than any gowns your wife or your daughters ever *wore*."[23]

Two other candidates appeared, but when the final count came "I beat them all by a majority of two hundred and forty-seven votes, and was again returned as a member of the Legislature from a new region of the country."

Crockett served in the Legislature once more from 1823 through 1824. As in the past, he represented the underdog, and proved the bane of the wealthy and privileged. He was rapidly becoming a folk hero along the way, a game hunting pioneer in the footsteps of Daniel Boone, who had died just a few years before at the age of 85.

It was during this time that Andrew Jackson ran for the senate against Colonel John Williams. Old Hickory had accused Williams of spreading rumors that he invaded Florida to protect personal land investments in the Pensacola area. Jackson won the election, but not with Crockett's help, who recalled. "I thought the colonel had honestly discharged his duty, and even the mighty name of Jackson couldn't make me vote against him.... I let the people know as early as then, that I wouldn't take a collar around my neck with the letters engraved on it, MY DOG. Andrew Jackson."[24]

There was dissatisfaction with Congressman Colonel Adam Alexander, according to Crockett, and "They therefore began to talking of running me in Congress against him.... I told the people that I couldn't stand that; it was a step above my knowledge, and I know'd nothing about Congress matters. "However, I was obliged to agree to run."

I now avail myself of the privilege common to every freeman, of offering myself as a candidate for a seat in the next Congress of the United States ... sufficient time will intervene between now and the period of election, to see and converse with many of you—all I will now undertake to say is, that I feel so much interest in your welfare, and if elected, will bestow as much labor in promoting your interests as any other.

I am, very respectfully, your obedient servant,
David Crockett
Nashville, 25th October, 1824[25]

These words appeared in a letter three days after the close of the final session of the Tennessee Legislature. It seems Crockett was ready to move up in the world. But the world was not yet quite ready for him. In the election of August 1825, he polled 2,599 votes to Alexander's 2,866. The downcast candidate, now used to victory, headed back to his log cabin and family to shoot a few more bears and wade a few more streams. He and his supporters, however, watched Alexander's performance with eagle eyes and, seeing chinks in his armor, "I concluded I would try him once more, and see how it would go."[26]

15

The Bloody Deeds of Gen. Jackson

When Colonel Crockett lost his bid for Congress in 1825, he may have taken comfort in General Jackson having lost his bid for the presidency the previous year. If the hero of New Orleans could take a tumble, why not a humble former sergeant like himself?

The formidable forces behind Old Hickory, however, rallied from the moment his election was lost, their sights firmly set on 1828. If they had their way, John "Corrupt Bargain" Adams would be a one-term president.

Jackson supporters proposed a constitutional amendment which would prevent important government posts being given to members of Congress for the term of the administration, plus two years. The likes of Henry Clay could not be made Secretary of State. Jackson used this proposal as an excuse to leave a job he found tiresome at best. "I could not, with any thing of approbation on my part, consent either to urge or encourage an alteration, which might wear the appearance of being induced by selfish considerations; by a desire to advance my own views."[1] He tended his resignation to the Tennessee Legislature and, with Rachel, headed for the cozy surroundings of the Hermitage. "From Baltimore to our farm we were honored by the most friendly and hospitable attentions," she wrote to Katherine Morgan, "for which I will forever feel grateful."[2] Rachel was delighted to be free of Washington politics, but this was to be a savage election campaign, with no holds barred, and for the potential First Lady there was much damage in store.

Although the proposed constitutional amendment never occurred, the push for Jackson was in full swing, and the alarmed Adams administration sharpened their knives for a desperate fight. Secretary of State Henry Clay accused Jackson of being a dangerous "military chieftain" who had abused his powers when declaring martial law in New Orleans. Old Hickory replied that martial law was declared not for, "personal aggrandisement, but for the preservation of all and everything that was valuable, the honor, safety, and glory of our country. Does this constitute a 'military chieftain'? And are all our brave men in war, who go forth to defend their rights, and the rights of their country, to be termed 'military chieftains' and therefore denounced?"[3] He noted that Clay had never fought for his country, but now implied that those who had should be excluded from political office. Demagogues like Mr. Clay were the danger, said Jackson, not honest soldiers.

A Washington newspaper hostile to Old Hickory suddenly changed tack and came out for the hero of New Orleans! Under new management, it had been purchased by

John Eaton and other Jackson men. Other newspapers in other cities went the same way. A barrage of good words for Andrew Jackson ran off the presses while Adams and Clay were derided.

Sam Houston was, of course, another Jackson advocate. "I have not in my life seen a cause rising so fast as *that of the people is, nor,* one sinking faster than the cause of a *wicked and corrupt coalition,*" Houston wrote to his hero. "Every movement tends to its more complete overthrow—Genl Coffee can give you particulars; which are too numerous to place on paper!"[4] No doubt Jackson was pleased to have the vocal support of the man who became Governor of Tennessee during the venomous election campaign.

The four secretaries of state to precede Henry Clay had gone on to become president of the United States. No doubt this was Clay's own ambition. But the barrage of "corrupt bargain" allegations from the hostile camp made his current job anything but a blessing, and his presidential chances obscure

The witty, eccentric congressman John Randolph had no time for Henry Clay. Politics aside, Clay, when House Speaker back in 1811, had ordered the bellicose Randolph to remove his pet dog from the House, something no previous speaker had dared to do. From the inauguration of the Adams administration, Randolph vehemently attacked both Adams and Clay from the Senate floor. He denounced them as "the combination, unheard of till then, of the Puritan and the blackleg." Adams could live with "Puritan," but Clay took exception to "black leg," and promptly challenged Randolph to a duel, despite having received a thigh wound from Senator Humphrey Marshall in a previous exchange.

On April 8, 1826, Clay and Randolph faced off in dense woods near Little Falls bridge on the Virginia side of the Potomac River. Randolph preferred Virginia because, should he fall, he wished it to be on soil "endeared to him by every tie of devoted loyalty and affection."[5] Randolph's second was none other than Thomas Hart Benton, the man who wounded Andrew Jackson in 1813. Randolph felt honor-bound to answer Clay's challenge, but said he would not return Clay's fire. The accidental discharge of his pistol, however, just before the signal, seemed to unsettle his nerves. With guns reloaded, the signal was given, and both pistols fired. Randolph's ball missed while Clay's ripped a hole through his coat. Clay, dissatisfied, demanded another round. Powder and shot were rammed home once more, and the signal given. Clay's gun fired—a total miss. Randolph pointed his weapon to the sky and fired, his ball shooting harmlessly into oblivion. "I do not fire at you, Mr. Clay," he said, "you owe me a coat." Clay walked forward. "I'm glad the debt is no greater," he replied, and shook Randolph's hand.

But Clay probably wished he had asked for a third shot. "Randolph loses no chance to abuse him," John Eaton wrote to Jackson one month following the duel, and "He spoke of the abuse you had received from various sources heretofore, then said that you would live and last with posterity when your detractors should have sunk to forgetfulness, that like the great father of rivers, the Mississippi, your fame and splendid efforts for your country would roll its mighty volume on."[6]

Thomas Jefferson died on July 4, 1826, aged 83, exactly 50 years after signing the Declaration of Independence. But even deceased, the famous statesman became a participant in the fractious election campaign. Henry Lee, son of Lighthorse Harry and brother of Robert E., had visited Jefferson just a few days before his death, and learned from the family that "he holds in abhorrence the men and measures of our present administration," and he wished for "change at the next presidential election."[7] The anti–Jackson forces, however, circulated rumors that Jefferson felt that Old Hickory's popularity was "evidence that the Republic would not last long." Jackson struck back by repeating Lee's assertions, and circulating copies of a complimentary letter from Jefferson following the Seminole War.

Adams' disciples searched Andrew Jackson's past for any dirt that could be found. They stressed his antagonistic background and personality as proof of a vicious nature, an unprincipled man with only a sham code of honor. Owning slaves was acceptable, of course, but he was accused of actually being a slave trader, a lowly occupation beneath the dignity of quality folk. Then there was his treatment of militiamen when on the campaign trail. The shooting of John Wood at Fort Strother in 1814 was raked up, along with the execution of the six militiamen shortly after the Battle of New Orleans. This saw a variety of sensational "coffin handbills" appear. "Some Account of Some of the Bloody Deeds of Gen. Jackson" read one, above an image of six coffins. Dozens of these were circulated, accusing Jackson of everything from murdering innocent, unarmed Indians to eating their dead bodies after the Battle of Horseshoe Bend. An inner circle of Jackson's friends, including Sam Houston, responded with denials, and mocked the allegations of killing innocent Indians by comparing it to New Orleans:

> COOL AND DELIBERATE MURDER: Jackson coolly and deliberately put to death upwards of fifteen hundred British troops on the 8th of January 1815, on the plains below New Orleans, for no other offence than that they wished to sup in the city that night.[8]

Jackson supporters stated that Adams, while ambassador to Russia, had procured girls for the Czar's pleasure. And, of course, John Adams ran a corrupt administration, as exemplified by the "corrupt bargain," which had denied the American public the president of their choice. A vote for Jackson would be a vote for the man of the people, for democracy. Convoluted issues of more substance, like tariff reforms, took second place as the two camps slogged it out.

The Cincinnati *Gazette* struck a new low with allegations that Jackson's mother had been a common prostitute who "married a MULATTO MAN, with whom she had several children, of which number General JACKSON is one!!!"[9]

Then Rachel Jackson came under attack. The pro–Adams press described her as a "dirty, black wench." Unknown to Rachel at the time, her divorce to her first, violent husband had not been finalized when she married Jackson in 1791. Her husband had only filed for divorce, and did not take final action till 1793, stating her adultery as the cause. Once the mistake was discovered, Jackson and his bride repeated their marriage in 1794. The Adams press described Rachel as "a loose, impetuous and immoral woman who had willingly cast off her lawful husband for an arrogant and impassioned young suitor." Jackson was described as having played a "serpentlike role" in the seduction of a married woman who, as First Lady, would "offend" Washington society and degrade "public morals."[10] Old Hickory and his bible-toting wife were displeased, to say the least. Jackson wrote to William Keene of

> the torrent of the vilest Slander wickedness & falsehood can invent, daily poured out against Mrs Js character as well as my own.... When the midnight assassin strikes you to the heart, murders

your family, and robs your dwelling, the heart sickens at the relation of the deed; but this scene loses its horrors when compared with the recent slander of a virtuous female propagated by the minions of power for political effect.[11]

Old Hickory interpreted this slander as an attempt to prod him into some "desperate act by which I would fall prostrate before the people." But he did not go after his antagonists, saber in hand, as they may have wished. He stood firm. "The day of retribution and vengeance must come, when the guilty will meet with their just reward."[12]

Their "just reward" occurred in December 1828. Andrew Jackson, the first president from outside Massachusetts or Virginia, swept home with an overwhelming majority. The popular vote was 647,000 for Jackson as opposed to 508,000 for the opposition. Old Hickory's 178 to Adam's 83 in the electoral college was even more decisive. In the congressional elections, the Democrats, as the Jacksonians were becoming known, achieved a majority in both the House and Senate.

But, despite the victory, "my mind is depressed," Jackson wrote to John Coffee. "I will write to you more fully shortly." In June of that year, amid the slanderous campaign, Lyncoya, the Creek boy adopted by Jackson, had died of tuberculosis at the age of 16. And perhaps Jackson had a foreboding of ill tidings, that inevitable balance that keeps mere mortals in their place. Jackson was well aware that the woman he adored, his soul mate, dreaded the prospect of being First Lady of the nation. She would be on public display in Washington where many considered her too common for such a role. Despite being attractive in her youth, the now corpulent Mrs. Jackson was seen, according to one officer's daughter, as "neither graceful or elegant," and "without any culture, and out of the way of refining influences."

Rachel, however, steeled herself for the trials to come: "I owe it to myself and my husband—to try to forget, at least for a time, all the endearments of home and prepare to live where it has pleased heaven to fix our destiny."[13]

But Heaven had fixed her destiny to remain forever in Tennessee. Three weeks after writing these words, Rachel Jackson was dead. She was sitting quietly as Jackson wrote a letter, but then felt an "excruciating pain in the left shoulder, arm and breast."[14] He called a doctor whose only solution was to bleed her, which did seem to provide temporary relief, but to no avail. She died four days later, the victim of a heart attack.

Her distraught husband had to be pried from her body to allow burial preparations. Laid to rest in the Hermitage garden, Governor Sam Houston led a funeral procession which brought thousands from all over the country. Newspapers that, a few months before, had scorned Rachel as an unworthy adulteress, now printed tributes commending her virtuous life.

"O, how fluctuating are all earthly things," Jackson recalled. "At the time I least expected it, and could lest spare her, she was snatched from me, and I left here a solitary monument of grief, without the least hope of happiness here below, surrounded with all the turmoil of public life."[15]

Jackson, "looking twenty years older," set out for Washington for his inauguration at the last possible moment. Despite his shattering sorrow, the president elect had a host of other issues to crowd his mind. One was Texas, home to an increasing number of Americans. Despite the Treaty of Florida in 1819, Old Hickory believed the Mexican province should rightfully be part of the United States.

16

A Thousand Wild Rumors

Thirteen months before Rachel Jackson's death, Sam Houston had been elected governor of Tennessee. He took to his new duties with relish, embarking on a program of changes which included relief for settlers who had committed themselves beyond their meager means to pay for public domain farm lands. Profits from the sale of further public lands would be used to build schools and fund a variety of other benefits for the community at large. He built a hospital in Memphis for travelers who became ill on Mississippi riverboats, and continued with reforms to the state banking system initiated by his predecessor, William Carroll.

But the duel reemerged when antagonist General White wrote a letter to the press. Houston would be "stripped of his little brief authority," he wrote, "and neither the name or influence of a great man, (Jackson) nor the misdirected sympathies of a deluded people," would screen him from "punishment."[1] No doubt the prophetic General White was delighted with scandalous events soon to erupt.

On Christmas Eve 1827, Houston hosted a grand dinner at the Nashville Tavern for Old Hickory, currently involved in the vitriolic election campaign. A few days later Jackson, Houston and their entourage headed downstream on board the paddle steamer *Pocahontas*. Rachel spent much of her time in seclusion, but when appearing put a brave face, despite the smears being perpetrated by the Adams campaign. Old Hickory was true to form, threatening to open fire on small boats that impeded the steamer's progress.

The gentry of New Orleans awaited their hero to celebrate the great victory of nine years earlier, and a ceremony was held on the battleground. This was followed by a grand dinner with speeches praising the Old Chief on January 9. Sam Houston had not visited New Orleans since having the Creek musket ball removed by an army surgeon. This wound still caused problems; one more thing he and Jackson had in common.

The festivities complete, it was back home and back to work. Houston toiled on behalf of Old Hickory as the 1828 presidential election approached, and headed up what was called the "Literary Bureau" whose main job was to refute base allegations, and sling mud back into the Adams camp.[2] Regardless of what Adams and Clay trumped up, Old Hickory looked sure to win.

But Governor Houston, at 35, was still without a wife. A fine lady at your side, a brood of children, and perhaps a good dog or two was good for the public image; especially if the White House was the next logical step. Houston wrote a letter to his cousin

Jack in November of 1828, "I am not married yet, but it may be the case in a few weeks, and should it—*you* shall *hear* of it before the papers reach you"[3]

The intended bride was Eliza Allen of Gallatin township. The "dear girle" herself, about to turn 19, was 16 years the governor's junior. Houston had been a family friend of the auspicious Allen family for some years, and saw the young Eliza evolve into a beautiful young woman. With her father's approval, Sam proposed to Eliza, and she consented to be his bride.

Andrew Jackson was delighted, the good news received a little before his success at the polls and his own wife's death. Houston was mortified with "Aunt Rachel's" loss, and was already upset with "a small blow up" with his intended bride. "What the Dival is the matter with the Gals I can't say, but there has been Hell to pay and no pitch hot!" he wrote to his friend John Marable on December 4.[4]

But this trifle was a mere prelude to pitch hot events yet to come. A raven fell dead on the track before Sam as he rode to his wedding, he later said. The couple were married on January 22, 1829, at Allenwood, the Allen family mansion which graced bluffs overlooking the Cumberland River. Candles lit the proceedings, the large room filled with distinguished guests, the groom a "figure of elegance in a black suit of velvet, topped by a Spanish cloak lined with scarlet satin."[5]

Following the festivities, the newlyweds ascended the stairs to their quarters for the night. Next day they departed for Nashville, but due to bad weather stayed overnight at Locust Grove, the home of friends Robert and Martha Martin. The following morning, Houston was outside exchanging snowballs with the Martins' daughters when Eliza descended the stairs. She peered out the window at the frolic, and Martha Martin recalled:

> I said to her: it seems as if General Houston is getting the worst of the snowballing; you had better go out and help him. Looking seriously at me, Mrs. Houston said: "I wish they would kill him." I looked astonished to hear such a remark from a bride of not yet forty-eight hours, when she repeated in the same voice, "yes, I wish from the bottom of my heart that they would kill him."[6]

The astonished Mrs. Martin said nothing to the groom, and the newlyweds set off to Nashville where they spent a few days with Houston's cousin Robert McEwen and his wife. Their hosts noticed nothing amiss. The Houstons then took up residence in the Nashville Inn where they were visited by the Martins who, no doubt, were even more concerned when they saw the newlyweds, but never together in the same room.

Life at the Nashville Inn must have come as something of a shock for Eliza after living in the family mansion, cushioned from the harsh outside world by family and servants. The noisy Nashville Inn was frequented by Houston's political allies and drinking companions. And there was work to be done. On January 30 Houston announced his intention to run for governor once more. His opponent would be former incumbent William Carroll, most displeased with the loss and determined to retrieve his crown.

Sam and Mrs. Houston would soon oblige Carroll, and it became apparent that all was not well between them. One anecdote was related by the Reverend Burleson, as told by Eliza's cousin:

> One evening when cousin Eliza was worn out by fashionable dining and throngs of company and was seeking a little rest, a fashionable gossip entered the Governor's mansion, and she exclaimed involuntarily; "Oh, yonder comes that horrible Mrs S—to bore me to death. I wish she would stay at home and torment someone else." Yet she sprang up, adjusted her beautiful toilet, put on her

sweetest smiles, and met "the horrible Mrs S—" with a kiss and protestations of her joy at her coming.[7]

Houston supposedly "rebuked her sharply for such insincerity," not worthy of the governor's mansion, and his young wife wept all night. It is possible this did occur, but it seems unlikely anyone would call Nashville Inn the "Governor's mansion."

Houston's friend Frank Chambers, however, saw that that the marriage was in trouble. "Governor Houston looked years older. I saw that the beautiful young wife would be but dead sea fruit to him.... I saw that his heart was broken."[8]

The details are obscure, but the likely scenario was this: On April 11, Houston rode off for a debate with Carroll at Cockrell's Spring, ten miles from home. His friend, Nashville sheriff Willoughby Williams, went along to listen and report on the crowd's reaction. Williams gave Houston a positive account as they rode back towards Nashville, then they went their separate ways. Houston returned to the Nashville Inn only to find Eliza had flown the coop.

David Crockett later stated that Eliza stood the marriage "as long as she could and then wrote to her father that if he did not come and get her then she would go by herself. Accordingly Colonel Allen came for her ... departed with her father leaving a note to apprise the governor of the fact."[9]

What exactly was the cause of the marriage breakdown has been the subject of speculation. Rarely does a marital rift have such repercussions as it did for Sam Houston. The theories include his impotence, her abhorrence of his unhealed, oozing thigh wound or Houston's extreme jealousy—he sometimes locked Eliza in her room, so some claimed. It was, of course, in the Allens' family interest to place the fault with Sam.

But Houston gave more than a broad hint of events when he wrote to Eliza's father on April 9, shortly before the split. His somewhat rambling letter suggests perhaps having had one too many:

> Mr. Allen The most unpleasant & unhappy circumstance has just taken place in the family, & one that was entirely unnecessary at this time. Whatever had been my feelings and opinions in relation to Eliza at one time, I have been satisfied & it is now unfit that anything should be averted to. Eliza will do me the justice to say that she believes I was really unhappy. That I was *satisfied & believed her virtuous*, I had assured her on last night & this morning. This should have prevented the facts ever coming to your knowledge, & that of Mrs. Allen. I would not for millions it had ever been known to you. But as one human being knew anything of it from me, & that was by Eliza's consent and wish. I would have perished first, & if mortal man had dared to charge my wife or say ought against her virtue I would have slain him. That I have and do love Eliza none can doubt— that she is the only earthly object dear to me God will witness.
>
> The only way this matter can now be overcome will be for us all to meet as tho it had never occurred, & this will keep the world, as it should ever be, ignorant that such thoughts ever were. Eliza stands acquitted by me. I have received her as a virtuous wife, & as such I prey God I may ever regard her, & trust I ever shall.
>
> She was cold to me, & I thought did not love me. She owns that such was one cause of my unhappiness. You can judge how unhappy I was to think I was united to a woman that did not love me. This time is now past, & my future happiness can only exist in the assurance that Eliza and myself can be happy & that Mrs. Allen & you can forget the past—forgive all & find your lost peace & you may rest assured that nothing on my part shall be wanting to restore it. Let me know what is to be done.
>
> Sam Houston[10]

So Sam Houston was satisfied that his bride was virtuous—belatedly. Based on available evidence, including a story by Houston's pastor many years later, the probable scenario was as follows: Having retired after the wedding ceremony, Sam found his young bride cool towards his conjugal advances. When he inquired as to the problem, she broke down and admitted being in love with another man. Shattered, he accused her of having been intimate with a former lover. And how could she marry a man she did not love? Marrying the governor would enhance her family's position in society, she replied, and did so under parental pressure.

Houston reputedly walked to a desk, dashed out his resignation as governor of Tennessee, and handed it to her saying, "There, madame, is your position." His actual resignation would not come for another eleven weeks, but that piece of melodrama could well have occurred, sowing the seed for events to come.

Once the newlyweds moved to the Nashville Inn, Eliza, to prove her innocence, referred her distrusting husband to Dr. John Shelby, a friend of Sam's who had tended her family since she was a child. Houston spoke to Shelby and, assured of her chastity, attempted to make amends, thus his letter to Eliza's father on April 9.

These toxic events, however, had damaged the relationship beyond repair. News of the split spread like wildfire and Houston's "hopes for happiness in this life are blasted forever, his effigy was burned in Gallatin on Saterday night last," said a letter to an appalled Andrew Jackson. Another effigy was hung in the streets of Nashville, and troops were called out to maintain the peace. It seems political foes wanted the hard-drinking Houston to be responsible for this state of affairs. One was lawyer Henry Wise who wrote; "the family were flattered by the governor, and she was torn from her youth and her pure, natural maiden love, to become the victim of his jealousy, and his heartless, selfish ambition." Many believed it was Sam who had walked out, not the other way around.

Whether for love, to prevent career suicide, or a combination of both, Houston rode to Allenwood on the evening of April 15. He pleaded to see Eliza, who agreed to talk, providing they were not left alone. An elderly aunt witnessed Sam on his knees begging her forgiveness. But now that the bird had flown the coop she had no intention of returning. There was to be no reconciliation.

The following day Sam Houston wrote out his letter of resignation as governor of Tennessee. He made no mention of the rift with his wife, but felt, "I should retire from a position, which, in the public judgment, I might seem to occupy by questionable authority."[11]

David Crockett paid Houston a visit: "he told me he that he was going to leave the Country and go up the arkensaw and live with the Indians as he calls them his addopted brothers the Ballance of his days."[12]

On April 23, Houston went to the Nashville wharf on the Cumberland River and boarded the riverboat *Red Rover*, where he bade farewell to friends Dr. Shelby and Sheriff Williams. He was accompanied by a somewhat shadowy traveling companion, a Mr. H. Haralson, recently arrived from Ireland. Haralson had connections, and had possibly been sent to keep an eye on Houston by Andrew Jackson and friends. Houston steamed off to leave his political life behind—so he thought. His destination was Indian Territory, where he planned to disappear from the civilized world.

When the *Red Rover* docked in Clarksville, however, civilization caught up with him. Eliza's brothers had ridden across country to head him off:

They came aboard, greatly excited and heavily armed, and said: "Governor Houston, the manner in which you have left Nashville has filled the city with a thousand wild rumors, among others, that you are goaded to madness and exile by detecting our sister in crime. We demand that you give a written denial of this or go back and prove it." I replied: "I will neither go back nor write a retraction, but in the presence of the captain and these well known gentlemen, I request you to go back and publish in the Nashville papers that if any wretch ever dares to utter a word against the purity of Mrs. Houston, I will come back and write the libel in his heart's blood."

That evening as I was walking on the upper deck of the boat, reflecting on the bitter disappointment I had caused General Jackson and all my friends, and especially the blight and ruin of a pure and innocent woman who had trusted her whole happiness to me, I was in an agony of despair and strongly tempted to leap overboard and end my worthless life. But at that awful moment an eagle swooped down near my head, and soaring aloft with wild screams, was lost in the rays of the setting sun. I knew that a great duty and glorious destiny awaited me in the west.[13]

Only one month had passed since Eliza's departure, when more strange rumors began to circulate: the marriage breakdown was merely a ploy to give Houston and Jackson an excuse to raise an army of Texan "liberation." But, in fact, the last thing Old Hickory wanted was some hair-brained filibustering expedition. Such a venture would derail his plans to acquire Texas by peaceful means. Houston was well aware of this, and on May 11 wrote to Jackson, from Little Rock, Arkansas:

Tho' an unfortunate, and doubtless the most unhappy man now living, whose honor, so far as depends upon himself, is not lost, I can not brook the idea of your supposing me capable, of an act that would not adorn, rather than blot the escutcheon of human nature! This remark is induced, by the fact, as reported to me, that you have been assured that I meditated an enterprize calculated to injure, or involve my country.... To you any suggestion would be idle, and on my part, as man; ridiculous—You Sir, have witnessed my conduct thro life—You saw me draw my first sword from its scabbard—you saw me breast the fore front of Battle, and you saw me, encounter successive dangers, with cheeks unblanched, and with nerves, which had no ague in them! You have seen my private, & my official acts—to these I *refer* you—To what would they all amount, and for what would I live? but for my own honor, and the honor and safety of my country? Nothing! And now that domestic misfortune, of which I say nothing; and about which there are ten thousand imputed slanders; has come upon; as a black cloud at noonday I am *hunted down!* What am I? an Exile from my home; and my country, a houseless unshelter'd wanderer, among the Indians! Who has met, or who has sustained, such sad and unexpected reverses? Yet I am myself, and will remain, the proud and honest man! I will love my country and my friends—You Genl. will ever possess my warmest love and most profound veneration! In return I ask nothing—I would have nothing, within your powers to give me! I am satisfied with nature's gifts—*They* will supply natures wants![14]

One evening in late June 1829, Houston and Haralson arrived onboard the *Facility* at Cantonment Gibson, in Indian Territory. Remote and rough, Gibson was the westernmost military outpost of the United States. It had been established five years earlier on the Grand River as part of a string of forts built from north to south to protect the American frontier. Who better to command such a place than Colonel Matthew Arbuckle, the man who had burned Fowltown in 1817.

In a clearing at Webber's Falls Houston was welcomed with open arms by his Cherokee foster father, Chief John Jolly. "I have heard that a dark cloud has fallen on the white path you were walking, and when it fell in your way you turned your thought to my wigwam. I am glad of it ... it was done by the Great Spirit." The chief told Houston his people were living in difficult times. "You will tell our troubles to the great father, General Jackson. My wigwam is yours—my home is yours—my people are yours—rest with us."[15]

17

A Wicked, Unjust Measure

The two freight boats splashed and foamed through the mighty Mississippi's swirling current. David Crockett had discovered far too late "how much better bear-hunting was on hard land, than floating along on the water, when a fellow had to go ahead whether he was exactly willing or not."[1]

Crockett ordered the two boats lashed together, but this made the situation worse, the unwieldy bulk virtually impossible to manage. Racing waters were about to terminate the woodsman's latest business venture, as they had with the gunpowder factory and gristmill on Shoal Creek. "Our boats were so heavy that we couldn't take them much any way, except the way they wanted to go, and just the way the current would carry them." Crockett was below decks when he heard a mad scramble of feet and a commotion above. "We went broadside full tilt against the head of an island where a large raft of drift timber had lodged." Crockett found his craft being sucked under the debris and attempted to open the deck hatch but, "the water was pouring thro' in a current as large as the hole would let it, and as strong as the weight of the river could force it." The vessel heeled over on a mad angle, about to capsize, and he bolted for the only escape, a port hole in the cabin's upper side. Being a tight squeeze, he thrust his arms through and yelled for help as water filled the cabin behind him. His arms were seized by other men, who pulled him through "skin'd like a rabbit" to the boat alongside. Cut free, the craft behind him disappeared beneath the swirling water and debris to be "never seen any more to this day." Also gone was the precious cargo of wood staves for barrel construction. The staves on the rescue craft had also been swept overboard, so the penniless Crockett, now deeper in debt, floated downstream on the surviving boat with his sodden companions. But ever the optimist, "I felt happier and better off than I ever had in my life before, for I had just made such a marvelous escape, that I had forgot almost every thing else in that; and so I felt prime."

The following morning they were taken on board a passing boat with a seasoned crew who could handle the turbulent waters. They splashed and steered their way along the Mississippi to Memphis where news of Colonel Crockett's inglorious adventure had already arrived. Amid the waiting crowd was Marcus Brutus Winchester, "the most graceful, courtly, elegant gentleman that ever appeared on main street," wrote one admirer.[2] Winchester had worked with Andrew Jackson and others in the founding of Memphis, and was the town's first mayor. He supplied Crockett and the waterlogged crew with fresh clothes from his store, and his wife Amarante served them a fine meal that very evening. "Mary" was beautiful and educated in France, but being one-sixteenth black, her status was that of a freedman. This was tolerated in the town's early days, but would cause the couple much trouble in years to come.[3]

A few days following his arrival, Crockett traveled by steamboat to Natchez in search of his abandoned boat. It had been seen, only to be swept away following a failed salvage attempt. Crockett accepted the loss and returned to Memphis where he and his new friend Marcus Winchester discussed his future. The gentleman from the cane had lost his first bid for election to Congress in 1825, but with Winchester's financial support: "I now returned home again, and as the next August was the Congressional election, I began to turn my attention a little to that matter, as it was beginning to be talked about a good deal by the people."[4]

Opposing Crockett in 1827 was Colonel Adam Alexander, who had defeated him in 1825, and General William Arnold. "Taking both together, they take a pretty considerable of a load for one man to carry," recalled Crockett. Both were well educated with distinguished military careers, and apparently felt Crockett's candidature something of a joke. The bear hunter had lost once, and would do so again. "They, therefore, were generally working against each other, while I was going ahead myself, and mixing among the people in the best way I could."

The *New York Sunday Morning News* would recall: "His voice was loud and well suited to stump oratory. If his vocabulary was scanty, he was master of the slang of the vernacular, and was happy in his course figures. He spurned the idle rules of the grammarians, and had a rhetoric of his own."[5]

At one debate before a crowd of Tennessee folk, Crockett gave a short talk, to be followed by Alexander, then Arnold. The general went to some lengths to reply to Alexander's assertions, but Colonel Crockett's were ignored, apparently not worthy of a response. But during his talk, Arnold stopped to request that a flock of noisy guinea-fowls be driven away. Following his lengthy speech, Crockett walked up in front of the crowd and told Arnold he was "the first man I ever saw who understood the language of guinea fowls." Arnold was astonished, and Crockett recalled:

> I told him he had not the politeness to name me in his speech, and that was when my little friends, the guinea-fowls, had come up an began to holler "Crockett, Crockett, Crockett," he had been ungenerous enough to stop and drive *them* all away. This raised a universal shout among the people for me, and the general seemed mighty bad plagued.

No doubt both opponents felt "mighty bad plagued" when Crockett polled 5,867 votes to Arnold's 2,417 and Alexander's 3,646.[6]

So David Crockett found himself a member of Congress, elected by those who related to him; the storekeeper, the farmer, the wheelwright, the baker, the hunter, the common man. But he had much to learn, later telling Colonel John Swisher, "he never knew why the people of his district elected him to Congress, as it was a matter he knew precious little about at the time and had no idea what he would be called on to do when he arrived in Washington; but his friends assured him he would soon find out."[7]

Crockett had been elected as a member of Old Hickory's Democratic Party, Jackson's rising popularity no doubt a boost for Crockett's election. At this time, Jackson was preparing for his second run at president, the vitriolic "corrupt bargain" campaign in full swing. Crockett was said to be basically a Jackson man, but was obviously not wholly so, having previously voted for Colonel Williams over Jackson for senator while in the Tennessee Legislative Assembly.

Shortly after his election, Crockett, with his wife and eldest son John Wesley, now 24, traveled towards Elizabeth's parents' home in South Carolina. It was not often the Crockett family had any substantial time together, and Crockett no doubt enjoyed the prestige of his new place in the world among the myriad of Crockett and Patton relatives. The bear hunter from the canes had made good, the warm public glow blurring the dark shadow of debt behind the scenes.

In Nashville they met Elizabeth's relative, John Patton Erwin, whose appointment as paymaster had led to Sam Houston's duel with General White. Erwin, allied to Henry Clay, was surprised by the visit from a man he thought to be in the Jackson camp. Crockett, however, told him he was determined "to pursue his own course" once in Congress, and this would prove to be the case. Erwin wrote to Henry Clay saying Crockett wished to meet him, and would vote for the house speaker Clay advised. He also wrote his impression of the new congressman:

> he is not only illiterate but he is rough and uncouth, talks much & loudly, and is by far, more to his proper place when hunting a bear, in a Cane Break, than he will be in the Capital, yet he is a man worth attending to, he is independent and fearless and has a popularity at home that is unaccountable ... he is the only man that I now know in Tennessee that could openly oppose Genl. Jackson in his District & be elected to Congress.[8]

But beauty is in the eyes of the beholder, so 'tis said. William Foster, son of Senator Ephraim Foster, would later write of remembering Crockett "with pleasure," and:

> He was very often a guest of my father, always a pleasant, courteous, and interesting man, who, though uneducated in books, was a man of fine instincts and intellect and entertained a laudable ambition to make his mark in the world.[9]

Crockett would certainly achieve that aim, but the pinnacle would come in a crumbling Texas mission, not Congress. Based on Foster's recollection, perhaps Washington society had ironed out some of the bear hunter's rough edges by the time they met.

While trekking to South Carolina they visited Crockett kinfolk and friends in eastern Tennessee. At the home of old friend James Blackburn, Crockett threw off his coat to give a hand shucking corn with the other workers. One of them, John Jacobs, recalled meeting the "wonderful man," and left this description: "He was about 6 feet high, weighed two hundred pounds, had no surplus flesh, broad shouldered, stood erect, was a man of great physical strength, of fine appearance, his cheeks mantled with a rosy hue, eyes vivacious, and in form, had no superior."[10]

Despite suffering another bout of malaria, Crockett witnessed a duel on November 6, 1827. His friend Sam Carson had beaten political opponent Robert Vance for a seat in Congress. They had exchanged insults and Vance had accused Carson's grandfather of being a cowardly Tory during the American Revolution. The adversaries met across the border in South Carolina, where dueling was still legal. When the smoke cleared, Carson still stood while Vance lay mortally wounded. Crockett, overwhelmed with relief, mounted his horse and galloped back to Carson's home where his anxious family awaited news. "David Crockett was the first man who brought news to Pleasant Gardens," wrote one of the daughters, "he rode his horse almost to death, beat his hat to pieces & came dashing up yelling 'The victory is ours.'"[11]

While his wife and son returned to Tennessee with three slaves, gifts from Elizabeth's father, Crockett continued the journey to Washington to discover "what he had been called on to do." Now forty, he was about to enter the vicious world of 19th century Washington politics. The 1828 election fight was an example of what could be expected. Perhaps having killed and skinned varmints was good training for events to come, but he did not appear with a coonskin cap, buckskins, and a tomahawk. Dressing like other members of Congress, he wore a gentleman's high collared coat, vest and dress shirt with a cravat. His "uncouth" origins, however, would be used against him at every turn.

He arrived in company with duel survivor Sam Carson, then took a room at Mrs. Ball's reasonably-priced rooming house in Pennsylvania Avenue. Here he met several politicians from various states who were also in residence. Many of the Washington establishment did not know how to take this talkative, stubborn woodsman of little learning. He spoke directly, often swimming against the tide, come what may, diplomacy not blunting his forthright style.

Crockett continued his advocacy for the common man—but not with the degree of success he would have preferred. During his three terms in congress he would push to have his treasured Tennessee Land Bill become the law of the land. He wanted 160 acres each for poor farmers and squatters. But this would not come to pass.[12] Those poor folk he attempted to support, however, knew he was one of them, and writers seized on this eccentric from the canebrakes as good copy for their readers; someone new, something different.

Despite mythical perceptions, David Crockett sat in Congress attired as a gent, not a bear hunter from the canebrakes of Tennessee (Library of Congress).

One news story from 1828 read "One of the most eccentric and amusing members of Congress is Mr. Crockett from Tennessee. He has his coat of arms upon a seal, and characteristic enough truly they are of the owner, being a rifle, butcher's knife and a tomahawk, surrounding his name." Crockett had said he was not afraid to address the House of Representatives because he "can whip any man in it," and had boasted that he "could wade the Mississippi, carry a steamboat on his back and whip his weight in wildcats," said the writer. He "was a very clever fellow" fond of field sports, and the article described him competing in a shooting match. "His antagonist prudently paid forfeit, and

Tennessee was triumphant."[13] Over the years what Crockett actually said and did became blurred with concocted yarns, all adding to the fame of the backwoodsman.

But, despite the prestige of his place in the world, he shared the same opinion as Old Hickory regarding the day-to-day grind of political life. "There's too much talk," Congressman Crockett observed:

> Many men seem to be proud they can say so much about nothing. Their tongues keep working, whether they've any grist to grind or not. Then there are some in Congress who do nothing to earn their pay but listen day after day. But considering the speeches, I think they earn every penny, amounting to eight whole dollars a day—providing they don't go to sleep. It's harder than splitting gum logs in August, though, to stay awake.[14]

But dirty politics outside the House helped keep him awake. On November 25, 1828, the *National Banner and Nashville Whig* published a story about Crockett's supposed antics at a presidential dinner the year before. The ignorant backwoodsman had sipped water from finger bowls, then accused a waiter of stealing his dinner when the plates were cleared for the next course. Then he kept one hand on his plate so no one could "steal" it again—so said the story.

Crockett responded by having those seated near him write to newspapers with denials. Congressman Clark of Kentucky wrote that Crockett's behavior was "marked with the strictest priority" and Congressman Verplanck of New York wrote his behavior was "perfectly becoming and proper." President Adams himself noted in his diary, "Colonel Crockett was very diverting at our dinner," presumably due to Indian fighting and bear hunting stories rather than sipping from finger bowls. But this was not an isolated attack. Crockett would be accused of everything from gambling to drunkenness and adultery. He denied all, and wrote to brother-in-law George Patton:

> I have altered my cours in life a great deal sence I reached this place and have not tasted one drop of Arden Spirits sense I arrived here nor never expect to while I live nothing stronger than cider.... I trust that I was called in good time for my wickedness by my dear wife who I am certain will be no little astonished when she gets information of my determination.[15]

Old Hickory won his bid for the presidency in 1828, with the ever-present John Calhoun as vice-president. They were sworn in during March 1829. Jackson opened the inauguration ball to the general public and a motley crowd flocked into the White House. Drinks were spilt and dishes were smashed as muddy shoes clambered onto furniture for a better look at the new president. To draw the mob outside, tubs were filled with punch on the White House lawn. For this, Jackson was dubbed "King Mob" by the opposition.

In August of the same year, Crockett ran for his second term in Congress against his old adversary, Colonel Adam Alexander. Crockett scored 6,733 votes to Alexander's 3,641. But Crockett's desire to "pursue his own course" often saw his views at odds with his own party and the pro–Jackson Tennessee Legislature. He opposed a bill Jackson supported, for $100,000 for Susan Decatur, wife of naval hero Stephen Decatur, killed in a duel in 1820. Two days later Crockett wrote a letter criticizing the Old Chief: "Some large dogs I have Seen here with their Collers on with letters engraved on the collar *My dog*—& the mans name on the Coller. I have not got a Coller Round my neck marked my dog with the name of Andrew Jackson on it."[16]

Crockett also wanted to see funding for the West Point military academy abolished as it was "managed for the benefit and the noble of the country." He also opposed Revolutionary War pensions for members of the regular army because it "excluded all the volunteers and militia who fought in the old war, who were old and had been knocking at the door of Congress for years." He himself had fought as in a volunteer in the War of 1812, he said, and "discovered who had fought the bravest, the regulars or the volunteers and the militia. When regular troops were living bountifully, the militia were in a state of starvation. I came here to do justice; and I will do justice, or I will do nothing."

The critical break with the Jackson camp came with Old Hickory's Indian Removal Act, introduced to Congress on February 24, 1830. Jackson considered American Indians an "ill fated race" and wanted treaties negotiated for the removal of not only his old enemies, the upper Creeks to west of the Mississippi, but also those who had helped defeat them—lower Creeks, Cherokees, Choctaws and Chickasaws. Jackson would attempt to justify this with soothing words; the removal would be for their own good, he claimed: "Towards the aborigines of the country no one can indulge a more friendly feeling than myself, or would go further in attempting to reclaim them from their wandering habits and make them a happy, prosperous, people." Jackson claimed he wished to save them from "utter annihilation," and the government generously "proposes to pay the whole expense of [their] removal and resettlement." He hoped there were those who would "unite in attempting to open the eyes of those children of the forest to their true condition, and by a speedy removal to relieve them from all the evils, real or imaginary, present or prospective, with which they may be supposed to be threatened."[17]

"If I had known that Jackson would drive us from our homes, I would have killed him at the Horseshoe," said Cherokee warrior Junaluska. At Horseshoe Bend a Creek prisoner had lunged at Jackson with a knife, only to be brought down by Junalaska. Old Hickory's savior was sent by Chief John Ross with a plea to let the Cherokees stay in their ancestral lands.

"Sir, your audience is ended and there is nothing I can do for you," was Sharp Knife's response. Junaluska would be removed to the west along with the other Cherokees. Two years after Jackson's death, however, he would be granted citizenship and land in North Carolina.

Crockett voted against the bill and vented his feelings regarding the Indian Removal Act:

> They said this was a favorite measure of the president, and I ought to go for it. I told them I thought it was a wicked, unjust measure, and that I should go against it, let the cost to myself be what it might; that I was willing to go with General Jackson in everything I believed was honest and right.... I voted against this Indian Bill, and my conscience yet tells me that I gave a good, honest vote, and one that I believe will not make me ashamed in the day of judgment.

But those who had voted Crockett into office did not agree. When the session closed and Crockett returned home:

> I found a storm had been raised against me sure enough; and it was echoed from side to side, and from end to end of my district, that I had turned against Jackson.... I was hunted down like a wild varment, and in this hunt every little newspaper in the district, and every little pin-hook lawyer was engaged.[18]

In April of 1831, Old Hickory wrote to his friend Samuel Hayes, "I trust for the honor of the state, your Congressional District will not disgrace themselves longer by sending that profligate man Crockett back to Congress."

During this year the Indian Removal Act came into force. A ruling in the supreme court in favor of the Cherokees was simply ignored by Jackson. Speaking of the chief justice, "John Marshall has made his decision, now let him enforce it." Over the next decade over 125,000 Cherokees, Creeks, Choctaws, Chickasaws and Seminoles would be forced to relocate west, in chains and at gunpoint if need be. By 1831 many Cherokees had already been sent to Indian Territory, but when most of the remaining 17,000 were removed in 1838, about 4,000 died of hunger and disease along the "Trail of Tears."

Jackson stalwart Judge William Fitzgerald ran against Crockett in the 1831 election. At one gathering, Fitzgerald repeated accusations of Crockett's supposed gambling and drinking habits. Crockett had warned him a thrashing would be in order if the libels were heard again, and attended his next speech. An unfazed Fitzgerald repeated the accusations, and Crockett moved from the crowd to carry out the threat. But Fitzgerald, ready and waiting, produced a pistol and threatened to shoot. With little choice, Crockett stopped, turned and pushed his way back through the crowd. Fitzgerald's resort to firearms did him no harm, but the incident did much to damage Crockett's reputation. A few days after his electoral defeat—8,534 votes to 7,948—Crockett wrote to a friend, "I would rather be beaton and be a man rather than be elected and be a little puppy dog."[19]

Andrew Jackson lost his wife in 1828, Sam Houston his in 1829, and now it was Crockett's turn. When he lost the election he also lost Elizabeth. His wife decided she'd had enough of a husband she rarely saw. He had been unable to attend the marriages of his son William, his daughter Margaret, and step-son George Patton.

To keep creditors at bay, Crockett sold off property, including his house and 25 acres, to George Patton, along with a ten-year-old slave girl named Adaline. On the bill of sale he wrote, "Be allways sure you are right then Go, ahead," the first known writing of what became his famous maxim in life. While Elizabeth Crockett and those children still under her wing moved in with Patton relatives in Gibson County, he leased 20 heavily wooded acres in Carroll County to live alone. He felled trees, built a log cabin, planted crops, and took to the woods with hunting dogs and gun. But, courted by Jackson's opposition, the Whig Party, he also prepared for the next congressional election.

18

A Citizen of the Cherokee Nation

Resettling with his old Cherokee friends did not isolate Sam Houston from the outside world. He wrote letters to friends saying "Houston is himself again" and received encouraging replies. "As I was never a friend in sunshine alone, neither can I now be the deserter of Friendship in adversity," wrote J.P. Clarke, "when the reality of your absence presses on me still it would seem a disturbed dream—a thing of air—and yet, at times, I can hardly trust the evidence of my senses upon the subject of your absence ... your friends here beg me to say—that you are not forgotten by them."[1]

But big Sam was not forgotten by enemies either. Back east sharp pens slashed like knives. "I had always looked upon him as a man of weak and unsettled mind," former Governor William Carroll wrote to Jackson, "without resources, and incapable of manfully meeting a reverse of fortune, but I confess I was not prepared to see him act as he did ... charity requires us to place it to the account of insanity."[2]

Insane or not, Houston found himself in demand with not only the Cherokees but other tribes as well. His well-known friendship with Andrew Jackson meant those who had Houston's ear may well have the ear of the Great White Father in Washington. Osage chiefs approached Houston with complaints of fraud against their agent, Major John Hamtramack. Houston and Haralson both wrote to Secretary of War John Eaton recommending he be replaced with Auguste Chouteau, a previous agent, who was well trusted by the Osages, having lived among them for 20 years. Washington Irving toured the plains and visited Chouteau's agency, "a motley frontier scene":

> There was a sprinkling of trappers, hunters, half-breeds, creoles, negroes of every hue; and all other rabble rout of nondescript beings that keep about the frontier, between civilized and savage life; as those equivocal birds the bats hover about the confines of light and darkness.
> The little hamlet of the Agency was in a complete bustle; the black-smith's shed, in particular, was a scene of preparation; a strapping negro was shoeing a horse; two half-breeds were fabricating iron spoons in which to melt lead for bullets. An old trapper, in leathern hunting frock and moccasins, had placed his rifle against the work-bench, while he superintended the operation, and gossiped about his hunting exploits; several large dogs were lounging in and out of the shop, or sleeping in the sunshine.[3]

Following Sam's visit, the Creeks requested that he mediate their disputes with the Osages, and the Choctaws requested that he write to Secretary of War John Eaton on their behalf.

Then John Jolly asked Houston to intervene in a dispute that threatened war. A band of Cherokees had crossed the border into Texas to be attacked by a war party of

Tawakonis. Some Cherokees had been killed and the survivors made to watch a scalp dance. A revenge raid was planned by young Cherokees and they asked neighboring Creek warriors to join them. Houston wrote to Colonel Arbuckle at Cantonment Gibson in July of 1829:

> I attended the Dance and Talk of the Cherokees, and Creeks, and had the mortification to witness (in spite of all my efforts) the raising of the Tomahawk of war.... The Creeks did not join and I trust that you may by attending their council prevent them any future day.... It is the project of a few restless and turbulent young men, who will not yield, or listen to the Talk of their Chiefs.... I have been informed (but vaguely) that some Osages, Choctaws, Shawnees, and Delawares are to join the Party, and in all make it some 250 or 300 warriors.[4]

Despite the entreaties of John Jolly and Houston, the war party set out for the Red River and evened the score with a raid on the Tawakonis. And there was other trouble afoot, eight Osages having been killed near the Red River by a Delaware war party. Secretary of War John Eaton appointed a commission which included Sam Houston, Colonel Arbuckle and Auguste Chouteau. They met with Osage subagent Nathaniel Pryor and Osage Chief Clermont at the mouth of the Verdigris River to "adjust the differences" between the tribes. Rather than attacking the Delawares, the Osages agreed to accept $100 worth of trade goods for each of the eight warriors killed. Stock including "standing blankets, butcher knives and vermilion" was provided from Chouteau's trading post.

Houston wrote to Andrew Jackson suggesting that the distribution of presents and medals among the tribes would help maintain not only peace between them, but also with the United States. The Osages and Pawnees had a long history of conflict, and an exchange of prisoners would leave "little difficulty in making peace."[5]

During that summer Houston rode hundreds of miles talking peace with the chiefs of various tribes, and upon return set up his own hewn-log trading post. Wigwam Neosho, as he called it, was between the Verdigris and Grand Rivers, about three miles from Cantonment Gibson. This not only provided a home for himself, but also his new wife. Tiana Rogers was a tall and attractive mixed-blood woman in her mid-thirties. She had two children by a former husband, David Gentry, a white blacksmith killed during a clash with Osage warriors. She was the daughter of Chief John Rogers and John Jolly's sister, Jenny Due. The marriage ceremony was according to Cherokee custom, and legally he remained married to Eliza Allen Houston.

Despite Sam's assurances that he had no plans to raise an army of Indians to conquer Texas, Old Hickory kept a close eye on his activities. He had been informed of Houston boasting "he would conquer Mexico or Texas, & be worth two million in two years." But this was while drunk during his trek to Indian Territory. Jackson did not take this too seriously, believing it "to be the effusions of a distempered brain." He informed Governor John Pope of Arkansas, however, that if such a project should be discovered to "adopt prompt measures to put it down & give the Government the earliest intelligence of such illegal enterprise with the names of all those who may be concerned therein."[6]

Once settled with the Cherokees and a new wife, Houston's drinking did not cease. Whatever else was in short supply on the frontier, alcohol flowed freely, especially in gambling dens near army posts like Cantonment Gibson. Here soldiers were quartered in cold, dismal cotton-wood and green oak log barracks, hastily built with no foundations. As they settled into the earth gaps appeared, doors and windows jammed. Public houses with crackling fires, goodtime girls and alcohol by the barrel were an enticement soldiers could not resist. Frequent drunken brawls were the result. The Indians also suffered, and post surgeon Dr. John Thornton reported that many deaths had occurred among them "from the intemperate use of intoxicants."[7]

Selling alcohol to the Indians was strictly banned. One soldier, Private Wilson, was caught and forced to stand on a barrel from sunrise to sunset for 10 days in front of the guard house. He had the sign "whiskey seller" on his back, and was made to hold a bottle in each outstretched hand.[8]

On October 29, 1829, for his services to the tribe, Sam Houston was granted "forever all the rights, privileges and immunities of a Citizen of the Cherokee Nation."

Late 1829 saw Houston on the paddle steamer *Amazon* as she wound her way along the Tennessee River carrying cargo and passengers back east. More Indians were expected to arrive in Indian Territory, and Houston was part of a delegation sent to Washington to discuss this and other issues which included food contracts for the Indians' journey. He arrived with the Cherokee delegation, booked in at Brown's Indian Queen Hotel, and was soon catching up with old friends.

He reunited with Old Hickory at a diplomatic reception; the first time they had met since Sam's flight from Tennessee. Dressed as a Cherokee, Houston was embraced by Jackson as a close friend and comrade. Houston would take comfort, no doubt, in knowing the warm welcome would be reported to his old enemy, Vice-President Calhoun, no lover of Cherokee garb. In recent times Jackson's relationship with Calhoun had also been strained. Word had reached his ear that, when Secretary of War, Calhoun had wanted him disciplined for the Florida invasion in 1817.

And then there was the "Petticoat Affair." Calhoun and his wife were currently refusing to socialize with Peggy O'Neill, the bride of Secretary of War John Eaton. Her previous husband had committed suicide because, gossips said, of his wife's scandalous affair with Eaton. This caused a rift within the government social scene. Jackson, a close friend of Eaton, complained of the "ridiculous attitude" of those shunning Mrs. Eaton, led by the Calhouns, and said they were a group of gossips "whose principal business is to run about the country and point to the mote in their brother or sister's eye without being conscious of the beam that lurks in their own."

But Jackson's niece Emily Donelson was one of these. With Rachel Jackson gone, Emily had become First Lady and hostess at the White House. While agreeing to greet Peggy under sufferance, Emily's cold treatment let the guest know she was most unwelcome.[9] This created friction between Jackson and Emily, and after a return visit to the Hermitage, she refused to return to Washington, much to Old Hickory's regret. Because of this scandal, Eaton would resign his post in 1831.

No doubt the subject of Texas was raised during Houston's visit. The president did not want some hair-brained filibustering expedition. Jackson taking Florida from Spain by force had been one thing, but Mexico had gained independence from Spain in 1821, thus Jackson was dealing with a neighboring government which was not going to disappear, unless Spanish threats to reconquer their old colony came to fruition.

The previous Adams administration had made a half-hearted attempt to purchase the province with an offer of one million dollars. This had been considered so paltry by the Minister to Mexico, Joel Poinsett, that he had declined to make the presentation.

Six months following his election, Jackson had Secretary Van Buren write to Poinsett with a fresh proposal suggesting various possible borders, a maximum of five million dollars to be paid depending on the territory ceded. Poinsett, however, had fallen into disfavor with the Mexican government, and was replaced by Colonel Anthony Butler of Mississippi. Jackson told Butler that the large number of American settlers moving into Texas were bound to declare independence sooner or later, and the United States would be accused of being responsible although "all constitutional powers will be exercised to prevent." But it had become well-known in Mexico that the Americans had previously wished to purchase Texas for a mere one million—a national insult. The anti–American mood among the Mexicans, fanned by the local press, made purchasing Texas, even for five million, most unlikely. Butler arrived in Mexico City in October of 1829, but kept the higher offer under wraps till a more opportune time.[10]

Houston's negotiations on behalf of the Cherokees meant a stay of a few months and he mingled once more in Washington society. On March 4, 1830, the *Cherokee Phoenix* reported: "It is stated that Governor Houston, who, as has been mentioned, is now in Washington, has abandoned entirely assumption of the Indian costume and habits, and mingles in social intercourse and gaiety as freely as formerly."[11]

During this stay however, Old Hickory introduced his Indian Removal Bill. Crockett may have denounced this, but Houston's first loyalty was to the Old Chief. He would justify his attitude by stating that the semi-civilized tribes in the southeast were "slowing up progress" in that part of the country and their removal, "with their consent into a country which would forever remain essentially Indian" would be in their own interest. "The United States have sworn, by the most solemn oaths, never to sell the lands contained within these limits, and never to allow the white race to work itself in by any means."[12] With such self-delusion Houston was able to accommodate Jackson's grand scheme.

One item under discussion was the provision of rations for those Eastern Cherokees during their western trek. Houston had witnessed the fraud that could result from this type of contract. To insure a fair deal for the Indians, while making a just profit, he placed a bid himself. His offer of 13 cents per ration of beef was about average, the other 12 bids ranging from 7 to 18 cents. His involvement raised a storm of protest from those with vested interests, including corrupt Indian agents like John Hamtramack, previously fired on Houston's recommendation. Houston was accused of being a fraudster and profiteer but, having been through a similar situation years earlier, was well prepared. His paperwork and facts correct, he was able to disprove the allegations. But the whole furor was in vain. No contracts were signed at this time and the issue was shelved.[13]

His work in Washington complete, Houston left for Indian Territory. He paused in Nashville along the way. He could beat William Carroll in another election for governor of Tennessee, so some said. Carroll saw the failed marriage debacle as the best way to prevent any future grasp for power. Eliza's parents packed her off to Carthage, about 30 miles from home, to prevent any meeting with Houston, who arrived in Nashville and met with old friends. Following his departure, a committee of gentlemen, friends of the Allens, announced in the press that they had investigated the marriage breakdown thoroughly. It comes as little surprise that they found in Eliza's favor, concluding that Houston's "unfounded jealousies" had "rendered his wife unhappy" and she was obliged by a "sense of duty to herself and her family, to separate from her infatuated husband and return to her parents." Since that time "she has remained in a state of dejection and despondency," that Houston was "a deluded man" and his wife was "of a character unimpeachable: and that she is an innocent and injured woman." As a *coup de grace* Sam's "What is to be done?" letter to Eliza's father was also published. This public reminder was a broad hint to Sam Houston that he should never return to Tennessee.

Once back at Wigwam Neosho and Tiana, Houston managed to prevent Creek and Cherokee warriors from staging another raid into Texas. But Colonel Arbuckle, while appreciating the success, came into conflict with Houston on another matter. As a Cherokee citizen, The Raven placed an order for nine barrels of various alcoholic beverages for his own use, so he said. Arbuckle, however, felt that such a large quantity must be intended for sale. Houston vehemently denied this, writing to Arbuckle: "I entertain too much respect for the wishes of the Government—too much friendship for the Indians; and too much respect for myself to make traffic of the baleful curse!"[14] The dispute reached Assistant Secretary of War Randolph, who decreed, in fence sitting fashion, that Houston was not to use his Cherokee citizenship to bypass the usual trade regulations, but allowed the acquisition to go ahead on provision that he post a bond. There is no evidence of Houston being a whiskey peddler, and he certainly had a big thirst himself. Often inebriated, he was called by some Cherokees "Oo-tse-tee Ar-dee-tah-skee" meaning "The Big Drunk," and to add insult to injury, these were Osage words, thus denying Sam even being a Cherokee. Tiana was known to have brought bring him home from Cantonment Gibson slung over a horse after a drinking binge.

While Old Hickory continued to hear rumors of Houston's supposed plans to conquer Texas, the exile himself became a father for the first time. During 1830 Tiana gave birth to Margaret Lewis Head Houston. Sam, meanwhile, continued to work towards maintaining peace between the tribes. Christian missionaries wanted peace too, but most wished to eradicate the Indians' way of life. This brought them into conflict with Houston who, while believing Indians could learn from the whites, felt they should be taught their own native culture in their own tongues. The Reverend Cephas Washburn had moved with the first Cherokees to relocate in the west, and was not happy with Houston's arrival among his flock. "We regard the residence of Governor Houston among the Indians, as a most injurious circumstance. He is vicious to a fearful extent, and hostile to Christians and Christianity. This I would not wish to have known as coming from me, as he has very considerable influence."[15] But not all missionaries shared this view, and took a different approach in their dealings with the tribes. Houston wrote of Dr. Marcus Palmer of the Fairfield Mission, as "a useful and intelligent Gentleman, and worth all the missionaries in the Nation."

Houston helped negotiate the Creek-Osage Treaty of May 10, 1831, which decreed that any tribal member who broke the peace would be tried by a joint council of Creek and Osage chiefs.[16] Thus it came as a shock 10 days later when Houston's application for a place on the Cherokee National Council was rejected. Mortified, he spoke angrily of leaving and resettling among the Choctaws, but such thoughts were put on hold when informed his mother was dying. He traveled back to East Tennessee with all due haste, and was at Elizabeth Houston's bedside when she passed away.

News of Sam's arrival back in Nashville caused joy among old allies, who invited him to a special dinner in his honor. But he gave no reason when he politely declined. Feeling, no doubt, the Carroll faction would be preparing an assault, he placed a sarcastic "PROCLAMATION" in the local press. This gave permission for all *"scoundrels whomsoever"* to "slander, vilify, and libel" him "to any extent" and he would provide "handsome gilt" copies of defamatory newspapers bound in "sheep" and "dog" to the "author of the most *elegant, refined and ingenious lie or calumny.*"[17]

Following his mother's funeral, Houston returned to Indian Territory and normal life at Wigwam Neosho. There were unresolved matters back in Washington, however, and he was asked to attend another conference on behalf of the Cherokees. He left Indian Territory in December 1831 for a roundabout trip that would take him to the capital via New Orleans. His friend Chief Opothleyahola of the Creeks gave him presents for the trip—a buckskin coat with a beaver collar, and a fine hunting knife.

19

Let Us Have Crockett's March

"My name is Nimrod Wildfire—half horse, half alligator and a touch of the airthquake—that's got the prettiest sister, fastest horse, and ugliest dog in the District, and can out-run, outjump, throw down, drag out, and whip any man in all Kaintuck." Decked out in buckskins and a massive wildcat fur hat, Colonel Nimrod Wildfire strode out on stage for the first time at the Park Theater, New York, on April 25, 1831. The play, *The Lion of the West, or A Trip to Washington*, was about a jocular, garrulous "b'ar killer" fresh from the frontier. The play and its star received massive applause from patrons and critics alike. A few days after the opening, a critic for the *Morning Courier and New York Enquirer* praised writer James Kirke Paulding, and stated that Colonel Wildfire was "an extremely racy presentation of Western blood, a perfect nonpareil—half steamboat, half alligator."[1] It was apparent to all that Nimrod, played by actor James Henry Hackett, was based on Colonel David Crockett, the famous frontier congressman.

But the real Crockett had lost his congressional seat just the month before. It seemed, however, that the play had intervened to keep Crockett in the public eye, bigger than ever, while he resumed his bear hunting life back in Tennessee—for the time being.

In 1833, the production traveled to the Royal Opera House at Covent Garden in London's West End. In a way not seen before, this reinforced tall tales of the American West, and was a great success despite puzzling American slang: "He'll come off as badly as a feller I once hit with a sledge hammer lick over the head—a real sogdolloger. He disappeared altogether; all they could ever find of him was a little grease spot in one corner."[2] That same year, Crockett attended a performance in Washington, and one observer recalled:

> This brought out a house full to overflowing. At seven o'clock the Colonel was escorted by the manager through the crowd to a front seat reserved for him. As soon as he was recognized by the audience they made the house shake with hurrahs for Colonel Crockett, "Go ahead!" "I wish I may be shot!" "Music! Let us have Crockett's March!" After some time the curtain rose, and Hackett appeared in hunting costume, bowed to the audience, and then to Colonel Crockett. The compliment was reciprocated by the colonel, to the no small amusement and gratification of the spectators, and the play then went on.[3]

The play's success awakened publishers to the financial possibilities of "Davy" Crockett, as he became known. Early in 1833, *The Life and Adventures of Colonel David Crockett of West Tennessee* was published in Cincinnati. After a few alterations the same book appeared in London and New York as *Sketches and Eccentricities of Colonel David Crockett of West Tennessee.* It was written anonymously, but the author seems to have heard Crockett stories first hand, then thrown in "whappers" of his own. The writer was originally supposed to have been novelist James S. French but, despite receiving royalties, he denied authorship. A more recent claim is that the writer was Matthew St. Clair Clark, a Whig supporter who had lost his position as clerk of the House of Representatives under the Jackson administration.[4] The book's style and language had much in common with the stage play: "I am that same David Crockett, fresh from the backwoods, half horse, half alligator, a little touched with the snapping turtle; can wade the Mississippi, leap the Ohio, ride upon a streak of lightning, and slip without a scratch down a honey locust." He could also whip his "weight in wildcats," "hug a bear too close," and for a ten-dollar bill, you could "throw in a panther," too.[5]

But while others made money from his name, it was wild game that provided meat for Crockett's table as the 1833 congressional elections loomed. Jackson had been returned to the presidency in 1832, but Crockett would not be reelected if the president had his way. Old Sharp Knife had Crockett's congressional district gerrymandered to assist the incumbent Jackson man, Adam Fitzgerald. "It was done to make a mash of me," complained Crockett. And then the *Book of Chronicles* appeared. Written in biblical prose, this made numerous attacks on Crockett and his political motives. It was authored by "old Black Hawk, as he is sometimes called (alias) Adam Huntsman," Crockett recalled, "with all his talents for writing *Chronicles,* and such like foolish stuff."[6] Huntsman was a rising Jackson Democrat who had lost a leg in the Creek War, and was now "timber-toed," wearing a wooden replacement. Crockett, however, went ahead, undaunted, and "when the election came on, the people of the district, and of Madison County among the rest, seemed disposed to prove to Mr. Fitzgerald and the Jackson Legislature, that they were not to be transferred like hogs, and horses, and cattle in the market: and they determined that I shouldn't be broke down."

Shortly after the election, the *Niles Weekly Register* reported:

> A great deal has been said in the newspapers concerning Col. Crockett, who has been again elected a member of Congress from Tennessee. It was the misfortune of the colonel to have received no school education in his youth ... but he is a man of strong mind and of great goodness of heart. The manner of his remarks are so peculiar that they excite much attention, and are repeated because of their originality; but there is a soundness, or point, in some of them which shows the exercise of a well disciplined judgment.... We have oftentimes been asked, "what sort of man is colonel Crockett?" and the general reply was—"just such a one as you would desire to meet with, if any accident or misfortune had happened to you on the high way."[7]

To the ordinary folk of Tennessee, a man could have no higher praise than that.

Crockett returned to Mrs. Ball's boarding house in Pennsylvania Avenue. When Congress convened on December 22, 1833, he immediately launched an attack on "King Andrew the First," as the Whigs called Jackson with derision.

Old Hickory had decided to reform the American government's financial system. He had no time for the Bank of the United States, and opposed their charter being renewed. It was an election promise, and he meant to see it through. He believed the bank operated as a monopoly, and its president, Nicholas Biddle, indulged in corrupt lending practices. Jackson, who had lost money himself in previous bank investments, withdrew all government funds from the Bank of America and placed them with various state banks. Crockett and other Whigs wanted the money returned. Biddle, however, had extended the repayment time for a loan to Crockett upon his reelection,[8] thus it would appear a conflict of interest occurred. But Jackson's anti-bank actions were widely condemned, bringing on recession, so Crockett's opposition may well have been genuine, regardless of his personal affairs.

Old Hickory had not been able to keep Crockett out of Congress, but he got his way with the Bank of America. The institution would lose its charter in 1836, and the United States would be without an official central bank until the establishment of the Federal Reserve System in 1913.

Crockett, however, riding high with his fame and reelection, had high hopes for his pet project, the Tennessee Land Bill. "I have no doubt of effecting this object before this Session Closes my prospects is much brighter than ever it was at any former Session," he wrote to his son, John. But, despite this optimism, the cherished Land Bill continued to meet a congressional brick wall.

There were men of influence, however, who saw a bright future for the gentleman from the cane. Delegates from the Whig Party approached him in early 1834 with the suggestion he run for president in 1836. Jackson's current vice-president, Martin Van Buren, was the likely Republican contender, and the Whigs felt Crockett's popularity in the west would see him win. And nothing would give Crockett more pleasure than beating Van Buren, a key Jackson man he loathed as much as Sharp Knife himself. Crockett responded, saying he doubted he had the makings for such high office, but "If you think you can run me in as President, then just go-ahead. I had a little rather not; but you talk so pretty, that I cannot refuse. If I am elected, I shall just seize the old monster party by the horns, and sling him right slap into the deepest part of the Atlantic sea."[9] Crockett's self esteem received a considerable boost, no doubt, and he began to see himself as the future president of the United States.

But "the best laid schemes of mice and men often go awry," Robert Burns had penned in 1786. *The Lion of the West* and *Sketches and Eccentricities* had made a heap of money for other people, but none for their inspiration, Colonel David Crockett of Tennessee. As a result he went to work at his own authorized biography. He claimed he was misrepresented in the earlier work and "In the following pages I have endeavoured to give the reader a plain, honest, homespun account of my state in life, and some few of the difficulties which have attended me along the journey, down to this time." His writing skills being somewhat basic, he needed help. Sharing his room at Mrs. Ball's was his friend, Congressman Thomas Chiltern of Kentucky. Both had started out as pro–Jackson men, but shared disillusionment with the Old Chief.

Together they went to work, Crockett writing the basic material, Chiltern then rewriting in backwoods, but acceptable, prose. "The manuscript of the Book is in his hand writing though the entire Substance of it is truly my own," Crockett wrote to the publishers. "The aid which I needed was to Classify the matter but the Style was not altered." Crockett planned a promotional tour, and wrote to John, "I intend never to go home until I am able to pay all my debts and I think I have a good prospect at present and I will do the best I can."[10]

The original hand-written manuscript arrived at the publisher's office, and the following announcement appeared:

> It may interest the friends of this genuine Son of the West to learn, that he has lately completed, with his own hand, a narrative of his life and adventures, and that the work will be shortly

published by Messrs. Carey & Hart, of Philadelphia. The work bears this excellent and characteristic motto by the author:

I leave this motto for others, when I'm dead:
Be always sure you're right—THEN GO AHEAD![11]

A Narrative of the Life of David Crockett of the State of Tennessee was an instant
best seller. Within a few months of release, the presses thumped out the sixth edition.
It is estimated Crockett's share of the royalties, with 10,000 books sold in the first year,
would have brought him about $2,000, a substantial sum at that time. Despite a "whap-
per" or two, including an embellishment of his Creek War service, the book remains
an important source of American frontier life and events. Crockett, surrounded by fans,
attended book signings during the spring of 1834, and spent time with an old comrade,
Sam Houston, who, no doubt, read a copy himself. "I didn't realize you were at the Enitachopco and Emuckfau fights," Houston may well have said. It's strange that Crockett
falsely added these dubious "victories" to his battle record. The Horseshoe Bend victory
would have made more sense.

"I take great pleasure in recording my name in Miss Octavia Walton's Album as a
testimonial of my respects for her Success through life," wrote Crockett, "and I hope
she may enjoy the happiness and pleasures of the world agreeable to her expectation
as all Ladys of her sterling worth, merits."[12]

The beautiful Octavia Walton was a noted socialite and hostess, the friend of many
literary and political luminaries of her day. She came from an illustrious Georgian
family, and was presented at European Courts and to the Pope. Houston and Crockett
were her guests on April 23, when both signed her visitor's book. Octavia, however,
despite becoming a published author, would not enjoy happiness without much trauma
as well. In 1836 she married Alabama Doctor Henry Le Vert and, despite reservations
about slavery and succession, nursed wounded Confederate soldiers during the Civil
War. Her husband died during the conflict, and one child was stillborn. Two of her
other four children died. Her entertainment of Yankee soldiers during the occupation
would see her branded as a traitor, and she would die in obscurity, reliant on the charity
of cousins, in 1877, aged 65.[13]

By 1834, Texas was home to Sam Houston and he would, no doubt, have spent
considerable time telling Crockett about the opportunities of those vast, fertile plains
to the southwest. And trouble was brewing: American colonists were smarting under
what they saw as oppressive Mexican rule.

Two days after signing Octavia's album, Crockett bade Houston farewell, and took
off on a three-week book-signing tour. He visited Baltimore, Philadelphia, New York,
Newport, Boston, Lowell, Providence and Camden, shaking hands, making speeches
and attending dinners. Whig supporters were in close attendance. He was able to cover
such a distance in such a short time due to that modern miracle of transportation, the
steam train. He also took his first trip on a sailing vessel.

Congress, however, was still in session, and Crockett absent—his political enemies
sharpened their knives. Perhaps the bear hunter was now feeling above mishap, due to
his popularity, and the prospect of becoming president. At the Philadelphia Stock
Exchange he delivered a speech which drew attention to the depressed state of the
economy due to Jackson's withdrawal of the Federal bank deposits.

Look at it now; and what do you see? You behold your commerce suspended, your laborers wandering about for employment; your mechanics starving; and above all you see the best currency in the world deranged; And, gentlemen, what is all this for? To gratify the will of a superannuated old man; a man whose popularity, like the lightning of heaven, blasts and withers all that comes within its influence! His leading object, in all the mischief he has done, has been to destroy the best moneyed institutions on earth. But, gentlemen, will you submit to this experiment?[14]

"Never! Never!" cried the crowd.

During a visit to Peale's Museum of Curiosities and Freaks, Crockett and others were entertained by a ventriloquist who also performed conjuring tricks. One was magically moving money from one closed box to another. "I am about to remove the deposits," the performer said.

"He can remove the deposits better than Old Hickory," Crockett called out, much to the mirth of the crowd.[15] One seventeen-year-old girl, Helen Chatman, was also in attendance. She wrote to her mother:

I went to Peale's Museum last evening and saw many wonderful things of course... . But what will interest you the most of all probably ... is that I have seen a great man. No less of one than Col. Crockett. I ... sat close by him so I had a good opportunity of observing his physiognomy... . He is wholly different from what I thought him. Tall in stature and large in frame, but quite thin, with black hair combed straight over the forehead, parted from the middle and his shirt collar turned negligently back over his coat. He has rather an indolent and careless appearance and looks not like a "go ahead" man.[16]

But go ahead he did, attending factories, dinners, and theaters, all arranged by Whig supporters. They laughed along with his frontier yarns and showered him with a host of gifts including a woolen suit, a watch-fob engraved "go ahead," and a hunting coat. His personal specifications for a fine new rifle were noted by the young Whigs of Philadelphia. This was presented at a ceremony after the tour by celebrated gunsmith J. M. Sanderson, along with a silver tomahawk engraved "Go Ahead Crockett." There was also a powder horn, an ornate flask filled with the best whiskey, a shot pouch and hunting knife. The rifle, richly decorated with animals on a silver stock had "Go Ahead" etched on the barrel. Crockett was most impressed, and vowed to use the fine weapon in defense of his country, should the need arise. His present flintlock was called "Betsy," and the new rifle would be called "Pretty Betsy."[17]

In Boston, he was "entertained like a prince," and received far too many invitations to handle. He visited the USS *Constitution*, known as "Old Iron Sides" due to her ability to withstand British fire during the War of 1812. A wooden Andrew Jackson figurehead adorned the bow, and Crockett joked about it being placed where the general had "fixed himself, that was—before the Constitution."[18] Two months later the figurehead mysteriously disappeared, then turned up as the table centerpiece at a Whig banquet.[19]

Crockett visited the nearby Bunker Hill battlefield where the British had been dismayed to find that it took 1,000 casualties to capture a bluff from American militiamen. Crockett paid tribute to men, "who fell in that daybreak battle of our rising glory," and wished he could "call them up, and ask them to tell me how to help to protect the liberty they brought for us with their blood." Perhaps the fallen heroes answered that call. Crockett's destiny at the Alamo was less than two years away.

He arrived back in Washington on May 13 somewhat worse for wear. He was, at 47, one year older than Andrew Jackson when first dubbed "Old" Hickory.

Despite the adulation, time was moving on for David Crockett. Back in Congress,

David Crockett waves farewell. Dressed as a hunter, the final portrait foretold his coming fame as the frontiersman who fought and died at the Alamo (Library of Congress).

he broke the monotony with unbalanced, vitriolic attacks on Jackson, to be reprimanded by the House Speaker. He sat through long-winded speeches where, he felt, "Many men seem to be proud they can say so much about nothing."

The painter John G. Chapman encountered him on the capitol steps. "You look tired, Colonel, as through you'd just got through a long speech in the House."

"Long speech to thunder," Crockett replied, "there's plenty of 'em up there for that sort of nonsense, without my making a fool of myself at public expense. I can stand *good nonsense*—rather like it—but *such nonsense* as they are digging at up yonder, it's no use trying to—I'm going home."[20]

During 1833 and 1834, Crockett had six portraits painted by five different artists, one of which was lost by accident when left behind on a steam boat. They portrayed "Congressman Crockett" in formal attire, not the backwoodsman image that spread his fame. In May of 1834, John Chapman was working on a portrait of Crockett for the next election, when the sitter came up with a fresh idea. "I admitted," recalled Chapman, "that I would be delighted to try it, but it would have to be a large picture, and as I never saw a harricane, or a bear hunt, I should be obliged to give him a great deal more bother to explain all about them, and to show me what to do."[21]

Over six weeks, Chapman's deft hand with brush and oil paint created an image to fit the woodsman's "b'ar huntin'" reputation. The artist talked with his subject and made the following observations:

> I cannot recall to mind an instance of his indulgence in gasconade or profanity. There was an earnestness of truth in his narrations of events, and circumstances of his adventurous life, that made it obvious: while the heroic type of his grand physical development, equal to any emergency of achievement—his clear unfaltering eye, and with all gentle and sympathetic play of features, telegraphing, as it were, directly from a true heart, overflowing with kind feeling and impulse, irresistibly dispelled suspicion of insincerity and braggartism.[22]

One day, however, Crockett's downcast demeanor revealed all was not well. His own feelings were reflected by the crumpled state of the letter in hand. Eldest son John had written with news of religious conversion, and rebuked Crockett for his way of life. No doubt John had read of his father's triumphal book tour, and felt the adulation misplaced for one who had got the family into debt and not tended their needs.

"Thinks he's off to Paradise on a streak of lightning," grumbled Crockett to Chapman. "Pitches into me, pretty considerable."

When Chapman finally laid down his brush, a life-size, oil on canvas, portrait had emerged. David Crockett was dressed in hunting clothes, trusty flintlock in hand, hunting dogs at his feet. And he held his hat aloft—as though waving goodbye. Crockett's time was drawing to a close, and it seems fate had intervened to dispel the politician, and produce that last, enduring image, the Davy Crockett of books and screen, the mythical king of the wild frontier.

20

Most Daring Outrage
and Assault

Sam Houston chatted with Senators Grundy, Buckner and Blair as they stood on Pennsylvania Avenue, Washington, D.C. It was the evening of April 13, 1832. Senator Blair peered down the avenue at an approaching, rotund figure, then quickly scurried away.

Houston turned to see the new arrival, and they came face to face. "Are you Stanbery?"

"Yes, sir."

"Then you are a damned rascal!"

Houston's walking cane flashed and Congressman William Stanbery's hat went flying. "Oh don't," he cried. Stanbery staggered back, attempting to ward off more blows as Houston, furious, continued to lash out. The victim turned as though to run, but Houston leapt upon him and clung on as the two struggled about the pavement, wheezing and groaning, like fighting bears. Stanbery managed to throw Houston off, but his corpulent bulk fell to the ground, tripped by Houston's cane. He rolled face upwards, pulling a pistol from his coat. He aimed at Houston's chest and pulled the trigger, but the weapon misfired. Houston wrenched the gun from his hand, then stood over him, continuing to beat him over the head, body and sides. Then Houston "struck him elsewhere," as described by Senator Buckner, and Stanbery, after a few more blows, lay still, as though deceased. Buckner stepped forward to intervene, but Houston, his fury spent, stepped back of his own accord.[1]

The following day House Speaker Andrew Stevenson received the following communication:

> Sir: I was waylaid in the street, near to my boarding house, last night, about 8 o'clock, and attacked, knocked down by a bludgeon, and severely bruised and wounded, by Samuel Houston, late of Tennessee, for words spoken in my place in the House of Representatives, by reason of which I am confined to my bed and unable to discharge my duties in the House, and attend to the interests of my constituents. I communicate this information to you, and request that you lay it before the House.[2]

Congressman William Stanbery of Ohio had previously given a long speech which included: "Was not the late Secretary of War removed because of his attempt fraudulently to give Governor Houston the contract for Indian rations?"

This appeared on April 2 in the *Daily National Intelligencer*, the capital's premier paper, and Houston, furious, sent Stanbery a note demanding to know "whether your remarks have been correctly quoted." Stanbery, possibly fearing a call to dueling pistols, refused to receive the note. It was ten days later that Houston, still fuming, encountered the unfortunate Stanbery in the street. Once informed, Jackson said he wished "there were a dozen Houstons to beat and cudgel the members of Congress."[3] It seems appropriate that Houston's hickory cane had been cut from a tree at the home of the bellicose Old Hickory himself.

"*Most Daring Outrage and Assault*" screamed *The United States Telegraph.* The editor, Duff Green, would himself be the victim of assault from Congressman James Blair in 1833. Blair would soon shoot himself after reading an "affectionate" letter from his wife to Governor John Murphy of Alabama. Such was political life in 19th century America.

Stanbery swore out allegations of assault against Houston before a justice of the peace and, accordingly, a warrant for Sam's arrest was issued on April 17. Members of Congress did not cherish the prospect of being beaten every time someone took offence to their sanctified words. Such shoddy behavior must be nipped in the bud.

Sam employed Francis Scott Key, author of *The Star Spangled Banner*, as his defense attorney, and appeared, on trial, in the House. But at least he appeared in "civilized" clothes, Old Hickory having lent him money to replace his Cherokee garb. Houston was put through a verbal grilling by anti–Jackson men, squabbles broke out between congressmen, and votes were taken on how best to proceed. Testimony was heard over several days, but it would be Sam Houston's closing address that would make or break him in the eyes of Congress and the public at large.

The night before delivering his speech, Sam got drunk with a group of cronies which included the man presiding over his trial, House Speaker Andrew Stevenson. A barber brought coffee and shaving gear the following morning, and Sam set out cleanly shaven and sprucely dressed.

Long and repetitive, Houston's speech boomed through the House. Not only congressmen followed his every word, but also a public gallery packed with the intrigued.

Stanbery had accused Houston of premeditated assault, deliberately waiting to launch his attack. This Houston denied, pointing out that it was Stanbery who came armed with a pistol, not himself. He had merely met Stanbery by chance, then acted on impulse, his name having been denigrated by a man who had refused to read his note which merely sought to clarify what was actually said. Houston denied that the assault had "been for words uttered in this place," but for the publication "in the *Intelligencer* of libelous matter to my injury" such as no member of this "honorable court" would ever submit to. But he also cast doubt on the validity of the honorable court. Was there a law of the land that gave members of Congress the privilege of conducting this trial, or was it merely a House rule? "Show it to me, that I may obey the law." He went on to deliver a lecture on parliamentary history and warn of the dangers of Congress abusing its powers with comparisons to Caligula, Bonaparte and Cromwell. "All history will show that no tyrant ever grasped the reins of power till they were put into his hands by corrupt and obsequious legislative bodies."

A young lady called out from the public gallery. She would rather be Sam Houston than those who accused him, she cried.

Houston pointed to the Stars and Stripes:

So long as that flag shall bear aloft its glittering stars—bearing them amidst the din of battle, and waving them triumphantly above the storms of the ocean, so long, I trust, shall the rights of American citizens be preserved safe and unimpaired, and transmitted as a sacred legacy from one generation to another, till discord shall wreck the spheresthe grand march of time shall cease—and not one fragment of all creation be left to chafe on the bosom of eternity's waves![4]

The House erupted in thunderous applause. Houston bowed to his appreciative audience. As he left, the famous actor Junius Booth, father of John Wilkes, shook his hand. "Houston! Take my laurels!" he said.

None of which altered the incriminating facts, 106 to 89 in favor of "Guilty" being the final vote. On Monday, May 14 he appeared in the House to hear sentence passed. Congressman William Archer accompanied him and entered a protest on Houston's behalf: "Although he believes the whole proceedings against him, as well as the sentence he now objects to, unwarranted by the constitution of this country, yet (he will) suffer in silent patience, whatever the House may think proper to enforce."

Speaker Andrew Stevenson opened by complimenting Houston for his intelligence and character. Then he announced the sentence; a reprimand by the Speaker. "I do reprimand you accordingly."

So that was it. Houston guilty, but then let off. Rather than punish Sam, this episode propelled him to national prominence, love him or hate him, once more. It comes as little surprise that Stanbery was furious, and still wanted his pound of flesh. With anti–Jackson supporters he won the right to investigate Houston and former Secretary of War John Eaton for fraud in regard to the Indian rations debacle. But this too backfired. Houston once again had facts and figures on hand which proved the innocence of both himself and Eaton. The accused were promptly cleared without reservation.

But Stanbery was still not done. At his instigation, the Federal Court issued an indictment against Houston for criminal assault. The trial was held at the end of June 1832, distinguished Chief Justice William Cranch presiding. The verdict was, once again, "Guilty."

"The old sinner fined me $500 and cost of suit!" Houston complained.[5] He was, however, given till the following winter to pay up.

During these vexatious proceedings, Houston was in contact with James Prentiss, a New York City land broker who held claim to large acreage in Texas. On June 1 he and Prentiss became partners in the Galveston Bay and Texas Land Company, intent on buying and selling real estate. At the end of July Sam Houston set out for Texas, stopping in Nashville along the way. He arrived on August 16. "I have seen several friends here lately from Texas" he wrote to Prentiss, "and all represent it as the most prosperous state, and say it is a lovely region! Thousands would flock there from this country, if the government were settled, but will not venture without it.... Several persons have said to me that I was looked for, and earnestly wished for, by the citizens of Texas."[6]

The Old Chief was taking a summer break at the Hermitage, and Houston paid him a visit. Prentiss was supposed to have financed Houston's journey, but investors in their new company were slow to pay up. Jackson reputedly filled the gap with a $500 loan. He also provided an official excuse for Houston to visit Texas, the Mexicans having banned further immigration from the United States in 1830. Houston would travel as an official agent of the United States to bring peace between Pawnees, Comanches and other plains tribes. A quiet western frontier would allow for easier resettlement of those Indians who were to be removed from the East.

Texas was in Houston's blood now, and he was going there come what may. There was certainly no future for him in Tennessee. When attending the theater in Nashville he was recognized and the crowd erupted in anger, demanding that he get out.[7] It would seem the Stanbery affair following the Eliza Allen debacle had done nothing for Houston's reputation in Tennessee.

Continuing west through Arkansas, he crossed into Indian Territory and returned to Wigwam Neosho. Here he said goodbye to his Cherokee family; a less traumatic parting than he had with Eliza Allen. He left Tiana and his daughter the trading post, stock, and surrounding land, so it seems he had no intention to return. Having burned his bridges, Houston set out for Texas where the inner flame of destiny told him his future lay.

He rode south carrying a passport from the U.S. Army which requested his safe passage through the territory of various Indian tribes. At Fort Towson, five miles north of the Red River border, he composed a lengthy report to the Commissioner of Indian Affairs. He stated that the way to contact the Comanches during winter was by entering Texas, "only practicable, by way of St. Antone. I wish to set out for that point in six days, and proceed as directly as possible."[8]

But this lengthy report was merely a cover to help legitimize his arrival in Texas. Secretary of War Cass received a letter from Albert Pike, a traveler who would later become the Confederate commander of Indian Territory. "Governor Houston will effect nothing with the Comanches. He goes to treat with the southern portion of them who are already friendly—he will never meet with one of the northern portion from whom is our only danger, and even should he do so he would be immediately scalped."[9]

On December 2, 1832, Houston's horse splashed through the waters of the Red River, and he rode for the first time onto Mexican soil. That evening he dined in Jonesboro, the oldest Anglo village in Texas, the first American settlers having arrived there in 1815. Riding via Nacogdoches, he rode the 300 miles to San Felipe de Austin, home of Stephen Fuller Austin, "The Father of Texas."

Colonel William Gray from Virginia visited San Felipe in early 1836: "San Felipe is a wretched, decaying looking place. Five stores of small assortments, two mean taverns, and twenty or thirty scattering and mean looking houses, very little paint visible. No appearance of industry, or thrift or improvement of any kind."[10]

Despite appearances, Stephen Austin had, in fact, been very industrious to get that far. With the blessing of the Mexican government, he had commenced bringing American families into Texas in 1821, the year Mexico had gained independence from Spain after a long and bloody fight. The Mexican government saw American immigration as a way of populating a vast region where the relatively few inhabitants were often under threat from hostile Indians. And Texas was a very attractive proposition to those who were not well off. Under the law of 1820, land in the United States cost $1.25 payable in gold or silver when purchased, with 80 acres the minimum. The Mexican government, by contrast, would sell 4,428 acres for $117, payable over six years.[11] Little wonder that Stephen Austin was, initially, a devoted and loyal citizen of the Mexican Republic. In 1829, he wrote to his sister: "This is the most liberal and magnificent Govt. on earth for emigrants—after being here one year you will oppose a change—even to Uncle Sam."[12]

Mexico allowing the Americans in, however, was like opening the gates to the Trojan Horse.

In 1821, the population of Texas, excluding Indians, was about 2,500. By 1836, this had mushroomed to more than 40,000. Of these, at least 35,000 were from the United States, including black slaves.[13] Bringing their own ideas of law and democracy, and many seeing Mexicans as inferior, it seemed only a matter of time before Texas split to become part of the United States—one way or another.

Stephen Austin was not in San Felipe, but Houston spoke with his deputy, Samuel May Williams, and applied for one league of land on Carancahua Bay.[14] The matter of settling Indians from the United States in Texas was discussed, as disclosed in a letter sent by Williams to Houston. Mexican official Tadeo Cortiz intended recommending "as a matter of policy & benefit to both parties, to designate a section of country North West of Bexar" to settle Choctaws of whom he had "heard a very good report."[15]

In San Felipe, Houston met various men who would be involved in significant events to come. This included an American who had become a local legend. Some say James Bowie's family can be traced back to Rob Roy, the famous Scot who was either outlaw or patriot, depending on one's point of view.[16] In the tradition of Rob Roy, Jim Bowie's father, Rezin, had been one of Colonel Francis Marion's "Swamp Fox" hit-and-run horsemen during the American Revolution.

Bowie was born in Kentucky in 1796. The family moved to Spanish Louisiana where Jim and his brother Rezin Jnr. gained a reputation as "those wild Bowie boys." Jim is reputed to have jumped on the back of an alligator that had killed one of his favorite hounds, and stabbed the creature to death.

Around 1814, Jim moved from home and made a sparse living by trading in timber. He was joined by brother Rezin and they became involved in a shady slave importation scheme which, by manipulation of existing laws, appeared to be legal. In league with them was the renowned pirate Jean Lafitte who helped Old Hickory at New Orleans. The enterprise flourished till Lafitte closed the operation in 1819, but by then the Bowie brothers had amassed a small fortune of $65,000. This they used to purchase land and establish plantations in Louisiana and Arkansas.

Jim Bowie took part in an 1819 attempt to rest Texas from the Spanish led by filibuster James Long, a surgeon who had served under Andrew Jackson at New Orleans. They captured Nacogdoches and declared the Republic of Texas; but not for long. 500 Spanish troops arrived and the new government fled.

The Bowie brothers established the first steam mill for grinding sugar in Louisiana, at the same time becoming involved in dubious land transactions and smuggling operations.

In 1827 the famous "Sandbar Fight" took place. Jim Bowie's friend Samuel Wells met Thomas Maddox to fight a duel on a partially wooded river sandbar outside Natchez, Mississippi. The combatants both fired and missed, reloaded, fired, and missed again. Satisfied, they shook hands. But then more bullets flew as a fight broke out between opposing onlookers. Jim Bowie was clubbed with an empty pistol, then shot in the chest by Norris Wright. Bowie charged at him, but a second bullet in the thigh fired by one of the Blanchard brothers brought him down. Wright and Alfred Blanchard drew sword canes and set upon Bowie, who savagely slashed back with what was to become his famous Bowie knife, designed by brother Rezin. One sword hit Bowie's breast bone and slid along a rib, but then Bowie seized Wright by the collar. As Wright drew back, he pulled Bowie up with him. He thrust his knife into Wright's chest, twisting, "to cut his heart strings." Blanchard, still thrusting at Bowie, was shot in the arm by Thomas Wells, and Bowie, pushing Wright's dead body away, inflicted a knife wound to Blanchard's side.

When the smoke cleared two men lay dead, and others nursed serious wounds. Doctors present to tend the unharmed duelists were able to render first aid, but Jim Bowie was not expected to live. The two bullets, however, had passed right through and, carried from the scene, he survived to fight another day.

Newspapers got wind of the fight, and stories of Bowie's strength and prowess with the big knife spread. Over time stories emerged of other knife, fist and gun fights, a combination of fact and fiction as was common on the frontier. "He was a foe no one dared to undervalue, and many feared," recalled his friend Caiaphas Ham. "When unexcited there was a calm seriousness shadowing his countenance which gave assurance of great will power, unbending firmness of purpose, and unflinching courage." He was a man not to cross, however, as "when fired by anger his face bore the semblance of an enraged tiger."[17]

Following the "G.T.T." trend—as "Gone to Texas" was commonly known, Jim Bowie traveled to San Antonio de Bexar in early 1828. He was in search of new vistas, fresh opportunities, and fertile land. He met and impressed both Vice Governor Don Juan Martín de Veramendi and his attractive daughter, Ursula. He acquired Mexican citizenship, became a Roman Catholic, and married Ursula on April 25, 1831. While establishing himself with the Mexican aristocracy, Bowie acquired about 750,000 acres of prime Texas land.[18]

In November of 1831, he set out with an expedition of 11 men in attempt to locate the legendary lost San Saba silver mine. They found no silver, but Bowie did enhance his reputation as a man who could fight and win. The expedition came under attack from a large Comanche war-party, and during a fourteen-hour stand-off, they claimed to have killed and wounded 85 hostiles, while suffering only one killed and three wounded of their own.

Jim Bowie, a knife-fighting man not to antagonize if possible (Wikimedia Commons).

In 1832, Mexico was rent with rebellion. Colonel José de las Piedras, commanding the garrison at Nacogdoches, demanded the surrender of all firearms from the local settlers. Piedras, however, was a supporter of the old regime, while most Anglos felt the rebels held their interests at heart.

The rebels included Generalissimo Antonio López de Santa Anna. The young lieutenant sited for bravery at the Battle of Medina in 1813 had established himself as the foremost soldier of the Mexican Republic during turbulent times of Spanish invasion, revolution and counter-revolution.

Texan militia companies were formed, and on August 2, 1832, shooting broke out in Nacogdoches. A fight from house to house took place, and the *soldados* were forced to take refuge in the town fort. They evacuated after dark, but Jim Bowie and 18 others followed on horseback, and engaged in a running fight. The demoralized Mexican force of 310 soldiers mutinied and surrendered. In San Antonio, the provincial capital, they were set free along with Colonel de la Piedras who was paroled before returning to Mexico.

The action was legitimized by the revolution within Mexico, and there were no repercussions, the Americans having backed the winning side. The settlers, furthermore, had learned that they could successfully defy Mexican troops if the need arose.

It was just six months after these events that Sam Houston met Jim Bowie in San Felipe. Having struck up a good rapport, Bowie rode the final 150 miles to San Antonio with Houston. Riding with them were two other men, Sterling Robertson, who had spent five months living with the Comanches, and Caiaphas Ham, a friend of Bowie's who had joined him in 1830.

Riding through Comanche country, they took turns standing guard, and Ham later told an amusing story about Houston, who had returned from standing guard during the night. Looking to one side, he had heard the zip of an arrow. He looked around to hear another, his head darted back to hear another. His head shot backwards and forwards as he tried to see the Comanches, an arrow zipping by with each turn. It was then he realized the arrow zip was actually his hat scraping along his raised coat collar.[19]

They arrived in San Antonio, where Houston was introduced to Bowie's Mexican in-laws. Don Veramendi was not present, having been called to Saltillo to be sworn in as governor of the state of Coahuilla y Tejas. To Houston's advantage, however, influential Southern Comanches were in town on a trading expedition. Sterling Robertson, an adopted member of the tribe, introduced Houston and talks began.

In preparation for the arrival of thousands of Indians from the East, Cantonment Gibson in Indian Territory had been upgraded to a more permanent post, Fort Gibson. Houston asked the Comanches to attend talks there, and they agreed. But they were merely being polite. Such a trek to the north would put them through country bristling with hostile tribes. These facts would have been well appreciated by Houston, but supposedly being in Texas to encourage peace between the tribes, he was obliged to go through the charade for appearances sake.

After two months of talking to a variety of people and assessing the local mood, Houston crossed the border to Natchitoches, Louisiana, from where, on February 13, 1833, he wrote to Andrew Jackson. Only briefly mentioning his Comanche dealings, he offered information which "may be calculated to forward your views, if you should entertain any, touching the acquisition of Texas." Houston stated that "nineteen-twentieths" of the population desired American rule. "Mexico is involved in Civil War.... The Government is essentially despotic.... The rulers have not honesty, and the people have not intelligence." He went on to say that settlers "are determined to form a State Government" and unless order and the constitution are restored, Texas will remain "separate from the Confederacy of Mexico." He said Mexican troops had been expelled, and Mexico, being "powerless and penniless," they could not return. He said now would be a good time to obtain Texas on fair terms. There was to be a convention which would form a State Constitution. Houston would attend, and inform Jackson of the outcome. He would probably be making Texas his abiding place, he wrote, but "in adopting this course *I will never forget* the country of my birth." Houston then mentioned the "Nullification Crisis"—a vitriolic tariff dispute with John Calhoun and the state of South Carolina which threatened to secede. He wrote,

> God grant that you may save the Union! It does seem to me that it is reserved for you, and you alone, to render to millions so great a blessing. I hear all voices commend your course,—even in Texas, where is felt the liveliest interest for the preservation of the Republic. Permit me to tender you my sincere thanks, felicitations, and my earnest solicitude for your health and happiness, and your future glory, connected with the prosperity of the Union.
>
> Your friend and obedient servant,
> Sam Houston[20]

One could get the impression Houston wished to stay on good terms with Old Hickory.

The convention met on April 1, 1833, at San Felipe de Austin, and Houston attended as one of five delegates from Nacogdoches. The aim was to petition the Mexican government for Texas to become a separate state in its own right, rather than a province which included neighboring Coahuila. An 1830 law prohibiting more American settlers, largely ignored, was a thorn in Anglo hides, and in 1832 the Mexican government had attempted to collect import duties and taxes, a moratorium on these fees to encourage settlers having expired. To enforce payment, Mexican troops were sent in and forts built at strategic harbors. The Americans were no more happy to pay these taxes than their forebears had been before the Boston Tea Party in 1773. The Mexican tax collectors, many corrupt, lacked diplomatic skills, there was an ill defined boundary between civil and military authority, and land titles became subjects of dispute. Mexico had outlawed slavery in 1829, but slaves remained as "indentured servants," thus slavery was not a prime concern, the issues varied and complex.

A young lawyer named William Barret Travis, out to make trouble, was jailed at the port of Anahuac. This led to shooting between armed volunteers and Mexican troops at Fort Velasco, and lives were lost on both sides. The Mexicans were forced to surrender, and Travis was released.[21]

A committee chaired by Sam Houston drew up a proposed constitution granting Texas the desired statehood, separate from neighboring Coahuila, and Stephen Austin set out to present the document to the authorities in Mexico City. Houston, meanwhile, made a return trip to Fort Gibson, where it came as no surprise that the Southern Comanches had not shown up. Houston then moved onto Hot Springs in Arkansas, before returning to Texas via Crow's Ferry, Louisiana.

In Nacogdoches, he learned Spanish from the beautiful daughter of an old acquaintance, Henry Raguet, a merchant from Cincinnati, Ohio. Anna Raguet was a clever 17-year-old who spoke four languages fluently. Sam Houston had an eye for the "dear girles" and, despite being 23 years her senior, soon had more than Spanish lessons in mind. In November of 1833, he filed for divorce from Eliza Allen. Under Mexican law, however, this was impossible, and the petition sat, ignored, in the Nacogdoches Court House for many years. Sam's pursuit of Anna over the next few years would not bear fruit, and she would eventually marry the man who carried letters between them, Dr. Robert Irion, of Tennessee, with whom she would have five children.[22]

Stephen Austin arrived in Mexico City on July 28, 1833. He met with Vice President Valentin Farias of the new government headed up by Santa Anna. Farias was tasked with running the country and implementing reforms while Santa Anna was pursuing forces hostile to his regime. Austin placed before Farias the wishes of the San Felipe convention. The proposals languished with no action taken, and Austin wrote home that Texas had best organize a state government itself; a bad mistake as it transpired. After writing this letter, Austin was granted concessions including a repeal of the law banning American immigration. Statehood, however, required a population of 80,000, while Texas had only 30,000.

With statehood rejected, Austin set out for home. Farias, however, received news of his indiscreet letter from Mexican supporters in San Antonio. In January of 1834 Austin was arrested in Santillo for inciting rebellion, and sent back in irons to a cold prison cell. This caused a wave of alarm in both Texas and the United States.

Sam Houston traveled to New York and Washington to attend to a variety of matters. To help him out at a time of need, he prevailed upon Andrew Jackson to pay the $500 fine from the Stanbery affair. A claim filed for reimbursement of costs incurred during the Texan Indian mission was met with doubt and delay by treasury officials, but this gave him time to catch up with acquaintances and old friends.

David Crockett was preparing for his book promotion tour, and the two Tennesseans spent some time together, including their visit to Miss Octavia Walton. With talk of Crockett possibly being the Whig presidential candidate, no doubt Houston took more than a casual interest in the gentleman from the cane. After all, it's not what you know, but *who* you know that counts. If Crockett were to become president, perhaps acquisition of Texas would be on his agenda? Perhaps Crockett and Texas were linked in some way?

Houston sought, without success, elusive money from James Prentice, who apologized for the "meanness and stupidity" of investors in the Galveston Bay and Texas Land Company.

"Take my word for it," wrote Houston, "they will *need* me more than I will *want* them!" He continued with prophetic words:

> I do think within one year that it will be a Sovereign State and acting in all things as such. Within three years I think it will be separated from the Mexican Confederacy, and will remain so forever—.... You need not hope for the acquisition (if ever) by this Government of Texas during the Administration of Genl Jackson—If it were acquired by a treaty, that treaty would not be ratified by the present Senate—!!!
>
> Texas will be bound to look for herself, and to do for herself—this present year, must produce events, important to her future destiny.
>
> Keep my predictions and see how far they are *verified!*[23]

21

I Will Go to Texas

"Since you have chosen a man with a timber toe to succeed me, you may all go to hell, and I will go to Texas."[1] So said David Crockett in 1835. Far from becoming president, he had just lost his seat in congress to Adam Huntsman, his peg-legged, Jackson-backed opponent.

Crockett's 1834 book tour, while spreading fame and gaining sales, was the beginning of his fall from grace. His opponents seized on this. What was a member of congress doing traipsing around the country on a self-promoting tour, signing autographs and selling books while his seat in the House sat cold and unattended? Is this what he had been elected for? And those poor folk back home wondered what had become of the Tennessee Land Bill that promised a fair deal when it came to buying property.

Crockett also spent much time working on two other books. Publishing the Crockett brand paid better than politics. At the same time he made vitriolic attacks on Andrew Jackson, the Hero of New Orleans, a president from his own state. On several occasions the Speaker of the House was obliged to bring the gentleman from the cane to order, for abusive, ungentlemanly behavior. Crockett wrote that he was looking "forward to our adjournment with as much interest as ever did a poor convict in the penitentiary to see his last day come. We have done but one act, and that is the will of Andrew, the first king, is to be the law of the land. He has tools and slaves enough in Congress to sustain him in anything he may wish to effect." Crockett then borrowed from Sam Houston's speech during the Stanbery affair. "I thank God I am not one of them, I consider him a greater tyrant than Cromwell, Caesar or Bonaparte."[2]

But Crockett was not alone in his assessment of the Old Chief. January 30, 1835, was damp and misty as President Jackson attended a memorial service in the House chamber for deceased Congressman Warren Davis. "Life is uncertain, particularly for the aged," preached the chaplain. As Jackson walked outside a man stepped from the crowd, raised a pistol, and pulled the trigger. "The explosion of the cap was so loud that many people thought the pistol had fired," recalled Thomas Benton.[3] But only the percussion cap had ignited, not the lethal powder charge. As Old Hickory raised his cane and made for the gunman, a second pistol appeared. Smoke flew as the cap banged, but another misfire occurred. Lieutenant Thomas Gedney of the U.S. Navy knocked the gunman to the paving, and others held him down. Among them was Colonel Crockett. "I wanted to see the d-mnd-st villain in the world," he recalled, "and now I have seen him."

Old Hickory was hustled aboard a carriage and, with the crack of a whip, was sent back to the White House. He had just survived the first attempted assassination of an American president. It was expected that Jackson, true to form, would be in a rage, but he appeared unruffled upon arrival.

"I went over to the old man," recalled Meriwether Randolph, "and found him as cool, calm, and collected, as though nothing had happened."[4] Old Hickory was no stranger to gunfire when all said and done. The pistols would be examined, the powder found to be dry, and the two misfires put down to Divine Providence.

The would-be assassin, Richard Lawrence, was a deranged house painter who thought himself King of England, Jackson's policies preventing a flow of money from his British estates.

A prime Jackson aim had been to pay off the national debt, and when the national accounts were tallied one month before the assassination attempt, the bottom line put the country in credit. This was an accomplishment many thought impossible, but the government's austerity had been at a cost to the community; roads not made, bridges not built. Found not guilty due to insanity, Richard Lawrence spent the remainder of his life in mental institutions.

Still in debt, but enjoying good returns from his autobiography, Congressman Crockett was paid an advance by his publishers for *An Account of Col. Crockett's Tour to the North and Down East in the Year of Our Lord One Thousand Eight Hundred and Thirty Four.* To do the final writing he employed a fellow lodger at Mrs. Ball's, Congressman William Clark of Pennsylvania. Crockett was also credited with writing a book attacking Vice-President Martin Van Buren, Jackson's chosen successor, actually ghostwritten by Congressman Augustin Clayton of Georgia. Wary of libel action, Carey and Hart omitted their own names.

As the 1835 congressional elections loomed, Adam Huntsman reentered the scene. Old Black Hawk was the man who had authored the *Book of Chronicles*, attacking Crockett before the last election. The lawyer, after losing a leg while fighting Creeks, had emerged as a Jackson stalwart and a man of promise in the Democratic Party. He was reputed to be an excellent speaker who would campaign hard to unseat the "buffoon" Crockett. But the *Adams Sentinel* had doubts, as expressed on November 24, 1834: "We take it the Colonel will care very little about such a 'varment as that are.' He will 'chaw him up in a flash.'"[5]

Old Black Hawk and Old Hickory, however, had different ideas. And many Tennessee voters saw Huntsman's wooden leg as a symbol of courage and sacrifice while fighting for flag and country.

Crockett was obliged to defend himself before a barrage of attacks; absenteeism; ignoring requests by voters for Jackson literature while using congressional franking to post anti–Jackson material; inflated travel expenses, failure to get the promised Tennessee Land Bill passed. He was painted by the opposition as a traitor to Old Hickory and the state of Tennessee.[6]

Martin Van Buren, Jackson's anointed successor, was known as the "The Little Magician,"[7] and with good reason. He was a canny politician who knew every trick in and out of the book, and enjoyed a large support base. The Whigs came to realize that the bear hunter was most unlikely to beat Van Buren in a race for president. And Crockett agreed. He signed a letter from the Tennessee Delegation requesting that Senator

Hugh White run as the Whig candidate. Originally a Jackson man, White had become disillusioned. Old Hickory asking Van Buren to run for vice-president at the last election, rather than himself, had been the last straw.

Crockett despised Van Buren, and if he was elected: "I will leave the united states for I never will live under his Kingdom before I will submit to his government I will go to the wildes of Texas I will Consider that government a Paridice to what this will be...."[8]

Adam Huntsman may have had one wooden leg, but this was no impediment to his extracurricular activities, apparently. Dirty tricks were part and parcel of political life, and the ever imaginative Crockett took advantage of Huntsman's reputation.

When on the campaign trail, the two candidates often stayed at the same lodgings. On one such occasion, so the story goes, Crockett stomped to the bedroom door of the farmer's attractive daughter using a wooden chair as a crutch. He rattled on the handle, the girl screamed, and Crockett hobbled noisily away. The irate farmer burst in on the bewildered Huntsman with accusations of attempted seduction. Crockett gained the farmer's vote, and probably those of his friends, who heard of the lecherous Huntsman's supposed lusting after the young lady.[9]

During one debate, Black Hawk handed Crockett a coonskin and asked him to assess its quality. Crockett ran his fingers through the pelt and looked closely. "No, sir, 'tis not good fur," Crockett replied. "My dogs wouldn't run such a 'coon, nor bark at a man that was fool enough to carry such a skin."[10]

But, unfortunately for Crockett, Huntsman carried not only the skin but the election too. It was close, though, Black Hawk garnering 4,652 votes to Crockett's 4,400.

Crockett heard rumors that that the Huntsman camp had paid $25 each for votes. "I have no doubt that I was completely Raskeled out of my election," Crockett wrote to his publishers. "I have Suffered my Self to be politically Sacrafised to Save my Country from ruin and disgrace if I am never again elected I will have the gratification to know that I have done my duty."

The *Charleston Courier* observed:

Col. Crockett, hitherto regarded as the Nimrod of the West, has been beaten for Congress by a Mr. Huntsman. The colonel has lately suffered himself to be made a lion, or some other wild beast, tamed, if not caged, for public shew—and it is no wonder that he should have yielded to the prowess of a Huntsman, when again let loose in his native wilds. We fear that "Go ahead" will no longer be either the colonel's motto or destiny.[11]

As coming events would prove, Crockett's "Go ahead" days were certainly numbered. But not just yet. Texas, that alluring Shangri-La of early 19th century America, now beckoned. If Texas was good enough for that other renowned ex–Tennessee politician, Sam Houston, it ought to be good enough for Colonel Crockett. Should Martin Van Buren be elected, what did it matter? David Crockett would be the resident of another country: Mexico. Unless, of course, Texas should split with the mother country and become part of the United States. But there was also talk of Texas becoming a Lone Star State—a republic in its own right.

The exact state of his relationship with wife Elizabeth before moving to Texas appears obscure, but according to an 1882 *Courier Newspaper* interview with daughter Matilda there was, at the very least, reconciliation in the air:

"He came in and said to mother, "Well, Bet, I am beat and I'm off for Texas.... He wanted to move right away but mother persuaded him to go first and look at the country and then if he liked it we would all go.... A few days before he started on his fatal trip he gave a big barbeque and barn dance and everybody far and near were invited. I tell you they had a glorious time. The young folks danced all day and night and everybody enjoyed themselves.... I remember distinctly the morning he started on his journey to Texas. He was dressed in his hunting suit, wearing a coon skin cap."

"I have concluded to drop you a line," Crockett wrote to brother-in-law George Patton on October 31, 1835. "I am on the eve of starting to the Texes—on tomorrow morning. Myself, Abner Burgen, Lindsay K. Tinkle, & our nephew William Patton from the lower country—this will make our company. We will go through Arkinsaw and I want to explore the Texes well before I return."[12]

Next day the four men rode out, their saddle bags well stocked and their powder horns full. Crockett was riding a fine chestnut horse with a white star emblazoned on its forehead. Despite Matilda recalling that he took his new "Pretty Betsy" for this trip, true and trusted old Betsy was the weapon of choice.

David Crockett was setting out in search of green pastures, not a battle. But well publicized events and tensions had been unfolding in Texas for some time now, and fighting had taken place between Texan militia and Mexican troops. In 1833, following the recent rebellion, Santa Anna was elected president of Mexico as a liberal who supported the Constitution of 1824. The following year, however, he recanted. Mexico was not ready for democracy, he said, and imposed autocratic, central power. The Constitution was revoked, many Mexicans were appalled, and revolts broke out. Santa Anna marched against the insurgents and a rebellion in Zacatecas was ruthlessly crushed. "Texas Committees" were organized in the United States to send money and volunteers to fight Mexican oppression.

One volunteer who rode towards Texas at the same time as Crockett was young Daniel Cloud of Kentucky. In December of 1835 he wrote to his brother:

Our Brethren of Texas were invited by the Mexican Government while republican in its form to come and settle, they did so, they

Antonio López de Santa Anna took leave from his presidential duties to teach the Texan rebels a lesson in Mexican justice (Library of Congress).

have endured all the privations & sufferings incident to the settlement of a frontier country and have surrounded themselves with all the comforts and conveniences of live. Now the Mexicans with unblushing effrontery call on them to submit to a Monarchical, tyrannical, Central despotism, at the bare mention of which every true hearted son of Kentucky feels an instinctive horror followed by a firm and steady glow of virtuous indignation. The cause of Philanthropy, of humanity, of Liberty & human happiness throughout the world call loudly on every man who can, to aid Texas.... Our rifles are by our sides and choice guns they are; we know what awaits us and are prepared to meet it.[13]

Daniel Cloud would die with Crockett at the Alamo. The old bear killer, while riding to Texas, must have known there was a good chance of becoming involved in a shooting war.

David Crockett had published his autobiography. He had sat for hist final portrait, in hunting clothes, his hat held aloft as though waving goodbye. The time had come for "Davy" Crockett to ride into the sunset one last time.

22

The Claws of Thirsty,
Rascally and Convict Soldiers

William Barrett Travis was no bear hunting backwoodsman, but he and David Crockett did have a few things in common. Both moved to the promised land for a fresh start leaving debt behind.

Born in Edgefield, South Carolina, in 1809, Travis was the eldest of ten children born to Mark and Jemima Travis. A farming family, they moved close to Sparta, Alabama, where William was educated at the Sparta Academy, founded by his uncle, and later at the academy of Professor William H. McCurdy in Claiborne. The smart young man became something of a bookworm, giving little hint of the firebrand to come. The tall, handsome teenager began teaching, and managed to fall in love with one of his students, the pretty Rosanna Cato. When Travis was 19, and she 16, they married in October of 1828. The newlyweds lived in Claiborne where, a little over nine months later, Charles Edward Travis was born.

A lifetime of teaching was not for Travis and, having studied under noted attorney James Dellet, he began practising law in February of 1828. He joined the Masonic order and was appointed adjutant of the local militia regiment. But business was slow, there being numerous attorneys in the area. The cost of providing for wife, child, and three slaves on loan from his father was more than the young lawyer could manage.

But he was ambitious, and started his own newspaper, writing, editing and publishing himself. This, however, incurred yet more debt, and the newspaper, growing ever thinner, printed its last edition in 1831. Legal action was taken against Travis for unpaid bills, and all was not happy in the marriage fold. "When poverty comes in at the door, love flies out of the window," as the old saying goes. He left his pregnant wife and child as the result of "a feud which resulted in our separation." There were rumors of Travis believing he had not fathered the unborn child. When seeking divorce, Rosanna later wrote that Travis had assured her that he "would return to his family or send for them as soon as he could obtain the means to make them comfortable."[1]

Despite the recent law prohibiting further American settlement, he rode across the Sabine River seeking a new life in Texas during the spring of 1831. He headed for the cluster of log buildings that comprised San Felipe de Austin where he met Stephen Austin and Francis "Frank" W. Johnson, the *alcalde* (mayor). Johnson had moved to Texas from New Orleans for his health and, as a surveyor, had laid out the town of Harrisburg. Hot tempered, he was one of a growing number in favor of Texas splitting from Mexico.

Travis placed a deposit on the league of land allowed new setters and, as he listed himself as single, it would seem reconciliation with Rosanna was not in the air.

He soon moved sixty miles to the new settlement of Anahuac on Trinity Bay. Anahuac means "Place by the water " in Aztec,[2] and being a port of entry for ships from around the globe, the young lawyer soon found sufficient work while he learned the Spanish language and laws. His practice flourished, and an acquaintance said he "enjoyed the respect, confidence and love of the colonists in general."[3]

But then, late in 1831, Mexican soldiers arrived. They were commanded by Colonel John (Juan) Davis Bradburn, an Anglo of Virginian birth. He had fought alongside rebels against Spain for Mexico's independence, and acted as emissary to the United States when the new regime sought recognition.

With the moratorium on import duties due to expire, a customs house along with rules, regulations and fees appeared. And construction of a brick fort began. Texans were not happy. They had become accustomed to free entry and trade for both legal and illegal merchandise, including slaves to be sold in the United States. Far from pacifying his fellow Anglos, Bradburn's rule resulted in friction and discontent, many of his soldiers being ex-convicts untrained in diplomatic skills.

And then word spread of attempted rape. Men answering cries for help burst into a home to find a woman fighting off four Mexican soldiers. Three bolted and made their escape, but the ringleader "was knocked down and securely bound." A posse gathered and some wanted to hang him there and then, but wiser heads prevailed and an alternative was found, as recalled by Creed Taylor, a boy of only 12 at the time:

> A bucket of tar was procured and a heavy coating was applied to the culprit from head to foot. Then, with her hands still bleeding from the effects of her terrible fight, the lady ripped open her feather bed and the trembling wretch was given an ornate dressing of feathers. He was then mounted astride a rail, and in this garb and manner was carried through the settlement and village, and finally turned loose near the fort with a message for Bradburn to the effect that should such another outrage be committed or attempted by his convict gang, the Texans would rise to a man.[4]

Bradburn found himself in a tight situation. He was obliged to apply Mexican law, but his soldiers were second-rate. It would appear, however, that his own attitude was of little help. Even Mexican officials attempting to resolve settlers' land claims found themselves jailed. Bradburn claimed this too came under his jurisdiction, but was ordered by his superiors to release the officials involved.

In January of 1832 Bradburn received a list of 10 men who were allegedly agitating for Texas independence. Along with Anglo antagonism to the new laws, and constant rumors of Texas splitting from Mexico, perhaps insurrection was on the horizon? Would his small garrison come under attack? Bradburn's fears were compounded when he heard an armed militia was being organized, supposedly for defense against Indians. But the nearest hostiles were hundreds of miles away, and militias were forbidden under Mexican law. He arrested their elected captain, Patrick Jack, a lawyer who shared office space with William Travis.

Judge Robert McAlpine Williamson was active in Texas politics and had little time for Mexican rule. At the age of 15, he had contracted tubercular arthritis causing his right leg to draw permanently back at the right knee. In order to walk, a wooden leg was fastened at the knee, giving rise to his nickname of "Three Legged Willie." Under pressure from Williamson, Bradburn ordered Patrick Jack's release.

Buck Travis, as friends called him, was hired to retrieve two slaves who had escaped from the United States. Bradburn had previously given escaped slaves sanctuary, employing them as laborers at the military barracks and on the fort under construction. The colonel ignored Travis' requests for the slaves' restitution, saying they had enlisted in the Mexican army.

Then, one rainy night, a guard was handed a letter by a mysterious, cloaked figure. Bradburn read that 100 militia were approaching, intent on freeing the two slaves by force. But a similar incident had occurred before, with troops deployed only to find out it was a hoax. Not believing "Wolf" when cried the second time, he decided to arrest the most likely culprit; the lawyer who would benefit if the slaves were released.

Bill Travis and Patrick Jack were in their office when a squad of soldiers arrived. Travis was placed under arrest, and Jack followed the squad back to Bradburn's office. There a heated argument took place. Exasperated, Bradburn had Jack also placed under arrest. He and Travis were put in the guard house where they sat for weeks while the colonel gathered evidence for a military trial in Matamoros, 300 miles away. Then guards intercepted a letter being smuggled out. It was a plea for Texans in San Felipe to come and rescue Travis and Jack "from the claws of thirsty, ra[s]cally and convict soldiers."[5]

A few weeks passed and more escape plans came to light. Bradburn had the prisoners moved from the guard house to a more secure location; a kiln used for making bricks for the fort's construction. Two small cannon were mounted to sweep the approach should anyone be so rash as to consider rescue. One of the plotters, Monroe Edwards, was also flung into the kiln.

Word spread through the Anglo colonies, and a force of over 100 militia gathered at Lynch's Ferry. These men were commanded by Brazoria *alcalde* John Austin, a friend of Stephen Austin, but not related, and San Felipe *alcalde* Frank Johnson. While Johnson would become involved in the war to come, John Austin would die the following year during a cholera epidemic.[6]

Bradburn, hearing of their approach, sent out an urgent call for reinforcements. Johnson, Austin and the militia arrived at Anahuac on June 10, 1832, and called for a parley. Johnson demanded the prisoners' release, but Bradburn stood his ground, refusing to capitulate to what he considered an unlawful mob. Austin threatened to attack and reduce the fort to rubble. The prisoners promptly found themselves bound to the kiln floor, soldiers standing over them, ready to shoot. Travis, undaunted, yelled at the top of his voice for the volunteers to forget him and "blaze away on the fort." Despite Travis' bravado, the Texans were confronted by two cannon, and they withdrew to the outskirts of town. Over the next two days shots were exchanged, and 19 Mexican cavalry scouting the militia position were taken prisoner. Johnson sent word for another parley, and offered to swap his captives for those in the kiln. Bradburn agreed to this, but then reneged once the soldiers were freed. He used the armistice to reinforce his position, and soldiers came in from outposts, swelling the garrison to about 160 men. Bradburn sent a challenge for Johnson to come and take the prisoners if he could. But more Texans arrived, boosting the rebel force to over 300, enough to isolate Bradburn's post. To legitimize their actions, the "Turtle Bay Resolutions" were draw up, stating that they were fighting on the side of Santa Anna, yet to show his true colors, and the *santanista* movement then in conflict with the central Mexican government.

A number of cannon were known to be in Brazoria, and on June 13 John Austin led a detachment to retrieve them and recruit more militia. The guns were loaded on a schooner, the *Brazoria*, for transportation down the Brazos River, but Colonel Domingo de Ugartechea at Fort Velasco refused to allow the vessel into the Gulf of Mexico. Austin, leading about 130 volunteers, attacked the post on the night of June 25, and a brisk fight ensued. The *Brazoria*, her mooring lines shot away, ran aground while receiving considerable damage from cannon fire, and the Mexicans counterattacked. The following day, however, their ammunition exhausted, the garrison was forced to surrender. They had lost five killed and sixteen wounded, and the Texans seven killed and fourteen wounded.

The day following Fort Velasco's surrender, a Mexican force approaching Anahuac from Nacogdoches encountered Johnson's volunteers. Negotiations were opened with Colonel José de las Piedras, Bradburn's superior, and agreement was reached on June 29. The prisoners would be released to stand trial, if at all, in a civilian court, and the hapless Juan Bradburn would be relieved of command. The volunteers would abandon hostilities and return to their homes.[7]

Piedras entered Anahuac and carried out his side of the bargain, placing Bradburn's adjutant, Lieutenant Juan Cortina in command, and releasing the prisoners from the kiln. They wasting no time in riding to Liberty township while Colonel Piedras undertook diplomatic action in Anahuac. He departed to Nacogdoches on July 8, leaving the deposed Bradburn behind. Fearing assassination, he begged Lieutenant Cortina to place a guard on his door. Travis, Jack, and Edwards returned to Anahuac on July 11 and, throwing a fandango, got the Mexican garrison rip-roaring drunk. It took only a little persuasion to have most declare for the revolutionary Santa Anna and the *santanista* movement.

Those soldiers wishing to remain loyal to the old regime asked Bradburn to resume command. Instead of mounting a counter revolt, however, the deposed colonel wisely fled. Unable to leave by sea due to Texan vessels blocking Trinity Bay, he and other loyalists took to their heels on land. Bradburn would eventually turn up in New Orleans and seek asylum with the Mexican consul.

The diplomatic Stephen Austin soothed Mexican pride by convincing the authorities that the Texans were hostile to Bradburn only, not Mexico in general. The authorities, already plagued by civil war, found it convenient to accept this. The last thing they needed was the deployment of additional troops to Texas.

William Travis now found himself with celebrity status. He closed his office, ransacked by *soldados* during the siege, and moved back to San Felipe. Here the hero's services were now in demand. Along with the usual legal work, Travis acted in the sale of slaves, and acquired some of his own. This included a woman named Matilda, and a young man named Joe who would accompany his master to the Alamo. He was later described as "five feet ten or eleven inches high, very black, and good countenance."[8]

Money came in. Travis rented one house while buying another, and he purchased more land including 100 acres to the east of town. He became involved in a river steamboat scheme. While business boomed, his social life also blossomed. Despite being a moderate drinker, he enjoyed parties, gambling, horse racing and balls. It comes as little surprise that the well-dressed, spruce young man enjoyed intimate encounters with more than one lady in town.

Rebecca Cummings was an attractive young lady who helped her brother John run an inn on Mill Creek, not far from San Felipe. Buck Travis became a frequent guest, and she soon became his single lady in life. With marriage in mind, he told Rebecca of his family back in Alabama, and she agreed to become his wife once a divorce was finalized. Fortunately Travis' wife had wedding plans of her own, and was prepared to grant not only a divorce, but also custody of son Charles, now aged four.

In 1833 Stephen Austin traveled to Mexico City with the convention's request for statehood and the repeal of the 1830 immigration laws. One month after Austin's arrest in January of 1834, Travis was appointed secretary to the San Felipe city council. This placed him amid local politics and other anti–Mexican firebrands, all surprised and angered by Austin's arrest. With Austin now virtually held hostage, many felt it was best to tread lightly while they sought his release. Thus far action against Mexican troops had supposedly been in support of the new, liberal regime, but Austin's arrest made it seem that President Santa Anna had become a threat as well.

And events would soon prove that to be the case. On June 12, 1834, Santa Anna dissolved the Mexican Congress, becoming virtual dictator, and abandoned the promised liberal reforms that had brought him to power. Rebellion broke out in the provinces, and Santa Anna needed money for his cash-strapped regime.

One way to do this would be to reestablish customs duties on the Anglo settlers who had deposed Mexican garrisons, supposedly in his name, and not paid a peso since.

23

Damn Him, Let Him Take the Horse

The Convention of 1833 had seen Sam Houston aligned with Stephen Austin and others against those who clamored for independence. On April 21, 1835, one year before the Battle of San Jacinto, he swore allegiance to the government of Mexico. By this time he was running a law practice in Nacogdoches, and was boarding with his friend *alcalde* Adolphus Stern and his wife Eva. Sam required little in the way of creature comforts, as seen on a legal document which listed his worldly goods: One table; four chairs; one wash stand; three pans; one set of fireplace implements; one candlestick and snuffer; one sauce pan with lid; one sword with scabbard, and nearly fifty books. These included a bible, texts on international and military law, a dictionary, and the classics, including Shakespeare, Plutarch, Burns, Byron and Homer. Not listed were his substantial holdings in land.

Under Mexican law, all Texan landholders must be of the Catholic faith. In the parlor of the Stern home Houston went through the ritual with the Eva acting as Godmother, and gave her the gift of a diamond ring as a baptismal present. As was the custom, he took a baptismal name and legal documents were signed, for a time, Paul Sam Houston. His certificate of good character records his name as Samuel Pablo Houston.[1]

Stephen Austin, meanwhile, had written from his prison cell accusing firebrands of courting disaster and being responsible for his imprisonment. This was published in Texas newspapers, causing furor, and in April 1835, Houston wrote to radical leader John Wharton, attacking Austin for his "public expose of his want of understanding" and he had "shewed the disposition of a viper without its fangs."[2]

But it was not only Anglos who were hostile to Santa Anna's regime. The native Mexicans in several states rebelled, and on May 12, 1835, the Napoleon of the West, as Santa Anna styled himself, defeated the most determined opposition. Zacatecas leaders had refused to disband their militia as instructed, and confronted Santa Anna with 4,000 men. Santa Anna won the battle, and the infamous "Rape of Zacatecas" took place. The generalissimo allowed his men 48-hours of rapine and pillage; a savage lesson to others who may consider opposition.

Even before hearing of Zacatecas, William Travis wrote to his friend, lawyer David Burnet, on May 22.

I have as much to lose by a revolution as most men in the country. Yet I wish to know, for whom I labor—whether for myself or a *plundering* robbing, autocratic, aristoctratical jumbled up govt.

which in fact is no govt. at all—one day a republic—one day a fanatical heptarchy, the next a military despotism—then a mixture of the evil qualities of all.[3]

The preceding January Mexican customs official José Gonzáles had arrived in Anahuac. To enforce his demands were Captain Antonio Tenorio and a company of troops. Despite a high-taxing regime, Santa Anna's coffers were empty, and the customs duties dropped after Bradburn's expulsion were to be resumed.

The disgruntled Texans undermined the unwelcome authorities; withholding supplies and sabotaging building works they undertook. The Mexicans seized the ship *Montezuma* and its cargo, and delayed incoming immigrants for indefinite periods. Anahuac merchant Andrew Briscoe appealed for help against exorbitantly high taxes on imported goods. His friend Buck Travis attended meetings of disaffected Texans at Harrisburg in early June. In the heat of the moment it was resolved to expel the soldiers and officials from Anahuac. But tempers cooled, and no action was taken.

But not for long. On June 10, in Anahuac, a scuffle took place as Andrew Briscoe and De Witt Harris were placed under arrest, and William Smith was wounded. Word quickly spread through the colonies and a meeting was held in San Felipe. After much discussion it was resolved to free the prisoners and expel the Mexicans; a repeat of proceedings in 1832.

The loud boom of a gun mounted on the sloop *Ohio* announced William Travis' arrival in Galveston Bay. He had with him two dozen other Texans out to make trouble for the Mexican garrison; their password "Victory or death." Two boats rowed ashore, and Travis commenced negotiations with Captain Tenorio. Travis demanded that the garrison of 48 men surrender and leave Texas. Tenorio requested that he be given till the following day to give his answer. Travis declined, giving him one hour.

Tenorio ordered his men to retreat from their quarters and take cover among the trees. The sloop's gun, brought ashore, was fired into the foliage to hasten a decision. Tenorio sent a note asking to meet Travis to discuss terms for surrender. They met under the moonlight, and Travis, despite having half the Mexican numbers, threatened to "put every man to the sword." His bluff worked and Tenorio, following a brief discussion with his officers, agreed to Travis' demands.

Next day the Mexicans were put aboard the *Ohio* and taken to Harrisburg. Travis was applauded by those out to ferment rebellion, but most Texans were upset with this turn of events. Peace advocate James Miller had no time for the pro-war mob, and wrote that "Travis is in a peck of troubles."[4] Resolutions were passed in several communities condemning Travis, and pledging allegiance to the Mexican government. After being wined and dined, however, Tenorio was shipped back to Mexico, not Anahuac. Perhaps even apologetic Texans looked forward free trade once more.

Travis wrote to Colonel Domingo de Ugartechea in command at San Antonio de Bexar to put his side of the story, but the only reply was an order for his arrest along with Frank Johnson and other troublemakers. Travis went into hiding with a $1,000 price on his head, but the local Americans, while apologetic, were not prepared to see the fugitives hang. Simply ignoring the order, they hoped for the best.

But then captured Mexican dispatches revealed that troops were on the way. This included a garrison of 200 men for San Felipe. "Let the towns be garrisoned, and we are slaves," wrote Travis in late August, "We shall give them hell if they come here.... Let us be men and Texas will triumph."[5]

Sam Houston, in his capacity as commander of the Nacogdoches militia, issued in late August a "law of the land" proclamation calling men to arms. They were to repel a supposed attack by a combined force of Mexican troops and Plains Indians. The Texan militia would be required only until reinforced by American troops under General Gaines!—so said Sam Houston. Such an incursion would be a violation of Mexican territory, possibly leading to war with the United States. This would have suited Houston nicely, but it was the last thing on Old Hickory's mind. A few weeks later the Nacogdoches Vigilance Committee, including Sam Houston, petitioned Jackson to enforce existing treaties and prevent Creek Indians from the United States invading Texas at the behest of the Mexican government. No such incursion took place, however, and Jackson took no action.[6]

Stephen Austin had been released by the Mexican authorities without formal charge or trial. He arrived back in San Felipe in mid–September, but the previous peace advocate had now changed his tune. "No more doubts," he said to friends, "no submission. *I hope to see Texas forever free from Mexican domination of any kind.*"[7] On September 21 he put out a call for volunteers to fight the Mexican threat, and volunteers arrived carrying rifles and Bowie knives.

"Come and Take it," had been the defiant words of Colonel McIntosh when told to surrender Fort Morris to the British during the Revolution. The British did not take the fort, and "Come and Take it" now appeared above the embroidered cannon on the flag of Texan volunteers at Gonzales.

Colonel Ugartechea at San Antonio had dispatched 100 dragoons to relieve the colonists of the old brass gun loaned to them in 1831 to repel Indian attacks. Amid early morning mist, a sortie against the Mexican camp took place on October 2. A truce was called, and a parley took place between Lieutenant Francisco de Castañeda and Colonel John Henry Moore. The American told Castañeda his volunteers were fighting to keep their cannon and uphold the Constitution of 1824. The officer replied that he was personally opposed to Santa Anna and sympathetic to their cause. Moore then invited him to join with them in their fight for the Constitution of 1824. Castañeda declined, saying he was a soldier and duty bound to follow orders.

With nothing resolved, the two commanders returned to their lines. The disputed cannon erupted and a load of scrap metal flew towards the Mexican lines. The volunteers fired a rifle volley, and Moore led an advance. Castañeda, having come with orders to avoid conflict if possible, ordered his dragoons to withdraw. They rode back to San Antonio, the "Come and Take It" cannon still firmly in rebel hands.

Sam Houston put pen to paper with a call to the United States for volunteers:

> *War in defence of our rights, our oaths, and our constitution is inevitable, in Texas!* If volunteers from the United States will join their brethren in this section, they will receive liberal bounties of land. We have millions of acres of our best lands unchosen and unappropriated.
> Let each man come with a good rifle, and one hundred rounds of ammunition—and come soon. Our war cry is "liberty or death." Our principles are support the constitution, and *down with the usurper!!*[8]

This appeared in American newspapers, along with numerous editorials, including: "*War in Texas—Gen. Cos landed near the mouth of the Brazos River with 400 men....*

He has issued his proclamation, 'declaring that he will collect the revenues, disarm the citizens, establish a military government, and confiscate the property of the rebellious.' ... Stephen F. Austin has written to several citizens of Nacogdoches, that a resort to arms is inevitable. They have hoisted a flag with 'The constitution of 1824' inscribed on it, and two hundred freemen gathered around it, determined to stand or fall with it."

On October 10, 1835, Texans attacked and captured the Mexican garrison at Goliad. Former black slave Sam McCulloch was wounded during the action, the first man to shed blood in the Texan Revolution.

The same day Houston issued general orders to the Nacogdoches volunteers:

The morning of glory is dawning upon us. The work of liberty has begun. Our actions are to become part of the history of mankind.... Let your valour proclaim to the world that liberty is your birthright. We cannot be conquered by all the arts of anarchy that despotism combined. In heaven and in valorous hearts, we repose our confidence.[9]

"The cause of Texas flourishes in every quarter of the U.S.," Angus McNeill wrote to Houston from Natchez, Mississippi. "You will be overrun with volunteers. 30 or 40 leave in this boat."

Colonel Jim Bowie had been through rough times. In 1833 his young wife Ursula and her parents had died in a cholera epidemic, and now he was on Santa Anna's "Wanted" list of Texan land speculators. He turned up in Nacogdoches on a lame horse and strode into Houston's office. "Houston, I want your horse."

"You can't have him. I have but one, and I need him."

"I'm taking that horse" he said, and strode out.

Houston turned to Caiaphas Ham. "Do you think it would be right for me to give up my horse to Bowie?"

"Perhaps it would be proper under the circumstances."

"Damn him," said Houston, "Let him take the horse."[10]

One week following the "Lexington of Texas," as the Gonzales skirmish became known, Santa Anna's brother-in-law, General Martín Perfecto de Cos, marched into San Antonio at the head of his 400 troops to join Colonel Ugartechea's 350 men already stationed there.

Stephen Austin had been appointed commander of the "Volunteer Army of the People," and advanced with about 300 men from Nacogdoches to remove the enemy from Texas soil. It says something for Texan self confidence that they would march with a far smaller force.

Veteran Noah Smithwick recalled:

Words are inadequate to convey an impression of the appearance of the first Texas army. Nothing short of ocular demonstration could do it justice.... Buckskin breeches were the nearest approach to uniform, and there was a wide diversity even there.... Boots being an unknown quantity; some wore shoes and some moccasins. Here a broad-rimmed sombrero overshadowed the military cap at its side; there a tall "beegum" rode familiarly beside a coonskin cap, with the tail hanging down behind.... Here a big American horse loomed above the nimble Spanish pony ... there a half-broke mustang pranced beside a sober, methodical mule ... there the shaggy brown buffalo robe contrasted with a gaily checkered counterpane.... In lieu of a canteen, each man carried a Spanish gourd ... a fantastic military array to a casual observer, but the one great purpose animating every heart clothed us in a uniform more perfect in our eyes than was ever donned by regulars on dress parade.[11]

Presumably the dapper Buck Travis, riding with them, stood out from the homespun crowd.

Houston did not go with Austin, having been elected a delegate to a "Consultation" of people's representatives at San Felipe. Jim Bowie had also stood for election, but had not received enough votes.[12] Sam Houston arrived to find a quorum was lacking. Most delegates had gone off, guns in hand, and joined Austin's troops. Realizing the importance of defining political issues and aims in legal form, Houston rode out to bring the delegates back. Noah Smithwick recalled Houston's arrival at Cibilo Creek where the volunteers were encamped. Apparently Bowie still had Houston's splendid mount, as Sam "rode into our camp alone, mounted on a little yellow Spanish stallion so diminutive that Old Sam's long legs, incased in the traditional buckskin, almost touched the ground."

"Victory or death" wrote William Barret Travis. Reputed to be drawn from life by compatriot Wiley Martin (Wikimedia Commons).

Houston argued that the advance was premature, and they should fall back and form a disciplined army at Gonzales before taking on Mexican regulars. Austin, however, wanted to push forward, but did agree that other delegates should return to the Consultation. Prominent firebrand Mosley Baker was furious with what he considered Houston's defeatist attitude. Eight years later he falsely accused Houston of getting drunk that night and calling for a pistol to shoot himself, only saved by Bowie's intervention.[13]

Houston and the delegates returned to San Felipe while the rustic Texan army approached San Antonio. Their numbers swelled to about 500 men with new arrivals joining along the way.

Austin ordered Jim Bowie and Captain James Fannin forward with a detachment of 90 men to scout the town and return that evening "with as little delay as possible." Being close to the enemy, Austin wisely wanted his small force intact and undivided.

Near San Antonio Mexican cavalry appeared. Shots were exchanged, then the *sol-dados* rode off. Bowie, ignoring Austin's orders to return, led his command to a bend in the San Antonio River near Missión Purísima Concepción de Acuña, and set up a defensive camp. Towards sunset he sent a courier to inform Austin of his actions. Austin had awaited Bowie with "great discomfortsure," and could not sleep after dark for fear of Mexican attack. Bowie, on the other hand, was reported to have slept soundly all night.

The following morning, October 28, a heavy mist drifted above the river and through Bowie's camp. A Texan sentry saw something through the haze; a Mexican horseman. The crack of two guns broke the morning stillness. The sentry missed while the dragoon shot his powder horn away. Bowie's men sprang to arms and took position around the camp. Soon the mist dispersed to reveal a solid line of Mexican infantry with one field piece across the bottleneck. On the opposite bank cavalry were deployed with another cannon to prevent escape. In all the 92 Texans were confronted by 475 *soldados.* Colonel Ugartechea appeared to be employing a leaf out of Old Hickory's Horseshoe Bend book of 1814.

"When the fog rose it was apparent to all that we were surrounded and a desperate fight was inevitable," Bowie recalled. Unlike Jackson, however, Ugartechea did not press his attack. This allowed Bowie to redeploy his men, cut away brush and throw up defensive works. At 8 a.m. the first heavy firing broke out, the Mexicans delivering disciplined volleys while the Texans fired at will. The Mexican field piece to their front came into play firing canister, the scatter-shot of small metal balls only damaging pecans and foliage amid the trees. Finally the Mexicans charged.

Noah Smithwick recalled:

> "Fire!" rang out the steady voice of our leader, and we responded with a will. Our long rifles—and I thought I never heard rifles crack so keen, after the dull roar of the cannon—mowed down the

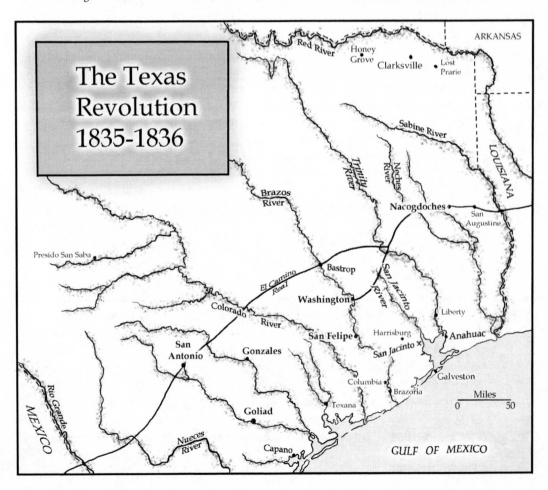

Mexicans at a rate that might have well made braver hearts than those encased in their shriveled little bodies recoil. Three times they charged, but there was a platoon ready to receive them. Three times we picked off the gunners, the last one with a lighted match in his hand; then a panic seized them, and they broke.[14]

The Mexicans, hampered by poor gunpowder and shorter range muskets, had no chance. Bowie had taken a squad around the riverbank and yelled "to the cannon and victory." The Texans scrambled over the bank and, having overrun the position, turned the Mexicans' own gun on them. Blasted with canister, they made a disorderly retreat. And then Travis arrived from Austin's command with a company of mounted men. They pursued the Mexicans as they fled back to San Antonio, leaving at least 60 killed or wounded, while Bowie's loss was one dead and one wounded.[15]

If Gonzales had been the Texan Lexington, Missión Concepción was the Concord Bridge.

24

The Enemy Is Closely Shut Up in Bejar

Just four days after the Concepción fight, David Crockett and his three companions rode south, bound for Texas. Word spread that the famous "b'ar killin'" politician was on his way, and at each town they received a warm reception. They were joined by others, some just to share the ride for a short time. "I rode with Crockett," they'd be able to tell their grandchildren.

On November 10, about thirty men rode into Memphis, Tennessee. Here Crockett was reunited with his old friends Marcus and Amarante Winchester who had helped out after the flatboat debacle in 1826. Unfortunately for Winchester, financial troubles and increasing racial intolerance were now the cause of vexing problems. In 1837, the town council would introduce an ordinance banning "citizens keeping colored wives."[1] Aimed at the partly colored Amarante, Winchester moved his family to a farm outside Memphis where she died two years later.

Crockett took time off for a few days, drinking and socializing with local folk. Despite losing his seat in Congress, they wanted to hear stories and shake hands with one of the most celebrated men of the day. "You may all go to hell, and I will go to Texas," he told them with a laugh.[2]

Once ferried across the Mississippi, Crockett set out once more. Some of those with him had remained in Memphis, and others would depart along the way. The bear hunter and his companions reached the territorial capital of Arkansas, Little Rock, on November 12, 1835.

"Among the distinguished characters who have honored our City with their presence, within the last week, was no less personage than Col. David Crockett—better known as Davy Crockett—the real critter himself," said the *Arkansas Gazette* on November 17. Editor William Woodruff assumed that they were "on their way to Texas, to join the patriots of that country in freeing it from the shackles of the Mexican Government." News of the arrival spread and "hundreds flocked to see this wonderful man, who, it is said, can whip his weight in wild cats, or grin the largest panther out of the highest tree."[3] Crockett was honored with a dinner at the Jeffries Hotel organized by "several anti–Jackson men, merely for the sport of hearing him abuse the administration, in his outlandish style," Woodruff wrote. The backwoodsman took part in a shooting match, was entertained with a puppet show, and told admirers "If I could rest anywhere it would be Arkansas, where the men are the real half-horse, half-alligator breed such as grow nowhere else on the face of the universal earth but just around the backbone of North America."[4] One reporter claimed that Crockett said he would "have Santa Anna's head and wear it as a watch seal."[5]

"The colonel and his party," said the *Arkansas Gazette*, "all completely armed and well mounted, took their departure on Friday morning for Texas, in which country, we understand, they intend establishing their future abode, and in the defense of which we hope they may cover themselves in glory."

Crockett splashed crossed the Red River at the Jonesborough Crossing into northeast Texas. His first night on Mexican soil was spent under the roof of Kentuckian John Styles. Crockett met local settler Isaac Jones and exchanged his watch and $30 for the engraved pocket watch presented by Philadelphia admirers during his 1834 book tour. "I was gratified at the exchange," recalled Jones, "as it gave me a *keepsake* which would often remind me of an honest man, a good citizen and a pioneer in the cause of liberty, amongst his suffering brethren in Texas."[6] The watch would eventually be returned to Elizabeth Crockett, back in Tennessee.

James Clark founded the settlement of Clarksville, about 30 miles south of the Red River. He was away with a party tracking hostile Comanches when his wife Isabella received news of David Crockett's approach. She and another young woman rode out to warn the party of the Indian danger. She found their trail and overtook Crockett on Becknell's Prairie, about five miles west of Clarksville. Here Isabella "prevailed upon him to wait for a guide and recruits to pursue a course bearing towards the east."[7] They rode to the home of Captain John Becknell, a well known pioneer who had opened the famous Santa Fe Trail in 1821. Crockett was advised to "turn south down the Choctaw trail and strike the Spanish trail into San Antonio at Nacogdoches, thus avoiding these wild tribes who were then on the warpath west of here," recalled Isabella's grandson Pat Clark.[8] But it seems the thought of hostile Indians did not concern the bear hunter, as it was decided to go *west* on a hunting trip. While bagging game the party arrived at a grove swarming with bees and honey-laden hives. Crockett liked what he saw and named the place "Honey Grove." A few years later the first settlers arrived, and the township of Honey Grove, Fannin County appeared, where it stands today; the "sweetest town in Texas."

When riding towards the headwaters of the Trinity River they encountered the party led by James Clark. Crockett told him of the young woman who had ridden out to warn them of the Indian threat. "That was my wife," said Clark. "For no other woman would do a thing like that."[9]

Once returned from the hunting trip, Crockett and his companions bade farewell to John Becknell, and continued south towards Nacogdoches. Above them, Halley's Comet was in the sky. Many considered this celestial visitor a harbinger of doom, being blamed for any earthly disaster while it loomed overhead. In 1456 Pope Callixtus 111 had excommunicated the "heavenly" body as an "instrument of the devil."[10] The Great Comet of 1811 had given Tecumseh's words great power, foreshadowing the fall of Fort Mims. Perhaps the more famous Halley's Comet foreshadowed the fall of a more famous fort in Texas.

At Misión Concepción, meanwhile, the battle smoke had scarcely cleared when Stephen Austin and the bulk of the troops arrived. Seeing the captured cannon and dead Mexicans strewn about, Austin wanted an immediate advance against the demoralized enemy in San Antonio. As he issued orders, however, firstly Bowie, and then Fannin, implored him to stay put. They felt that the enemy defenses, including artillery, were far too strong. An attack now with their small force would see the Texans receive a bloody repulse. Austin, in ailing health, reluctantly gave in.

It was decided to isolate the town and attempt to starve the enemy out. Austin sent a dispatch to the Consultation in San Felipe complimenting Bowie and Fannin "on the brilliancy of their victory," but, behind the scenes, felt the chance for a bigger triumph had been lost. Had his orders been obeyed the entire force may well have been in action, and San Antonio captured. He issued new instructions: "Any officer who disobeys orders, shall be immediately arrested and suspended from his command, until a court martial decides his case."[11]

Austin's desire to isolate San Antonio was not helped by 150 men leaving to secure winter clothing. He estimated the enemy at 700, while he had only 450 in camp. "This force," he wrote to the Consultation on November 4, "is but undisciplined militia and, in some respects of very discordant materials. The officers, from the commander in chief down, are inexperienced in military service. With such a force Bexar cannot be effectually invested."[12] The following day he wrote saying 180 reinforcements had arrived with three cannon, and "In the name of Almighty God send no more ardent spirits to this camp. If any is on its way have it turned back or have the head knocked out."

But what exactly were the Texans fighting for? At the Consultation a minority wanted complete independence, but most, including Houston, favored a different course. On November 6, by a vote of 33 to 14, the Consultation commenced organization of a provisional government of Texas as a Mexican state, separate from Coahuila. They demanded restoration of the Constitution of 1824. By not declaring independence, they were keeping on side the many native Mexicans, or *Tejanos*, as they were called, who were hostile to Santa Anna and fighting alongside the American settlers.[13]

The pro-independence men were mollified, no doubt, when one of their own, Henry Smith, was elected governor. Smith had been wounded at the Battle of Velasco in 1832, became *alcalde* of Brazoria, and was appointed political chief of the Department of the Brazos by the Mexican government in 1834. He had the unusual distinction of being married to three sisters of the one family—at different times. Despite the decision for Texas to remain within Mexico, Smith continued to favor independence and was plagued by a contentious relationship with the provisional legislature, known as the "General Council."

On November 12, as David Crockett was arriving in Little Rock, Colonel Ugartechea rode from San Antonio with 250 men to meet Mexican reinforcements marching from Mexico. That same day Sam Houston received a commission from the Consultation: "We, reposing special trust and confidence in your patriotism, valor, conduct and fidelity, do by these present constitute and appoint you to be Major General and Commander-in-chief of the armies of Texas." The commission went on to detail Houston's duties, but also issued a veiled warning: "And you are to regulate your conduct in every respect by the rules and discipline of war adopted by the United States of North America...."[14]

In other words, stay sober and don't thump anyone (other than Mexicans) with a hickory cane.

By concentrating on consultation rather than combat, Houston had worked himself into a more powerful position than sitting with the undisciplined volunteers besieging San Antonio. The Consultation, however, was split by opposing factions, and there were those who loathed Sam Houston, who realized he was the commander of an army that scarcely existed. He was going to need more men and arms, properly trained. But the ragtag army was doing well with what it had. Two days after his appointment, Houston received a letter from Thomas Jefferson Rusk:

> I marched a detachment of forty cavalry within 300 yards of the wall & remained there 20 minutes they were afraid to come out and they fired their cannon but done us no damage all we want is two or three hundred reinforcements ... & some thing like organization. Much depends on you & what you do must be done quickly or it will be too late all that can be done shall be done here but you know we have no organization. Make one forceful appeal to the Convention ... & make the war bear on all alike & whatever may be our fate (not) give up the ship.[15]

Rusk, a lawyer and protégé of John Calhoun, had come to Texas chasing embezzlers who had fled with money invested in a mining company. This money had been gambled away, but Rusk liked what he saw and settled in Nacogdoches with his family. When the troubles broke out, he raised a company of volunteers and took part in the Gonzales "Come and Take It" skirmish.

On November 14 Austin wrote: "The enemy is closely shut up in Bejar, and more and more discouraged every day. All we need is perseverance, and reinforcements to keep up the army. I entreat the Convention to hurry on reinforcements with all possible dispatch.... There is very little prospect that the enemy will get any aid from the interior."[16]

San Antonio de Bexar had a population of about 2,000, some of whom had flown once the shooting started. Tejano Joseph López described the town as:

> built of stone houses one story high, and so placed to form a square before the Church, the streets commencing at each of its Corners, While each one of those streets was well fortified, at the end towards the public square, and a Cannon placed there, that could cut up any body of men to pieces, had they attempted to come that way.[17]

Across the San Antonio River, to the west of town, was the Alamo. The original had been established on the east bank in 1718 by Franciscan Friar Antonio Olivares as Missión San Antonio de Valero. Its purpose was to convert the local Indians to Catholicism and Spanish culture, and keep at bay the French or other powers who may consider occupying the area. The first stick-and-straw buildings were relocated to the west bank in 1724, and moved again a short distance in 1756 where a stone chapel, a convent and white-washed outer walls enclosing about three acres were built. In 1793 the Franciscans moved on and the land was divided between the local Indians, control of the mission passing to the civil authorities. How the name "Alamo" came about is not certain, but in the early 19th century it was occupied by Spanish troops called the Alamo company, named for their hometown south of the Rio Grande, Alamo da Paris. As a result, it became known as Pueblo de la Compañía del Alamo, or simply "the Alamo." An alternate explanation was it being named for cottonwood trees, or *los alamos* which grew alongside irrigation ditches.[18] The Mexican troops reinforced the defenses, but basic construction remained that of a mission, not a purpose-built fortress.

The Alamo
1836

Paul Williams
2013

Drawing by the author.

For the Texans besieging town and fort, change was in the air. The ailing Austin was pleased to hear that he was relieved of command. "I believe my wornout constitution is not adapted to a military command, neither have I ever pretended to be a military man."[19] The Consultation appointed Austin as Commissioner to the United States, along with independence faction leader William T. Wharton, and Branch T. Archer. It would be their job to seek money and arms from within the United States. On November 24 Edward Burleson, frontier Indian fighter and former Tennessee militia colonel, was elected the new commander of the army besieging San Antonio.

Scout Erastus "Deaf" Smith had intended to remain neutral, but upon being barred from his home by the Mexicans, had joined the Texan cause. He brought Burleson word of a Mexican pack train approaching San Antonio, and word spread that it was carrying silver to pay the Mexican troops. Burleson dispatched Bowie with a cavalry detachment, and sent infantry to follow up the attack. What became known as the "Grass Fight" took place when the Texans pitched into the escorting Mexican dragoons. General Cos sent out reinforcements and a fight took place on foot amid ravines until Texan reinforcements drove the Mexicans back into San Antonio. The pack mules were left behind, but elation turned to mortification when the captured "silver" turned out to be grass for the Mexicans' horses, the prairie having been burned by the Texans.

No doubt Bowie's men felt a similar chagrin to that of Caller's men after Burnt Corn Creek when barrels thought to contain valuable gunpowder were found to hold Liverpool salt.

The Texans returned to camp where despondency, low morale and drunkenness became the order of the day. There was little money to support the troops, and a proposed attack was called off due to lack of will. Men started packing their kits and heading for home. Travis, despite praise for capturing 300 Mexican mounts and their escort, returned to San Felipe. The plan was to abandon the siege and spend the winter in Goliad, 95 miles to the southeast. Jim Bowie departed to strengthen the fortifications at Goliad's Presidio La Baha, a fort and mission built by the Spanish in 1747.

But some were not happy to see the campaign dissolve. Benjamin Milam rode in from a scouting expedition, and erupted in fury when told the siege was to be abandoned. He had escaped from a Mexican prison before helping chase Mexicans from Goliad, and had no intention of quitting now. Then a Mexican deserter arrived in camp. The lieutenant told of low morale and hunger among the garrison. The town would fall easily if attacked, he said.

"Who will go with old Ben Milam into San Antonio?"[20] the veteran bellowed with a wave of his hat. A cry went up. There were many volunteers who would follow Ben Milam into San Antonio.

The following morning, December 5, about 200 hundred men formed in two columns under Milam and Frank Johnson for the assault from the south while Burleson kept another 200 in reserve.[21] At 5 a.m. a cannon opened up on the Alamo's north wall, fired by Horseshoe Bend and Gonzales veteran, Captain James Neill. A small force feigned a general attack against that side of the fort.

Drums rattled and bugles blared as Mexican soldiers scrambled from the township towards the Alamo, exactly as the Texans planned. Their main attacking force moved into the sparsely defended town streets from the south, then shooting broke out as a sentry opened fire, wounding Deaf Smith in the wrist. He shot back, wounding the sentry. The alarm was raised, orders rattled out, and *soldados* scrambled back towards the town. The seven cannon in the plaza boomed and Texans ducked for cover as grapeshot and canister flew between the stone and adobe buildings. But they still groped their way forward, digging sheltering trenches and occupying houses along the way, "And the process of cutting port holes commenced," recalled Tejano Joseph Lopez, "which in less than one hour made the houses look like a pigeon nursery, from whence flame and lead poured out as fast as the men could load and fire."[22]

The main streets being death traps from grapeshot, men of the New Orleans Greys scrambled onto rooftops, but came under musket fire from the church steeple. As night came on the gunfire died away, and provisions were brought in to feed the hungry troops. At first light next morning one musket cracked, then another, sleeping men were quickly wide awake, and back on the firing line. A rebel cannon brought in during the night opened fire on the church steeple. "In spite of its being built of stone" the structure trembled, chunks of masonry flew, and "dislodged those rascals," recalled Joseph Lopez.

Burleson kept cavalry on the move around the town in an attempt to prevent Mexicans from escaping. While on the job they gathered beef cattle and grain from surrounding ranches. Most of the horsemen were Tejanos commanded by Captain Juan Seguin, the former *alcalde* of San Antonio.[23]

The battle continued into the next day, and then the next, digging trenches. "The tremendous fire of the Mexicans would have been alarming had it not been for the composed countenance of Milam and Johnson and several Brave Captains," recalled Henry Dance.[24]

It was a slow business, the supposedly demoralized Mexicans putting up a stiff resistance, as recalled by López:

> Several outside batteries were now playing on the Mexicans, and the process of digging trenches had progressed so far, as to enable the Texans to take possession of several houses from which they fired as fast as they could, but they could produce little or no effect on the Mexicans, who were behind shelters some ways off, and well furnished with ammunition. They kept up a hail storm of bullets at a distance.[25]

The Veramendi home, formerly occupied by Jim Bowie's in-laws, was occupied by a Texan squad commanded by Frank Johnson. Mexican officers could be seen darting in and out of a building south of the main Plaza; General Cos' headquarters, apparently. Ben Milam arrived with a plan to assault the building and take Cos prisoner. He stepped outside with a small telescope, but in the next instant fell, a bullet through his temple. A puff of smoke had been seen from a cypress tree alongside the river. A rebel volley rang out, leaves flew, and crack shot Felix de la Garza fell onto the bank before rolling into the San Antonio River.

Ben Milam's loss "put a considerable damper on the army," recalled Henry Dance, but Frank Johnson remained determined to execute their dead leader's strategy. That night, as a cold drizzle fell, a stone house was seized a little distance north of the church. Despite four days with little sleep, fighting, digging trenches, the Texans were finally within yards of the heavily fortified Main Plaza. Many Mexicans felt the fight was lost, and a body of dragoons deserted, riding for the Rio Grande.

But the following day, December 8, there was a joyous blare of music from the military band behind the Alamo's walls. Over 400 Mexican reinforcements had arrived, escorted by Colonel Ugartechea and the 250 men who had left San Antonio on November 12. The mission gates swung open, and the *soldados* tramped in followed by accompanying women and children.[26] Cheers went up from behind the walls; deliverance was at hand, and the plan to capture General Cos was thwarted when his headquarters were moved into the Alamo.

The impressive rescue scene, however, was an illusion.

Having marched hundreds of miles through bad weather on poor rations, the new arrivals, mostly convicts and raw recruits, were exhausted and in no state for a prolonged fight. Rather than bolstering the Mexican force, Cos was now obliged to feed and supply men of little value from his dwindling reserves.

Growing desperate, Cos planned a counterattack. Unable to dislodge the rebels, he decided to go round them and menace their main camp with both cavalry and infantry. Hopefully this would cause a withdrawal from the town.

Herman Ehrenberg recalled:

> About three o'clock in the afternoon we saw and heard for the first time the fanfare of a Mexican assault. A unit of the blue coats numbering about five hundred or six hundred came streaming forth from inside the walls of the Alamo.... After the enemy had paraded around a while in all his splendor, but at a respectable distance from us, and after he had taken a few loads from our cannons, he marched very quietly and without fanfare back into the Alamo. He saw that his ruse had not worked.[27]

That night the New Orleans Greys under Captain William Cooke made a dash on two Mexican guns in the town plaza, but were driven back by a bayonet charge. They forced *soldados* from what was called the Priest's House, and from there continued the fight. Enemy cannon opened fire on the stone building at close range. The Greys threw heavy furniture against the wall, but some balls burst through. Short of powder, and cut off from retreat, Cooke gave his men the option of surrender. But they would stay fighting, they said, and hold this post to the death.

But, from a distance, it appeared that the Greys had been wiped out. Burleson summoned Johnson for an assessment. They had one keg of gunpowder left and the supply of bullets was rapidly dwindling. They were in a desperate situation. Perhaps the game was up; time to withdraw.

But General Cos had his own problems. To consolidate his defense, he ordered a retreat from the town into the Alamo. The demoralized *soldados* had little food, and the starving horses were eating anything including woodwork and the troops' cloaks. The unshackled convict "reinforcements" were mutinous, women and children cried, and a mutinous throng was gathering. Cos went out in an attempt to calm the situation, but was knocked over and trampled in the darkness. The mob were soon quieted down, and Cos, injured both physically and morally, retired to bed.

At dawn the following morning he summoned Captain José Sánchez to his quarters. Seeing no other way out, he told Sánchez to approach the detested *norteamericanos* and get the best possible terms for surrender. In the face of protests from officers determined to fight on, Sánchez raised a flag of truce in the town's central square. Despite the battering of the Priest's House, no New Orleans Grey had been killed, and only one badly wounded. William Cooke emerged from the crumbling building and spoke to Sánchez, who was then escorted through the lines to an astonished Frank Johnson. The Greys had returned from the dead with a Mexican officer wanting to discuss surrender terms. No doubt Burleson, on the brink of withdrawing, could not believe his good fortune.

The resulting agreement allowed for Cos and the Mexican officers to be paroled, and "not in any way oppose the re-establishment of the Federal Constitution of 1824."[28] The troops would return to Mexico with their arms and a small cannon for protection against Indian attack. The bulk of munitions and about 20 cannon would remain in Texan hands. The Mexicans had suffered about 150 casualties, as opposed to about 35 for the Texans, including five dead, a tribute to the accuracy of the long rifles over the Brown Bess muskets of the Mexican force.[29]

On December 14 General Cos and his command left San Antonio, and trudged dejectedly down the El Camino Real towards the Rio Grande. Those too badly wounded to travel were left in Texan hands. With all enemy troops expelled from Texas soil, the war was won—so many thought.

25

Farewell

Three weeks after the Mexican withdrawal from San Antonio, a cannon shot echoed through the streets of Gonzales. But this was not to repel a Mexican attack. A salute had been fired to honor the arrival of David Crockett and his entourage. That night, January 6, 1836, the former congressman was treated to a banquet in his honor, and he addressed the crowd:

> I am told, gentlemen, that when a stranger like myself arrives among you, the first inquiry is, what brought you here. To satisfy your curiosity at once as to myself, I will tell you all about it. I was, for some years, a member of Congress. In my last canvas, I told the people of my district that if they saw fit to reelect me, I would serve them as faithfully as I had done before. But, if not, they might go to hell, and I would go to Texas. I was beaten, gentlemen, and here I am.[1]

The crowd clapped and cheered. Naturally they assumed the famous bear hunter had come to whip several times his own weight in Mexican wildcats, and Crockett rose to the occasion: "We'll go to the city of Mexico and shake Santa Anna as a coon dog would a possum."

Santa Anna would save Davy Crockett the trip. Stephen Austin, even before taking leave, had received word of a huge Mexican force being mustered. The Napoleon of the West was going to lead the army in person, and teach the Texan rebels a lesson, Anglos and Tejanos alike.

Sam Houston knew the war was not won when General Cos trudged despondently towards the Rio Grande. On Christmas day 1835, Houston had arrived at the new settlement of Washington-on-the-Brazos, now serving as the provincial capital. Colonel Fairfax Gray passed through and stayed at John Lott's tavern, "a frame house, covered with clapboards, a wretchedly made establishment, and a blackguard, rowdy set lounging about. The host's wife and children, and about thirty lodgers, all slept in the same apartment, some in beds, some on cots, but the greater part on the floor." The township itself was 'laid out in the woods; about a dozen wretched cabins or shanties constitute the city; not one decent house in it, and only one well defined street, which consists of an opening cut out of the woods. The stumps still standing."[2]

From here Sam Houston was supposed to organize the Texan Army, but "I very soon discovered that I was a General without an army, serving under and by authority of a pretended government, that had no head, and no loyal subjects to obey its commands."[3]

But he proceeded to do what he could. Although San Antonio had been taken from the enemy, he did not see a post that far west as important to defend. The prominent Anglo settlements were in East Texas, and he saw the vital defense line running from

170

the small Gulf port of Capano, northwest to Goliad, then north to Gonzales.[4] He issued instructions for volunteer fighters to concentrate at Goliad and Gonzales, and ordered a company of volunteers, recently arrived from the United States, to Capano.

But others took a different view. San Antonio had been fairly won in combat, they felt, and should be held at all costs. It was on the road to the eastern colonies; the first point of defense.

On December 27 Houston sent out a dispatch:

> To all volunteers and Troops for the Aid of Texas in her conflict.
> I now recommend you come by sea and land at Copano, Coxes Point, or Matagorda. The time employed will be less than one-fourth that which would be needful to pass by land.
> To those who would prefer to pass by land, I would recommend to bring Baggage Wagons; and to bring NO HORSES, unless for teams, or for packing.
> By the first of March the campaign will open.
> Sam Houston[5]

Apparently Houston felt he had enough horses on hand. A man on horseback was far more trouble to feed and maintain than a man on foot, as the Mexicans had experienced when bottled up in San Antonio. Horses required vets, blacksmiths and proper fodder. A cavalry company encumbered with unhealthy animals was virtually useless. Mounted troops, while extremely useful for scouting, raiding, and pursuit, were considered by military men as "the most easily dispensable arm."[6] As a rule, infantry and artillery were the ultimate deciding factors in 19th century combat.

Assuming "campaign opening" referred to first shots fired, Houston's estimation of March 1 would have been accurate had the Alamo not been defended. The first Mexicans would arrive at San Antonio on February 23.

With new responsibilities, Houston attempted to change his drinking ways. On January 2 he wrote to his friend Don Carlos Barrat to tell his friends that, "I am most miserably cool and sober ... instead of egg-nog I eat roasted eggs in my office."[7]

There were about 400 Cherokee Indians residing in East Texas. There was always the chance of the Mexicans sending envoys with promises of land in exchange for attacking the rebellious Texans behind their lines. Houston arranged to meet with the Cherokees for treaty negotiations to keep them out of the coming fight. But first priority was organizing an army. He set off from Washington on January 8, 1836, and rode to Goliad to take command of mustering volunteers.

The following day, David Crockett wrote a letter from San Augustine, about 25 miles east of Nacogdoches. It was addressed to his daughter Margaret and her husband Wiley Flowers in Gibson County, Tennessee:

> My dear Sone & daughter,
> This is the first time I have had the opportunity to write to you with convenience I am now blessed with excellent health and am in high spirits although I have had many difficutys to encounter I have got through safe and have been received by every body with the open arm of friendship I am hailed with a hardy welcome to this country a dinner and party of Ladys have honored me with an invitation to participate with them both in Nacogdoches and this place the cannon was fired here on my arrival and I must say as to what I have seen of Texas it is the garden spot of the world the best land and the best prospect for health I have ever saw is here and I do believe it is a fortune to any man to come here there is a world of country to settle it is not required here to pay down your League of Land every man is entitled to his head right of 400–428 (4,428) acres they may make the money to pay for it off the land
> I expect in all probability to settle on the Bodark or Choctaw Bayou of Red River that I have found no doubt the richest country in the world good land and plenty of timber and the best

springs and good mill streams good range clear water and every appearance of good health and game plenty It is in the pass where the Buffalo passes from north to south and back twice a year and bees and honey plenty

I have a great hope of getting the agency to settle that country and I would be glad to see every friend I have settle there It would be a fortune to them all I have taken the oath of the Government and have enrolled my name as a volunteer for six months and will set out for the Rio Grand in a few days with the volunteers from the United States all volunteers is entitled to vote for a member of the convention or to be voted for and I have but little doubt of being elected a member to form a constitution for this Province

I am rejoiced in my fate I had rather be in my present situation than to be elected to a seat in Congress for life I am in hopes of making a fortune for myself and family as bad has been my prospects

I have not wrote to William but have requested John to direct him what to do I hope you show him this letter and also your brother John as it is not convenient at this time for me to write to them

I hope you will do the best you can and I will; do the same do not be uneasy about me for I am with friends

I must close with great respects your affectionate Father Farewell

David Crockett[8]

"Farewell"—A fitting final word, as this is the last known letter from David Crockett.

The gentleman from the cane had ridden from Nacogdoches to San Augustine after taking an oath of allegiance to the provisional government of Texas. This was required if he was to get a land grant, and if he ever wished to run for elected office at some future time. He signed his oath in the presence of Judge John Forbes but, not happy with the original wording, insisted that the word "republican" be inserted when referring to the government. Crockett was not going to take an oath to some dictatorship that could possibly emerge in future. The judge obliged, and Crockett signed the following:

> I do solemnly swear that I will bear true allegiance to the Provisional Government of Texas, or any future republican Government that hereafter may be declared, and that I will serve her honestly and faithfully against all her enemies and oppressors whatsoever, and observe and obey the orders of the Governor of Texas, the orders and decrees of the present and future authorities and the orders of the officers appointed over me according to the rules and regulations for the government of Texas, so help me God.

Crockett's nephew William Patton also signed an oath. Lindsay Tinkle and Abner Burgin, however, decided that "the greenest state in the land of the free" was still home to them. They packed their saddle bags, bade farewell and good luck to their companions, and rode north towards Tennessee.

Crockett, Patton and some others rode to San Augustine where they were greeted with another cannon salute and welcoming banquet. He stayed in the home of Creek War veteran Judge Shelby Corzine, from where he wrote that last letter to his "dear Sone & daughter." The ex-congressman was approached with the suggestion that he represent San Augustine in the Constitutional Convention, but he was not ready for another bout of politics just yet. Having signed up for military service he had come to Texas to fight, he said, but would "rather be a member of the Convention than of the Senate of the United States."[9] Perhaps Crockett saw a brighter future for veterans who had fought for the Texan cause; be that the Constitution of 1824, or possibly independence if some outspoken men had their way.

Crockett and his companions returned to Nacogdoches where volunteers were mustering. On January 15 he sold two spare rifles to the government for $60, receiving

$2.50 upfront, the rest to be paid at a later date. His horse, rifle Betsy, and other accoutrements went the same way, but to be retained for his own use. For these he was issued another voucher for $240. For the journey ahead, he requisitioned a small tent from the local military supplies.

On January 16, 1836, Crockett rode out with the "Tennessee Mounted Volunteers." It seems more than likely the company was given this name to honor of the famous bear killer from the Volunteer State. Most had arrived from other places, including young commander Captain William B. Harrison of Ohio.[10] The volunteers rode west through native woods which gave way to prairie, the rolling grass only broken by clusters of trees along meandering streams. They crossed the Trinity River and made their way south over 130 miles to Washington-on-the-Brazos to find that Sam Houston was absent, having ridden out on January 8 to organize troops at Goliad.

The General Council, deluded with the capture of San Antonio, had authorized an expedition to sack the Mexican town of Matamoros at the mouth of the Rio Grande. But Houston knew every man and gun were needed to defend Texas soil. Dr. James Grant, as deputy president of the former legislature and *Jefe de Armes*, called himself "acting commander-in-chief," and took men, horses and munitions from San Antonio for the venture.[11] Houston had written to Governor Henry Smith complaining of the Council's actions while "no aid has been rendered for raising a regular force for the defense of the country." He quoted from a letter written by Colonel James Fannin that troops on the expedition should be "paid out of the first spoils taken from the enemy," which, Houston wrote, "divests the campaign of any character save that of a piratical or predatory war." He considered the Council no longer a "constitutional body, nor their acts lawful ... and therefore I am compelled to regard all their acts as void."[12]

Houston rode from Goliad and caught up with the Matamoros expedition at Refugio. He addressed the men, imploring them to stay and defend Texas against the coming threat. Four of the six companies complied, but Grant arrived with authorization for the expedition from the Council. Expecting reinforcements, he continued towards Mexico with the remaining troops.

Lieutenant Colonel James Neill had helped take San Antonio from the Mexicans and now commanded the garrison there. He sent an appeal for men to bolster his depleted garrison. Houston dispatched James Bowie and about 20 men, but not to reinforce the post. They were to blow up the fortifications in town and, subject to Smith's approval, blow up the Alamo and retreat with the artillery to Gonzales.

An exasperated Sam Houston returned to Washington-on-the-Brazos where Governor Smith and the General Council were at each other's throats. Smith, opposed to the Matamoros expedition, had attempted to dissolve the Council who in turn decided to impeach him, nominating James Robinson as his replacement. But Smith refused to resign, insisting he was the lawful authority. Lieutenant Colonel Henry Millard had been dispatched on a recruiting expedition, and wrote to Houston bitterly complaining of broken promises and lack of support: "I have paid no attention to orders received from Gov. Robinson or the council since their dissolution with Gov Smith under whom and yourself I can only acknowledge the right to command operations.... I had reason enough to curse the Dmd council before I left them but their late acts I believe justly brought down the curses of the country."[13]

Houston and others now wanted a new convention; a fresh start with a new, unified government. Nothing was going to be achieved with the current situation. Independence now seemed the best hope to unite the dysfunctional factions, and on February 1 elections were held. The representatives were to meet at Washington-on-the-Brazos to form a new administration on March 1.

Amid this turmoil, on February 5, Houston rode from Washington with Judge John Forbes, who had administered Crockett's oath of allegiance, for the previously arranged Cherokee Treaty Council. Houston's sense of priorities at this time would forever be open to question. Perhaps he was motivated by frustration, simply wishing to rid himself of the bickering and backstabbing which divided the Texan government. He would later state that he had been made commander-in-chief of the Texan army at the Convention, but the General Council then appointed another commander-in-chief, as they had already appointed another governor.[14] "You have no idea of the difficulties I have encountered," he wrote to Smith on January 17. But considering Smith's own vexing problems, he probably had every idea.

James Fannin commanded the garrison at Goliad, and he now recognized alternate Governor James Robinson as the legitimate Texan authority. Robinson wrote to him on February 15:

> Fortify & defend Goliad and Bexar if any opportunity fairly offers, give the enemy battle as he advances, but do not hazard much until you are reinforced as a defeat of your command would prove our ruin—all former orders given by my predecessor, Gen. Houston, or myself, are so far countermanded as to render it compatible to now obey any orders you may deem Expedient.

Robinson signed the letter "Acting Governor and Commander-in-Chief of the Army of Texas.[15]

Unfussed by political turmoil, David Crockett and the Tennessee Volunteers were on the road to San Antonio, about 170 miles west of Washington-on-the-Brazos. They paused at the Chriesman Settlement, later called Gay Hill, where Crockett spent time with the Swisher family including 17-year-old John who would fight at the Battle of San Jacinto. "He conversed about himself in the most unaffected manner," John recalled. "He was of a florid complexion, with intelligent gray eyes. He had small side whiskers, inclined to sandy. His countenance, although firm and determined, wore a pleasant and genial expression. Although his early education had been neglected, he had acquired such a polish from his contact with good society that few men could eclipse him in conversation. He was fond of talking and had an ease and grace about him which, added to his strong natural sense and the fund of anecdotes that he had gathered, rendered him irresistible."[16]

The Tennessee Volunteers had been dispatched to San Antonio by John Lott, proprietor of the Washington Tavern. He was also the local government agent and, with Houston on the road, was responsible for directing companies to their posts.[17] Had Sam Houston been in town at this time, the Tennessee Volunteers would have been directed elsewhere; the history of David Crockett taking a different course.

26

The Key to Texas

On February 8, 1836, Crockett arrived at San Antonio de Bexar. He and a few others were in advance of the main party, due to arrive a few days later. The new arrivals paused on the edge of town and sent word of their arrival to garrison commander, Lieutenant Colonel Neill. Buck Travis and Jim Bowie were also with the garrison. The arrival of the famous Crockett was a tonic for men who felt they were all but forgotten by a dysfunctional government. Jim Bowie guided Crockett's company into the town plaza where the bear hunter, asked to make a speech, stood atop a packing crate. Dr. John Sutherland recalled, "Its sound was familiar to many who had heard it in days past, while the hearts of all beat a lively response to the patriotic sentiments which fell from his lips." Crockett told amusing stories of his past career, including his "go to hell" line, then finished with:

> And fellow citizens, I am among you. I have come to your country, though not, I hope, through any selfish motive whatever. I have come to aid you all that I can in your noble cause. I shall identify myself with your interests, and all the honor that I desire is that of defending as a high private, in common with my fellow-citizens, the liberties of our common country.[1]

So Texas had become Crockett's country. And despite his title of "Colonel," he refused the offer of a command, only considering himself a "high private." This speech made many a man "Colonel Crockett's friend," recalled Dr. Sutherland. The doctor had studied Samuel Thompson's method of treating illness with steam and herbs in Alabama before moving to San Antonio in 1835. His elder brother George had come to Texas as a homesteader in 1829.

Bowie took Crockett to the home of Erasmo Seguin, prominent in Texas politics, and the father of Captain Juan Seguin, where quarters were provided.[2]

Three weeks earlier Bowie had arrived in San Antonio with instructions from Sam Houston. The original order no longer exists, but a January 17 letter from Houston to Governor Smith stated:

> I have ordered the fortifications in the town of Bexar to be destroyed, and if you think well of it, I will remove all the cannon, and other munitions of war to Gonzales and Capano, blow up the Alamo, and abandon the place as it will be impossible to keep up the Station with volunteers. The sooner I can be authorized the better it will be for the country.[3]

The actual removal of guns and blowing up of the Alamo, as opposed to the fortifications in town, are subject to Smith's authorization. This would lead to dispute as Houston would later claim his orders to Jim Bowie were, in fact, to destroy the Alamo. The General Council were under this impression, denouncing him on January 30 for ordering the destruction of all defenses and abandonment of the post.[4]

James Neill felt that San Antonio should be held at all costs and Bowie, taking no more notice of Houston's orders than he had those of Stephen Austin, came to the same conclusion. Bexar was, after all, the provincial capital, and on the road to the eastern colonies. Both Bowie and Neill had fought to take San Antonio from the Mexicans, and they had no desire to hand it back. Men, horses and supplies had been lost to the Matamoros expedition, but Bowie was impressed with Neill's ability to keep the 120-man garrison intact despite the scant resources at hand.

"Colonel Neill and myself," wrote Bowie, "have come to the conclusion we will rather die in these ditches than give it up to the enemy."[5] But it seemed unlikely, even with reinforcements, that they would have enough men to hold the post against a sizable enemy force. And Private David Cummings was not impressed with many volunteers: "Many it is true have left the country and returned home to their friends and pleasures, but of such Texas has no use for and her Agents in the U. States should be careful whom they Send us for assistance we want men of determined spirit that can undergo hardships and deprivation."[6]

Unable to hold both town and fort, preparations were made to defend the Alamo only. Twenty-seven-year-old Green B. Jameson, a lawyer, was appointed chief engineer. It was his task to reinforce the mission's fortifications, and on January 18 wrote to Sam Houston, "You can plainly see by the plot that the Alamo never was built by a military people for a fortress."[7] John Sutherland recalled, "There being no portholes in the walls, it was necessary for them to make an arrangement by which they could shoot over it. This was done by throwing up an embankment against it on the inside."[8]

On January 26 there was a mass meeting of volunteers and town citizens organized by Jim Bowie. Held initially in support of the beleaguered Governor Smith, it evolved into a rousing rally to hold the Alamo at all costs. James Neill presided as a resolution was signed which condemned the General Council for land speculation, illegal appointment of officers for the Matamoras Expedition, and misappropriation of funds. "We cannot be driven from the Post of Honor and the sacred cause of freedom," the declaration said. It expressed unqualified support for Sam Houston who, in fact, wanted the post abandoned. Regardless of the orders, the garrison had no funds to support any defense. Bowie, however, was a man with connections, and raised a $500 loan.

Rumors spread, and on February 2 Bowie wrote to Smith that a rider had come in and "the forces at the Rio Grande are two thousand complete; he states further that five thousand more a little back and marching on.... My informant says they intend to make a descent on this place in particular and there is no doubt about it."[9]

The following day William Travis rode into San Antonio with 30 men. He was now a lieutenant colonel, but far from happy with the lack of support. The company he had raised at Governor Smith's direction had never amounted to the 100 men requested, only totaling 39. Since then he had suffered from nine desertions, and wrote to Smith on January 23 saying his reputation was at stake. He was unwilling to go "into the enemy's country with so little means, so few men, and these so badly equipped."[10] If ordered to proceed, "I feel it is due to myself to resign my commission." He and his small command camped on the Colorado River and awaited a reply. Hearing nothing, Travis finally succumbed to the inevitable. He told his men to mount up, and they rode on into San Antonio to reunite with Bowie and Neill.

The Convention to restore a functional government, due to commence on March 1, was only weeks away. On February 7 Jesse Badgett and Sam Maverick were elected to represent the San Antonio garrison.

David Crockett and companions arrived the following day, boosting morale, and preparations to repel the enemy continued.

Buck Travis walked every day to the Alamo from his headquarters on Main Plaza. He frequently stopped at the last house before the bridge, the home of Tejano Ambosio Rodriguez and his family. Rodriguez heard from a "reliable source" that Santa Anna was on the march with 7,000 men. He told Travis and "advised him to retire to the interior of Texas and abandon the Alamo," recalled Rodriguez's son, Jose. But Travis "could not believe it, because General Cos had only been defeated less than three months." It seemed impossible that Santa Anna "could organize in so short a time an army as large as that.'"[11]

To celebrate Crockett's arrival, a fandango was held in the local cantina on the night of February 10. During the festivities a dusty courier rode in and asked to see Juan Seguin. Told that he was not there, he opened the letter and showed it to Jose Antonio Menchaca, a friend of Bowie's.

According to reporter Charles Merritt Barnes, Menchaca recalled:

> As he was reading the letter, Bowie came opposite him and asked to see it, and while reading it, Travis came up, and Bowie called him to read the letter; but at that moment he could not stay to read letters, for he was dancing with the most beautiful woman in San Antonio. Bowie told him that the letter was one of grave importance, and for him to leave his partner. Travis came and brought Crockett with him.[12]

They discussed the letter's contents; news of a scarcely believable 13,000 Mexicans on the march. But Travis was having a good time, apparently, and said, "Let us dance tonight and tomorrow we will make provisions for our defense." The fandango continued till 7 a.m.

James Neill, meanwhile, had received word of sickness in his family, his wife very ill. The day after the fandango he mounted up and rode out on twenty days leave. Before departure, he placed Buck Travis in command. But Bowie's volunteers had little time for the 26-year-old Travis. The 40-year-old knife fighting legend was their leader of choice.

Travis wrote to Governor Smith on February 13:

> Colonel Neill left me in command, but wishing to give satisfaction to the volunteers here and not wishing to assume any command over them, I issued an order for the election of an officer to command them with the exception of one company of volunteers that had previously engaged to serve under me. Bowie was elected by two small companies, and since his election has been roaring drunk all the time, has assumed all command & is proceeding in a most disorderly and irregular manner—interfering with private property, releasing prisoners sentenced by court-martial & by the civil court & turning every thing topsy turvy.... I am unwilling to be responsible for the drunken irregularities of any man.[13]

Captain Juan Seguin, in his role as magistrate, had Private Antonio Fuentes seized and put back behind bars after Bowie released him. Despite having been on the jury that convicted Fuentes of theft, Bowie was infuriated. His volunteers took up arms and tramped back and forth across the Main Plaza shouting abuse.

But the following day the knife fighter sobered up. A truce between himself and Travis was called. Despite their differences, they agreed on at least one thing: "It is more important to occupy this post than I imagined when I last saw you," Travis wrote to Smith, "It is the key to Texas."

Bowie acknowledged his young rival's existence, and they agreed to share command; Travis the regulars and volunteer cavalry, and Bowie the remaining volunteers. All orders would be jointly signed. They wrote to Governor Smith saying they had overextended their credit in San Antonio and required the $5,000 understood to be in the governor's hands. Without financial support, the men would leave. "There is no doubt that the enemy will shortly advance upon this place, and that this will be the first point of attack. We must therefore urge the necessity of sending reinforcements as speedily as possible to our aid."[14]

The commanders may have known that Santa Anna was on the way, but it seems they kept this to themselves. Private David Cummings wrote from San Antonio the same day, February 14, to his father in Pennsylvania that an attack was not expected "before a month or six weeks as the enemy have not yet crossed the Rio Grande." They were not expected to "make any movement this way until the weather becomes warm or the grass is sufficiently up to support their horses." The defenders must prepare for attack "in the Spring."[15]

As these words were written, Santa Anna was a mere eight days away. Oblivious to the looming danger, Cummins left San Antonio to peruse a land grant on Cibolo Creek. He would be absent when the siege began, but return with the doomed Gonzales Ranging Company on March 1.[16]

David Crockett and ordnance chief Robert Evans spoke to some men tending the horse herd to the east of the Alamo. They asked Crockett if he thought they would be seeing any action. If not, they would end the tedium by returning home. Crockett said that men were leaving as fast as others arrived, and if he were in command he would have given those leaving "shit long ago."[17] What they needed was someone to "carry orders back to hurry up the drafted men and all soldiers at home." Private David Harman promptly volunteered. They walked to Bowie's quarters, but apparently the slightly built 20-year-old did not look the part. He looked awfully young to be a soldier, Bowie said. Harman protested, saying he was quite capable of carrying dispatches, so Bowie gave him the job. He rode out to San Felipe, Liberty, and other places with a plea for men to hasten to the Alamo. Reassigned by Sam Houston to scouting duties along the Brazos, Harmon did not return to share his comrades' fate.[18]

On February 16, Chief Engineer Jameson wrote to Governor Smith with his plans for improving the Alamo's defenses. Regarding the previous Mexican fortifications, he wrote, "They have shown imbecility and want of skill in the fortress as they have in all things else." And two days later he penned, "in case of an attack we will move into the Alamo and whip 10 to 1 with artillery."[19]

This attitude, derived from the previous defeat of Mexican troops, exposed an underestimation of the enemy. But Santa Anna would ultimately make the same mistake himself.

The Alamo bustled with activity, men moving to and fro across the bridge from town to fort, storing supplies in the old stone and adobe buildings behind the mission walls. Under Jameson's direction men toiled in their shirt sleeves with pick and shovel reinforcing fortifications. This included the gun ramparts, and the weak northern wall

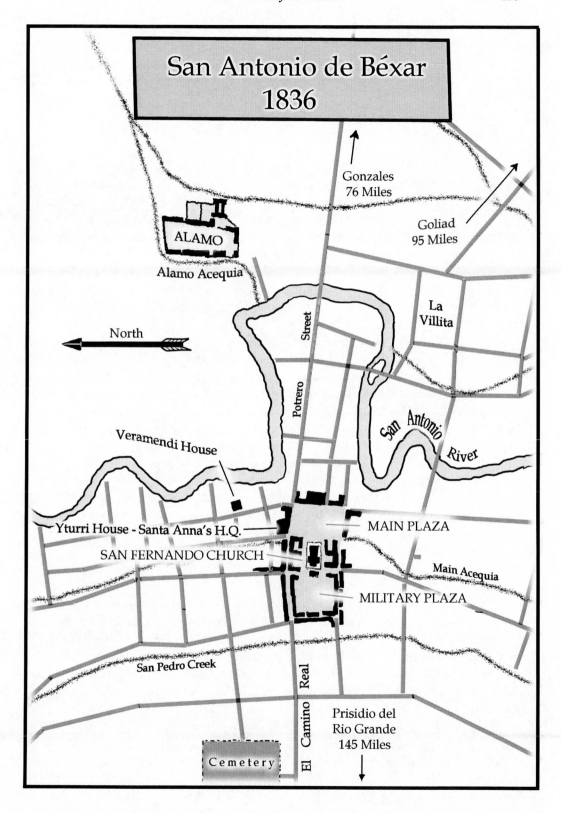

San Antonio de Béxar
1836

Gonzales
76 Miles

Goliad
95 Miles

ALAMO

Alamo Acequia

La
Villita

North

Street

Potrero

San Antonio River

Veramendi House

Yturri House - Santa Anna's H.Q.

SAN FERNANDO CHURCH

MAIN PLAZA

Main Acequia

MILITARY PLAZA

San Pedro Creek

El Camino Real

Prisidio del
Rio Grande
145 Miles

Cemetery

where a system of log bracing backed with earth was under construction. Regarding the fort's cannon, John Sutherland recalled:

> Of these they had some thirty or forty pieces of various caliber, amongst them an eighteen pounder. Most of them had been taken in the previous December when Cos had surrendered. Though they had so many, they were not all mounted. I think not more than twenty were put to use during the siege. They had also obtained from the same source a considerable number of muskets, swords and bayonets, together with any amount of ammunition, which came in play, for of their own they had but a small supply. All were armed with good rifles, single barrel pistols, and good knives.[20]

Purchased by Travis for $12 a head, 65 cattle were driven into the stock pens inside the eastern wall. With cash scarce, only a signed claim was issued as payment. Lead was melted and molded into bullets, barrels were cleaned, knives sharpened, and flint-locks oiled. The percussion cap had been invented over a decade earlier, but flint and flash pan were still the most common firing mechanism. The American and British armies would not adopt the percussion cap as standard issue till the 1840s.

The tools and equipment of blacksmith Antonio Saez were dismantled and moved behind the Alamo's walls. He shod horses and repaired guns while ordnance officer Sam Blair had men cut up old horseshoes to make "grapeshot" for use in the captured artillery.

Artillery Captain Almaron Dickinson, a Pennsylvanian by birth, had eloped with his Tennessee bride Susanna in 1829. They moved to Gonzales in 1831. He was a volunteer in the "Come And Take It" skirmish, then took part in the siege of Bexar. Susanna and their fifteen-month-old daughter Angelina now resided with him in their quarters on Main Plaza. Dickinson drilled his men to load and fire their pieces from their positions around the walls, and barrels of gunpowder were stored in side rooms of the church.

The second story of the long barracks housed the hospital quarters where post surgeon Dr. Amos Pollard cared for the ill with what medical supplies and instruments he had on hand. If San Antonio were to be attacked, there would be casualties, and every military surgeon had a sharp saw handy, removal of disabled limbs being the most common cure. Pollard had been at the opening Gonzales fight, then marched as a volunteer private with Stephen Austin's troops on San Antonio. Not wanting to waste Pollard's medical expertise, Austin had appointed him regimental surgeon the previous October.

But Pollard was unable to help Jim Bowie as a creeping illness set in. Living in the Veramendi house, he was cared for by his father-in-law's niece Juana, recently married to Texan volunteer Dr. Horace Alsbury.[21] Perhaps Bowie's drunken bout had been the final straw for a body already in decline. With Pollard's meager supply of medicines exhausted, Dr. Sutherland and his chest of herbal cures were called in to give a hand. But Bowie's illness was "of a peculiar nature," he recalled, "not to be cured by an ordinary course of treatment."[22]

While Jim Bowie became less active, Travis kept restlessly on the move. Rumors kept arriving of a Mexican advance. He deployed what reliable scouts he had, mostly Tejanos commanded by Juan Seguin. Scout Deaf Smith, wounded in the Bexar siege, rode from the Alamo on February 15. He was concerned with caring for his family who had already traveled east. Travis had him pause at San Felipe to make a report to Henry

Smith. He carried a letter of introduction informing the governor that Erastus Smith "has proven himself to be the bravest of the Brave" and in time of need Texas ought to "protect him and his helpless family."

Governor Smith, however, was in a somewhat helpless position himself. With a rival governor, backed by the dysfunctional General Council, there was little he could do to help either the Alamo or Deaf Smith. The General Council had not managed to assemble a quorum since January 18, and alternate Governor Robinson relied on an advisory council of a few men. Feeling San Antonio was adequately garrisoned, they recommended incoming recruits be dispatched to other towns.

Colonel James Fannin was stationed at Goliad with 400 men. On February 17 Travis dispatched Lieutenant James Butler Bonham with a plea for reinforcements. Bonham was well at home taking part in a revolution. In 1827 he had been expelled from South Carolina College for instigating a student protest against what he said were poor conditions. He studied law and set up a practice in 1830, and became an officer of the Charleston artillery at a time when the states' rights "Nullification Crisis" had threatened war between Old Hickory and South Carolina.

In court, Bonham displayed an apparent empathy with Sam Houston when he caned the opposition, having accused an opposing lawyer of insulting his lady client. An apology was demanded by the judge, but Bonham merely threatened to tweak His Honor's nose. Behind bars for 90 days, the chivalrous Bonham was brought food and flowers by the local ladies who appreciated his stance for women's rights. He moved his practice to Montgomery, Alabama, and when news of troubles in Texas arrived, he helped raise the volunteer "Mobile Greys." He crossed the border and met Sam Houston, who recognized a kindred spirit when he saw one. Bonham was commissioned a second lieutenant of cavalry, and was with Jim Bowie when he arrived at the Alamo on January 19, 1836.[23]

Fannin had arrived at Goliad with troops on February 12. Unlike the Alamo, the La Bahia presidio in Goliad had been purpose built as a fortress by the Spanish. "A square of about three and a half acres is enclosed by a stone wall of eight or ten feet in height," recalled Dr. Joseph Barnard. It had ample barracks and a solid stone church. "The whole structure impresses one strongly the idea of solidity and durability."[24] A lottery for a new name had been held, "Fort Defiance" being the result. Fannin had tried to instill regular army discipline on the volunteers, causing a rift, and an earlier ambitious zeal had been replaced with self doubt. On February 22 he wrote to Governor Robinson, a personal friend, that he wished to be relieved of command. "I feel, I *know*, if you and the council do not, that I am incompetent.... If General Houston will give up all other considerations, and devote himself to the military, I honestly believe he will answer the present emergency.... I would feel truly happy to be in the bosom of my family, and rid of the burden imposed on me."[25]

Two days later he wrote to Robinson again, this time requesting permission to comply with Travis' request and shift his force to San Antonio. This, however, was not approved, and he was obliged to hold "Fort Defiance."

Travis had dispatched others in search of aid, and on February 19 sent Captain James Vaughan southeast to the Rio Grande. He was to recruit men from towns south of the border, and ride to Matamoros. If James Grant's expedition had met with success, at least some men may return to the Alamo once they had pillaged the town. Grant had said there were many Mexicans in that vicinity opposed to Santa Anna. If so, Vaughn was to recruit them as well.

After dark on February 20 scout Blas Herrera galloped into San Antonio. He rattled on the door of his cousin, Juan Seguin, with alarming news. Travis was immediately informed, and at about 9 o'clock held "a council of war." Herrera was brought in, and John Sutherland recalled:

> He reported that he had seen the army crossing the river (Rio Grande) and through enquiry had ascertained that the main body of the force, numbering thirty-five hundred, would travel slowly, but that the cavalry, fifteen hundred strong, would make a forced march for taking the Texians by surprise.

Seguin vouched for Herrera's reliability, but even now "a majority" were not convinced.

> So many false alarms had been given by a degraded class of "Greasers" continually passing to and fro through the west, that no danger was apprehended. Many had persuaded themselves that Santa Anna would never attempt to conquer Texas and the most general reply to any argument to the contrary was that he was afraid to meet us.[26]

Thus their was no firm resolve as the officers returned to their quarters for a good night's sleep.

The following morning Juan Seguin's family, their bags packed, left San Antonio. It was obvious they believed Herrera's account. Travis, not knowing what to believe, issued orders for soldiers outside of town to return. If the report was true, he was determined not to retreat. And, of course, there was still the hope that Fannin's reinforcements would arrive.

On Monday, February 22, thunder rumbled as a light drizzle fell from a dark, cold sky. But the day's work was rewarded that night as the men danced and sang in the cantina. It was George Washington's birthday, a good excuse for a little frivolity. Some warmed themselves by a glowing fire, and pretty *señoritas* danced beneath flickering lanterns as corn liquor, mescal and tequila put worrying rumors out of mind. Live for the moment, live life to the hilt. Tomorrow, the 23rd, was another day.

27

The Enemy Are in View

The following morning, Mexican civilians were on the move. They made their way east with worldly possessions in bumping donkey carts, or carrying them on their backs; infants, pots, pans, garments, blankets, and religious statuettes. Mrs. Rodriguez buried $800 beneath the floor of her home. No doubt many others also buried their savings before joining the flight.

A perturbed Travis must have known why, but he asked some why they were on the move. He wanted the worst confirmed. Going farming, they said. A likely story. He issued orders for the exodus to cease, and his men turned people back. John Sutherland recalled:

> Finally he was informed secretly by a friendly Mexican, that the enemy's cavalry had reached the Leon, eight miles from the city, on the previous night, and had sent a message to the inhabitants , informing them of the fact, and warning them to evacuate the city at early dawn, as it would be attacked the next day.[1]

Travis borrowed one of Sutherland's two mounts and sent a rider to gather the horse herd on the Salado River. The mounts were to be driven back to town with all haste. Travis, Sutherland and another man hastened to the San Fernando Church, situated between Main and Military Plazas. They climbed the old stone bell tower, the highest structure in town, and peered to the southwest. Nothing could be seen. Travis and Sutherland left the soldier with instructions to toll the bell should the enemy come in sight.

Travis returned to his quarters while Sutherland accompanied Nat Lewis to his store. Lewis believed the enemy was near and asked Sutherland to help him take an inventory of his stock, saying that he had "some suspicion" that the Mexicans would soon clean him out.

Then the bell clanged, loud and clear. "The enemy are in view," the sentinel cried. Running from the store, Sutherland joined Travis and an excited crowd gathering outside the church. Men scrambled up the bell tower and peered as the sentry pointed southwest. But nothing could be seen except grass and foliage. "False alarm," a man yelled down. The sentry, however, insisted he had seen troops, but "they had hid behind a row of brushwood."

Another false alarm, most thought—no Mexicans, yet again. The crowd disbanded. But Sutherland felt a quick scout was in order. He asked Travis to assign a good man to accompany him, and John W. Smith got the job. Smith, known as "El Colorado," was a local civil engineer and surveyor who had drawn out the town plans for the successful attack on General Cos.[2] He knew the area intimately. As Sutherland mounted up he told Travis that if they returned "in any other gait than a slow pace" he could be sure the enemy was in sight.

Sutherland and Smith rode from town along the main road at "a moderate gait." They had not gone far before they topped a rise to see a host of Mexican cavalry

> well mounted and equipped; their polished armor glistening in the rays of the sun as they were formed in a line between the chaparral and mesquite bushes mentioned by the sentinel, the commander riding along the line, waving his sword, as though he might be giving directions as to the mode of attack.[3]

The two riders wheeled their mounts around and began to gallop back through puddles and mud. Sutherland's horse began slipping and, attempting to halt, somersaulted, throwing rider and gun overhead. Sutherland landed on the roadway, and in the next instant the horse rolled over his knees. Smith dismounted and attempted to pull the stunned animal off the trapped man. The horse, regaining its senses, got up, and Smith assisted the injured doctor to his feet. Sutherland picked up the pieces of his gun, "broken off at the breech," and, despite injuries, remounted. They galloped back towards San Antonio, their rapid pace alerting the garrison that the sharp-eyed sentinel had been right.

The church bell clanged as they galloped into the Main Plaza where David Crockett rode up. He told them that Travis had moved his headquarters from town into the Alamo, and the entire garrison was ordered to do likewise. While many were already quartered behind the fort walls, others occupied the barracks of Military Plaza and houses in town. Gathering possessions, they moved from their quarters and hastened east up Potrero Street. An old woman called out, "Poor fellows. You will all be killed. What shall we do"[4]

In the Alamo, Travis wrote out the first of his letters appealing for help. It was addressed to "Andrew Ponton, Judge and Citizens of Gonzales, February 23, 1836":

> COMMANDANCY OF BEXAR, 3 o'clock P.M. The enemy in large force are in sight. We have 150 men and are determined to defend the Alamo to the last. Give us assistance.
> P.S. Send an express to San Felipe with news night and day.[5]

Smith returned to his house, while Crockett and Sutherland rode towards the Alamo. They splashed cross the river, where they encountered Captain Philip Dimitt and Lieutenant Ben Nobles. Dimitt had designed two distinctive flags of the revolution, the Mexican "1824" tricolor, then another for independence; a blood red arm and dripping red sword.[6] But, according to Sutherland, today Dimitt had no intention of brandishing any sword, bloody or otherwise. He said "there were not enough men at Bexar to defend the place, that it was bound to fall." He insisted that the injured Sutherland leave town and he "would see me safely out," before riding east and seeking reinforcements. Sutherland, however, replied that he must report to Travis first, and may not join Dimitt even then. The captain rode on saying he would wait for Sutherland at his house. Crockett and Sutherland rode in through the Alamo gate amid others who were carrying possessions. Some men "who had sold their rifles to obtain the means of dissipation were clamoring for guns of any kind."[7] Fortunately, muskets and bayonets captured from Cos were on hand. A flock of Tejano women and children took refuge along with their menfolk.

Jim Bowie, along with Juana Alsbury and her younger sister Gertrudis Navarro, vacated the Veramendi House. Despite his failing health, Bowie led a detachment to search deserted houses near the Alamo, and about 90 bushels of corn were lugged behind the walls. Amid chaotic disorganization, the usually inebriate Irish Sergeant William Ward set a sobering example. He stood quietly by the guns on the south wall, "ready to use them." Thirty cattle had been seized and were being herded into the stock pens along the east wall.

The injured Sutherland dismounted and "my knee gave way and I fell to the ground." Crockett helped him to his feet, and they entered Travis' latest headquarters, a room of the Travino home along the Alamo's west wall. The colonel's nib was busily scratching away as he wrote a dispatch. Travis "by this time no longer doubted that the enemy were upon him," recalled Sutherland. The doctor reported what he had seen and, despite his injuries, offered to be of further service. "He replied that he wished me to go forthwith to Gonzales, and rally the settlers, if possible, to his relief." Then Crockett spoke up. "Colonel, here am I. Assign me a position, and I and my twelve boys will try to defend it." Travis assigned him the picket defence line between the church corner and the barracks on the south wall.

Sutherland painfully remounted his horse, then rode out. He moved down the river a short distance, thinking he would encounter Captain Dimitt, but found he had flown the coop. Dimitt would later state that he and Nobles had been dispatched by Travis to scout the enemy, and received word that they would not be able to return due to the presence of Mexican troops.[8]

Near the ford Sutherland encountered El Colorado Smith. He had gathered provisions, locked his store, and was now on his way to Gonzales. His pregnant wife and children were already there, headed for New Orleans. A bugle blared and the two men looked around. Mexican cavalry were moving into Military Plaza in "regular order."

On Main Plaza Captain Dickinson rushed into his home. "Give me the babe; jump on behind me and ask me no questions!" The family mounted up and splashed across the ford, soon joining the throng behind the Alamo's walls."[9]

Nat Lewis, on foot, encountered Sutherland and Smith. Lewis carried whatever he could in saddle bags across his shoulders. The future "Cattle King of Texas" later said he departed because, "I'm not a fighting man, I'm a business man."[10]

Sutherland and Smith were headed for Gonzales, 76 miles to the east, but galloped off down the Goliad road. This was a ruse to delude any Mexicans watching their movements. About one mile down the track they veered left and rode "into mesquite and chaparral brush, following the winding paths that lead through it."

Cavalryman John B. Johnson rode behind them. He was headed for Goliad carrying a dispatch signed by both Travis and Bowie to Colonel James Fannin:

COMMANDANCY OF BEXAR: We have removed all the men to the Alamo where we make such resistance as is due our honor, and that of a country, until we can get assistance from you, which we expect you will forward immediately. In this extremity, we hope you will send us all the men you can spare promptly. We have one hundred and forty six men, who are determined never to retreat. We have but little provisions, but enough to serve us till you and your men arrive. We deem it unnecessary to repeat to a brave officer, who knows his duty, that we call on him for assistance.[11]

But Travis had sent previous requests to Fannin for reinforcements. This latest dispatch has an air of desperation.

Colonel José Vincente Miñon led a 60-man advance guard of the elite Matamoros Battalion into town. Miñon was a veteran hero of Zacatecas and the revolution against Spain. He had taken the central Mexican city of Queretaro defeating 400 soldiers with only 30 of his own. With him was Santa Anna's private secretary Colonel Juan Nepomunceno Almonte, who recalled: "The enemy, as soon as the march of the division was seen, hoisted the tri-color flag with two stars, designed to represent Coahuila and Texas. The President with his staff advanced to Campo Santo (burying ground). The enemy lowered the flag and fled, and possession was taken of Bexar without firing a shot."[12]

Miñon entered San Antonio's Military Plaza to find only wounded Mexican soldiers in the barracks; too badly hurt to evacuate with General Cos. With them was a Mexican doctor and two aides who had stayed to tend their needs as best they could.[13] Miñon's men spread out around the plaza, guns primed, as the gates on the Alamo closed.

Then Santa Anna arrived. Behind him the cavalry, lancers, infantry and artillery of the main army, in five separate units, were spread over many miles. They had begun their march from Saltillo following El Camino Real, the Royal Road, at the very end of January. Following along were hundreds of women and children; families of the soldiers. The disgraced General Cos, in violation of his parole, marched north with a smaller force on February 6. The troops were a combination of conscripts, Indians who spoke no Spanish, and seasoned veterans. And, of course, the much-derided convicts, looked upon with disdain by Santa Anna. Lieutenant Colonel José Enrique de la Peña, however, recalled that General José Urrea, leading a separate command, "found them quite useful, for they were well acquainted with the country, and he had in them excellent guides, skilful scouts who would lead him along suitable routes and would give him timely and important reports."[14]

With Mexico virtually bankrupt, Santa Anna had been forced to give a personal security of 10,000 pesos, extract money from the Catholic Church, purchase rations on credit at twice the normal price, and make deals with loan sharks at unreasonable terms.[15] He had much riding on a successful outcome, and, along the way, had addressed his troops:

> Comrades in arms, our most sacred duties have brought us to these uninhabited lands and demand our engaging in combat against a rabble of wretched adventurers to whom our authorities have given benefits that even Mexicans do not enjoy, and who have taken possession of this vast and fertile area, convinced that our own unfortunate internal divisions have rendered us incapable of defending our soil. Wretches! Soon will they become aware of their folly! Soldiers, our comrades have been shamefully sacrificed at Anahuac, Goliad and Bejar, and you are those destined to punish these murderers. My friends: we will march as long as the interests of the nation we serve will demand. The claimants of the acres of Texas land will soon know to their sorrow that their reinforcements from New Orleans, Mobile, Boston, New York, and other points north, whence they should never have come, are insignificant, and that Mexicans, generous by nature, will not leave unpunished affronts resulting in injury or discredit to their country, regardless of who the aggressors may be.[16]

Mexican Minister of War José Tornel had no doubt of the outcome: "The superiority of the Mexican soldier over the mountaineers of Kentucky and the hunters of Missouri is well known. Veterans seasoned by twenty years of wars can't be intimidated by the presence of an army ignorant of the art of war, incapable of discipline, and renowned for insubordination."[17]

Which bears a remarkable similarity to the British attitude before the Battle of

New Orleans. General Manuel Castrillón agreed with Tornel, predicting that the Americans would not manage a single volley. But Colonel Carlos Navarro had been with General Cos at San Antonio. The Texans were formidable, he replied, who were bound to get off thousands of shots, and those who thought otherwise were badly underestimating the enemy.

Before coming to grips with the rebels on the fertile plains of Texas, there lay a 450 mile trek, much of it through arid conditions, with little forage for cavalry horses and animals dragging artillery and supply wagons. And it was winter. Frigid rain and snow saw wagons bogged and abandoned in muddy quagmires, others swept away by swollen streams. Men, women and children died. Dispirited soldiers deserted. Lieutenant Colonel de la Peña recalled reaching, in early March, the Tinaja de Arroyo Hondo river

> where we found water but, as in the previous journey, no pasture for the beasts. The troops passed the night along a riverbed that protected them somewhat from the north wind but not the snowfall.... Written messages could not be sent the next day, because the ink had frozen in the inkwells and bottles.[18]

No doctors had been provided and no priests were brought along. Hostile Indians swooped on stragglers, and corrupt officers syphoned off funds. But, despite all, Santa Anna was determined to teach the rebels a lesson, and made the expedition happen, something many complacent Texans thought not possible. And the Napoleon of the West may well have had bigger ideas. The previous November he had boasted to French and British diplomats that he would sweep through Texas and "continue the march of his army to Washington and place upon its *Capitol* the Mexican flag."[19]

But it was not the Mexican tricolor that fluttered from the San Fernando belfry on the afternoon of January 23. It was a blood-red flag—no quarter, no prisoners taken. A loud boom and a cloud of smoke was Travis' answer, fired from the Alamo's biggest cannon, the eighteen-pounder on the southwest corner. Santa Anna was entering the plaza with his staff when the ball whistled into town and splashed along a soggy street. De la Pena recalled, "immediately the artillery commander was ordered to set up two howitzers and to fire four grenades."[20] These exploded over the Alamo's walls, but a quick look around revealed no casualties. According to de la Peña, however, these shots "caused the enemy to raise a white flag." But Juan Seguin later claimed, "after the firing a parley was sounded and a white flag raised by the invaders."[21]

Without consulting Travis, Jim Bowie dictated a note to Juan Seguin for delivery to the Mexican commander:

> Because a shot was fired from a cannon of this fort at the time that a red flag was raised over the tower, and a little afterward they told me that a part of your army had sounded a parley, which, however, was not heard before the firing of the said shot. I wish, Sir, to ascertain if it be true that a parley was called, for which reason I send my second aid, Benito Jameson, under guarantee of a white flag which I believe will be respected by you and your forces.[22]

When signing, Bowie crossed out Seguin's traditional "Dios y Federación México" to wrote "God and Texas."[23]

Travis, no doubt, wondered what Green Jameson was doing when he galloped through the gate, white cloth in hand, then rode towards the foot bridge crossing into town. He dismounted and handed Bowie's note to Colonel Juan Almonte. Fluent in English, Almonte was well known in Texas, having traveled through the province in

1834 on a fact finding tour. His report to Santa Anna had revealed the rebellious nature of American colonists who had little regard for Mexican customs and laws.

Bowie's note was sent to Santa Anna, who was busily "quartering the corps of the division." The general took time off to read Bowie's letter and "becoming indignant of its contents, I ordered an aide, who was the nearest to me to answer it."[24] The aide, Colonel José Batras, wrote the response:

> I reply to you, according to the order of his Excellency, that the Mexican army cannot come to terms with rebellious foreigners to whom there is no other recourse left, if they wish to save their lives, than to place themselves immediately at the disposal of the Supreme Government from whom alone they may expect clemency after some considerations are taken up. God and Liberty![25]

Santa Anna appeared to be offering to spare their lives. But for what? Indefinite imprisonment? And those final words, "may expect clemency after some considerations are taken up," was a serious cause for concern. Obviously there would be no marching out to safety with their colors and arms intact. But in any case Travis had not stayed simply to surrender his post. And he was furious with Bowie for having sent his own note. This was a *joint* command, was it not? Travis dispatched Captain Albert Martin, a veteran of Gonzales and the Bexar siege, to the Mexicans with a verbal message. If Colonel Almonte wished to parley with Travis, he was more than welcome. But Almonte said such discussion would be in vain, only able to repeat those terms already presented. According to Juan Seguin, "When informed of this, Travis harangued his men and administered to them an oath that they would resist to the last."[26]

As more troops marched in, Mexican engineers set about cutting off the Alamo's water supply, an *acequia* that ran by the west wall with a separate channel to the interior. The defenders, however, had been hard at work digging a well behind the walls. About a dozen wives and children were given quarters inside the Alamo chapel. No doubt a few mothers glanced with apprehension at the ominous gunpowder barrels stored in rooms nearby. Despite the chapel windows having been enclosed in stone, one fiery spark and the battle would be over for them.

Some Mexicans moved into abandoned homes, or occupied the barracks of Military Plaza. After the privations of the long march, just having a proper roof overhead was a luxury. The infantry battalions were directed to campsites on the Alamo side of the river just south of the clutter of cabins and shacks called La Villita. Some officers set up quarters in the San Fernando Church, beneath the red flag, while others occupied homes around Main Plaza. Civilians who had not fled now found themselves obliged to either move out or share, but many welcomed their fellow countrymen, regardless of what they said when the Texans controlled the town.

Santa Anna set up his headquarters in the Yturri House on Main Plaza, while Colonel Almonte and two other officers, Fernando Urriza and Marcial Aguirre, moved into the deserted home of Major George Nixon, in Nacogdoches at this time. Almonte had brought along his own cook, a free black named Benjamin Harris, hired during a previous trip to the United States.

Eulalia Yorba, 35 at the time, recalled the Mexican arrival:

> Of course, I kept at home with my little boys and never stirred out once, for we women were all terribly frightened. Every eatable in the house, all the cows, lumber and hay about the place were taken by the troops, but we were assured that if we remained in the house no personal harm

would come to us.... I can never tell the anxiety that we people on the outside felt for the mere handful of men in the old fort ... for whom we few residents had previously formed a liking.[27]

In the Alamo, as day's light faded to dark, lanterns were lit. The work of reinforcing the walls with earth continued into the night. Jim Bowie's volunteers must have understood by now that they were going to be taking orders from Travis, like it or not. Bowie was ill, and it was Travis who had given the rousing Liberty or Death speech after hearing Santa Anna's terms. The Mexican arrival had a galvanizing effect. Regular soldiers and volunteers were all in the same boat; or fort, as it turned out. Time to put aside fractious bickering, time for Texans to unite. Peering over the Alamo's west wall, San Antonio de Bexar looked very different this evening. *Soldados*, banners and horses could be seen, and bayonets flashed by lantern light. Campfires sprung up on the adjacent plain where 24 hours earlier only an inky blackness could be seen. Then a Mexican military band struck up, drums rolling, the trumpets playing.

To the Alamo garrison, the fandango of only the night before must have seemed like a distant dream.

28

War Is Raging on the Frontiers

Despite the arrival of more troops—about 1,000 that first day—Santa Anna did not have enough men or time to place the Alamo under siege,[1] and people moved between town and fort. Juan Seguin had meals prepared in town and delivered behind the walls. But during January 24th more troops arrived, and the rest of the army, despite being slowed by rain and mud, plodded inevitably towards San Antonio. The two 7-inch howitzers had already seen action, and six light cannon arrived; two 8-pounders, two 6-pounders, and two 4-pounders. Trailing a long way behind with General Antonio Gaona's infantry were two 12-pounders.[2] These could do serious damage to the old mission walls. Even Cromwell's rudimentary artillery, two centuries earlier, had no problem shattering the solid stone walls of medieval castles during the English Civil War. The Alamo's north wall had been hit by Texan fire during the attack on General Cos. Perhaps James Neill would have been less pleased with his handiwork had he known the rebels would have to make repairs themselves.

But spirits were high. Sam Houston would be rallying troops, and it would take Fannin only three or four days to march to their relief. His gallant 400 were only 95 miles away.

The Mexican troops swept through San Antonio like locusts in a search for food. Breaking into one storehouse, they discovered a cache of shoes. Possibly Santa Anna felt this a good omen. Despite having brought no priests along, the Almighty was on side, making up for the shortcomings of his own commissary department. Had the Texans not underestimated Santa Anna, such supplies would have been destroyed before the Mexican arrival. The shoes were gratefully received by infantrymen whose own footwear was either nonexistent or in tatters after the gruelling march.

But His Excellency had more important things in mind than shoes and sore feet. He ordered a battery to be installed near the Veramundi house which would have a direct firing line of less than 400 yards to the fort. That afternoon the guns boomed and projectiles hurtled towards the mission walls. Inside, shells exploded, women rushed their children inside, and men took cover as shrapnel flew. Round shot hit the west wall while others flew overhead crashing into structures, or bounced across the plaza dirt. These were eagerly gathered by the defenders; so convenient to have the enemy boost their ammunition supply. Despite the barrage, no injuries occurred.

Jim Bowie was already out of harm's way. It seemed as though fate had decreed there was to be only one commander of the Alamo. But the old knife fighter was used to having his own way, like the time he simply took the great Sam Houston's horse.[3]

Now Bowie's illness forced him to relinquish command to Buck Travis, of all people, that stiff, legalistic boy. Bowie, however, was fortunate to have the tender care of Juana Alsbury, assisted by Gertrudis. These ladies were far more agreeable nurses than some bewhiskered volunteer. But, fearing his illness would spread, Bowie had himself removed from the ladies' quarters to a room near the main southern gate. "Sister, do not be afraid," he told Juana, "I leave you with Colonel Travis, Colonel Crockett, and other friends. They are gentlemen and will treat you kindly."[4]

That evening William Travis took stock of their situation, and picked up his eloquent pen once more:

> To the People of Texas & All Americans in the World
> Fellow citizens & compatriots
> February 24, 1836
>
> I am besieged, by a thousand or more of the Mexicans under Santa Anna—I have sustained a continual Bombardment & cannonade for 24 hours & have not lost a man—The enemy has demanded a surrender at discretion, otherwise, the garrison are to be put to the sword, if the fort is taken—I have answered the demand with a cannon shot, & our flag still waves proudly from the walls—I shall never surrender or retreat. Then, I call on you in the name of Liberty, of patriotism & everything dear to the American character, to come to our aid, with all dispatch—The enemy is receiving reinforcements daily & will no doubt increase to three or four thousand in four or five days. If this call is neglected, I am determined to sustain myself as long as possible & die like a soldier who never forgets what is due to his own honor & that of his country—VICTORY OR DEATH.[5]

Travis included a postscript saying corn and cattle had been taken into the fort. "The Lord is on our side," he wrote. Later that night the fort gate swung open, and Captain Albert Martin galloped east with the dispatch. From Gonzales it would be carried to San Felipe where Governor Smith would have 200 copies printed for distribution throughout the colonies. One copy was carried by David G. Burnet to Washington-on-the-Brazos where the Convention delegates, including Sam Houston, assembled on March 1.

From the Mexican viewpoint, José de la Peña recalled:

> In spirited and vehement language, they called on their compatriots to defend the interest so dear to them and those they so tenderly cherished. They urged mothers to arm their sons, and wives not to admit their consorts in their nuptial beds until they had taken up arms and risked their lives in defense of their families. The word liberty was constantly repeated in every line of their writings; this magical word was necessary to inflame the hearts of the men, who rendered tribute to this goddess, although not to the degree they pretend.[6]

News of the earlier messages from the Alamo had already spread. Alternate Governor Robinson had advised Fannin to disregard Houston's orders, but on January 26 he threw factional rifts to the wind: "Gen. Sam Houston Wherever he may be. Send this by express day and night." He wrote of the Alamo situation and asked, "Come quickly and organize your countrymen for Battle. Call the militia out en masse, send your orders East by this Express for that purpose."[7]

Sam Houston had concluded a proposed treaty with the Cherokees, to remain neutral, and upon arrival in Washington-on-the-Brazos his appearance was "that of an Indian chief," noted one observer, "A piece of red flannel with a hole cut in it for his great head to go through for a shirt with a buckskin over-shirt and buck-skin breaches."[8]

On March 2 the Convention, in a drafty, incomplete building, declared Texas independent from Mexico. They were now a lone star republic—if they had their way. As fate would have it, March 2 was Houston's forty-third birthday. "Travis sending for assistance—none to give—had to make a constitution on my birthday—had a grand spree—eggnog—everybody—two days—bad busines—hated it." So wrote historian Mary Austin Holley during an interview with Houston in 1844.[9]

Despite the grand spree, on March 4 Houston was confirmed as the military commander in chief. Noted duellist Robert Potter was the only delegate opposed. The former North Carolina congressman had previously been jailed for castrating a Methodist minister and teenage boy who, he suspected, had violated "the sanctity" of his marriage bed.[10] He had previously served as a young midshipman in the American navy, thus the pugnacious Potter would soon be appointed secretary of the Texan Navy. He would die as violently as he had lived, however, gunned down during a vicious feud in 1842.

Some demanded that they abandon the Convention and rush to the Alamo's aid, but Houston spoke against this. Having gone through factionalized hell, with rival commanders and rival governors issuing contradictory orders, he was determined that a solid, unified government be established if the war was to be won. There were numerous tasks to perform, including the installation of an interim president and office holders till a democratic election could be held.

Houston would later be accused of stating that reports of the Alamo being besieged were "a damn lie, & that all these reports from Travis and Fannin were lies, for there were no Mexican forces there and he believed it was only electioneering schemes on Travis and Fannin to sustain there own popularity."[11] Houston had no shortage of political enemies who well knew once mud is thrown it tends to stick, no matter how improbable the accusation. In his call to arms of December 27th, Houston had predicted the arrival of Mexican troops by March 1,[12] and on March 2 issued:

> ARMY ORDERS—War is raging on the frontiers.... By the last report, our force in Bejar, was only 150 strong. The citizens of Texas must rally to the aid of our army, or it will perish.... INDEPENDENCE IS DECLARED—It must be maintained. Immediate action, united with valor alone, can achieve the great work.[13]

For Houston to be denying the Alamo siege while issuing these words is doubtful to say the least, and it defies logic for him to think Travis would falsify reports which must eventually expose himself as a fraud.

On March 6, Houston rode from the convention leaving the other delegates to complete essential work. He would take command of the troops mustering in Gonzales, he said, to organize the Alamo's relief—too little and too late.

Dawn's first light over the Alamo on January 25, the third day of siege, revealed that many *soldados* had not slept after dark. The clanks of picks and shovels at work had carried through the cold night air as two more batteries were entrenched to the Alamo's south. But the Mexicans had learned to respect the rebels' long rifles, as recalled by Santa Anna's secretary, Ramon Caro: "His Excellency ordered Colonel Bringas to cross a small bridge with five or six men ... the enemy opened fire on this group and killed one man. In trying to recross the bridge the colonel fell into the water and saved himself only by a stroke of good luck."[14]

The Mexican guns opened fire in the morning, doing little damage and taking no lives. The Texans responded with cannon mounted on the western wall.

But at 10 o'clock the picture changed. About 300 *soldados* were seen to advance, sheltered by the structures of La Villita, about 100 yards to the Alamo's south. Ramon Caro recalled that these buildings were "occupied by our troops who suffered the loss of several killed and wounded in the operation." These were elite light infantry under General Castrillón, trained as highly mobile skirmishers. They were armed with the short-barrelled British Baker rifle with an accurate range of over 200 yards. The bulk of the army, trained to fight standing shoulder to shoulder delivering volleys, were armed with "Brown Bess" smooth-bore muskets with an accurate range of only 60 yards. In the field, the light Baker rifle could achieve an average hit score of 1 in 20 shots compared to 1 in 200 for the Brown Bess.[15] The defenders were armed with a variety of firearms including Brown Bess muskets captured from Cos, and possibly Baker rifles from the same source. Many, like Crockett, carried Kentucky long rifles. Although slower to load than the Brown Bess, the long rifle had a range of over 200 yards. Buck Travis carried a double-barrelled shotgun.

The Mexicans advanced until "within virtual point blank shot," according to Travis. The Texans opened fire from outer entrenchments, the south wall, and the timber palisade manned by Crockett and his men. The Mexicans fell back to La Villita which was then raked with grapeshot and canister by Alamo cannon. "Our soldiers, in order to carry out their orders to fire," recalled Caro, "were obliged to abandon the protection that the walls afforded them, and suffered the loss of one or two men, either killed or at least wounded, in each attempt to advance."[16] Charles Despallier, a personal aide to Travis, and volunteer Robert Brown bravely dashed out and set closer houses ablaze. The Mexican artillery on the west bank continued their fire, but after two hours of shooting the assault infantry withdrew. A few rebels had been scratched by flying stone fragments, but none killed. According to Santa Anna, he lost one scout and one corporal killed, and eight wounded.[17] Ramon Caro's account suggests more.

But this skirmish had been no serious assault. It was merely a probe to test the enemy's firepower, and will to resist. Santa Anna knew from townspeople that he was opposed by about 150 effectives. An attacking force would need at least three times the number of determined, fortified defenders to have any hope of success.

Once the battle smoke cleared, Travis returned to his room and picked up his pen. He had written to "All Americans in the World" but now decided to write to just one American in particular: "Major-General Sam Houston, February 25, 1936." Travis wrote that he did not have enough men to defend both town and fort, and had answered the Mexican demand for "surrender at discretion" with a cannon shot. He had sent out couriers seeking help, he wrote, then described that morning's Mexican assault. He also gave the impression of more enemy casualties, writing they "retreated in confusion, dragging many of their dead and wounded." He commended all for their heroism, and mentioned the bravery of certain men, including "The Hon. David Crockett was seen at all points, animating the men to do their duty." Travis concluded with:

> Do hasten on aid to me as rapidly as possible, as from the superior number of the enemy, it will be impossible for us to keep them out much longer. If they overpower us, we fall a sacrifice at the shrine of our country, and we hope prosperity and our country will do our memory justice. Give me help, oh my country! Victory or Death.[18]

But it was more Mexican troops who arrived, not Texan saviors. Santa Anna made plans to encircle the Alamo with entrenchments, and deploy his artillery to the best advantage. But for a hard-working commander, a little recreation was in order. Word had arrived of a very pretty *señorita* residing in town. Her good mother, however, insisted that any intimate relationship be sanctified by marriage. This included even His Excellency Antonio López de Santa Anna. Colonel Miñon happily arranged for one of his men to act out the role of priest. Vestments were borrowed from a clergyman in town, and instructions taken in wedding procedure. The charade was conducted in Santa Anna's quarters, and the groom retired with the beguiled bride for the night. The young lady and a companion later traveled by Santa Anna's carriage to Mexico with 2,000 pesos in hand. Needless to say, Santa Anna's real wife and children, back home, were oblivious to these proceedings.[19]

That night two more batteries were entrenched several hundred yards to the southeast of the mission walls, and the Matamoros Battalion encamped a short distance away. A little further to the east the Doloros Cavalry Regiment pitched their tents. This effectively sealed off the Gonzales Road. But there was more to investing a fort than simply ordering troops to surrounding positions. Replacement munitions and food must be supplied, entrenchments and latrines dug. Despite logistical challenges, the net around the old mission grew tighter.

Again the garrison were called to arms as a sharp-eyed sentry saw a movement in the dark. "On the night of the 25th they made another attempt to charge us at the rear of the fort," wrote Travis, "but we received them gallantly by a discharge of grape shot and musquertry, and they took to their scrapers immediately."[20] But forays of this sort would keep the defenders alert, unable to sleep.

It was decided to send another plea to Goliad for help. There were no volunteers, the result being the selection of Juan Seguin by vote. Travis was not happy with this. Being Mexican, he was best qualified to negotiate with the enemy should the need arise. But being Mexican also gave him the best chance to slip through enemy lines. Under pressure, Travis agreed. At about eight that night, Seguin crept out on foot to the *acequia* east of the fort. Keeping low, he made his way into town where a fellow Tejano, Antonio Cruz y Arocho, had a horse waiting. Together they rode for Goliad.[21]

But that same day, February 25, Fannin had received the plea sent out on the 23rd, "We deem it unnecessary to repeat to a brave officer, who knows his duty, that we call on him for assistance." Fannin decided to leave 100 men to hold Fort Defiance, while the other 300 would march to the Alamo's relief. But there would be no fast, mad dash. They would take four small field pieces, and wagons to carry provisions, powder and shot. The following day they marched out, but had not gone 200 yards when a wagon broke down. After yoking extra oxen, they managed to push, pull and splash the wagons and guns across the San Antonio River, but by nightfall a freezing wind had come on. They set up camp to shelter for the night.

At daybreak their oxen were nowhere to be seen, having strayed during the night. Then news arrived that Mexicans under General José Urrea were advancing from the south. Standing in the cold wind by the river, the bleak situation was discussed; few provisions, ragged clothes and unreliable transport. And Goliad itself was under threat. As "we may expect an attack on this place, it was deemed expedient to return to this post and complete the fortifications," Fannin wrote to Robinson later that day.[22]

While Fannin's men unpacked, the same cold wind that swept through Goliad sent a shiver through the garrison at the Alamo. And it rained. The firearms of the day could fail with damp flints and priming powder, and the Mexican infantry made no real attack. But Mexican cavalry were seen sweeping around to the east, and rebels rode out in defiance. Shots were exchanged to keep them at bay before falling back behind the Alamo's walls.[23]

The Mexicans continued to dig entrenchments in the mud and slush, and their artillery lobbed an occasional shell or cannon ball. These were fired by the two howitzers and two nine-pounders on the town side of the river, at a distance of 400 yards. More Mexican troops marched in, their numbers ever swelling and deploying. But Fannin, no doubt, was marching to the rescue—or so the rebels thought. The damp sentinels peered hopefully through the gloom at the distant hills.

Unless more men arrived, it would be impossible to defend the Alamo's extensive walls against a four-sided attack. Men were put to work cutting gunports in the barracks walls, and entrenchments were dug around the doorways. This created redoubts for a last stand should the Mexicans breach the mission walls.

A squad moved out to demolish abandoned shacks, and timber was dragged in. This provided firewood for heating and cooking fresh meat supplied by the cattle in the eastern pens. Other shacks were torched to prevent their use by the enemy, and to provide a clear line of fire.

The following day, the 27th, Travis dispatched James Bonham again to hurry Fannin along. At the very latest his reinforcements should arrive by March 3.[24]

The generalissimo wrote a dispatch to his second-in-command, General Vicente Filisola, who was still marching towards San Antonio with the rear guard. Santa Anna commended the march of General Ramírez y Sesma's "meritorious division," the first to occupy San Antonio, "which the traitors shall never again occupy." He summarized events over the last few days, and concluded with:

> From the moment of my arrival I have been busy hostilizing the enemy in its position, so much so that they are not even allowed to raise their heads over the walls, preparing everything for the assault which will take place when at least the first brigade arrives, which is even now sixty leagues away. Up to now they act stubbornly, counting on the strong position which they hold, and hoping for much aid from their colonies and from the United States of the North, but they shall soon find out their mistake.[25]

29

My Orders Must Be Obeyed

"These men were defiant to the last. From the windows and parapets of the low buildings, when taunted by the Mexican troops, they shouted back their defiance in the liveliest terms. A tall man, with flowing hair, was seen firing from the same place on the parapet during the entire siege. He wore a buckskin coat and a cap all of a pattern entirely different from those worn by his comrades. This man would kneel or lie down behind the low parapet, rest his long gun and fire, and we all learned to keep at a good distance when he was seen to make ready to shoot. He rarely missed his mark and when he fired he always rose to his feet and calmly reloaded his gun seemingly indifferent to the shots fired at him by our men ... this man I later learned was known as 'Kwocky.'"[1]

This recollection, attributed to Mexican Captain Rafael Soldana, may be true. And according to child survivor Enrique Esparza, "Crockett seemed to be the leading spirit. He was everywhere. He went to every exposed point and personally directed the fighting. Travis was chief in command, but he depended more on the judgement of Crockett and that brave man's intrepidity than upon his own."[2] Perhaps this recollection is also true.

But it's hard to know where truth ends and myth begins in regard to Davy Crockett and the Alamo. "Col. Crockett was a performer on the violin, and often during the siege took it up and played his favorite tunes," recalled Susanna Dickinson.[3] Speaking of which, we have Crockett and Scotsman John McGregor playing "duelling" instruments, fiddle and bagpipes, to entertain the garrison with their own music rather than that of Santa Anna's military bands. Perhaps this story, handed down from Susanna Dickinson's granddaughter, was true.[4] It is also said that Crockett narrowly missed shooting Santa Anna himself. Colonel Almonte noted on February 27, "In the afternoon the President was observed by the enemy and fired at."[5] If the bear hunter did the shooting he did not know who the target was. Despite having heard otherwise, Travis thought General Joaquín Ramírez y Sesma in command, Santa Anna yet to arrive.[6]

The weather warmed again over the next few days, but the Mexicans kept up a constant harassing fire as more troops trudged in. Santa Anna deployed both them and his artillery around the Alamo, moving closer, growing bolder. But spirits behind the old walls remained high. "I have so fortified this place, that the walls are generally proof against cannon-balls," Travis wrote, "and I shall continue to entrench on the inside, and strengthen the walls by throwing up dirt."[7]

Santa Anna did all in his power to wear down the enemy before any large-scale attack. Of a night time bugles blew, men shouted and shots were fired as though the walls were about to be stormed. Then the Mexicans would fade back into the dark, leaving the defenders tense and alert. No doubt David Crockett recalled that chilling, firsthand account of Fort Mims heard over two decades earlier, "having forced the inhabitants to one side of the fort, where they carried on the work of death as a butcher would in a slaughter pen." Perhaps this prompted, "I think we had better march out and die in the open air. I don't like to be hemmed up," as recalled by Mrs. Dickinson.[8]

On January 29 more Mexican reinforcements marched into Bexar, and during the afternoon the battalion of Allende were deployed to the east of the fort. The Napoleon of the West and his staff rode around the Alamo and planned the coming assault. His two 12-pounders could wreak havoc on the walls, and most likely force the rebels to surrender. But these larger guns had not arrived as yet, and there would be little glory if there was no battle. No artist would want to paint that, the enemy merely surrendering. "It was therefore necessary to attack him," recalled José de la Peña, "in order to make him feel the vigor of our souls and the strength of our arms." Prudent men, however, "understand that the soldier's glory is the greater, the less bloody the victory and the fewer the victims sacrificed."[9]

But Napoleon Bonaparte was famous for victorious battles, not sparing lives. Perhaps the famous painting of the *Empereur* crossing the Alps on a white charger passed through Santa Anna's mind. Perhaps he considered commissioning such an image of himself. At least he was scouting the Alamo on a fine horse, not crossing the Alps riding a mule, led by a guide, as did Napoleon in reality.

Santa Anna had received news of Fannin marching from Goliad. At midnight General Sesma moved out with a force of infantry and the cavalry who had been stationed on the Gonzales road. They marched towards Goliad to intercept Fannin, not knowing he had turned back. "Try to prepare yourself to fall on them at daybreak, and in a way that you are able to surprise them," ordered Santa Anna. "In this war you know there are no prisoners."[10]

The following morning, March 1, Santa Anna received word from Sesma saying he had scouted the countryside as far as Tinaja without seeing any sign of an enemy advance. His exhausted troops marched back into San Antonio during the day. The only achievement had been to leave the Gonzales road open for Alamo reinforcements the previous night. At 3 a.m. 32 volunteers from Gonzales had ridden in. One man was wounded in the foot, but not by a Mexican bullet, a sentry having shot from the wall first and asked questions later. With the "Gonzales Ranging Company of Mounted Volunteers" was John "El Colorado" Smith who had ridden out to get help the day the Mexicans arrived. Private David Cummings, of the original Alamo garrison, also rode with them. He had been off inspecting land when the Mexicans arrived.

On the outskirts of San Antonio an English speaking stranger had offered to guide the company in. They accepted and followed, but as he kept his distance, Smith smelt a rat. "Boys," he said, "I think it's time to be after shooting that fellow." The stranger dug in his spurs and bolted into the night.[11]

The arrival of reinforcements was like a tonic to the garrison. But only 32? Surely more were on the way. Travis had been very sparing with return fire, conserving powder and ammunition, but the arrival prompted some celebratory target practice. Much activity had been noticed around one house on Main Plaza, perhaps occupied by the

Mexican commander. From a 12-pounder on the west wall two shots were fired. One ball crashed into the plaza, while the other struck home, bits flying from Santa Anna's headquarters, the Yturri house. The Texans put up a cheer, but the generalissimo was spared any injury, having ridden out at midday to inspect troops entrenched around an old mill some 800 yards to the north of the fort.[12]

The following day General Sesma took breakfast with Santa Anna. While discussing progress, word was received of corn in abundance at the Sequin farm. Lieutenant Menchaca was dispatched with *soldados* to bring the corn in, every bushel needed to feed the hungry troops. In the afternoon Santa Anna reconnoitred once more and discovered a "covered road," presumably a rough track barely visible through the brush, which led to the Alamo. Possibly this was where the Gonzales volunteers had ridden in. He ordered in troops to seal the breach.[13]

The following day, March 3, dawned bright and clear with no wind. An ideal day to keep the powder dry, and for the rebels to remind the Mexicans they were ready to fight. Men lined up along the western wall, and a cloud of gun smoke erupted as the long rifles spoke. Then the cannons roared, sending balls flying into San Antonio. Despite the Mexicans having encircled the fort with entrenchments, and fired at least 200 shells, not a single rebel had died, morale remaining high.

And the Mexicans were still not able to seal the gaps. In broad daylight, courier James Bonham galloped in from between the powder house and the enemy's upper encampment where a second blood-red flag fluttered in the breeze. He had encountered no resistance, and no cavalry rode in pursuit. Bonham carried a dispatch from Major "Three Legged Willie" Williamson, the friend of Travis from those Anahuac events which had eventually led to war.

Williamson wrote that 60 men had set out from Gonzales, Fannin was marching with 300 men and four pieces of artillery, and another 300 were mustering in various towns "and no time will be wasted in seeking their help for you.... For God's sake, hold out until we can help you."[14] All this sounded encouraging, but of the supposed Gonzales 60, only 32 had arrived.

"Col. Fannin is said to be on the march to this place with reinforcements," wrote Travis the same day, "but I fear it is not true, as I have repeatedly sent to him for aid without receiving any."[15]

Not only Americans had entered the Alamo, but also Tejanos who had no time for Santa Anna's rule. With no sign of help, however, ammunition dwindling, entrenchments closing in, some had slipped away by March 3. Travis wrote "we have but three Mexicans now in this fort; those who have not joined us in this extremity, should be declared public enemies, and their property should aid in paying the expenses of the war." How many Tejanos were actually in the Alamo at this time is a matter of dispute.

A sudden burst of distant cheering. Rebels moved to the ramparts and peered towards town. The church bell began to ring, and cannon fired a salute. More troops were marching in to the rousing music of the bands. Travis assumed Santa Anna had finally arrived. But de la Peña described the real scene:

> We marched towards Bejar arriving between four and five in the afternoon within sight of the enemy, who observed us from inside their fortifications.... There were 846 combatants, which,

with the commanders, officers and drivers, came to that number. We entered Bejar just as the roar of cannon and martial music were announcing General Urrea's victory.[16]

General Urrea's victory. The Matamoros expedition, which had depleted San Antonio's garrison, had come to an abysmal end on March 2. De la Pena described the news:

> General Urrea had news that Dr. James Grant was returning from Rio Bravo, where he had marched with a party of select riflemen in an exploratory excursion to round up horses ... next morning he dealt Grant a decisive blow; forty-two men were killed including Grant ... his capture would have been more useful than death ... but the bait of his silver saddle, of his flashy firearms and other valuable jewels provoked one of the "cossack" officers shamefully to murder him, thus bringing ignominy upon himself. Eyewitnesses assert that Grant defended himself courageously, and on many occasions we have heard General Urrea lament his death.[17]

The victory was a small one, but for the Mexicans important; the tide turning, revenge for the humiliations of the past.

Santa Anna now had 2,400 men on hand to do battle with the defenders of the Alamo. He tightened the siege, and "a battery was erected to the north of the Alamo within musket shot," recalled Colonel Almonte. Santa Anna rode on a tour of inspection with brother-in-law General Cos who listened to His Excellency's plans to breach the same walls he had previously defended. But at least the enemy had let Cos live and return to Mexico. They had not hung a blood-red flag from the belfry, and decreed "no prisoners."

Captain José Sánchez, riding with Santa Anna, had mixed feelings, "the eagerness that his excellency presents himself to needless danger (God holds him in his hand)." But a few days later, "The assault has been decided upon. Why does senor Santa Anna always want his triumphs and defeats marked with blood and tears."[18]

The blood and tears yet to come, Travis sat in his room and wrote his final words from the Alamo, dated March 3, 1836. He wrote to a friend, Jesse Grimes, enclosing a separate letter to be forwarded, to his fiancée Rebecca Cummings. To Grimes he described events including the "shower of bombs and cannon balls" and urged the Convention to declare for independence and "we will then understand, and the world will understand, what we are fighting for."

Another letter was written "To the President of the Convention." Travis outlined events to date, and "during this period the enemy has been busily employed in circling us with entrenchments on all sides, at the following distance, to wit—in Bexar, four hundred yards west; in Lavilleta, three hundred yards south; at the powder-house, one thousand yards east by south, on the ditch, eight hundred yards north." He expressed doubt that Fannin was coming, and "I look to the colonies alone for aid; unless it arrives soon, I shall have to fight the enemy on his own terms ... the victory will cost the enemy so dear, that it will be worse for him than defeat. I hope your honorable body will hasten on reinforcements, ammunition, and provisions to our aid, as soon as possible." Travis gave details of the munitions required, and said the garrison was to be put to the sword if the Alamo was taken, but "Their threats have no influence on me or my men, but to make all fight with desperation, and that high-souled courage which characterizes the patriot, who is willing to die in defense of his country's liberty and his own honour.... God and Texas! Victory or Death!!"

But this was not the final Travis letter. He hastily wrote on a scrap of paper, just before the courier left, to his friend David Ayers at Washington-on-the-Brazos whose family had been caring for Travis's young son, Charles.

Take care of my little boy. If the country should be saved, I may make for him a splendid fortune; but if the country be lost and I should perish, he will have nothing but the proud recollection that he is the son of a man who died for his country.

El Colorado Smith was to carry these last dispatches, along with letters from others in the garrison. Travis told Smith the reinforcements should bring 10 days rations, and he would fire the big 18-pounder; morning, noon and night. This would let the world know the Alamo still held out.

Slumbering *soldados* encamped around the old sugar mill sprang from their blankets when a rattle of gunfire broke out. Were the rebels attempting to break out to the north under cover of dark? As troops moved in and the Mexicans returned fire, Smith rode from the main gate in the south, then turned eastward towards Gonzales.

Next day, March 4, Santa Anna called a council of war. To his senior officers he "expounded on the necessity of making the assault," recalled de la Peña. Colonel Almonte was present and recalled "After a long conference, Cos, Castrillón, Orisnuela, and Romero were of the opinion that the Alamo should be assaulted." Castrillón, however, felt prisoners should be taken.

Santa Anna was eating a chicken leg as the conference went on, and held it up. "What are the lives of soldiers more than of so many chickens? I tell you, the Alamo must fall and my orders must be obeyed at all hazards. If our soldiers are driven back, the next line in their rear must force those before them forward, and compel them to scale the walls, come what may."[19] But some wanted to await the arrival of the two 12-pounders, due on March 7. These heavier guns would shatter the fort's walls. Santa Anna, Almonte and Sesma said they did not wish to wait, while others prompted caution. "In this state things remained—the General not making any definite resolution," recalled Almonte.

As the Mexican officers discussed their options field pieces battered the Alamo's north wall. In response the Texans employed the same tactics as Sailing Master Loomis 20 years earlier. Their red-hot, glowing cannon balls, however, struck no powder supplies and the bombardment continued. Colonel Ampudia felt the use of such tactics was "in violation of the rights of man and of war."[20] Perhaps he had heard of the mangled bodies at Negro Fort.

By March 5 the Mexicans had fired 68 exploding shells and 334 cannon balls at the Alamo.[21] During the night they advanced their northern battery, now only about 250 yards away. Being entrenched in a dry water course, it was relatively safe from return fire. The defenders could no more silence these guns than they could the howitzers and the two 9-pounders west of the river. Only a few days before Travis had written of how the walls were "generally proof against cannon-balls." Despite claims of projectiles crashing through the north wall this may have remained the case, or effective repairs were promptly carried out. Mexican accounts reveal this wall being intact at the time of the final assault. It had to be scaled, there being no breach to storm through.

But Santa Anna made his decision, if ever it was in doubt. The attack must proceed. "Some, though approving this proposal in the presence of the commander in chief, disagreed in his absence," recalled de la Peña, "a contradiction that revealed their weakness, others chose silence, knowing that he would not tolerate opposition, his sole pleasure being in hearing what met with his wishes."[22]

The Mexican artillery became silent; a change in tactics was under way. The rebels peered over the Alamo's walls. The *soldados* were seen working like ants on some new venture. They were constructing something—scaling ladders. There was to be an all-out frontal attack, the numbers involved overwhelming.

If the legend is to be believed, now was the time for William Travis to unsheathe his sword and draw a line in the sand. Although no proven fact, such a gesture would have been consistent with the man. Mrs. Dickinson recalled something similar having taken place: "On the evening previous to the massacre, Col. Travis asked the command that if any desired to escape, now was the time, to let it be known & to step out of the ranks. But one stepped out. His name to the best of my recollection was Ross."[23]

Having assembled his men, he confirmed the dire situation they already knew. There was no longer any hope of reinforcements. He would stay and fight—Victory or Death. But others could depart with honor if they so wished. He asked those who chose to stay and fight to cross the line. All took those fateful steps except one—50-year-old Frenchman Louis Rose. It was a wall of the Alamo he crossed that night, not the line in the sand.[24] He was not prepared to die, he said, and, speaking Spanish, he had a good chance of making it through the enemy lines.

So Travis had prevailed, the rest would stay and fight; Crockett, Bonham, Dickinson; even Jim Bowie had asked that his cot be carried across the line—so the story goes. But that blood-red flag on the church steeple told the full story—there was little hope any would survive.

Time for reflection, perhaps. Travis must have seen the inevitable result; weeping sweethearts, wives and children of the slain. And what of the women and children still in the fort? This included Susannah Dickinson and her infant child. Would they all end up impaled on Mexican bayonets? The men had chosen to fight, Victory of Death. But did he still not have an obligation to avoid, if possible, the coming bloodshed and grief?

Santa Anna later claimed that he offered to spare the garrison's lives "characteristic of Mexican kindness" before the final assault.[25] But General Filisola told a different story. The "same evening" that plans for the attack were made, "March 5," Travis, "through the intermediary of a woman," proposed the surrender of fort and arms on condition that all lives would be spared. "No guarantees for traitors," was the response. Like a toreador in the bullring, Santa Anna's final victory must come with the thrust of a bloody sword. "With this reply it is clear that all were determined to lose their existence, selling their lives as dearly as possible," recalled Filisola. "Consequently they were to exercise vigilance in order not to be surprised at any time of the day or night."[26]

One last courier, 21-year-old Kentuckian James Allen, rode from the Alamo towards Goliad with a plea for help. Then William Travis did his rounds, chatting to the men, and visiting the women and children in the chapel. He took a gold ring with a black cat's-eye stone from his finger, and threaded it on some twine, which he then placed around the neck of little Angelina Dickinson. Surely Santa Anna's blood-red flag would not apply to a 15-month-old girl.

The determined men kept a brave face, despite the apparent oblivion that awaited them. Should they die, the Alamo and their sacrifice would always be remembered. Dr. Joseph Barnard, in San Antonio a few months after the battle, wrote a letter which appeared in the *Missouri Argus* on August 26, 1836:

There were several friends who were saved, and who informed me that the men, with the full prospect of death before them, were always lively and cheerful, particularly Crockett, who kept up their spirits with his wit and humor. The night before the storming, he called for his clothes that had been washed, stating that he expected to be killed the next day, and wished to die in clean clothes, that they might give him a decent burial.[27]

While David Crockett donned his clean clothes, and checked flintlock Betsy, Santa Anna made final preparations for the storming of the Alamo. He was much agitated, according to Almonte's cook, an African American freedman named Ben Harris, and ordered that coffee should be available all night. The general and Almonte went out at midnight, and returned at about 2:30 a.m. when Santa Anna ordered coffee. He threatened to run Ben through if it was not brought instantly. Almonte remarked that the assault "would cost them much." Santa Anna replied, "It was of no importance what the cost was, that it must be done."

Senior officers had received Santa Anna's orders signed by General Juan Valentín Amador: "2 o'clock P.M.—Secret.... At 4 o'clock a.m., the columns of attack shall be placed at musket-shot distance from the first entrenchments, ready for the charge, which shall commence at a signal to be given with the bugle from the Northern Battery." Four columns would make the assault from different directions, but the north wall would be the principal target. General Cos with would lead the assault on the northwest corner, Colonel Francisco Duque the north wall center. Between them they would command about 750 men. Colonel José Romero, with about 430, would assault the east, and Colonel Juan Morales, with 125, the south. General Sesma's 375 cavalry would stay back, deploying principally to the east. It would be their task to prevent the escape of either rebels, or *soldados* who found a blaze of grapeshot not to their taste. About 1,700 men would take part in the initial assault, and Santa Anna himself would command an additional 400 reserve troops from the northern battery.[28]

"The first column will carry ten ladders, two crowbars and two axes; the second, ten ladders, the third, six ladders, and the fourth, two ladders. The men carrying the ladders will sling their guns on their shoulders, to be enabled to place the ladders wherever they may be required." No doubt Santa Anna knew of the New Orleans debacle when the redcoats left the scaling ladders behind. He would show the great, imperial British how to win a fight. And those in the assault "will wear neither overcoats nor blankets, or anything that may impede the rapidity of their motions. The Commanding Officers will see that the men have the chin-straps of their caps down, and that they wear either shoes or sandals.... The arms, principally the bayonets, should be in perfect order."

And finally, "His Excellency expects that every man will do his duty."[29] Lord Nelson had signalled "England expects that Every Man will do his Duty" just before his historic naval victory at Trafalgar in 1805. No doubt Santa Anna felt confident that what these words had done for Nelson, they would also do for him.

Except, of course, the commander's death.

30

A Horrible Carnage Took Place

"Come on boys, the Mexicans are upon us, and we'll give them hell!" So yelled Buck Travis as he rushed to the north wall, shotgun in hand, sword at his side. His slave Joe ran with him, rifle primed and ready to fire. Officer of the day John Baugh had rushed to Travis' quarters yelling that the assault was under way.[1] Outlying rebel pickets had given no warning before being overrun.

"Viva Santa Anna!" could be heard along with the roll of drums and blare of trumpets. Those defenders who had been slumbering leapt to their feet. The *soldados* "were hit by a hail of shrapnel and bullets that the besieged men let loose on them. The attackers at the first sound of the trumpet were all on their feet at their respective posts with their arms at the ready," recalled General Filisola.[2]

"Ladders, beam, bars, pick axes &c were carried," recalled one *soldado*, "although the distance was short, we suffered through canister shots that shot down more than forty men."[3]

José de la Peña charged with Duque's column from the northern battery:

> The bands from all the corps, gathered around our commander, sounded the charge; with a most vivid ardor and enthusiasm, we answered that call which electrifies the heart, elevates the soul, and makes others tremble.... Alerted to our attack by the given signal, which all columns answered, the enemy vigorously returned our fire, which had not even touched him but retarded our advance. Travis, to compensate for the reduced number of defenders, had placed three or four rifles by the side of each man, so the initial fire was very rapid and deadly. Our columns left along their path a wide trail of blood, of wounded, and of dead.... It could be observed that a single cannon volley did away with half a company of cazadores from Toluca, which was advancing a few paces from the column.[4]

Ramon Caro, recalled," The first charge was met with a deadly fire of shot and shell from the enemy, the brave colonel of the Toluca Battalion, Francisco Duque, being among the first who fell wounded. His column wavered as a result of his fall while the other three columns were held in check on the other fronts."[5]

Stormed with rifle ball and canister, Cos' column attacking the northwest corner diverged left and met with Duque's column along the north wall. At the same time Romero's force attacking the east diverged right to avoid fire from the eastern wall where three cannon were mounted on the church upper platform. "All united at one point, mixing and forming a confused mass." Despite Santa Anna's planning, the infantry found themselves like the British at New Orleans. "The few poor ladders that we were bringing had not arrived because the bearers had either perished on the way or had escaped," recalled de la Peña, "Only one was seen of all those that were planned." But

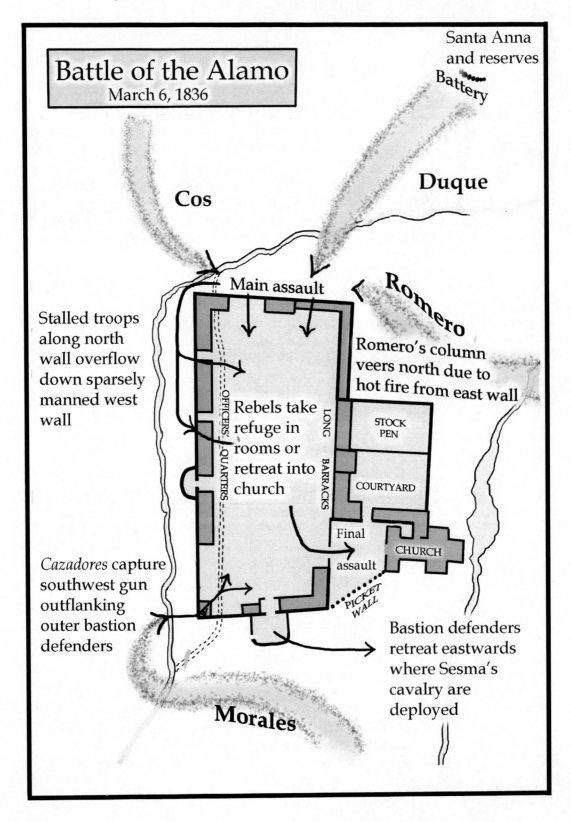

Battle of the Alamo
March 6, 1836

Santa Anna and reserves

Battery

Duque

Cos

Main assault

Romero

Romero's column veers north due to hot fire from east wall

Stalled troops along north wall overflow down sparsely manned west wall

OFFICERS' QUARTERS

LONG BARRACKS

STOCK PEN

Rebels take refuge in rooms or retreat into church

COURTYARD

Final assault

CHURCH

PICKET WALL

Cazadores capture southwest gun outflanking outer bastion defenders

Bastion defenders retreat eastwards where Sesma's cavalry are deployed

Morales

the *soldados* were able to grasp obtrusions from timber repairs carried out on the north wall, and at various points missing ladders soon appeared.

Travis discharged his gun into the Mexicans, but was then hit by a shot to the head. His piece dropped over the wall as he fell back on the earthen slope against a cannon wheel. Joe, his gun discharged, retreated back to the rooms along the west wall.

"A lively rifle fire coming from the roof of the barracks and other points caused painful havoc, increasing the confusion of our disorderly mass," recalled de la Peña. "The first to climb were thrown down by bayonets already waiting for them behind the parapet, or by pistol fire, but the courage of our soldiers was not diminished as they saw their comrades falling dead or wounded, and they hurried to occupy their places and to avenge them, climbing over their bleeding bodies."[6]

Seeing the attack waver, Santa Anna ordered in not only his 400 reserves, but the general staff as well. Within the township, civilians watched the frightening spectacle with awestruck fascination. Eulalia Yorba, watching from the house of a Spanish priest recalled:

> It seemed as if there were myriads of soldiers and guns about the stone building. There was volley after volley fired into the barred and bolted windows…. Occasionally we heard muffled volleys and saw puffs of smoke from within the Alamo, and when we saw, too, Mexican soldiers fall in the roadway or stagger back we knew the Texans were fighting as best they could for their lives.[7]

"Before the Sapper Battalion, advancing through a shower of bullets and volley of shrapnel, had a chance to reach the foot of the walls, half their officers had been wounded," recalled de la Peña. On the north wall the crack of gunfire mingled with the cries of men as knives and bayonets slashed. Santa Anna recalled that the garrison "defended themselves relentlessly. Not one soldier showed signs of desiring to surrender, and with fierceness and valor, they died fighting."[8]

Eulalia Yorba continued to watch:

> It seemed as if ten thousand guns were shot off indiscriminately …The smoke grew thick and heavy and we could not see clearly down at the Alamo, while the screams of crazy, exultant Mexicans increased every moment…. Next several companies of soldiers came running down the street with great heavy bridge timbers. These were quickly brought to bear as battering rams on the mission doors, but several volleys from within the Alamo, as nearly as we could see, laid low the men at the timbers and stopped the battering for a short time.[9]

The rebels held their own, but the press of Mexicans at the north led to an overflow, *soldados* moving along the undermanned western and eastern walls. The Mexicans scrambled up and over, outflanking the defenders who were now forced to abandon the north wall. The Mexicans "rushed into the grounds after about three quarters of an hour of terrible fighting," recalled one *soldado*.[10]

"Great God, Sue, the Mexicans are inside our walls!" yelled Almaron Dickinson to his wife in the church, "All is lost! If they spare you, save my child."[11] With "a parting kiss," she recalled, "he drew his sword and plunged back into the strife."

Amid the battle smoke and struggling mass, it was hard to tell friend from foe. "Some of our men suffered the pain of falling from shots fired by their comrades, a grievous wound indeed, and a death even more lamentable," recalled de la Peña. A young officer, José Torres, seized the flag of the New Orleans Greys, only to be cut down moments later. "He died at one blow without uttering a word, covered with glory, lamented by his comrades."[12]

Outflanked and vastly outnumbered, those rebels still standing fell back to the barracks rooms previously fortified as a final redoubt. "Not all of them took refuge, for some remained in the open looking at us before firing," recalled de la Peña. He saw one man he thought to be Travis who "would take a few steps and stop, turning his proud face towards us to discharge his shots; he fought like a true soldier. Finally he died, but he died after having traded his life very dearly." From the rebels in the fortified barracks there "issued an infernal fire."

To the south, Colonel Morales force of 125 *cazadores* captured the 18-pounder on the southwest corner. Having charged from the south, the main gate protected by the outer bastion would have been their primary target. But "Three or four brass cannon," recalled Yorba, "were placed directly in front of the main doors of the mission. They did serious work." Forced to veer left by grapeshot and rifle fire, the *cazadores* headed for the southwest corner where they took "advantage offered by some small jacales with walls of stone and mud," stated Filisola. Here Morales regrouped his men. The two ladders carried by the *cazadores* were thrown up against the west wall where "by a daring move they seized a cannon which was placed on a platform." The southwest corner and cannon were now in the hands of 100 or more Mexicans. Colonel Morales left no account of his assault, but logically his men would have delivered angled musket fire down on those Texans who had forced them to veer left; the defenders of the outer bas-

The Mexicans capture the 18-pounder on the southeast corner. Outflanked, the defenders holding the main gate bastion are forced to abandon the post. Sesma's cavalry await them in the distance (drawing by the author).

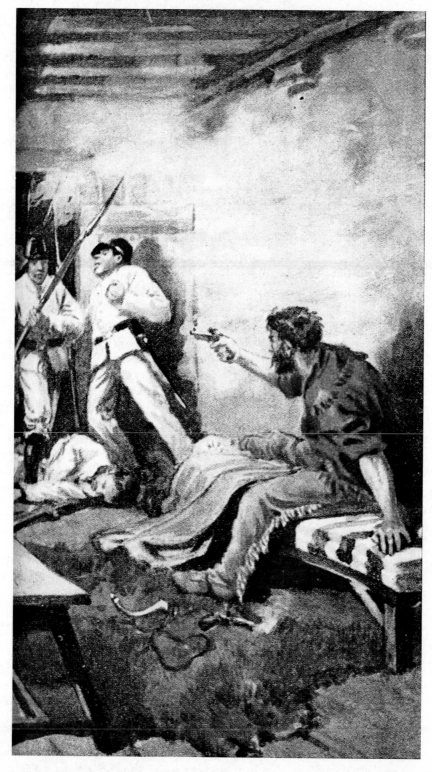

How exactly Jim Bowie died is not certain, but may well have gone down fighting as portrayed in this illustration (Wikimedia Commons).

tion. Morales' other men, meanwhile, moved down the gun ramp into the compound behind the main gate. The bastion defenders were now totally outflanked and isolated from their compatriots fighting inside. At Fort Mims, the battle lost, some had fled the carnage, and the same occurred at the Alamo. Those defenders outside the gate were now forced to abandon their post, the only hope of escape east towards Gonzales where no Mexicans could be seen.

But, in the dark, the lances of Sesma's cavalry awaited them.

As the bastion rebels beat a hasty retreat, Morales' *cazadores* moved to support the efforts of General Amador who, according to Filisola,

> made use of the enemy's own artillery and turned them towards the doors of the small inner rooms in which the rebels had taken cover. From there they opened fire on the troops who were coming down from the parapet to the patio or plaza of the aforesaid enclosure so that all were finally killed by shrapnel, bullets and bayonets. Our losses were great and deplorable.[13]

"A horrible carnage took place, and some were trampled to death," recalled de la Peña. And Ramon Caro recalled, "Generals Amador and Ampudia trained their guns on the interior of the fort to demolish it as the only means of putting an end to the strife."[14] The Mexicans, their blood running hot with the fury of the moment, burst into the rooms and fought hand-to-hand with those inside. Other *soldados*, following on through the smoke, "fired their shots against friends and enemies alike." Jim Bowie died in his sickbed, delirious, or perhaps fighting back with pistols and a Bowie knife.

De la Pena continued his description of the chaos:

> In the midst of this thundering din, there was so much confusion that orders could not be understood, although those in command would raise their voices when the opportunity occurred. Some may believe that this narrative is exaggerated, but those who were witnesses will confess that this is exact, and in truth, any moderation in relating would fall short.[15]

Seeing the battle lost, some rebels attempted to surrender. But that red flag had meant no quarter, and the Mexicans, furious with so many comrades killed, were in no mood for mercy. If any remained in the hospital, they too died. But disabled men threatened with death can not only fight but act with heroism. (Despite his injured foot, hospital patient Corporal Scheiss was to receive the Victoria Cross for his valor at the Siege of Rorke's Drift in 1879.)

Sheltering indoors, Juana Alsbury, clutching her infant son, told sister Gertrudis to open the door and yell that only women were here; don't fire in. Gertrudis opened the door and called out only to be abused and have her shawl ripped from her shoulders, then the Mexicans burst in. A rebel also entered, attempting to protect Juana, only to be bayoneted and shot. Another came in seeking protection behind the women, but suffered the same fate. The soldiers ransacked the room before an officer arrived, then a Mexican sergeant, Manuel Perez, entered the room. A relative of Juana, he took the women in charge and placed them in safety with a colored woman belonging to Bowie.[16]

The last bastion to fall was the southeast corner; the church and the picketed courtyard. The rebels' own cannon were turned on the solid church doors, blowing them open, then the *soldados* rushed in. One rebel was killed while trying to fire the powder magazine. The remaining defenders on the artillery platform were either shot or bayoneted, as were those below. Three rebels rushed into the room where Susanna Dickinson cowered with daughter Angelina. Hotly pursued, the men fell beneath the enemy bayonets. In the fury of the moment, the woman and child may well have been killed, but through the acrid smoke a Mexican officer appeared. He called out for Mrs. Dickinson, "If you wish to save your life," he said in English, "then follow me." Clutching her little girl, "I followed him, and although shot at and wounded, was spared." The wound "between the knee and ankle," was superficial, probably a graze, but Angelina remained uninjured.[17] "I recognized Col. Crockett lying dead and mutilated between the church and the two-story barrack building, and even remember seeing his peculiar cap lying by his side," Susannah recalled.

A glow of sunlight filtered through the haze drifting between town and fort. "The roadway was thronged with Mexican soldiers with smoke and begrimed faces, haggard eyes and wild, insane expressions" recalled Eulalia Yorba. Daylight revealed a ghastly sight throughout the smoke shrouded fort. "The stones of the church wall were spotted with blood, the doors were splintered and battered in."[18] Wounded Mexicans groaned as their comrades stripped and mutilated dead rebels who lay strewn about the blood-soaked ground. Some continued to shoot into the lifeless bodies. A triumphant Santa Anna rode in and cast his eyes about. He dismounted and walked among the dead. "These are the chickens," he said to Captain Urriza. "Much blood has been shed, but the battle is over: it was but a small affair."[19] The Napoleon of the West had won bigger, bloodier victories than this, and another battle was yet to come. Sam Houston was out there somewhere to the east.

A small group of prisoners were brought out under the protection of General Castrillón. He asked that they be spared. But Santa Anna was displeased to have his red flag ignored. Several officers, "thrust themselves forward," recalled de la Peña," and with swords in hand, fell upon these poor defenceless men just as a tiger falls upon his prey."[20] He identified one of the victims as "the naturalist David Crockett." And he may have been correct. But de la Peña had misidentified another man as William Travis. Perhaps he was mistaken here, also.

There were other reports of Crockett being executed by Santa Anna's order. But San Antonio acting *alcalde* Francisco Ruiz said he asked to have the bodies of "Travis, Bowie and Crockett shown to him." Santa Anna's own report, written the same morning, stated: "Among the corpses are those of Bowie and Travis, who styled themselves colonels, and also that of Crockett, and several leading men."[21] These suggest Crockett already lying among the dead, not executed in front of Santa Anna. Ruiz said he saw Crockett's body in a different place to that sighted by Mrs. Dickinson: "Towards the west, and in the small fort opposite the city, we found the body of Col. Crockett."[22]

Mexican officers went into town to solicit help for the wounded. Eulalia Yorba was one who responded, and recalled:

> I remember seeing poor Colonel Davy Crockett as he lay dead by the side of a dying man, whose bloody and powder stained face I was washing. Colonel Crockett was about fifty years old at the time. His coat and rough woolen shirt were soaked with blood so that the original color was hidden, for the eccentric hero must have died of some ball in the chest or bayonet thrust.[23]

It will never be known for certain how and where Crockett met his end. It has been a matter of much debate. But, "The Hon. David Crockett was seen at all points, animating the men to do their duty," Travis wrote on February 24. It is fair to assume the old b'ar killer fought the same way on March 6, regardless of how he died.

Travis' slave Joe was taken prisoner. William Gray recalled his account:

The work of death being completed, the Mexicans were formed in hollow square, and Santa Anna addressed them in a very animated manner. They responded to it with loud vivas. Joe described him as a light build, slender man, rather tall—sharp, but handsome and animated features, dressed very plainly; somewhat *"like a Methodist preacher,"* to use the negro's own words.[24]

A Methodist preacher—dressed in black. It would seem the generalissimo took no chances and wore camouflage for the nighttime assault.

Exactly how many fell on either side is not known. One hundred eighty-three defenders killed would seem to be the most common figure; the 150 mentioned in Travis' letter plus the 32 Gonzales volunteers, but others state more. A few hours after the battle Santa Anna wrote the Mexican casualties as "about 70 men killed and 300 wounded." Others gave widely varying numbers, including Santa Anna's secretary Ramon Caro who claimed, "Three hundred were left dead on the field and more than a hundred of the wounded died afterwards."[25] But Mexican dead and wounded are generally thought to be between 400 and 600, many from their own gunfire. "Another such victory will ruin us," said Colonel Almonte.[26]

Defenders undoubtedly died outside the walls but, again, how many is not known. Even under the most favorable conditions errors occur. In this case darkness and battle smoke obscured the sharpest eyes, and soldiers, as a rule, inflate the number of enemy confronting them and the role they played.

During the Civil War Abraham Lincoln famously estimated, based on his generals' reports, that the Confederacy had well over one million men in the field; three times as many as the Union, which, in fact, had the larger force.[27]

Accordingly, Santa Anna claimed a total of 600 rebels killed and stated that "a great many who had escaped the bayonet of the infantry, fell in the vicinity under the sabres of the cavalry."[28] Sesma later claimed three groups emerged from the fort, to be cut down by lance and sabre. He stated that one group of "about fifty ... they resolved to sell their lives very dearly—they were swept away in minutes and suffered the knife."[29] But he went on to claim that his cavalry surrounded "the Alamo at a distance of fifteen paces in environs under fire from the enemy." By this time the rebels were fighting for their lives from inside buildings and were in no position to be firing on cavalry outside. It was in Sesma's interests to inflate his role as did Santa Anna with his claim of 600 dead. Sesma's 50 outside the walls in one group alone may have been, say, only 20.

Considering the "horrible carnage" as the battle raged any organized departure by rebels from inside the fort was impossible. And there is no account from survivors like Joe and Mrs. Dickinson of any predetermined plan to abandon the post. This comes as no surprise as such a plan would be impossible without foreknowledge of where the Mexicans would first breach the defences. Decades later an unknown Sergeant Loranca claimed 62 men "sallied from the east side of the fort" and were killed by lancers with only one resisting, but also claimed a highly inflated 283 dead.[30] And an "unknown Mexican officer" claimed 68 killed by cavalry, with 230 dead.[31] How credible are these recollections?

Post-battle accounts scarcely mention dead bodies outside the walls; e.g., Santa Anna: "when the battle was over, not a single man in the Alamo was left alive. At the battle's end, the fort was a terrible sight to behold."[32] And Eulalia Yorba: "The dead Texans lay singly and in heaps of three or four, or in irregular rows here and there all about the floor of the Alamo."

After Fort Mims, the officers' report stated: "The plains and the woods around were covered with dead bodies, in some places thinly scattered, in others lying in heaps as the men happened to fall in flight, or in a body resisted to the last."

There is no such testimony after the Alamo. Evidence of a large number of dead bodies outside is missing. If many died outside, their bodies would have received a notable post-battle mention. Combined with reports of the ferocious resistance inside, it would appear only a small number died beyond the walls; those defending the main gate bastion. They were the only ones in a position to make a cohesive departure and, outflanked, were forced to abandon their post. A few others may have made it across the walls in an unorganized attempt to escape the slaughter inside.

There is no precise figure for non-combatants who survived, but it seems there were at least 14. This included Mrs. Dickinson, her child, Travis' slave Joe, Juana Alsbury and her infant, he sister Gertrudis, and other Mexican women and children. Tejano rebel Brigida Guerrero escaped death by claiming he had been taken prisoner by the Texans.[33]

But, the battle won, how best to dispose of the bodies? His own brave men would be given a decent burial, Santa Anna decreed. Ruiz and others, however, later claimed some dead *soldados* ended up in the San Antonio River, as there were simply too many to be buried. The usurpers who rebelled against Mexican authority would not be given the honor of burial. All except one, Tejano Gregorio Esparza. His brother Francisco, who lived in San Antonio, was one of the local Presidial Company of Bexar who had served under General Cos during the Texan siege. Upon Santa Anna's arrival, they had been told to hold themselves in readiness for active service, but had not been called upon to fight.

Francisco received permission to bury Gregorio in consecrated ground, and found him "in one of the rooms of the Alamo," where he "had received a ball in his breast and a stab from a sword in his side." With two other brothers, Francisco carried the body to the "burying ground on the west side of the San Pedro Creek, where it still lies."[34]

Francisco Ruiz recalled that Santa Anna

> sent a company of dragoons with me to bring dry wood and dry branches from the neighboring forest. About 3 o'clock in the afternoon they commenced laying the wood and dry branches, upon which a file of dead bodies was placed; more wood was piled on them, and another file brought, and in this manner they were all arranged in layers. Kindling wood was distributed through the pile, and about 5 o'clock in the evening it was lighted ...

But, by burning the defenders of the Alamo, did Santa Anna subconsciously do them honor?

Viking warriors were sent on their way to Valhalla from a funeral pyre or a burning boat. In P.C. Wren's famous novel of the French Foreign Legion, *Beau Geste*, an Alamo-like siege takes place. The garrison is wiped out by Tuareg tribesmen. Legionnaire Geste had wished for a "Viking Funeral," thus his brother torches Fort Zinderneuf, the dead garrison consumed by flames.

As in *Beau Geste*, Santa Anna gave the defenders of the Alamo a funeral fit for heroes; a Viking funeral.

31

The Flash of a Musket

As flames engulfed the Alamo dead, an oblivious Sam Houston rode from the Convention at Washington-on-the-Brazos. He wore a red Indian blanket over buckskins and a feather in his hat.[1] Sam was to ride to the relief of the Alamo with the volunteers mustering in Gonzales, so the plan went. But the two-day ride took Houston five days. He was later accused of staying at the home of a Captain Burnum for two nights instead of getting on with the job. Why did he take so long?

The fact was "General" Houston had never commanded an army in combat. He was a mere lieutenant at Horseshoe Bend over two decades earlier, his bravado then almost causing his death. Since then, his duel with General White and the caning of William Stanbery were the only action he had seen.

Houston was now expected to defeat an army of 5,000 or more, commanded by a distinguished general who had defeated a Spanish invasion in 1829 and recently routed 4,000 militia at Zacatecas. He was supposed to save, with a few hundred volunteers, a fort he had wanted abandoned. Perhaps Houston knew in his soul that the Alamo must fall. Any troops he led to San Antonio would only add to the toll, himself included. And the fate of James Fannin and his command would prove that such reservations, if he had them, were quite valid.

As Houston rode towards Gonzales, other soldiers did likewise. He had dispatched recruiters to the United States and South Texas. James Fannin commanded the largest single Texan unit in the field, and Houston had ordered him to march to Gonzales. When Houston arrived on March 11 he found former Alamo commander James Neill in charge of about 300 volunteers.[2] Neill's ill wife had died shortly after his departure from San Antonio.[3] Not knowing the fort had fallen, he and Ed Burleson had attempted to reinforce the Alamo with 50 men on March 7 only to be driven off by Mexican dragoons.

Many of Neill's volunteers had no firearms and no military training. They were called to an assembly and Houston stood before them. He may have had enemies, both Mexican and Texan, but 13-year-old Private John Holland Jenkins, was not one of them—yet:

> I thought I had never seen so perfect a model of manliness and bravery, and my admiration knew no bounds. Calling the men together at DeWitt's Tavern in Gonzales, he delivered a short speech setting forth in stirring words the complications of troubles that threatened our Republic, finally closing with a rousing appeal to every Texan to be loyal and true in that hour of need and peril. I yet consider him about the finest looking man I ever saw, as he stood over six feet tall, in the very prime of mature manhood.[4]

That afternoon, Tejanos Anselmo Vergara and Andres Barcena arrived in town. They brought news of the fall of the Alamo, the garrison wiped out, devastating news for the families of Gonzales. It was from here the reinforcements had ridden. Private Jenkins' stepfather, John Northcross, was one of those who had ridden to his death at the Alamo. Houston immediately had the two Tejanos arrested as spies to create doubt in their report. The news spread, however, and Jenkins recalled, "I remembered most distinctly the shrieks of despair with which the soldiers' wives received the news of the death of their husbands.... I could now understand that there was woe in warfare, as well as glory and labor." Twenty men deserted, some possibly to protect their families. The disorganized militia were in no state to fight, and Houston gave orders to prepare for a retreat.

Deaf Smith and two others were sent towards San Antonio to scout the Alamo,[5] and a rider was dispatched to Fannin at Goliad with a change of plans. An immediate enemy advance was expected, Houston wrote, so Fannin was to leave Goliad promptly and fall back to Victoria, 25 miles to the east, with "such artillery as can be brought with expedition. The remainder will be sunk in the river ... you will take the necessary measures to blow up the fortress, and do so before leaving the vicinity."[6]

The awful truth was confirmed two days later, March 13, when Deaf Smith returned with Susannah Dickinson, her daughter, Almonte's former cook Ben Harris, and Travis' former slave, Joe. Survivors had been interviewed by Santa Anna following the battle and, with Almonte translating, he spoke to Susannah of her impoverished situation. He offered to adopt Angelina and have her brought up with "every advantage that money could procure" in Mexico. Susannah replied that she would "rather see the child starve than given into the hands of the author of such horror."[7] After a few days she and the other women were given two pesos and a blanket, then released with a written proclamation to spread news of what rebels bearing arms could expect. A donkey was provided for Susannah and her child.

The desperate women of Gonzales begged Mrs. Dickinson for news of their husbands and sons, only to be told all had died in the desperate fight. Susanna and Angelina were taken to the home of James Tumlinson and his wife Elizabeth, distraught with news of their own son's death. She told what she knew of the struggle from her position in the church, Sam Houston listening with tears in his eyes.

Houston assembled his men and read aloud Santa Anna's proclamation. All would be pardoned who lay down their arms, the generalissimo declared, but those who chose to keep fighting would die. Houston hurled the paper down, then ground it underfoot. "Death to Santa Anna, and down with despotism!" he shouted.[8] The rebels cheered and vowed revenge. But Houston knew his force, despite more volunteers arriving, had no hope of stopping the Mexican juggernaut, and orders to retreat went down the line. Women wept and children cried as wagons were loaded ready for flight. One officer came to Houston's tent, "General, my company is ready to march." But Houston was not impressed. "In the name of God, sir, don't be in haste—wait till we are ready and let us retreat in good order."[9]

After Fort Mims there had been a surge of fleeing refugees. The same thing now happened in Texas, and the "Runaway Scrape" began. Two field pieces without teams were pushed into the river, and the army pulled out at about 11 that night. Civilians, including the families of the Alamo dead, trudged along on foot, or by horse and wagon. Behind them a squad put Gonzales to the torch. There would be no shelter or supplies for the Mexicans there. The volunteers and refugees walked for ten long miles in the darkness until, a little before dawn, they stopped by the banks of Peach Creek to rest. A wave of panic swept through the refugees when the rumble of Santa Anna's artillery was heard. The Mexicans were on their heels, many thought. But then calmer heads prevailed. The Mexicans could not be so close, they said. The explosions were merely gunpowder and spirits stored in Gonzales set off by the flames.

In San Antonio, meanwhile, the remaining Mexican troops had arrived, and Santa Anna had been planning his next move. Orders went out, and General Morales marched southeast towards Goliad with two infantry battalions. He was to form a junction with General Urrea's southern column, then move eastwards along the Texas coast. Another force under General Sesma marched east towards Gonzales with two infantry battalions, fifty cavalry, and two field pieces. He planned to destroy any rebel resistance in the central eastern colonies and march as far as Nacogdoches, only 40 miles from the American border at the Sabine River. General Gaona marched with 700 men on a northern sweep to Bastrop. He was to whip any rebels before reuniting with Sesma at Nacogdoches. A supremely confident Santa Anna would soon follow and direct operations from Sesma's central command. Thus three columns; north, central and south, were to crush any resistance and wind up the campaign.[10] Texas would be secure, the rebellious *norteamericanos* taught a lesson they would never forget. *Viva Santa Anna!*

As Houston's march from Peach Creek resumed, he "rode slowly from the front to the rear of the army," recalled one volunteer, "pointing towards the ranks with his finger, evidently counting the men." He then rode to the front, saying "in his peculiar deliberate and distinct utterance, 'we are the rise of eight hundred strong, and with a good position can whip ten to one of the enemy.'"[11] More volunteers had joined them, but presumably Houston had counted, multiplied by two, and added a few more for good measure. But these words would pass down the line, encouraging the men that there was a fight to be won.

At Navadad on March 15, Houston wrote by candlelight to Chairman of the Military Committee, James Collingsworth, explaining his position. He had 374 men, he said, but many without arms or ammunition, and most were untrained and undisciplined. Rumors indicated 2,000 enemy of Sesma's central column in pursuit, and he "deemed it proper to fall back and take a position on the Colorado Creek.... By falling back, Texas can rally, and defeat any force that can come against her." Houston was well aware that the fall of the Alamo would see accusing fingers pointed in his direction. "Our forces must not be shut up in forts, where they can neither be supplied with men nor provisions. Long aware of this fact, I directed, on the 16th of January last, that the artillery should be removed, and the Alamo blown up; but it was prevented by the expedition on Matamoros, the author of all our misfortunes."[12]

The same day that Houston wrote this letter, news was received at the Convention in Washington-on-the-Brazos that an attack on the Alamo had been repulsed. "All hoped it true, but many feared the worst." But then the bleak truth arrived. "Still some did, or effected to, disbelieve it," wrote diarist William Gray.[13] Despite the tragic news, there was unfinished business at hand, and the delegates resolved to stay put for the moment, but plans were also made for a hasty retreat. Late the following night a vote was taken approving the constitution of the Republic of Texas. A provisional government was elected, and at 4 a.m. of March 17, David Burnet was hastily sworn in as interim president.

Rumors had flown through town of General Gaona's northern column fording the Colorado River at Bastrop, 75 miles to the northwest. The enemy were closing in, and the first government of Texas now made an undignified retreat. "The members are now dispersing in all directions with haste and in confusion," wrote Gray, "A general panic seems to have seized them." But the delegates were not alone, as "A constant stream of women and children, and some men, with wagons, carts and pack mules, are rushing across the Brazos night and day."[14]

Houston's retreat continued, many volunteers disillusioned with the flight. One man, Creed Taylor, later claimed half the troops had seen previous action, and Houston "didn't have a man in his army who didn't have a blood grievance against the Mexicans and that did not know that he could do as we had done before—whip ten-to-one of the carrion-eating convicts under Santa Anna."[15] Had a bolder man been in command, Taylor claimed, the war would have ended a lot sooner. He may well have been right—but who would have won?

Ahead of the retreating command, news spread and families packed belongings, abandoned homesteads, and headed east towards the border with the United States. Despite Santa Anna's boast of carrying his flag to Washington, D.C., it was most unlikely he would test his forces against the American army at this time or place.

Frustrated with the lack of discipline, Houston shouted at his young admirer, John Holland Jenkins, "God damn your soul!!! Didn't I order you to ride right here?" The general had allowed the tired young private to ride for a time, but despite instructions not to move ahead, Jenkins "allowed him to go a little too fast, and was rudely aroused and shocked by the voice of my hero." The mortified young private dismounted and returned to trudging on foot. Jenkins admitted that "he had cause to rebuke me," but "with those few harsh words, General Houston completely changed the current of my feeling toward him, and my profound admiration and respect was turned into dislike I could never conquer."[16] Jenkins would be detached from the command by Ed Burleson to look after his family, and miss the final action.

On March 17 the retreating rebels crossed the wide, fast flowing, lower Colorado by ferry as rain came down. Once on the opposite bank, despite the damp timbers, the craft was set ablaze. Houston moved the command 30 miles downstream to Beason's Crossing, all the while attempting to instil a sense of discipline. When returning to camp, a young sentry refused Houston access. The general must have written permission, said the private, as per his orders. "Well, my friend," Houston replied, "if those were your orders, you are right." He patiently waited till an officer arrived to allow him through.[17]

Protected by the rising waters of the Colorado, Houston paused to train his men and make a fresh assessment. Others troops, including 200 Kentucky volunteers under Colonel Sidney Sherman arrived. The longer Houston delayed battle, the stronger he became through reinforcements and the training of his men.

In Goliad meanwhile, on March 14, James Fannin had received Houston's order to fall back on Victoria with his 400 troops. That day before, however, Colonel William

Ward with 80 men had moved out to aid volunteers under Captain Amon King. They had been surrounded in a church near Refugio by Urrea's advancing force. Fannin was reluctant to march without word from the detached troops, and decided to stay behind the solid walls of Fort Defiance, a far stronger post than the Alamo. On March 17 he learned that the force under Ward and King had been attacked and scattered. Fannin finally gave orders to prepare for retreat to Victoria as per Houston's orders. The following day a Mexican patrol was seen on nearby hills. A detachment rode out and a skirmish took place before the Mexicans fell back. The following morning, having spiked heavy cannon and destroyed supplies, the command of about 300 men slipped away through a sheltering fog, Goliad in flames behind them. They carried plentiful ammunition, but in their haste, scarcely enough food for a prolonged retreat.

General Urrea and his *soldados* arrived at the abandoned fort later the same day. Local Mexicans pointed out which way the rebels had fled, and Urrea's cavalry moved swiftly in pursuit.

Fannin, stalled once again by broken wagons and exhausted oxen, was forced to halt in open prairieland a few miles short of sheltering forest and the refreshing waters of Coleto's Creek. Then warning arrived that Mexican cavalry were closing in. Fannin took up the march again, prodding the exhausted and thirsty oxen, but half a mile from shelter the Mexican vanguard rode round the Texans to block their retreat. Fannin ordered his wagons formed into a square, cannon defending each corner. Urrea's main force arrived and deployed, then charged the rebel square. Cannon boomed and rifles cracked, as the Mexicans were driven back. They regrouped and attacked twice more, each time repulsed with numerous casualties. Behind the wagons, there were seven dead and 60 wounded including James Fannin who performed with courage, despite being badly hit in the thigh.

Night fell and under cover of dark Mexican sharpshooters kept the Texans on edge while fresh troops and artillery arrived. The rebels dug trenches and threw up fortifications from anything at hand; boxes, carts and dead animals.[18] Water was in short supply and the wounded suffered.

Dawn's first light saw Mexican cannon poised to wreak havoc on the rebel square. As Fannin pondered his desperate situation, the enemy opened fire, hurling round shot into the rebel position. Outnumbered and outgunned, a white flag was shown, and a parley arranged. Fannin demanded that they be treated as prisoners of war and paroled to the United States. Urrea refused this, saying he was bound by Santa Anna's orders; unconditional surrender. He would, however, intercede with His Excellency on their behalf. The surrender document signed by Fannin said they were to be treated as prisoners of war but, "subject to the disposition of the supreme government." This last condition was withheld from the Texans, who believed they were to be paroled to the United States.[19]

The prisoners were escorted back to Goliad and imprisoned in the church within the fort, to be joined a few days later by Colonel Ward and his company, previously captured. Another 33 men, including Captain King, had already been captured, but then executed; an unfortunate portend of things to come. Juan Holzinger, a German officer serving with the Mexicans, had spared eight of King's men found to be Texan colonists, not recently arrived "pirates" from the United States.[20]

Urrea left Gonzales and continued his march eastwards towards the Sabine, leaving Lieutenant Colonel José de la Portella with orders to treat the captives well. Arrangements were made to have them shipped back to New Orleans. Urrea had written to Santa Anna requesting clemency, and it seemed to the captives that they were in safe hands. But de la Portella received orders direct from the generalissimo; all prisoners to be shot. De la Portella had no desire to carry out Santa Anna's orders. He had established a rapport with Fannin, dined with him, and together they had drunk a toast to Urrea's health.[21]

On Palm Sunday, March 27, however, all prisoners who could walk were mustered in the plaza, then marched out the gates escorted by troops with loaded muskets. They marched in four separate groups down four different roads. Dillard Cooper, a volunteer from South Carolina, recalled that his group was ordered to halt about half a mile down the road. They were lined up along a brush fence, their backs to the Mexican troops. Realizing what was about to happen, some pleaded for their lives. Robert Fenner called out, "Don't take on so, boys; if we have to die, let's die like brave men." Cooper recalled:

> At that moment, I glanced over my shoulder and saw the flash of a musket; I instantly threw myself forward on the ground, resting on my hands. Robert Fenner must have been instantly killed, for he fell with such force upon me as almost to throw me over as I attempted to rise, which detained me a few moments in my flight, so that Simpson, my companion on the right, got the start of me. As we ran towards an opening in the brush fence, which was almost in front of us, Simpson got through first, and I was immediately after him. I wore, at that time, a small, round cloak, which was fastened with a clasp at the throat. As I ran through the opening, an officer charged upon me, and ran his sword through my cloak, which would have held me, but I caught the clasp with both hands, and tore it apart, and the cloak fell from me. There was an open prairie, about two miles wide, through which I would have to run before I could reach the nearest timber, which was a little southwest of the place from where we started.[22]

From the four groups, 26 men managed to bolt through the smoke. They splashed across the San Antonio River and made their escape. Back at the fort, about 50 wounded were also shot, James Fannin was last. He asked that he be shot in the heart, and his pocket watch be sent to his wife. Seated on a chair, he was shot in the face, his watch kept by the officer commanding the execution.[23]

32

Their Forlorn Situation

Houston stayed encamped at Beason's Crossing, drilling his men as more volunteers arrived. They were spoiling for a fight when, on March 21, scouts reported Mexican troops of General Sesma's column camped only one mile from the opposite bank. Houston's officers urged him to attack but, expecting Fannin's force, he refused to make any general assault before it arrived. He did, however, allow Captain Henry Karnes to take 64 men across the river to probe the enemy camp. Another company under Captain John Bird was dispatched to cover their withdrawal.

The approach of Carnes' troops caused "great confusion" in the Mexican camp. But Houston had correctly doubted his own inexperienced volunteers' ability to avoid confusion, as Dr. Nicholas Labadie recalled:

> Captain Carnes, (Karnes) though brave, had not the experience necessary in a commander ... we were about to wheel to the right, expecting to make a dash in full gallop to take the enemy's cannon, but, at this moment Carnes rides up to the orderly, and gives the order, "Wheel to the left, to the left!" Just as he spoke, the whistle of a ball from the cannon, passing over our heads, was heard, and the report had scarcely subsided before another, and then another followed, our line causing to break in three or four places, as our horses became almost unmanageable. The balls struck the ground some distance beyond us, throwing up a cloud of dust. Upon looking back, I found myself at the head of only four men, the company haven fallen back fully 600 yards to the rear, whom we then joined, as the order to retreat was given.[1]

Two men had dashed forward, and now drove captured Mexican horses back. But the rebels also saw "the enemy mounted and coming towards us in good order." Along the river bank the Texans dismounted and prepared to open fire from the cover of trees, stumps and long grass. But, "the enemy was prudent enough not to approach within a quarter of a mile, when they turned and retreated." At twilight, the rebels having "failed in our purpose," recrossed the river to the campsite, "and reaching it, lo! we found it entirely deserted." They followed and rejoined the army and refugees, retreating once more. The opportunity for final victory was yet to come.

On March 23 a galloper arrived with the bad tidings of Fannin's surrender; a bitter blow with worse news to yet to come. Houston wrote to Secretary of War, Thomas Rusk:

> You know I am not easily depressed, but before my God, since we parted, I have found the darkest hours of my past life! If what I have learned of Fannin to be true, I deplore it and can only attribute the ill luck to his attempts to retreat in daylight in the face of a superior force. He is an ill-fated man.[2]

On March 26 Houston assembled the army and divulged the unhappy news. He told them they were "the only army in Texas now present.... There are but few of us,

218

and if we are beaten, the fate of Texas is sealed. The salvation of the country depends on the first battle had with the enemy. For this reason I intend to retreat, even if I am obliged to go to the banks of the Sabine."[3] His army was disgruntled with the decision but, despite numerous desertions, was still basically intact. The same day the retreat resumed, three fresh companies arrived, two from the United States and one from within Texas. They brought with them a large store of ammunition and supplies.

The following day, March 27, as Houston's army marched towards a new campsite near San Felipe, Fannin's command were being shot down, the wounded finished off with sword and bayonet.

The refugees trudging with the troops made a distressing sight, as recalled by Nicholas Labadie:

> The road was filled with carts and wagons loaded with women and children, while other women, for whom there was no room in the wagons, were seen walking, some of them barefoot, some carrying their smaller children in their arms or on their backs, their children following barefooted; and other women again were seen with but one shoe, having lost the other in the mud ... the cries of the women were still more distressing, as they called our attention to their forlorn situation, raising their hands to heaven and declaring they had lost their all ... and encouraging us to be of stout heart and avert, if possible, the disasters that were threatening the country.[4]

Two of Houston's company commanders, Moseley Baker and Wiley Martin, were indignant. They refused to retreat beyond the Brazos River. Martin, 60, had been a captain under Andrew Jackson at Horseshoe Bend and had no time for the upstart Houston. He had been one of Austin's first settlers, the "Old Three Hundred" and served as *alcalde* at San Felipe. He had drawn the only image from life known to exist of his deceased friend, Buck Travis.

Mosely Baker, once Speaker of the Alabama House of representatives, had arrived in Texas after being jailed for fraud and making his escape. He and Houston had hotly disagreed when Baker wanted the Consultation abandoned. Sam insisted they remain. "I had rather be a slave" he said, "and grovel in the dust all my life, than a convicted felon." Baker was another Houston hater.

Martin moved downstream with his company to defend the crossing at Fort Bend, and Baker to the crossing at San Felipe. Should the Mexicans attempt to cross the Brazos at these points, Baker and Martin would have their desire to fight well satisfied.

Houston addressed his impatient troops, now numbering about 750. "I am told that evilly disposed persons have told you I am going to march you to the Redlands. This is false. I am going to march you into the Brazos bottom near Groce's to a position where you can whip the enemy ten to one, and where we can get an abundant supply of corn."[5] The Redlands was the red earth area around Nacogdoches, about 40 miles from the American border. Jared Groce owned a large plantation about 20 miles north of San Felipe, Groce's Retreat. Here the troops could get food and rest. The lawyer George Childress had written the first draft of the Texas Declaration of Independence while staying there.[6]

"I hope I can keep them together. I have, thus far, succeeded beyond my hopes," Houston wrote to Rusk on March 31. "Be assured, the fame of Jackson could never compensate me for my anxiety and mental pain."[7]

And the famous Andrew Jackson watched Texan events with an eagle eye from his perch in the White House. Not only Mexican and rebel troops were on the move, but

American forces as well. An 1831 treaty with Mexico allowed troop movements in the border region to repel Indian attacks. In command of the southwest district was Sharp Knife's old comrade from the Seminole War, General Edmund Gaines. He too scrutinized Texan events. Gaines wrote to American Secretary of War Lewis Cass, "I take leave to suggest whether it may or may not be become necessary, *in our own defence*, to speak to the contending belligerents in a language not to be misunderstood—a language requiring *force*." But the pro–Houston Gaines was particularly interested in "speaking" to the Mexicans. He would hold his troops in readiness, he said, "to anticipate their lawless movements, by crossing our supposed or imaginary national boundary, and meeting the savage marauders wherever to be found, in their approach towards our frontier."[8]

Mexico claimed Texas to the Sabine, but Jackson claimed Louisiana to the Neches River, which would place Nacogdoches in American territory. And Nacogdoches was the planned rendezvous point for Mexican troops. Cass responded to Gaines that Jackson did not wish to take advantage of the situation and "thereby obtain possession of any portion of Mexican territory." He did, however, authorize Gaines to "prevent a violation" of American ground, and he may assume "such position, on either side of the imaginary boundary line, as may be best for your defensive operations."[9] Gaines could advance as far as Nacogdoches "which is within the limits of the United States, as claimed by this Government." The American territorial claim was dubious, to say the least. The treaty of 1819 clearly stated the Sabine as the border. But Jackson claimed the Neches was actually the western branch of the Sabine as the two rivers flow into the Sabine Lake before entering the Gulf of Mexico.[10]

"My intention has never been to cross the Brazos," Houston asserted, the rumor supposedly spread "by men who have basely deserted the army of Texas." But he acquired the services of the steamboat *Yellow Stone* to cross the Brazos, if need be. Captain John Ross had cotton bails on board that could provide protection, and "I have four cords of wood on board, & everything ready to 'go ahead.'" Perhaps news of Crockett's death at the Alamo had inspired those last two words.

Despite Baker, Martin and others, there were many who "reposed unlimited confidence in General Houston, and were willing to follow him blindly," recalled 15-year-old Private William Zuber:

> Some wondered how he held his army together. *They* held themselves together as a last resort. But the General helped them to do so by his inflexibility, confidence of success, and courtesy to his soldiers. Also he kept no bodyguard. When we were encamped, the door of his tent generally stood open, and any soldier who wished could enter at liberty.... He was skilled in inspiring men with hope, and his sympathy with his men was remarkable.[11]

Houston's army marched to Groce's Retreat and "Our camp was pitched near a deep ravine which had the appearance of having once been the bed of a river, and this miserable hole was our hiding place for about two weeks," recalled Labadie. And then horrific tidings arrived. On April 4 "some three of Fannin's men, wounded, barefoot and ragged, came into camp and related all the particulars of their disaster."

That same day Secretary of War Thomas Rusk arrived in camp. He carried a heated message from President Burnet: "The enemy are laughing you to scorn. You must fight them. You must retreat no farther. The country expects you to fight. The salvation of the country depends on you doing so."[12]

"I am sorry that I am so wicked," Houston replied, "'for the prayers of the righteous shall prevail.' That you are so, I have no doubt, and hope that Heaven, as such, will help and prosper you, and crown your efforts with success in behalf of Texas and humanity."[13]

Houston explained his strategy to Rusk. The secretary of war then placed himself under Houston's command with the rank of colonel, and fended off critics within the government ranks. Houston had previously said he was going to "retreat to the Sabine," if necessary, and had couriers riding between himself and Gaines.[14] If, in fact, Houston's plan was to lure Santa Anna into conflict with the United States, the ploy certainly made sense. Instead of confronting a small Texan army Santa Anna would also be fighting American troops, the likely outcome annexation by the United States. Thus the retreat meant short-term pain for the colonists, their homes destroyed, but the Napoleon of the West would suffer the same fate as his French hero after his attempt to conquer Russia in 1812—defeat and ignominious retreat.

But, if such was the intention, it must remain secret. Despite giving Gaines much latitude, Andrew Jackson made it clear he wanted no war with Mexico. The neighboring country would not disappear, as had the Spanish from Florida.[15]

The Runaway Scrape baffled and dispirited Houston's men. Critics and desertions were abundant. Privates Garner and Scales were court-martialled for mutiny and desertion. Guilty was the verdict, and they were sentenced to be shot the following day. But the court also recommended clemency. Andrew Jackson's shooting of soldiers had created vitriol at the time, and was used against him by political opponents in following years. No doubt Sam Houston wished to avoid a repetition. "This, being the first instance, is directed as an admonition," he read to the troops, but "the next *must* be an example."[16] When Private Scales deserted again three days later, he beat a hasty retreat. And Sam Houston probably wished him God speed, thus avoiding the need for an execution.

On April 7 Sesma's column, now commanded by Santa Anna himself, arrived at San Felipe on the west bank of the Brazos—or what had been San Felipe. All that remained of the timber buildings were charred ruins, burned by Moseley Baker's men. He would claim it was done on Houston's orders. Captain Isaac Moreland stopped by Houston's tent. "Moreland, did you ever hear me give orders to burn the town of San Felipe?"

"General. I have no recollection of it."

"Yet, they blame me for it," said Houston.[17]

Once at San Felipe, Santa Anna did not head 20 miles north to do battle with Houston's army at Groce's Retreat. He wished to kill the Texan snake by severing its head. The rebel government, in flight east of the Brazos, was the generalissimo's prime target.

A Mexican attempt to cross the river by flatboat was abandoned when Baker's men opened fire from the eastern bank. Santa Anna unlimbered two cannon, and for the next two days grape, round shot and musket balls whistled through a haze of gun smoke across the Brazos. Outraged by his advance being stalled by so few rebels, Santa Anna moved south to seek a ford elsewhere while Sesma continued the fight at San Felipe. The generalissimo arrived at Thompson's Ferry with the bulk of his force on April 12.

Here he wisely decided to use stealth rather than might. Colonel Almonte hailed the ferryman in English, and the craft was brought across from the opposite bank. Santa Anna and his staff burst from the bushes and captured the craft.[18] The troops commenced crossing while a courier rode to Sesma with orders to break off the fight with Baker's men and join Santa Anna. Wiley Martin's company 12 miles downstream at the Fort Bend crossing, meanwhile, remained blissfully unaware as the Mexicans established themselves on the eastern bank.

That same day, smoke bellowed into the broad Texas sky as the *Yellow Stone* commenced the first of seven trips over the river. She took three days to move Houston's men to the opposite bank.[19] April 14 saw both armies east of the Brazos where reinforcements arrived in Houston's camp. They brought with them two light cannon, a gift from the citizens of Cincinnati. The United States being politically neutral, the guns had been shipped to Texas as "hollow ware." Elizabeth and Eleanor Rice, twin sisters, were present when the guns were presented to the Texans in Galveston, thus the "Twin Sisters" became the two guns' name.

With Santa Anna across the Brazos, Martin and Baker, outflanked, withdrew their men from the fords and rejoined the main command.

The Thompson's Ferry boatman arrived in Houston's camp riding a mule. He had a message from Santa Anna written in English by Colonel Almonte. "Mr. Houston: I know you're hiding up there in the bushes. As soon as I catch the other land thieves, I'm coming up there to smoke you out."[20] So nice of the over-confident Santa Anna to divulge his plans. And captured Mexican dispatches revealed he was far in advance of his main command, racing to capture the rebel government, now in Harrisburg. The following day, April 15, Santa Anna arrived and put the town to the torch. President Burnet and his colleagues had slipped away just in time. They fled to New Washington and boarded a boat for Galveston Island. The Mexicans galloped onto the shoreline and prepared to open fire, the boat within musket range. Colonel Almonte, however, refused to give the order. The chivalrous gentleman could see that a lady, Burnet's wife, was on board.[21]

On the same day, April 15, Stephen Austin, attempting to raise money in the United States, wrote to Andrew Jackson and senior government officials requesting financial aid for the Texan cause. Jackson's response gave no cause for comfort:

> The writer did not reflect that we have a treaty with Mexico, and our national faith is pledged to support it. The Texans before they took the step to declare themselves Independent which has aroused all Mexico against them ought to have pondered well—it was a rash and premature act, our neutrality must be faithfully maintained.[22]

On April 17 the Texan army and accompanying refugees approached a fork in the road; the fork of destiny, so to speak. The left track headed northwest towards Nacogdoches, the right veered southwest to Harrisburg where scouts reported the enemy had arrived. The weathered branches of an old tree, the "Which-way tree" seemed to point along both roads, offering the alternatives; battle to the right, or further retreat to the left. Some say Houston ordered, "Columns right," others say the men marched to the right themselves. According to Nicholas Labadie, local farmer Abram Roberts raised his hand and cried out, "That right-hand road will carry you to Harrisburg just as straight as a compass." Houston was just riding up when the men shouted, "To the right, boys, to the right!"[23] But Private John Washington Winters recalled: "Early next morning we received orders to commence a forced march in the direction of Harrisburg.... I never heard any talk as to Houston's not designing to fight; or of officers or men insisting on his taking the road to Harrisburg; or of any one doubting his intention to do so."[24] Captain Robert Calder, with the leading troops, recalled, "I received an order to take the right-hand road. I do not recollect to have seen or heard any altercation, nor do I think there was any mutinous conduct."[25]

Houston and the army of Texas turned right towards Harrisburg while the refugees took the left fork to Nacogdoches, Wiley Martin and a large detachment with them as a guard. Nicholas Labadie recalled seeing, " 'Three-legged Willie' galloping up to General Houston dressed in buckskin and with a coonskin cap ornamented with some half dozen old coons' tails that were dangling on his shoulders."[26]

A crusty pioneering woman, Pamela Mann, produced a pistol to retrieve the oxen she had loaned to the army. She had understood they were all marching towards Nacogdoches.

Houston's force tramped into Harrisburg the following day, April 18. There was little to be seen but smouldering ruins. Anything of value had been taken either by fleeing inhabitants or Santa Anna's troops. Scouts brought in three Mexican prisoners, one an officer. He revealed that Santa Anna was "within the sound of the drum" with only 500 men, so he said, but another 1,000 were only 40 miles away. Houston had at hand about 700 men. Thomas Rusk sent out an appeal for the men of Texas to prove themselves by "rallying at once to your country's standard. Your general is at the head of a brave and chivalrous band, and throws himself, sword in hand, into the breach, to save his country, and vindicate her rights." And Sam Houston added: "Rally to the standard, and be no longer the scoff of mercenary tongues! Be men, be freemen, that your children may bless their father's names."[27]

Houston knew battle was at hand, finally the time had come. As his men prepared to cross Buffalo Bayou, he stood before them and made a rousing speech, concluding with, "The army will cross and we will meet the enemy. Some of us may be killed and must be killed; but, soldiers, *remember the Alamo, the Alamo!*"[28]

33

That Is Sam Houston's Writing

On April 20 the Texans, encamped near Buffalo Bayou, had just commenced breakfast when agitated scouts galloped in. They had exchanged gunfire with Mexicans dragoons near Morgan's Point. Men scrambled for powder horns and guns as a call to arms was heard throughout the camp. Hot coffee was hastily downed as eggs were pulled from the boil—a last chance to eat for who knew how long. But some, once cracked open, were found to contain chickens. "I surrendered my share to others," recalled Labadie, "who, finding them well cooked, swallowed them quickly."[1]

Colonel Sidney Sherman galloped out with a cavalry detachment to scout the enemy advance. The rebels' flintlocks had been loaded for two weeks, and many decided to reload with fresh gunpowder to prevent misfires. Triggers were pulled to clear the loads, and a deafening crescendo echoed across the bayou as those with dry powder discharged. Sam Houston was not happy. "Stop that firing! Stop that, God damn you. I say, stop firing!" But more guns went off. Houston, rising himself in his saddle to full height, drew his sword. "I'll run the next shooter through," he yelled.

Bang went another gun right before his eyes. "General," the soldier said, "it won't do for you to try that game on us." Old Hickory may well have run that shooter through.

Houston ordered the men to fall back amid sheltering timber along Buffalo Bayou. The Twin Sisters, commanded by James Neill, were positioned a little outside the trees where they commanded a clear line of fire across open grassland. A company was dispatched to hold Lynch's Ferry, a short distance to the left. Shortly a barge carrying supplies for Santa Anna's troops appeared. Guns cracked, musket balls flew and the Mexican crew jumped overboard. The craft was brought to shore and an American captured at Harrisburg was found still on board.

Sherman's detachment galloped back with urgent news. The enemy's main force was making a rapid advance. Orders rapped out, and men scrambled into battle order, their rifles primed. All eyes peered to the south and soon Mexican horsemen rode into sight. They "advanced towards us in fine order with trumpets sounding," recalled Labadie. "As the dragoons approached, over sixty of us stood before our two pieces of artillery." Most men, however, lay flat on the grass to hide their numbers as Houston paced restlessly, peering at the enemy advance. "In the stillness of that moment, not a word, nor a whisper, was heard, nothing save the penetrating sounds of the instruments and the thrilling notes of the bugle."

"Clear the guns and fire!" yelled Houston. The Twin Sisters erupted in cloud of smoke. Despite taking no casualties, the gallant, trumpeting advance came to an abrupt halt. They wheeled about and rode back to their main body, much to the chagrin of the rebels who thought they were about to taste proper action after the long retreat.

Santa Anna had with him a single cannon, a 12-pounder. It was seen being positioned in a cluster of oaks midway between the two armies. Smoke belched as it opened fire and grapeshot flew towards the rebel lines. Their aim was too high, however, and leaves fell and a spray of water erupted as the balls fell into Buffalo Bayou. The Twin Sisters replied bringing down two artillery mules and a horse, shattering an ammunition box, and wounding one officer.[2] Houston ordered Sherman to advance with mounted men towards a cluster of trees, but *soldados* concealed there opened fire. A few horses came down, and the rebels fell back. Those now without mounts ran back to their own lines. Then the Twin Sisters opened fire and it was the Mexicans who were forced to retreat as grapeshot ripped through the grove.

Thinking the enemy 12-pounder could be captured, Sherman pressed Houston to allow an attack. Preferring to stay on the defensive, however, he agreed to a reconnaissance only. With 60 mounted men, including Thomas Rusk, Sherman bolted from the trees and, disobeying orders, charged directly for the 12-pounder. The rebels opened fire from horseback but, carrying long rifles rather than short barrelled carbines, had to dismount to reload. Bugles shrilled and Mexican dragoons galloped to counterattack.

Without orders, Captain Jesse Billingsly led his company out to reinforce Sherman followed by Ed Burleson with more men. But Houston, wanting his force to remain intact, sent out orders to return. Ignored, he ordered artillery support, and one cannon was moved forward by hand. "With my rifle in one hand,'" recalled Labadie, "I took hold of the rope with the other, and we moved forward pretty briskly about 300 yards; but it required all our strength to move the carriage over the hag-bed prairie, and a halt was ordered. The combatants were advancing, then receding, with sudden evolutions and rapid movements."

Sherman's men fought off the attack before the reinforcements could intervene. Mexican infantry moved to cut them off, but the rebels made it back to their own lines with the loss of one dead, two wounded and several horses killed. The contested cannon remained in Mexican hands.

Houston, livid that the command had been placed at risk for no result, gave Sherman a tongue lashing that ensured another enemy for life.[3] Private Mirabeau Buonaparte Lamar, however, was promoted to colonel that same evening and replaced Sherman as head of cavalry. Better known as a poet than a warrior, Lamar had saved Rusk's life, and carried a wounded man back to safety on his own mount. That night many spoke of Sherman's bravery rather than his failure, and some thought he may well make a better commander than Sam Houston. Among the casualties of the day was James Neill who had been "seriously wounded" by grapeshot to the hip. He had fired the war's first shot at Gonzales, but would miss the climactic battle the following day.

Thursday morning, April 21, saw the Mexicans camped within easy striking distance; about 1,000 meters away. Despite warnings from his officers, Santa Anna had camped with his back to Peggy's Lake and boggy marshland.

The Texans were alarmed to hear a rattle of drums and the blare of bugles as more troops arrived—General Cos with 400 reinforcements. But they had been forced-marched during the night and were in no shape to fight. Santa Anna, however, now had a force of about 1,350 men, and with even more troops on the way, all he had to do was wait. Houston downplayed the arrival of Cos, saying it was a ruse, Santa Anna having sent out troops during the night to arrive once more to daunt the enemy. Deaf Smith, knowing better, suggested he go out and destroy Vince's Bridge to delay the arrival of any more reinforcements. This would also impede retreat for either side. Houston agreed, and Smith rode for the bridge with six men to do the job.[4]

Private John Winters recalled:

> There had been so many "split ups" and differences that Houston preferred the opinions of the men themselves, feeling that before hazarding battle he must find whether they would enter the engagement with a will. For the men had marched so long without food or rest that, perhaps, they might not be physically prepared.[5]

Houston walked among the campfires and asked the men if they wanted to fight. "We replied that we were most anxious to do so," recalled Winters.

At noon Houston had a senior officers' call. What was their best course of action? The Mexicans had constructed a protective breastwork of brushwood, baggage and saddlebags during the night, and the rebels had no bayonets; a vital assault weapon in close combat once the flintlocks were discharged. Of the seven officers present, five, including Lamar and Sherman, voted not to attack. They felt the best strategy was to prepare for a Mexican assault. Perhaps Colonel Sherman was feeling a little less confident after his brush with Mexican dragoons the day before.

José de la Peña later wrote that "a slave appeared before Houston at 3 o'clock" who informed him that "Santa Anna was sleeping," his camp having "a feeling of confidence and great abandon." Houston then "hurried to take advantage of the beautiful opportunity" afforded him. "This circumstance explains why he decided to battle an enemy who had just received reinforcements of four hundred men when the previous day he had not accepted combat offered to him with inferior numbers."[6]

A roll call of the Texans at 3 o'clock revealed 783 men ready to fight. More volunteers had arrived in camp over the past few days. It was now or never, Houston decided. The vengeful rebels might not have bayonets, but there was no shortage of Bowie knives.

He determined that the company of Tejanos would not be in the fight. Sergeant Tony Menchaca recalled that they were "ordered to remain and guard horses and equipages." He went to Houston with Captain Seguin, and told him that he had come to fight "and that I wanted to do so even if I died facing the enemy. I did not enlist to guard horses and would not do such duty," and he would "go and attend to my family who were on their way to Nacogdoches without escort or servants." Houston replied that he had "spoken like a man"; the Tejanos would take their place in the ranks.[7] But as a precaution against "friendly fire" he had them place pieces of cardboard in their hatbands.

The Texans were lined up, ready to fight, in two ranks across a 900-yard front in a depression between themselves and the Mexican camp. Houston positioned himself on horseback in the center with the Twin Sisters. Alongside Houston was the Texan battle flag, a bare-breasted warrior woman with a "Liberty or Death" sash draped across her sword. To his left two regiments under Sherman and Burleson formed up, and to his right were two regiments under Rusk and Millard. Colonel Lamar, as a mere private

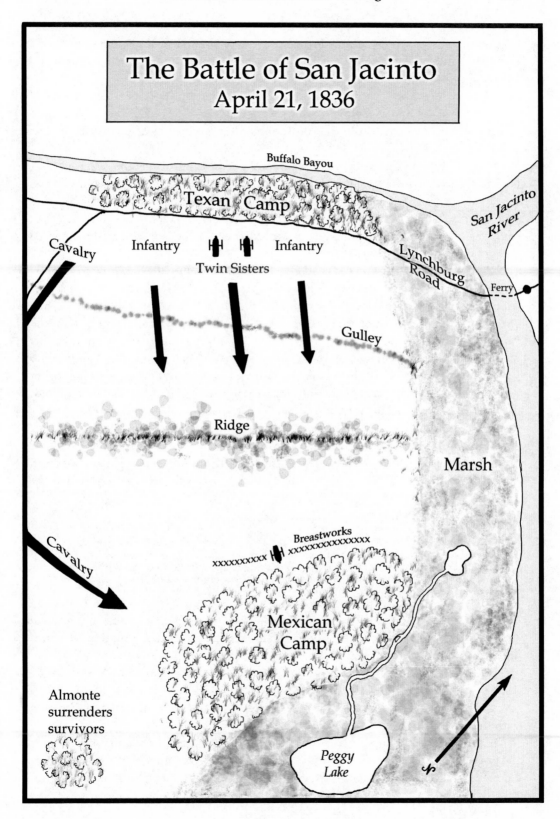

The Battle of San Jacinto
April 21, 1836

the day before, would never have believed he was to lead the cavalry in battle one day later. It was his job to cut off a Mexican retreat to the left of the enemy line, while marshland and San Jacinto Bay would do the same to their right. More marshland and Peggy's Lake would impede enemy flight to the rear.

Houston drew his sword. "Trail arms, forward," he said. The general rode several yards ahead of the line as the Twin Sisters were wheeled alongside by hand. A fife and drum were heard to play above the soft tramp of hundreds of feet on grass as the line advanced.

Ahead of them lay a totally unprepared Mexican camp. Dragoons watered their horses, the tired reinforcements napped. It was siesta time, after all, and Santa Anna was, in his own words, "in a deep sleep."[8] The nap came to an abrupt halt when a dozing sentry looked up to see the enemy cresting the ridge between themselves and the Texan camp. He gave the alarm and a bugle blared. Moments later the Twin Sisters boomed and grapeshot ripped through the tents.

Ben McCulloch, a friend of David Crockett, would eventually die as a Confederate general, but today he commanded one of the guns. "The fire from it opened upon the enemy about two hundred yards distant," he recalled. "We advanced after each discharge, keeping in advance of the infantry, until we were within less than one hundred yards of their breastwork." Houston was riding "in advance of every man in that part of the field,"[9] and McCulloch had to delay one shot as he galloped across "some thirty yards in front of the gun." The Texans paused and fired a volley. Some said an order was given to halt and reload. Either not heard or ignored, the unfettered men did not even waver, and rushed forward with vengeance in their blood. "*Remember the Alamo! Remember Goliad!*" The Mexicans had scrambled for muskets and hastily returned fire. Houston hit the ground, his horse shot from under him, but he scrambled into another saddle and continued forward. Then grapeshot ripped into his left ankle and his fresh mount came down. He regained his feet to mount a third horse and continued the charge, sword in hand.[10]

Santa Anna, abruptly awakened, recalled:

> I immediately perceived we were attacked, and had fallen into frightful disorder. The enemy had surprised our advance posts. One of their wings had driven away the three companies posted in the wood on our right, and from the trees were doing much execution with their rifles. The rest of the enemy's infantry attacked us in front with two pieces of cannon, and their cavalry did the same on our left.[11]

Santa Anna said he tried to organize a defense, but "Then I saw His Excellency," recalled Colonel Pedro Delgado, "running about in a most excited manner, wringing his hands and unable to give an order."[12]

The rebels dashed whooping over the barricade and cut through the Mexicans like a scythe, shooting, clubbing, knifing anything that moved. A 12-year-old fifer who survived the carnage, Luis Espinosa, thought "judging by the yells" Indians were fighting with the rebels.[13]

Lamar's cavalry galloped in on the Mexican left forcing many *soldados* back towards the bog alongside San Jacinto Bay while others retreated into marshland around Peggy Lake. General Castrillón had predicted the rebels would not manage a single volley, but the Alamo had proved otherwise. Taking charge of the 12-pounder, however, he

Sam Houston led from the front and defeated the Mexicans under Santa Anna in 18 minutes (drawing by the author).

attempted to rally his men. "I have been in forty battles and never once shown my back. I am too old to do it now," he said. Seeing his desperate valor, Rusk yelled that his life was to be spared and knocked rifle barrels aside. But, standing defiantly on an ammunition box, Castrillón died where he fell.[14]

The Napoleon of the West, meanwhile, sensed Waterloo in the air. He mounted his charger and fled. "The enemy was rapidly advancing with loud hurrahs," he recalled, "and in a few minutes obtained a victory, which they could not, some hours before, even have dreamed of."[15]

The battle was a disaster for the Mexicans from start to finish. There was no strong point that held out. With the Texans among them, they broke and ran. *Remember the Alamo* did for the rebels what *Remember Fort Mims* had done for the volunteers at Tallushatchee, and the avengers showed little mercy. "Me no Alamo, no Goliad," *soldados* cried before falling under a clubbed rifle or Bowie knife.

They fled through the woods into the marshes, and splashed into Peggy Lake, the battle over in 18 minutes, "but the minute they would raise their heads they were picked off by our men," recalled Private Winters.[16] The rebels stood along the shoreline firing, then hastily ramming fresh powder and shot down barrels as a haze of acrid gun smoke drifted across the water and through the trees, "Here the Mexicans and horses killed made a bridge across the bayou."

Sickened by the ongoing slaughter, some officers ordered the men to stop firing only to be ignored. "General Wharton tried to get us to cease," recalled Winters, "and grabbed a Mexican and pulled him up behind him on his horse, saying that it was his Mexican, but Jim Curtis shot the Mexican." Colonel Delgado recalled: "It would have been all over with us had not providence placed us in the hands of the noble and generous captain of cavalry, Allen, who by great exertion, saved us repeatedly from being slaughtered by the drunken and infuriated volunteers."

Houston rode up, blood seeping from his ankle. For him, this was Horseshoe Bend all over again; wounded amid bloody carnage, the enemy shot down like dogs. Thomas Rusk recalled, "The men were entangled and in great confusion" at the quagmire, "and the General ordered a halt to form the men."[17] But the rejoicing, undisciplined militia could not be reformed. "Houston gave the order three times and still the men paid no attention to him," recalled Winters, "And he turned his horse around and said 'Men, I can gain victories with you, but damn your manners, and rode into camp.'"

Some time later Houston, in pain from his wound, saw an organized file of Mexican troops moving across the field. He assumed they were General Filisola's reinforcements arriving. The rebels, scattered and disorganized, were in no state to organize a defense. "All is lost; all is lost; My God, all is lost," he said. But Captain Turner handed him a telescope and suggested he take a closer look. Houston peered through the glass to see a file of several hundred Mexican prisoners being escorted back to camp.[18] Despite the carnage, tempers had soon cooled and many *soldados* had been spared.

Not among the prisoners, however, was Santa Anna. The generalissimo recalled:

> I remembered that General Filisola was only seventeen leagues off, and I took my direction towards him, darting through the enemy's ranks. They pursued me, and after a ride of one league and a half, overtook me on the banks of a very large creek, the bridge over which was burned by the enemy to retard our pursuit. I alighted from my horse, and with much difficulty succeeded in concealing myself in a thicket of dwarf pines. Night coming on I escaped them, and the hope of reaching the army gave me strength. I crossed the creek with the water up to my breast, and continued on foot. I found, in a house which had been abandoned, some articles of clothing, which enabled me to change my apparel. At eleven o'clock, a.m., while I was crossing a large plain, my pursuers overtook me again. Such is the history of my capture.[19]

Santa Anna was wearing a private's tunic. It seems unlikely he would have found it in an abandoned home. More likely it was stripped from a *soldado*, alive or dead. A detachment of Kentucky cavalry from Sherman's command came across the disheveled generalissimo, but they had no idea who their prisoner was. Near the camp they encountered Major John Forbes, and the prisoner let it be known that he wished to see Sam Houston. He produced a letter addressed to Don López de Santa Anna, revealing his identity. Forbes and Colonel George Hockley took him towards Houston's tent. "El Presidente! El Presidente!" prisoners murmured as they passed by.

Houston was lying on a mattress beneath the spreading branches of a big oak tree, a "red badge of courage" swathed around his left ankle (often incorrectly stated as his right).[20] Roused by Forbes, Houston looked up, and Santa Anna surrendered himself as a Prisoner of War.

The word went round that the oppressor was in camp. "Shoot him, hang him," many yelled as they gathered around the nervous prisoner.[21] Houston had guards keep the avengers kept at bay, and sent for Ramon Caro and Colonel Almonte, also taken prisoner. They both confirmed Santa Anna's identity. The prisoner was seated on a box, and Almonte interpreted as they spoke. The exact words were never recorded, but

Santa Anna reputedly told Houston that the man who defeated the Napoleon of the West was born to no common destiny, and could afford to be generous to the vanquished. Houston reminded Santa Anna of his treatment of prisoners; execution. He replied that the Alamo was taken by storm, a fair battle, and he had no knowledge of the terms supposedly offered to Fannin by General Urrea. The insurrectionists had no legal government and those who had invaded from the United States were not Mexican citizens but pirates, for whom death was prescribed by law.[22]

Despite Santa Anna's atrocities, Houston knew he was far more use to Texas alive than dead. He held in his hand a bargaining chip that could help ensure Texas remained free from Mexican control while showing the world that the rebels operated by a code of honor that Santa Anna had not. The former dictator was put under close guard while there was a count of the captured, wounded and dead.

Some *soldados* were still on the loose, and few days later a well-dressed Mexican was captured by Deaf Smith. The scout asked the prisoner if he had seen General Cos, who said he had not. "He offered $1,000 for my head," Smith said, "and if I find him I will cut his head off and send it back to Mexico." Once in camp, the prisoner was recognized as the parole-violating Cos.[23] "He was the most frightened man I ever saw," recalled Private Winters, "He covered his head with a blanket. I could see it tremble twenty feet off." But Cos kept his trembling head. More than enough retribution had already been taken, and no Mexican captives faced a rope or firing squad. According to Houston's official report, 630 Mexicans had died, 730 taken prisoner, and "very few escaped." His own loss was "two killed and twenty three wounded, six of whom mortally."[24]

David Burnet and other officials arrived from Galveston Island on board the *Yellow Stone* to view the sight of the great victory. Santa Anna and about 80 prisoners were put on board and taken back to the island to be held under guard.

Five days after the battle, Sam Houston scribbled a note to General Gaines on the Sabine. "Tell your friends all the news, that we have beat the enemy, killed 630." He reduced the number of captured from 730 to 570, and gave other details including Santa Anna's capture, and the weapons taken. Gaines immediately ordered one of his officers, Lieutenant Hitchcock, to Washington with an official dispatch and Houston's original note. When Hitchcock arrived he was quickly shown into Old Hickory's presence. Jackson had previously said the Revolution was "rash and premature," but now changed his tune, as recalled by Hitchcock:

I never saw a man more delighted than President Jackson. He read the dispatch over and dwelt particularly on the one from Houston, exclaim-

Jackson's old comrade from the Seminole War, General Edward Gaines, sent word to him of the Mexican defeat (Wikimedia Commons).

ing over and over, as though talking to himself, "Yes, that is his writing. I know it well. That is Sam Houston's writing. There can be no doubt about what he says." Then the old man ordered a map and he and I spread it and tried to locate San Jacinto. He passed his finger excitedly over the map in search of the name, but it was not there. He would say, "It must be here. No, it is over there," as he ran his fingers back and forth over the map, but finally gave up the search. So great was his enthusiasm that I think he would have promoted me to a captain of dragoons on the spot had there been a vacancy.[25]

Two treaties were signed by David Burnet and Santa Anna at Velasco, Texas, on May 14, 1836. One was for immediate publication, the other to remain secret until the conditions of the other had been fulfilled. In essence, the public treaty provided that hostilities cease, all Mexican forces would withdraw south of the Rio Grande, property confiscated by the Mexicans would be restored, and an equal number of prisoners on both sides would be exchanged. Santa Anna would be returned to Mexico when "deemed proper."

The secret document pledged Santa Anna's immediate return to Mexico where outstanding matters regarding the recognition of Texas independence would be finalized, and a binding treaty arranged. He would refrain from further hostilities, and the border with Texas would be the Rio Grande.[26]

34

Wisdom and Humanity Dictates

"There will be jealousies, persecutions, treacheries starting up among little men of narrow minds, who will endeavor to cast a slur over your brightest acts.... Such ever, from time immemorial, has been the case and you cannot hope to escape," wrote George Boyd to his friend Sam Houston on June 6, 1836. Boyd was the city marshal of Lafayette, Louisiana.[1]

The smoke had scarcely cleared at San Jacinto before another battle broke out. President Burnet and his Houston-hating cohorts started plotting to rid themselves of the man who had resisted their demands for premature battle, and in doing so saved their hides. With Houston's fame spreading like wildfire, he was a serious threat. Navy Secretary Potter, who had literally castrated men in the past, now wished to do the same to Sam Houston. Potter wanted charges laid against the general for distributing Santa Anna's captured treasury among his victorious troops. Wiser heads, however, thought better of this. The Texan government could well be used for target practice by Houston's men.

But Burnet, out for revenge, refused permission for Houston to get medical treatment in New Orleans. Captain Ross of the *Yellow Stone*, however, refused to cast off without Houston on board. Burnet reluctantly backed down, and Thomas Rusk took the reins as acting commander-in-chief.[2] Houston was accompanied by army Surgeon General Alexander Ewing, who was stripped of his post for desertion by newly appointed Secretary of War, Mirabeau Lamar. The man Houston had promoted from private to colonel at San Jacinto had joined the Burnet camp. Despite their differences, however, Houston and Burnet agreed on one thing; Santa Anna alive was far more use to Texas than dead.

Houston arrived in New Orleans onboard the schooner *Flora*. Awaiting him was a jubilant, welcoming crowd who jostled for a glimpse of the wounded Hero of San Jacinto. What New Orleans had done for Old Hickory, San Jacinto did for Sam Houston.

With Houston gone, Burnet announced that Mirabeau Lamar was to replace Rusk as the army's acting commander-in-chief. But senior officers had other ideas, and a democratic election confirmed Rusk's position. A perplexed Lamar still attempted to issue orders until persuaded to desist. Despite the unrest in Texan ranks, all Mexican troops followed Santa Anna's written orders and retreated back across the Rio Grande, much to the fury of the Mexican government.

Burnet and Lamar argued that Houston, by leaving Texas, had no right to resume his role as commander-in-chief. "I have by rumor heard it suggested," wrote Felix Huston, (no relation) that "no orders should be given you. There are a precious set of scoundrels in Texas. Accept my best wishes for your speedy recovery and soon join the army."[3] Santa Anna, meanwhile, also put pen to paper:

> Friends, I have seen how brave you are in battle, how generous you are in its aftermath. You may count on my friendship forever and you will never regret having dispensed these considerations upon me. In returning to my place of birth thanks to your generosity, please admit this most sincere farewell.[4]

But not just yet. The generalissimo had been put aboard the Texas schooner *Invincible* for return to Mexico. On July 1, however, General Thomas J. Green arrived at Velasco on board the vessel *Ocean* with 130 New Orleans volunteers. *Remember the Alamo*, they said, and ordered the ship's captain to hand the tyrant over. Santa Anna could see a hostile mob waiting ashore. He immediately wrote to Burnet asking "to grant me the one wish of being shot aboard this ship; there is no scarcity of soldiers to execute such an order, and I will not leave this boat unless I am dead."[5] Guaranteed protection, however, he reluctantly went ashore to be placed in a cell under armed guard. He wrote to Burnet protesting this breach of the treaty, being made a spectacle of, and the treatment he received from the guards. But the prisoner had come under the "tender" care of General Rusk who had little regard for his captive's well-being.

Santa Anna now wrote to Andrew Jackson in Washington, D.C., the very place he had boasted of planting his flag. He asked Old Hickory to intervene. "Let us establish mutual relations, to the end that your nation and the Mexicans may strengthen their friendly ties and both engage amicably in giving existence and stability to a people that wish to figure in the political world."[6]

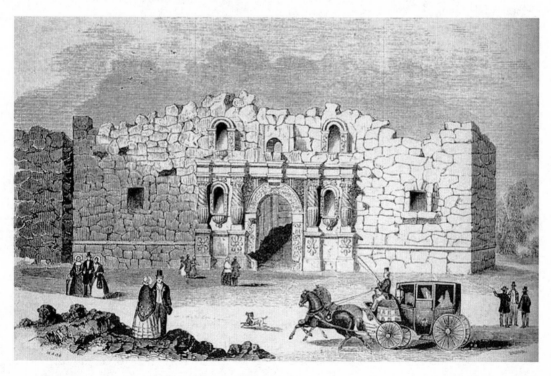

The scarred and battered Alamo Chapel as it appeared in 1854 before restoration by the United States Army (Wikimedia Commons).

Burnet sent Santa Anna 30 miles up the Brazos to the Phelps plantation, where he was held during the summer and autumn. Napoleon had once attempted suicide with poison, and Santa Anna now tried the same. Like Napoleon, however, he survived. On another occasion, assassins arrived at the plantation. The intended victim was saved when Mrs. Rosetta Phelps threw her arms and about him and pled for his life.[7] Rumors circulated of an escape plot, and the former dictator found himself in irons shackled to a live oak tree.

A recuperating Sam Houston returned to Texas from New Orleans. He met with friends and supporters, and quickly reestablished himself amid the log cabins of power. Burnet's interim government had not been chosen by the voters, and preparations were made for the first democratic election, to be held on September 5, 1836. The candidates for president were Stephen Austin, Henry Smith and Sam Houston. When the votes came in, it became clear that there was no better candidate than a wounded hero who had won a great battle. Houston scored 5,119 votes to Smith's 743 and Austin's 586.[8] It had taken Andrew Jackson 14 years from New Orleans to become president of the United States, but only six months after San Jacinto for Sam Houston to become president of Texas. Houston, however, wanted Texas to become part of Old Hickory's domain. Mirabeau Lamar, the new vice-president, had different ideas. He favored Texas remaining as a sovereign nation, and advocated the conquest of Mexican territory to the Pacific Ocean. The presidential vote, however, had included a referendum. Only 94 voters had favored independence over annexation by the United States.

Houston was inaugurated in Columbia on October 22, 1836:

> I, Sam Houston, President of the Republic of Texas, do solemnly and sincerely swear, that I will faithfully execute the duties of my office, and to the best of my ability, preserve, protect and defend the Constitution of the Republic.[9]

Shortly before the election, real estate entrepreneurs Augustus and John Allen from New York had purchased land along Buffalo Bayou with the intention of creating a new settlement close to the hallowed battleground. The town of Houston was established and served for some time as the new republic's capital. The renowned naturalist John James Audubon visited Houston when heavy rains had caused the waters of Buffalo Bayou to overflow.

> We approached the President's mansion wading in water above our ankles. This abode of President Houston is a small log house consisting of two rooms and a passage through, after the Southern fashion. The moment we stepped over the threshold on the right hand of the passage we found ourselves ushered into what in other countries would be called the antechamber. The floor, however, was muddy and filthy; a large fire was burning, and a small table covered with writing materials was in the center; campbeds, trunks and different materials were strewed around the room.... The president was engaged in an opposite room on some national business and we could not see him for some time.[10]

A few days after his election, President Houston's received a letter from Santa Anna. He was desperate to get home before a hangman's rope or a firing squad brought such plans to a mortal end. The longer he remained a prisoner, he said, the less influence he could have on Mexican political affairs. If he was to support Texan independence, he must be released. Houston also received a letter from Old Hickory:

> I have seen a report that General Santa Anna was to be brought before a military court, to be tried and shot. Nothing could now tarnish the character of Texas more than such an act at this

late period. It was good policy as well as humanity that spared him. It has given you possession of
Goliad and the Alamo without blood or loss of the strength of your army. His person is still of
much consequence to you. He is the pride of the Mexican Army and the favorite of the priest-
hood, and while he is your power the priests will not furnish the supplies necessary for another
campaign, nor will the regular soldiers *voluntarily* march when their reentering Texas may endanger or cost their favorite general his life. Therefore preserve his life and the character you have
won, and let not his blood be shed unless it becomes necessary by an imperative act of just
retaliation for Mexican massacres hereafter. This is what I think true wisdom and humanity dic-
tates.[11]

On November 5, 1836, Santa Anna wrote to Houston again saying that as Texas was
now independent, the critical issue was the precise border with Mexico, and the American president would be an ideal mediator for these discussions. Houston, hoping for
annexation, agreed. On November 25 Santa Anna rode with Almonte, three Texan officials and a small escort for Washington, D.C.[12] Old Hickory had agreed to a meeting but,
"Until the existing Government of Mexico ask our friendly offices between the contending parties, Mexico and Texas, we cannot interfere."[13] The Mexican government had
disowned the Treaties of Velasco signed by Santa Anna; a prisoner fearing for his life,
and he had forfeited his position as president of Mexico—for the time being, at least.

Traveling by steamer up the Mississippi and Ohio Rivers, Santa Anna arrived in
Louisville, Kentucky, on Christmas Day. Here he was delighted to receive a hero's welcome by abolitionist northerners who thought the Texas Revolution a Southern con-
spiracy to add one more slave state to the Union.[14]

Continuing overland, they paused in the town of Frederick, Maryland, where Santa
Anna met General Winfield Scott, his future opponent in the Mexican-American War.
Other officers were present, including the young officer who had taken news of San Jacinto to Andrew Jackson. Lieutenant Hitchcock seemed somewhat impressed by the
Napoleon of the West: "He is a Spaniard, a slight figure, about 5 ft. 10, of very commanding, dignified appearance, graceful manner and benign countenance. He smiled
at his misfortunes, and for my life I could not believe he ever gave the order for the
massacre at Goliad."[15]

Similar things were said about William Weatherford after Fort Mims.

Santa Anna met Old Hickory in the White House in early 1837, primarily a cour-
teous exchange, especially as the president was in the last days of his administration.
But it was still possible to sow seeds for future action should Santa Anna regain power.
Jackson again suggested the acquisition of Texas by the United States. But the 5 million
dollars, considering Mexico's recent defeat, was reduced to 3.5 million. In view of Santa
Anna's situation, it comes as no surprise that he appeared receptive to the idea, especially as a trip home on an American naval vessel was on offer.

Santa Anna and Almonte set sail on board the recently launched bark USS *Pioneer*.
But they were lucky to make it back home. Designed for polar exploration, the exper-
imental craft exhibited dangerous sailing qualities, and her new-fangled anthracite
stoves almost sent the ship up in flames.[16] Despite all, Santa Anna and Almonte returned
in safety to a joyous welcome at Veracruz in late February 1837. With an amazing power
to not only survive, but thrive, Santa Anna would be returned to power in 1839. He was
not quite his old self by that time, however, having lost a leg in a fight with the French
at Veracruz the year before. True to form, the generalissimo had the severed limb buried
with full military honors.

Andrew Jackson, approached by Houston to recognize Texan independence, handed the issue to Congress. On February 28, 1837, the House of Representatives authorized funds for recognition, and decreed that a *chargé d'affaires* be dispatched to Texas. The following day the Senate voted 23 to 19 for formal recognition.[17] Old Hickory, 11 days short of his 70th birthday, left the White House on March 4 to retire from public life. His final official act was recognition of the Republic of Texas by the United States.

So ended the Texas Revolution. Despite Mexican incursions in the following years, Texas remained independent. The attack on Fort Mims in 1813 and the following Creek War had brought to light three men who all had their part to play. The famous David Crockett, whose death helped revere the Alamo legend; Sam Houston, the avenger who won independence, and Andrew Jackson, the first head of state to recognize the Republic of Texas.

Old Hickory would die just six months before Texas became the 28th state of the Union in December 1845. Annexation would lead to war with Mexico under Santa Anna who, in all, was president of Mexico at eleven different times. After living in exile, he would return to Mexico City and die there in 1876.

Sam Houston would be President of the Texas Republic once more, from 1841 to 1844. He legally divorced Eliza Allen in 1837, and married 21-year-old Margaret Moffett Lea of Alabama in 1840. Between 1843 and 1860 they had eight children. He was elected governor of Texas in 1859, but was removed from office the following year for refusing to take an oath of allegiance to the Confederacy. Despite opposing secession and warning the South it could not win the coming war, he declined an offer from Abraham Lincoln to hold Texas with Union troops. He would die in 1863 of pneumonia, aged 70, just a few weeks after the Confederate disasters at Gettysburg and Vicksburg which vindicated his position.

David Crockett would have taken comfort had he known his son John would be elected to his old seat in Congress. Adam Huntsman, whose victory had driven him to Texas, and possibly some voters to hell, did not stand for election against the famous Crockett name.[18] And John would, in 1841, get through an amended land rights bill allowing poor farmers to acquire land for twelve and a half cents per acre. No doubt his father's name and death at the Alamo helped push the bill through.[19] Crockett was dead, but his fame lived on through "Davy Crockett Almanacs" as publishers continued to profit with fictional adventures as the bear killer continued to tame the wild frontier.

Crockett's son Robert went to Texas where he was made a first lieutenant in the cavalry. He received $240 for his father's military service, and in 1854 settled in Texas on land that was due to his father upon death.[20]

The victors at Fort Mims and the Alamo; William Weatherford and Santa Anna, both won the battles, but both lost their wars, and both lost vast territory to the United States. Santa Anna's image has remained that of a villain, while Weatherford's duplicity and eloquence has seen him emerge as the noble Red Eagle—judged by words rather than deeds. In 1855 Alexander Beaufort Meek published *The Red Eagle: A Poem of the South.* The lengthy work, excerpted in this book, portrayed Weatherford as a tragic hero with a *fictional* lover, Lilla, who dies at Fort Mims. Despite this, Meek claimed in his introduction, "The love-life of Weatherford,—here truthfully narrated." Meek went on to commend, "his dauntless gallantry, his marvelous personal adventures and hair-breadth escapes, and, chief of all, his wonderful eloquence, which eventually saved his life, when all other means would have failed."[21]

At least Meek got the last part right.

Red Eagle and the Wars with the Creek Indians in Alabama by George C. Eggleston was published in 1878, reinforcing the Red Eagle myth, and other publications have appeared since then.

The Alamo is well remembered. Countless books have been written, numerous films made. Disney's TV series released in 1954, also cut to a feature film, saw an unforeseeable burst of interest in Davy Crockett, king of the wild frontier. With this, Hollywood wrote a screen-friendly, fictional story woven through the facts. In the public mind, the fiction became the reality. Disney is often sited as the source of people's belief that Davy died swingin' ol' Betsy at the Alamo. But this is not actually seen. The picture fades as Davy swings, so who is to say he was not taken prisoner?

John Wayne's 1960 epic was also fiction woven through fact, and portrayed Davy impaled on the church doors. Disney (Touchstone) tried again in 2004 with a more factual version, but once again, where history became inconvenient, it was rewritten to suit the required image. Santa Anna was portrayed as a unattractive, grinning buffoon rather than a handsome man who could exude charm when required. The television series *Texas Rising* gave a fairer rendition of Santa Anna's person, despite fiction being woven through fact once more.

But what of that other fort taken in 1813. By comparison, there have been precious few words written about Fort Mims, and not a single feature film made. A flaming, animated arrow destroying an illustrated fort in Disney's Crockett is the only Hollywood depiction. Today a reconstructed blockhouse and picket wall represent the long gone Fort Mims, the rural countryside isolated enough to avoid the urban obliteration suffered by most of the Alamo site.

Daniel Beasley and William Travis were both among the first to die. But the incompetent Beasley whipped a well-meaning slave while leaving the fort gates wide open. A hideous massacre of women and children occurred; best ignored, best forgotten.

But from all accounts there were those at Fort Mims who fought just as valiantly as the men of the Alamo; people like Captain Dixon Bailey, his company on the north wall, and the lone, unnamed defender of the blockhouse. From both forts there were those who fled once the battle was lost. Combatants survived Fort Mims while no soldier survived the Alamo—some say. But it was simply impossible for Sesma's 375 dragoons to seal off the countryside on all sides. A week prior to news being heard of the Alamo's fall, The *Arkansas Gazette* carried a story of two men, one wounded, arriving in Nacogdoches, "who said San Antonio had been retaken by the Mexicans, the garrison put to the sword—that if any others escaped the general massacre besides themselves, they were not aware of it."[22] Possible contenders were Henry Warnell and William Cannon, who later claimed to have escaped. But as with much else to do with the Alamo, doubt has been placed on their accounts.[23]

It has been said by some that the Alamo was a useless sacrifice; San Antonio of no real strategic importance. But it did delay Santa Anna's advance for at least 13 days while independence was declared; something solid to fight for. Sam Houston put out a call for volunteers, and they gathered at Gonzales under James Neill while the Alamo held Santa Anna at bay. They would be the core of Houston's army, the men who would crush Santa Anna and win independence for Texas. And there is more to winning wars than logistics and strategy. It also takes morale and a will to fight.

José de la Peña recalled,

> The cry *Remember the Alamo!* that the enemy shouted as he delivered his death blows served to increase his fury during that terrible moment, to make the conflict more bitter for our men, and to avenge twice over their comrades who had fallen at the place of that name.

It could well be argued that the Texas Revolution was won at the Alamo.

In the same sense, it could be argued that the Battle of New Orleans was won at Fort Mims. The Creek War brought about the concentration of veterans needed to win the battle, and brought Jackson's leadership to light. Without this victory, would Old Hickory have taken Florida, become president of the United States and would Sam Houston have achieved his place in the world without the famous general's patronage? Another Texan commander may well have fought Santa Anna's full force too early. With the battle lost, Texas could still be part of Mexico today.

The Alamo, now a World Heritage Site, is well remembered. But perhaps Fort Mims should be remembered also.

Chapter Notes

Prologue

1. Meek, *The Red Eagle*, 22.
2. Notes furnished to A. J. Pickett by Patrick May, July 16, 1847.
3. *Ibid.*
4. A. J. Pickett interview with Dr. Holmes, June 3, 1847.
5. Claiborne, *Life and Times of General Samuel Dale*, 74.
6. Pickett, *History of Alabama*, Chapter 36 (online).
7. Claiborne, *Life and Times of General Samuel Dale*, 79–80.
8. Halbert and Ball, *Creek War of 1813 and 1814*, 141.

Chapter 1

1. Encyclopedia of Alabama (online).
2. Halbert and Ball, *Creek War of 1813 and 1814*, 69.
3. Blaisdell, *Great Speeches by Native Americans*, 58.
4. Miller, *The Taking of Lands in the Southeast*, 107.
5. Owsley, *Struggle for the Gulf Borderlands*, 13.
6. Thrapp, *Encyclopedia of Frontier Biography*, 1284.
7. Owsley, *Struggle for the Gulf Borderlands*, 188.
8. Kanon, *Tennesseans at War, 1812–1815*, 61.
9. Waselkov, *A Conquering Spirit*, 89.
10. *Ibid.*, 102.
11. *Ibid.*, 20.
12. Listed in a compensation claim to the U.S. Congress in 1815, Lackey, *Frontier Claims*, 31.
13. Waselkov, *A Conquering Spirit*, 120.
14. Pickett, *History of Alabama*, Chapter 37 (online).
15. Dr. T. H. Holmes Notes, Pickett Papers (online).
16. Waselkov, *A Conquering Spirit*, 229–231.
17. Notes furnished to A. J. Picket by Patrick May, July 16, 1847 (online).
18. Waselkov, *A Conquering Spirit*, 109.
19. Fowler, *Santa Anna of Mexico*, 28–29.
20. Encyclopedia of Alabama (Online).
21. J. D. Dreisbach to Lymann Draper, July 1874. Vol. 1 Series V, Georgia, Alabama and South Carolina Papers.
22. Owsley, *Struggle for the Gulf Borderlands*, 33.
23. Waselkov, *A Conquering Spirit*, 93–94.

24. Woodward's reminiscences of the Creek or Muscogee Indians (online).
25. Claiborne, *Life and Times of General Samuel Dale*, 128–129.

Chapter 2

1. Halbert and Ball, *Creek War of 1813 and 1814*, 184.
2. Owsley, *Struggle for the Gulf Borderlands*, 14.
3. Pickett, *History of Alabama*, Chapter 37 (online).
4. Stiggins, *Creek Indian History*, 108.
5. Waselkov, *A Conquering Spirit*, 114.
6. *Ibid.*, 124.
7. *Ibid.*, 190.
8. Halbert and Ball, *Creek War of 1813 and 1814*, 153.
9. *Ibid.*, 174.
10. Dr. T. H. Holmes Notes, Pickett Papers.
11. *Ibid.*
12. Draper Manuscripts, Vol. 1 Series V Georgia, Alabama and South Carolina Papers.
13. Meek, *The Red Eagle*, 47.
14. Meek, *Romantic Passages in Southwestern History*, 254.
15. *The Evening Post*, (New York) October 14, 1813.
16. Dr. T. H. Holmes Notes, Pickett Papers.
17. Pickett, *History of Alabama*, Chapter 37 (online).
18. Halbert and Ball, *Creek War of 1813 and 1814*, 158–159.

Chapter 3

1. Greenblatt, *War of 1812*, 118.
2. *Tennessee Gazette*, Oct. 3, 1804.
3. Halbert and Ball, *Creek War of 1813 and 1814*, 184–199.
4. *Ibid.*, 202–203.
5. Claiborne, *Life and Times of General Samuel Dale*, 118.
6. Waselkov, *A Conquering Spirit*, 192.
7. *Ibid.*, 149–150.
8. *Ibid.*, 152.
9. Crockett, *Narrative*, 87–88.
10. *Ibid.*, 88.

Chapter 4

1. Crockett, *Narrative*, 92–93.
2. Claiborne, *Life and Times of General Samuel Dale*, 127.

3. Meek, *The Red Eagle*, 59.
4. Halbert and Ball, *Creek War of 1813 and 1814*, 233–234.
5. Owsley, *Struggle for the Gulf Borderlands*, 69.
6. Patterson, *The Generals*, 110.
7. Kanon, *Tennesseans at War*, 91.
8. *Ibid.*, 93.
9. Halbert and Ball, *Creek War of 1813 and 1814*, 274.
10. *American Historical Magazine*, July 1901, Court-Martial Proceedings, 258–259.
11. Owsley, *Struggle for the Gulf Borderlands*, 76.
12. Letter from Doherty to Jackson from "Four Spring Camp," March 2, 1814.
13. *American Historical Magazine*, July 1901, Court-Martial Proceedings, 258.
14. Brand, *Andrew Jackson*, 214–215.

Chapter 5

1. Brand, *Andrew Jackson*, 215.
2. Kanon, *Tennesseans at War*, 101.
3. O'Brien, *In Bitterness and in Tears*, 149.
4. Brand, *Andrew Jackson*, 292.
5. *Ibid.*, 220.
6. Owsley, *Struggle for the Gulf Borderlands*, 56.
7. Meek, *The Red Eagle*, 88.
8. *Ibid.*, 48.
9. Waselkov, *A Conquering Spirit*, 171.
10. Buell, *History of Andrew Jackson*, 335–336.
11. Waselkov, *A Conquering Spirit*, 174–175.
12. Claiborne, *Life and Times of General Samuel Dale*, 129.
13. Owsley, *Struggle for the Gulf Borderlands*, 86–87.
14. Brand, *Andrew Jackson*, 233.
15. *Ibid.*, 234.
16. Owsley, *Struggle for the Gulf Borderlands*, 181.

Chapter 6

1. *Washington Globe*, Nov. 30, 1838 2.
2. Letter from Percy to Vice Admiral Cochrane Sept. 16, 1814.
3. Andrew Jackson Papers 111.
4. Owsley, *Struggle for the Gulf Borderlands*, 93–94.
5. Wallis, *David Crockett; the Lion of the West*, 130–131.
6. Crockett, *David Crockett Narrative*, 101.
7. Crockett, *Ibid.*, 104–106.
8. Brand, *Andrew Jackson*, 244.
9. *Ibid.*, 245.
10. Owsley, *Struggle for the Gulf Borderlands*, 118.
11. Brand, *Andrew Jackson*, 266.
12. Owsley, *Struggle for the Gulf Borderlands*, 174.
13. Crockett, *Narrative*, 107.
14. *Ibid.*, 109–110.
15. *Ibid.*, 115–116.
16. *Ibid.*, 122.
17. *Ibid.*, 123.

Chapter 7

1. Heidler, *Encyclopedia of the War of 1812*, 190.
2. Brand, *Andrew Jackson*, 259–260.
3. *Ibid.*, 142–143.

4. Brand, *Andrew Jackson*, 268.
5. Owsley, *Struggle for the Gulf Borderlands*, 131.
6. Latour, *Historical Memoir of the War*, 132.
7. *Ibid.*, 134.
8. *Ibid.*
9. Nolte, *Fifty Years in Both Hemispheres*, 219.
10. Owsley, *Struggle for the Gulf Borderlands*, 170.
11. James, *A Collection of the Charges and Sentences of Courts Martial*, 691.
12. Ward, *Andrew Jackson, Symbol for an Age*, clxv.
13. Latour, *Historical Memoir of the War*, 154–155.
14. Gleig, *The Campaigns of the Army at Washington and New Orleans 1814–1815*.
15. Owsley, *Struggle for the Gulf Borderlands*, 162.

Chapter 8

1. Haley, *Sam Houston*, p.15.
2. *Cherokee Advocate*, May 11, 1878, p.1.
3. Texas State Historical Society biography online.
4. Haley, *Sam Houston*, 9.
5. *Ibid.*, 12.
6. *Cherokee Advocate*, May 11, 1878, p.1.
7. Tegawa, *Sam Houston's Republic*, 44.
8. Lester, *Life of Sam Houston*, 27.
9. Letter, March 1, 1815, A. J. Houston Collection, Texas State Library.
10. Letter, May 31, 1817, Penny Thornall Remick Collection, Houston Research Center.
11. Haley, *Sam Houston*, 21.
12. James, *The Raven*, 42.
13. General Orders, March 1, 1818, Penny Thornall Remick Collection, Houston Research Center.

Chapter 9

1. *Memoirs of Andrew Jackson*, 315.
2. Brands, *Andrew Jackson*, 290.
3. *Niles Weekly Register*, April 29, 1815.
4. Nolte, *Fifty Years in Both Hemispheres*, 238–239.
5. Brands, *Andrew Jackson*, 308.
6. *Ibid.*, 298–299.
7. Remini, *Andrew Jackson*, 128.
8. Warshauer, *Andrew Jackson and the Politics of Martial Law*, 42.
9. Brands, *Andrew Jackson*, 305.
10. Wasserman, *A People's History of Florida*, 112.
11. Brands, *Andrew Jackson*, 311.
12. Fort Scott—ExploreSouthernHistory.com.
13. Owsley, *Struggle for the Gulf Borderlands*, 184.
14. *Army and Navy Chronicle*, Vol. 2, Jan. 1 to July 30, 1836, 115.
15. McReynolds, *The Seminoles*, 77.
16. *Army and Navy Chronicle*, Vol. 2, Jan. 1 to July 30, 1836, 115–116.
17. McReynolds, *The Seminoles*, 78.

Chapter 10

1. Crockett, *Narrative*, 125.
2. Wallis, *David Crockett, Lion of the West*, 132.
3. Thompson, *Born on a Mountaintop*, 228–235.
4. Crockett, *Narrative*, 127.
5. Chrzan, *Alcohol: Social Drinking in Cultural Context*, 38.

6. Shackford, *David Crockett, the Man and the Legend*, 34.
7. Crockett, *Narrative*, 81–82.
8. *Ibid.*, 127–128.
9. Wallis, *David Crockett, Lion of the West*, 140.
10. Crockett, *Narrative*, 132.
11. Shackford, *David Crockett, the Man and the Legend*, 37.
12. Jones, *Crockett Cousins*, 23.
13. Wallis, *David Crockett, Lion of the West*, 145–147.
14. Crockett, *Narrative*, 132–133.
15. Wallis, *David Crockett, Lion of the West*, 148.
16. York, *Sergeant York, His Own Life Story and War Diary*, March 1918 entry.
17. Wallis, *David Crockett, Lion of the West*, 152.
18. Shackford, *David Crockett, the Man and the Legend*, 38.
19. Crockett, *Narrative*, 137.
20. Wallis, *David Crockett, Lion of the West*, 156.

Chapter 11

1. *Dictionary of American Biography*, 145–146.
2. Letter, McMinn to Houston, April 22, May 1, 1818, Houston Papers, Catholic Archives of Texas.
3. Letter, McMinn to Houston, June 13, 1818, Houston Papers, Catholic Archives of Texas.
4. Haley, *Sam Houston*, 31.
5. *Tennessee Historical Quarterly*, V (1946) 286.
6. Haley, *Sam Houston*, 34.
7. *Ibid.*, 36.
8. Crane, *Life and Select Literary Remains of Sam Houston*, 250.
9. "Audited Expense Account" April 29, 1824, Houston Papers, Catholic Archives of Texas.
10. Letter from Houston to Worth, Jan. 24, 1826, Barker and Worth, *Writings of Sam Houston*.
11. James, *The Raven*, 56.
12. Letter by White written on Dec. 21, 1826, Nashville History online, story by Debie Cox.
13. *Ibid.*
14. *Niles Register*, Aug. 18, 1827, 412.
15. Haley, *Sam Houston*, 46.
16. *Niles Register*, Nov. 10, 1827, 164.

Chapter 12

1. American State Papers, Class V, Military Affairs Vol. 1 723.
2. The Battle of Fowltown, ExporeSouthernHistory.com.
3. Wasserman, *A Peoples History of Florida*, 179.
4. The Scott Massacre of 1817, ExporeSouthernHistory.com.
5. *Niles Register*, March 27, 1819, 91.
6. *Ibid.*
7. *Niles Register*, December 19, 1818 507.
8. Montgomery, *Georgians in Profile*, 124.
9. *The National Register*, No. 16. Vol. V, 1818, 254.
10. Brands, *Andrew Jackson*, 328.
11. Moser, Hoth, Hoemann, *The Papers of Andrew Jackson*, Vol. 1V, 190.
12. British and Foreign State Papers, 1818–1819, Vol. V1, 410–411.
13. *Ibid.*, 414.

14. History of Fort St. Marks, ExporeSouthernHistory.com.
15. Milly Francis—The Creek Pocahontas, ExporeSouthernHistory.com.
16. *Niles Register*, May 9, 1818 192.
17. Moser, Hoth, Hoemann, *The Papers of Andrew Jackson*, Vol. 1V, 192.
18. Tucker, *Encyclopedia of the War of 1812*, 460.
19. *Civil and Military History of Andrew Jackson*, 350.
20. Waldrep, *Lynching in America*, 44.

Chapter 13

1. Moser, Hoth, Hoemann, *The Papers of Andrew Jackson*, Vol. 1V, 202.
2. *Ibid.*, 213.
3. Brands, *Andrew Jackson*, 348.
4. Moser, Hoth, Hoemann, *The Papers of Andrew Jackson*, Vol. 1V, 79–81.
5. Holloway, *The Ladies of the White House*, 292.
6. American State Papers, Class V, Military Affairs Vol. 1 806.
7. Brands, *Andrew Jackson*, 360.
8. Moser, Hoth, Hoemann, *The Papers of Andrew Jackson*, Vol. V, 100.
9. British and Foreign State Papers, 1821–1822, 326.
10. Brands, *Andrew Jackson*, 364.
11. Moser, Hoth, Hoemann, *The Papers of Andrew Jackson*, Vol. V, 170.
12. Moser, Clift, *The Papers of Andrew Jackson*, Vol. V1, 386–387.
13. Brands, *Lone Star Nation*, 131.
14. Brands, *Andrew Jackson*, 378.

Chapter 14

1. George, *History of Tennessee; From Earliest Discoveries to 1894*, 60–61.
2. *Ibid.*, 61.
3. Levy, *American Legend*, 73.
4. Downing, *Tennessee Encyclopedia of History and Culture* (online).
5. Crockett, *Narrative*, 138.
6. *Ibid.*, 139.
7. *Ibid.*, 141–142.
8. Wallis, *David Crockett*, 162.
9. *Sketches and Eccentricities of Col. David Crockett*, 57–59.
10. Crockett, *Narrative*, 139.
11. *Ibid.*, 145.
12. Wallis, *David Crockett*, 168.
13. Smith, *The Land Holdings of Col. David Crockett in West Tennessee*, 11.
14. Thompson, *Born on a Mountaintop*, 96.
15. Wallis, *David Crockett*, 170.
16. Crockett, *Narrative*, 147.
17. *Ibid.*, 153.
18. *Ibid.*, 154.
19. Shackford, *David Crockett*, 57–58.
20. *National Banner and Nashville Whig*, Aug. 14, 1822.
21. Crockett, *Narrative*, 155.
22. *Ibid.*, 168–169.
23. Shackford, *David Crockett*, 64.

24. Crockett, *Narrative*, 172.
25. Wallis, *David Crockett*, 188–189.
26. Crockett, *Narrative*, 173.

Chapter 15

1. Goodwin, *The Biography of Andrew Jackson*, 288.
2. Mosser, Clifft, *The Papers of Andrew Jackson*, Vol. VI, 1825–1828, 72.
3. Brands, *Andrew Jackson*, 390.
4. Mosser, Clifft, *The Papers of Andrew Jackson*, Vol. VI, 1825–1828, 269–270.
5. Pope, *Hidden History of Alexandria, D.C.* 70.
6. Smith, Owsley, *Papers of Andrew Jackson*, 169–170.
7. Brands, *Andrew Jackson*, 398.
8. Brady, *The True Andrew Jackson*, 298.
9. Danielson, *The Color of Politics*, 37.
10. Smith, *Religion in the Oval Office*, 139.
11. Mosser, Clifft, *The Papers of Andrew Jackson*, Vol. VI, 1825–1828, 343–344.
12. Brands, *Andrew Jackson*, 401.
13. *Ibid.*, 405.
14. Meacham, *American Lion*, 4.
15. Reynolds, *America, Empire of Liberty*, 176.

Chapter 16

1. *The Southwestern Historical Quarterly*, Vol. 94, July 1990, 10.
2. Haley, *Sam Houston*, 48–49.
3. Letter, Nov. 10, 1828, Records of the Governor, Texas State Library and Archives.
4. Correspondence of John Hartwell Marable (1786–1844) (Online).
5. Williams, *Sam Houston*, 63.
6. James, *The Raven*, 138–139.
7. Hayens, *The Life and Writings of Rufus C. Burleson*, 584.
8. Haley, *Sam Houston*, 51.
9. The Southwestern Historical Quarterly, Vol. 94, July 1990—April 1991, 14.
10. Williams, *Sam Houston*, 66–67.
11. The Southwestern Historical Quarterly, Vol. 94, July 1990—April 1991, 16.
12. Shackford, *David Crockett*, 125.
13. Hayens, *The Life and Writings of Rufus C. Burleson*, 552.
14. Feller, Moser, Moss, Coens, *The Papers of Andrew Jackson*, Vol. VI1, 1829, 212–213.
15. Haley, *Sam Houston*, 65.

Chapter 17

1. Crockett, *Narrative*, 196.
2. Heiskell, *Andrew Jackson and Early Tennessee History*, 456.
3. De Costa-Willis, *Notable Black Memphians*, 352.
4. Crockett, *Narrative*, 200.
5. Groneman, *David Crockett: Hero of the Common Man*, 104.
6. Wallis, *David Crockett*, 200.
7. *Austin Weekly Statesman*, March 5, 1891.

8. Hargreaves, Hopkins, *The Papers of Henry Clay*, Vol. 6, 1827 1098.
9. Groneman, *David Crockett: Hero of the Common Man*, 103.
10. Wallis, *David Crockett*, 203.
11. *North Carolina Historical Review* 313.
12. Thompson, *Born on a Mountaintop*, 333.
13. *The Adams Sentinel*, Dec. 17, 1828.
14. Wallis, *David Crockett*, 212.
15. Bradle, *Goliad; the Other Alamo*, 95.
16. Shackford, *David Crockett*, 118–119.
17. Jackson's Second Annual Message to Congress, Dec. 6, 1830.
18. Crockett, *Narrative*, 206–207.
19. Wallis, *David Crockett*, 225–226.

Chapter 18

1. Haley, *Sam Houston*, 67.
2. Feller, Moser, Moss, Coens, *The Papers of Andrew Jackson*, Vol. VI1, 1829, 240.
3. Irving, *A Tour on the Prairies*, 11.
4. Gregory, Strickland, *Sam Houston with the Cherokees, 1829–1833*, 65.
5. *Ibid.*, 67.
6. Feller, Moser, Moss, Coens, *The Papers of Andrew Jackson*, Vol. VI1, 1829, 193.
7. *Muskogee Daily Phoenix*, Feb. 7, 1932.
8. Gregory, Strickland, *Sam Houston with the Cherokees, 1829–1833*, 76.
9. Brands, *Andrew Jackson*, 423–424.
10. *American Historical Review*, Vol. 12 No. 4 (July 1907) 788–790.
11. *Cherokee Phoenix*, March 4, 1830, 3.
12. Haley, *Sam Houston*, 79.
13. *Ibid.*, 73.
14. Gregory, Strickland, *Sam Houston with the Cherokees, 1829–1833*, 77–76.
15. Haley, *Sam Houston*, 79.
16. Gregory, Strickland, *Sam Houston with the Cherokees, 1829–1833*, 64.
17. *Niles Register*, Vol. 40, page 464.

Chapter 19

1. Aderman, Kime, *Advocate for America: the Life of James Kirke Paulding*, p.137.
2. Wallis, *David Crockett*, 234.
3. Perley, *Perley's Reminiscences*, 181.
4. Shackford, *David Crockett*, 258–265.
5. Thompson, *The Alamo: A Cultural History*, 120.
6. Crockett, *Narrative*, 210.
7. *Niles Register*, Sept. 7, 1833, 20.
8. Thompson, *Born on a Mountaintop*, 150.
9. Wallis, *David Crockett*, 258.
10. Shackford, *David Crockett*, 148.
11. Wallis, *David Crockett*, 250.
12. Shackford, *David Crockett*, 308.
13. Encyclopedia of Alabama (online).
14. *Working Man's Advocate*, May 3, 1834.
15. Davis, *Three Roads to the Alamo*, 391.
16. Briscoe Center for American History, University of Texas (online).
17. Wallis, *David Crockett*, 270.
18. Crockett, *An Account of Col. Crockett's Tour*, 64.

19. Thompson, *Born on a Mountaintop*, 151.
20. Brands, *Lone Star Nation*, 328.
21. Davis, *A Legend at Full Length*, 165.
22. Wallis, *David Crockett*, 266.

Chapter 20

1. *Niles Register*, April 28, 1832 172.
2. Haley, *Sam Houston*, 82.
3. Wallis, *David Crockett*, 254.
4. Brands, *Lone Star Nation*, 199.
5. Haley, *Sam Houston*, 86.
6. Brands, *Lone Star Nation*, 202.
7. Haley, *Sam Houston*, 90.
8. Williams, Barker, *Writings of Sam Houston*, 271.
9. Gregory, *Sam Houston with the Cherokees*, 67.
10. Star of the Republic Museum, Vol. 1V, No. 3 (online).
11. *The Alamo Official Commemorative Guide*, 12.
12. Hatch, *Encyclopedia of the Alamo*, 46.
13. Thompson, *Born on a Mountaintop*, 166.
14. Donovan, *Blood of Heroes*, 13.
15. Haley, *Sam Houston*, 92.
16. Hatch, *Encyclopedia of the Alamo*, 53.
17. Davis, *Three Roads to the Alamo*, 214.
18. Hatch, *Encyclopedia of the Alamo*, 56.
19. Haley, *Sam Houston*, 93.
20. Bruce, *Life of General Houston*, 81–83.
21. Davis, *Three Roads to the Alamo*, 272.
22. Texas State Historical Association—Irion, Anna W. Raguet (online).
23. Haley, *Sam Houston*, 101.

Chapter 21

1. Jones, *In the Footsteps of Davy Crockett*, 93.
2. Shackford, *David Crockett*, 167.
3. Brands, Andrew Jackson, 503.
4. Oliver/Marion, *Killing the President*, 9.
5. Wallis, *David Crockett*, 272.
6. Groneman, *Crockett, Hero of the Common Man*, 130.
7. Jones, *In the Footsteps of Davy Crockett*. 168.
8. Shackford, *David Crockett*, 173–174.
9. Davis, *Three Roads to the Alamo*, 404.
10. *Ibid.*, 405.
11. Wallis, *David Crockett*, 275.
12. Bouffard, *Defiance, a Saga of David Crockett and the Alamo*, 107–108.
13. Daughters of the Republic of Texas Library the Alamo.

Chapter 22

1. Jackson, White, *Joe, the Slave Who Became an Alamo Legend*, 102.
2. Donovan, *Blood of Heroes*, 14.
3. Davis, *Three Roads to the Alamo*, 262.
4. Baugh, *Rendezvous at the Alamo*, 152–153.
5. Davis, *Three Roads to the Alamo*, 267.
6. Texas State Historical Association (online).
7. Davis, *Three Roads to the Alamo*, 272.
8. Hansen, *The Alamo Reader*, 84.

Chapter 23

1. Haley, *Sam Houston*, 104.
2. Williams, *Sam Houston* 118.
3. Davis, *Lone Star Rising*, 125–126.
4. Edmundson, *The Alamo Story*, 204.
5. Roberts, Olson, *A Line in the Sand*, 41.
6. Haley, *Sam Houston*, 107.
7. Davis, *Three Roads to the Alamo*, 459.
8. *Niles Register*, Oct. 31, 1835, 144.
9. Tagawa, *Sam Houston's Republic* 112.
10. Haley, *Sam Houston*, 112.
11. Fehrenbach, *Lone Star*, 66.
12. Haley, *Sam Houston*, 113.
13. *Ibid.*, 114.
14. Smithwick, *Evolution of a State*, 80.
15. Davis, *Three Roads to the Alamo*, 443.

Chapter 24

1. De Costa-Willis, *Notable Black Memphians*, 352.
2. Wallis, *David Crockett*, 283.
3. Herndon, *The High Lights of Arkansas History*, 65.
4. Wallis, *David Crockett*, 284.
5. Olson, *A Line in the Sand*, 92.
6. Shackford, *David Crockett*, 214.
7. *Ibid.*, 215.
8. Wallis, *David Crockett*, 285.
9. Shackford, *David Crockett*, 215.
10. Newton, *Chemistry of Space*, 173.
11. Davis, *Three Roads to the Alamo*, 472.
12. Barker, *Life of Stephen F. Austin* p.486.
13. Haley, *Sam Houston*, 117.
14. Starr, *History of the Cherokee Indians*, 201.
15. Haley, *Sam Houston*, 116.
16. Muster at Gonzales & Battle of Bexar (online).
17. Pension Application of Joseph Lopez, Texas State Library and Archives (online).
18. Hatch, *Encyclopedia of the Alamo*, 14.
19. Donovan, *Blood of Heroes*, 74.
20. Bradle, *Goliad, the Other Alamo*, 63.
21. Donovan, *Blood of Heroes*, 80.
22. Pension Application of Joseph Lopez, Texas State Library and Archives (online).
23. Texas State Historical Association (online).
24. Muster at Gonzales and Battle of Bexar (online).
25. Pension Application of Joseph Lopez, Texas State Library and Archives (online).
26. Donovan, *Blood of Heroes*, 86.
27. Hardin, *J.C. Neill, the Forgotten Alamo Commander* (online).
28. Brooks, *A Complete History of the Mexican War*, 32.
29. Siege of Bexar, Texas State Historical Association (online).

Chapter 25

1. Wallis, *David Crockett*, 289–290.
2. Star of the Republic Museum, Vol. 1V, No. 3 (online).
3. Shackford, *David Crockett*, 220.
4. Haley, *Sam Houston*, 118.

5. Chariton, *Exploring Alamo Legends*, 157.
6. Von Clausewitz, *On War*, 286.
7. Haley, *Sam Houston*, 120.
8. Wallis, *David Crockett*, 292–293.
9. Davis, *Three Roads to the Alamo*, 414.
10. Texas State Historical Association (online).
11. *Ibid.*
12. Edmondson, *The Alamo Story*, 253–254.
13. Haley, *Sam Houston*, 121.
14. Shackford, *David Crockett*, 220.
15. Bradle, *Goliad: The Other Alamo*, 138.
16. Wallis, *David Crockett*, 295.
17. Donovan, *The Blood of Heroes*, 165.

Chapter 26

1. Ford, *Origin and Fall of the Alamo*, 26–27.
2. Memoir of José A. Menchaca, *Eyewitness to the Alamo*, 167.
3. Williams, *The Alamo Defenders*, 36.
4. Hansen, *The Alamo Reader*, 728.
5. Lord, *A Time to Stand*, 79.
6. Hansen, *The Alamo Reader*, 675.
7. *Ibid.*, 570.
8. *The Fall of the Alamo*, the account of Dr. John Sutherland (online).
9. *Southwestern Historical Quarterly*, Vol. 36, July 1932—April 1933, 277.
10. Bradle, *Goliad: The Other Alamo*, 91.
11. Memoir of José A. Menchaca, *Eyewitness to the Alamo*, 168.
12. *Ibid.*, 168.
13. Baugh, *Rendezvous at the Alamo*, 195.
14. *Southwestern Historical Quarterly*, Vol. 36, July 1932—April 1933, 284.
15. Hansen, *The Alamo Reader*, 675.
16. Hatch, *Encyclopedia of the Alamo* 82.
17. Donovan, *Blood of Heroes*, 184.
18. *Patriot Ancestor Album, Daughters of the Republic of Texas*, 123.
19. Tucker, *Exodus from the Alamo*, 142.
20. *The Fall of the Alamo*, the account of Dr. John Sutherland (online).
21. Hatch, *Encyclopedia of the Alamo* 39.
22. Sutherland's account, 5—*Battle of the Alamo—Individual Accounts* (online).
23. Hatch, *Encyclopedia of the Alamo* 52–53.
24. Journal of Dr. Joseph H. Barnard (online).
25. Chariton, *Exploring the Alamo Legends*, 138.
26. *The Fall of the Alamo*, the account of Dr. John Sutherland (online).

Chapter 27

1. *The Fall of the Alamo*, the account of Dr. John Sutherland (online).
2. Texas State Historical Association (online).
3. *The Fall of the Alamo*, the account of Dr. John Sutherland (online).
4. Lord, *A Time to Stand*, 96.
5. William Barret Travis Alamo letters (online).
6. Texas State Historical Association (online).
7. Potter, *The Fall of the Alamo*, 1860 pamphlet.
8. Dimmit to Kerr letter, *Eyewitness to the Alamo*, 10.
9. Hansen, *The Alamo Reader*, 55.

10. Hatch, *Encyclopedia of the Alamo*, 19.
11. William Barret Travis—Alamo Letters (online).
12. Almonte Journal, *Eye Witness to the Alamo*, 29.
13. Donovan, *The Blood of Heroes*, 197.
14. de la Peña, *With Santa Anna in Texas*, 69.
15. Lord, *A Time to Stand*, 65.
16. de la Peña, *With Santa Anna in Texas*, 40.
17. Olson, *A Line in the Sand*, 85.
18. de la Peña, *With Santa Anna in Texas*, 36.
19. Olson, *A Line in the Sand*, 85.
20. de la Peña, *With Santa Anna in Texas*, 38.
21. Potter, *The Fall of the Alamo*, 1860 pamphlet.
22. Groneman, *Eyewitness to the Alamo*, 3.
23. Donovan, *The Blood of Heroes*, 202.
24. Santa Anna's report of Feb. 27, 1836.
25. Unidentified Mex. soldier, *The Alamo Reader*, 231–232.
26. Potter, *The Fall of the Alamo*, 1860 pamphlet.
27. Testimony of Eulalia Yorba, *Eyewitness to the Alamo*, 132–133.

Chapter 28

1. Travis dispatch, Feb. 24, 1836 (online).
2. Donovan, *The Blood of Heroes*, 208.
3. Haley, *Sam Houston*, 112.
4. Story of Juana Alsbury, *Eyewitness to the Alamo*, 90.
5. Lord, *A Time to Stand*, 14.
6. de la Peña, *With Santa Anna in Texas*, 41.
7. Lindley, Notes from an 1844 interview, *Alamo Traces*, 103.
8. Donovan, *The Blood of Heroes*, 255.
9. Lindley, *Alamo Traces*, 14.
10. Haley, *Sam Houston*, 122–123.
11. Davis, *Three Roads to the Alamo*, 547–548.
12. Haley, *Sam Houston*, 123.
13. Hansen, *The Alamo Reader* 511–512.
14. Ramon Caro pamphlet, *Eyewitness to the Alamo*, 56.
15. Edwards, Eric W. *The Baker Rifle*, Pitt River Museum (online).
16. Ramon Caro pamphlet, *Eyewitness to the Alamo*, 56.
17. Santa Anna's report Feb. 27, *Eyewitness to the Alamo*, 8.
18. William Barret Travis—Alamo Letters (online).
19. Donovan, *The Blood of Heroes*, 255.
20. Travis letter to Jesse Grimes, March 3, 1836.
21. Donovan, *The Blood of Heroes*, 219–220.
22. Olson, *A Line in the Sand*, 135–136.
23. Lord, *A Time to Stand*, 114.
24. *Ibid.*, p.133.
25. Santa Anna's report Feb. 27, *Eyewitness to the Alamo*, 9.

Chapter 29

1. Story of Raphael Soldana, *Eyewitness to the Alamo*, 188.
2. Hansen, *The Alamo Reader* 103.
3. Testimony of Susanna Dickinson, *Eyewitness to the Alamo*, 88.
4. Thompson, *Born on a Mountaintop*, 313.
5. Almonte Journal, *Eyewitness to the Alamo*, 31.
6. Travis dispatch, Mar. 3, 1836 (online).

7. *Ibid.*
8. Groneman, *David Crockett: Hero of the Common Man*, 151.
9. de la Peña, *With Santa Anna in Texas*, 42.
10. Santa Anna order to Sesma, *Eyewitness to the Alamo*, 10.
11. Sutherland's account, Hansen, *The Alamo Reader*, 147.
12. Lord, *A Time to Stand*, 128–129.
13. Almonte Journal, *Eyewitness to the Alamo*, 32.
14. Hansen, *The Alamo Reader* 601.
15. Travis dispatch, Mar. 3, 1836 (online).
16. de la Peña, *With Santa Anna in Texas*, 37.
17. *Ibid.*, 68–69.
18. Sánchez journal, *Eyewitness to the Alamo*, 199. As this did not come to light until 1936, some doubt is cast on its authenticity. But as the facts written are brief, appear authentic, and contain nothing controversial, there would seem to be little point in fabrication.
19. Testimony of Fernando Urriza, *Eyewitness to the Alamo*, 78.
20. Donovan, *The Blood of Heroes*, 264.
21. Davis, *Three Roads to the Alamo*, 556.
22. de la Peña, *With Santa Anna in Texas*, 43.
23. Testimony of Mrs. Hannig (Dickinson) *Eyewitness to the Alamo*, 111.
24. Donovan, *The Blood of Heroes*, 270.
25. Santa Anna Memoir, 1837, *Eyewitness to the Alamo*, 54.
26. Filisola account, 1849, *Eyewitness to the Alamo*, 68.
27. Donovan, *The Blood of Heroes*, 441.
28. *Ibid.*, 265–266.
29. Hansen, *The Alamo Reader* 337–338.

Chapter 30

1. Testimony of Joe, *Eyewitness to the Alamo*, 27.
2. Filisola account, 1849, *Ibid.*, 68–69.
3. Testimony of anonymous soldier, *Ibid.*, 22.
4. de la Peña, *With Santa Anna in Texas*, 47.
5. Ramon Caro pamphlet, *Eyewitness to the Alamo*, 57.
6. de la Peña, *With Santa Anna in Texas*, 49.
7. Testimony of Eulalia Yorba, *Eyewitness to the Alamo*, 133.
8. Santa Anna memoir, *Ibid.*, 219.
9. Testimony of Eulalia Yorba, *Ibid.*, 133.
10. Hansen, *The Alamo Reader*, 486.
11. *Ibid.*, 46.
12. de la Peña, *With Santa Anna in Texas*, 49.
13. Filisola account, 1849, *Eyewitness to the Alamo*, 69.
14. Testimony of Ramon Caro, *Ibid.*, 57.
15. de la Peña, *With Santa Anna in Texas*, 51.
16. Testimony of Juana Alsbury, *Ibid.*, 91.
17. Testimony of Susanna Dickinson, *Ibid.*, 97.
18. Testimony of Eulalia Yorba, *Ibid.*, 134.
19. Attributed to Col. Fernando Urriza, *Ibid.*, 78.
20. de la Peña, *With Santa Anna in Texas*, 53.
21. Santa Anna report, *Eyewitness to the Alamo*, 17.
22. Testimony of Francisco Antonio Ruiz, *Ibid.*, 80.
23. Testimony of Eulalia Yorba, *Ibid.*, 135.
24. Account attributed to Joe, *Ibid.*, 28.
25. Ramon Caro, pamphlet, *Ibid.*, 57.

26. Attributed to Ben, *Ibid.*, 61.
27. Beringame, *Abraham Lincoln; A Life*, 324.
28. Santa Anna report, March 6, *Ibid.*, 17.
29. Sesma's report March 11, *Eyewitness to the Alamo*, 229–230.
30. Manuel Lorenca 1878 account, *Eyewitness to the Alamo*, 95.
31. Journal of unidentified Mexican officer, *Ibid.*, 222.
32. Santa Anna Memoir, *Ibid.*, 219.
33. Lord, *A Time to Stand*, 209–210.
34. Deposition of Francisco Esparza, *Eyewitness to the Alamo*, 76.

Chapter 31

1. Donovan, *The Blood of Heroes*, 302.
2. *Ibid.*, 303.
3. Lindley, *Alamo Traces*, 316.
4. Jenkins, *Recollections of Early Texas*, 36–37.
5. Haley, *Sam Houston*, 124.
6. *Southwestern Historical Quarterly*, 1897, 273–274.
7. Hansen, *The Alamo Reader*, 59.
8. Donovan, *The Blood of Heroes*, 307.
9. Bradle, *Goliad, the Other Alamo*, 178.
10. Hatch, *Encyclopedia of the Alamo*, 189.
11. Haley, *Sam Houston*, 126.
12. Hansen, *The Alamo Reader*, 519–520.
13. *Ibid.*, 192.
14. Donovan, *The Blood of Heroes*, 311.
15. Brands, *Lone Star Nation*, 412.
16. Jenkins, *Recollections of Early Texas*, 40.
17. Haley, *Sam Houston*, 127.
18. Donovan, *The Blood of Heroes*, 314.
19. Coleto, Battle of, Texas State Historical Association, (online).
20. Holzinger, Juan José, *Ibid.*
21. Donovan, *The Blood of Heroes*, 317.
22. Goliad Massacre—Diverse Survivor Accounts (online).
23. Donovan, *The Blood of Heroes*, 317.

Chapter 32

1. Journal of Dr. Nicholas Labadie (online).
2. Hardin, *The Alamo 1836*, 67.
3. Haley, *Sam Houston*, 129.
4. Journal of Dr. Nicholas Labadie (online).
5. Haley, *Sam Houston*, 129.
6. Groce's Retreat, Texas State Historical Association (online).
7. Moore, *Eighteen Minutes*, 148.
8. *Niles Register*, May 21, 1836, 208.
9. Brands, *Andrew Jackson*, 521.
10. *Ibid.*, 515.
11. Zuber, *My Eighty Years in Texas*, 71.
12. Hardin, *The Alamo 1836*, 72.
13. Tagawa, *Sam Houston's Republic*, 152.
14. Haley, *Passionate Nation*, 184.
15. Brands, *Andrew Jackson*, 521.
16. Haley, *Sam Houston*, 135.
17. Journal of Dr. Nicholas Labadie (online).
18. Thompson's Ferry, Texas State Historical Association (online).
19. Yellow Stone, *Ibid.*

20. Haley, *Passionate Nation*, 184.
21. Haley, *Sam Houston*, 139.
22. *American Historical Review*, Vol. 12 No. 4, Jul 1907 788–809.
23. Journal of Dr. Nicholas Labadie (online).
24. Winters, *Account of the Battle of San Jacinto* (online).
25. Haley, *Sam Houston*, 141.
26. Journal of Dr. Nicholas Labadie (online).
27. Moore, *Eighteen Minutes*, 242.
28. Journal of Dr. Nicholas Labadie (online).

21. Winters, *An Account of the Battle of San Jacinto* (online).
22. Haley, *Sam Houston*, 153.
23. Huffins, *The Texas War of Independence*, 77.
24. Houston's Report to President Burnet, April 25, 1836.
25. Wharton, *The Republic of Texas, A Brief History*, 165.
26. *Treaties of Velasco*, Sons of de Witt Colony Texas (online).

Chapter 33

1. Journal of Dr. Nicholas Labadie (online).
2. Haley, *Sam Houston*, 145.
3. *Ibid.*, 147.
4. Battle of San Jacinto, Harris County Historical Commission (online).
5. Winters, *An Account of the Battle of San Jacinto* (online).
6. de la Peña, *With Santa Anna in Texas*, p.131.
7. Moore, *Eighteen Minutes*, 247.
8. Maillard, *A History of the Republic of Texas*, 109.
9. Richardson (ed.) *The Texas Almanac for 1860*, 29.
10. Bradle, *Goliad, the Other Alamo*, 237.
11. Maillard, *A History of the Republic of Texas*, 109–110.
12. Haley, *Sam Houston*, 150.
13. de la Peña, *With Santa Anna in Texas*, p.127.
14. Hatch, *Encyclopedia of the Alamo*, 65.
15. Maillard, *A History of the Republic of Texas*, 110.
16. Winters, *An Account of the Battle of San Jacinto* (online).
17. Richardson (ed.) *The Texas Almanac for 1860*, 30.
18. Haley, *Sam Houston*, 151–152.
19. Maillard, *A History of the Republic of Texas*, 110–111.
20. (Archived) Sam's San Jacinto wound Issue Solved (online).

Chapter 34

1. Haley, *Sam Houston*, 160.
2. The *Yellow Stone*, Texas State Historical Association (online).
3. Haley, *Sam Houston*, 163.
4. Fowler, *Santa Anna of Mexico*, 179.
5. *Ibid.*
6. Brands, *Lone Star Nation*, 470.
7. *Captivity of López de Santa Anna*, Sons of de Witt Colony Texas (online).
8. Haley, *Sam Houston*, 164.
9. *Ibid.*, 166.
10. Buchanan, *Life and Adventures of Auburon the Naturalist*, 309.
11. Brands, *Andrew Jackson*, 524–525.
12. *Captivity of López de Santa Anna*, Sons of de Witt Colony Texas (online).
13. Brands, *Andrew Jackson*, 526.
14. Haley, *Sam Houston*, 163.
15. *Captivity of López de Santa Anna*, Sons of de Witt Colony Texas (online).
16. Lubin, Massom, *Polar Remote Sensing*, 15.
17. Hodge/Nolan *U.S. Presidents and Foreign Policy*, 70.
18. Donovan, *The Blood of Heroes*, 336.
19. Morgan, *Lions of the West*, 149.
20. Davis, *Three Roads to the Alamo*, 573.
21. Meek, *The Red Eagle*, 15.
22. Hansen, *The Alamo Reader*, 731.
23. *Ibid.*, 324–325.

Bibliography

Archives and Collections

ALABAMA DEPARTMENT OF ARCHIVES AND HISTORY

The A. B. Meek Manuscript
The Albert J. Pickett Papers
The John Coffee Papers
The Henry S. Halbert Papers

GEORGIA DEPARTMENT OF ARCHIVES

Benjamin Hawkins Papers
Collected letters of Benjamin Hawkins
Creek Treaties 1705–1839
Georgia House Journal
General John Floyd Papers
Georgia Military Affairs, Vol. 3, 1801–13

THE DOLPH BRISCOE CENTER FOR AMERICAN HISTORY, UNIVERSITY OF TEXAS

Don Carlos Barrett Papers
Samuel Erson Asbury Papers
Bexar Archives
Adina Amelia de Zavala Papers
Hassel Family Papers
John Henry Brown Papers
John Salmon Ford Papers
Mary Austin Holley Papers
Walter Lord Archive
Amelia Worthington Williams Papers
Louis Wiltz Kemp Papers

SAN JACINTO MUSEUM OF HISTORY

William Barret Travis Papers
William Physick Zuber Papers
Texas State Library and Archives Commission
Harbert Davenport Collection

Online Sources

American State Papers, Class V, Military Affairs Vol. 1 (memory.ioc.gov/amlaw/wplink.html).
Barnard, Dr. Joseph H., Journal of (www.tamu.edu/faculty/ccbn/dewitt/goliadbanard.htm).
Battle of San Jacinto, Harris County Historical Commission (www.historicalcommission.hctx.net/sanjacbattle.aspx).
Briscoe Center for American History, University of Texas (https://www.cah.utexas.edu/).
British and Foreign State Papers, 1818–1819, Vol. V1 (https://archive.org/details/britishandforei00sonsgoog).
Captivity of López de Santa Anna, Sons of de Witt Colony Texas (www.tamu.edu/faculty/ccbn/dewitt/santaanna4.htm).
Edwards, Eric W. *The Baker Rifle*, Pitt River Museum (england.prm.ox.ac.uk/englishness-baker-rifle.htm).
Encyclopedia of Alabama (www.encyclopediaofalabama.org/).
Goliad Massacre—Diverse Survivor Accounts (www.tamu.edu/faculty/ccbn/dewitt/goliaddiverse.htm).
Hardin, Stephen L. *J. C. Neill, the Forgotten Alamo Commander* (www.tamu.edu/faculty/ccbn/dewitt/adp/history/.../potter/frameset.html).
Labadie, Dr. Nicholas, Journal of—Texas and A&M University (www.tamu.edu/faculty/ccbn/dewitt/sanjacintolabadie.htm).
Marable, John Hartwell, Correspondence of (1786–1844) (www.marable-family.net/jlmarable/jhm-correspondence.html).
Muster at Gonzales & Battle of Bexar—Texas & and A&M University (www.tamu.edu/faculty/ccbn/dewitt/musterbexar.htm).
Pension Application of Joseph López, Texas State Library and Archives (https://www.tsl.texas.gov/treasures/contents.html).
Pickett's History of Alabama (homepages.rootsweb.ancestry.com/~cmamcrk4/pktfm.html).
Potter, R.M. *The Fall of the Alamo* (www.tamu.edu/faculty/ccbn/dewitt/adp/history/.../potter/frameset.html).
Star of the Republic Museum (www.starmuseum.org).
Sutherland, Dr. John, *The Fall of the Alamo* (www.tamu.edu/faculty/ccbn/.../history/.../accounts/sutherland/frameset.htm).
Tennessee Encyclopedia of History and Culture (https://tennesseeencyclopedia.net/).

Texas State Historical Association (https://tsha online.org/handbook/).

Texas State Library and Archives Commission (https://www.tsl.texas.gov/arc/index.html).

Travis, William Barret—Alamo Letters (www. ntanet.net/travis.html).

Treaties of Velasco, Sons of de Witt Colony Texas (www.tamu.edu/faculty/ccbn/dewitt/treatyvel asco.htm).

Winters, *Account of the Battle of San Jacinto (*www. jstor.org/stable/27784928).

Woodward's reminiscences of the Creek or Muscogee Indians (https://archive.org/details/wood wardsreminis00wood).

Newspapers, Magazines and Periodicals

Adams Sentinel
Alamo Official Commemorative Guide
American Historical Magazine
American Historical Review
Arkansas Gazette
Army and Navy Chronicle
Charleston Courier
Cherokee Advocate
Daily National Intelligencer
Houston Daily Post
Missouri Argus
Morning Courier and New York Enquirer
Muskogee Daily Phoenix
National Banner and Nashville Whig
New York Sunday Morning News
New-York Evening Post
Niles Weekly Register
North Carolina Historical Review
San Antonio Daily Express
San Antonio Light
The Southwestern Historical Quarterly
Telegraph and Texas Register
Tennessee Gazette
Tennessee Historical Quarterly
The Texas Almanac for 1860
United States Telegraph
Washington Globe
Working Man's Advocate

Books

Aderman, Ralph M., and Wayne R. Kime. *Advocate for America: the Life of James Kirke Paulding*. Selinsgrove: Susquehanna University Press, 2003.

Barker, Eugene C. *Life of Stephen F. Austin*. Seattle: Mockingbird Books, 2012.

Baugh, Virgil E. *Rendezvous at the Alamo*. Lincoln: University of Nebraska Press, 1985.

Blaisdell, Bob. *Great Speeches by Native Americans.* Mineola: Dover Publications, 2000.

Bouffard, James C. *Defiance: A Saga of David*

Crockett and the Alamo. Raleigh: Lulu.com, 2012.

Bradle, William R. *Goliad; the Other Alamo*. New Orleans: Pelican Publishing, 2013.

Brady, Cyrus T. *The True Andrew Jackson*. Whitefish: Kessinger Publishing, 2005.

Brands, H. W. *Andrew Jackson, His Life and Times*. New York: Random House, 2006.

_____. *Lone Star Nation*. New York: Random House, 2005.

Brooks, Nathan C. *A Complete History of the Mexican War*. Stoughton: Books On Demand, 2013.

Bruce, Henry. *Life of General Houston*. Ulan Press, 2012.

Buell, Augustus C. *History of Andrew Jackson.* Ulan Press, 2012.

Burlingame, Michael. *Abraham Lincoln: A Life*. Baltimore: John Hopkins University Press, 2008.

Chariton, Wallace. *Exploring Alamo Legends*. Boulder: Taylor Trade Publishing, 1992.

Chrzan, Janet. *Alcohol: Social Drinking in Cultural Context*. London: Routledge, 2013.

Claiborne, John F. H. *Life and Times of General Samuel Dale*. Whitefish: Kessinger Publishing, 2008.

Crane, William C. *Life and Select Literary Remains of Sam Houston*. Ulan Press, 2012.

Crockett, David. *A Narrative of the Life of David Crockett*. Lincoln: University of Nebraska Press, 1987.

_____ (purported). *Sketches and Eccentricities of Col. David Crockett*. Charleston: BiblioLife, 2008.

Danielson, Chris. *The Color of Politics: Racism in the American Political Arena Today*. Westport: Praeger Publishing, 2013

Davis, William C. *Three Roads to the Alamo*. New York, HarperCollins, 1998.

De Costa-Willis, Miriam. *Notable Black Memphians*. New York: Cambria Press, 2008.

de la Peña, José E. *With Santa Anna in Texas: a Personal Narrative of the Revolution*. College Station: Texas A & M University Press, 1975.

Dictionary of American Biography. New York, Scribner, 1946.

Donovan, James. *The Blood of Heroes: the 13-Day Struggle for the Alamo—and the Sacrifice That Forged a Nation*. New York: Back Bay Books, 2012.

Edmundson, J. R. *The Alamo Story, from Early History to Current Conflicts*. Boulder: Taylor Trade Publishing, 2000.

Fehrenbach, T. R. *Lone Star: A History of Texas and the Texans*. New York: Open Road Media, 2014.

Fowler, Will. *Santa Anna of Mexico*. Lincoln: Bison Books, 2009.

Free, George. D. *History of Tennessee; From Earliest Discoveries to 1894*. Charleston: Nabu Press, 2010.

Gleig, George R. *The Campaigns of the Army at*

Washington and New Orleans 1814–1815. London: John Murray, 1827.

Goodwin, Philo A. *Biography of Andrew Jackson.* Cincinnati: Tadalique & Co., 2014.

Greenblatt, Miriam. *War of 1812.* New York: Chelsea House Publishing, 2010.

Gregory, J., and R. Strickland. *Sam Houston with the Cherokees, 1829–1833.* Norman: University of Oklahoma Press, 1996.

Groneman, Bill. *Eyewitness to the Alamo.* Lanham: Republic of Texas Press, 2001.

Groneman, William. *David Crockett: Hero of the Common Man.* New York: Forge Books, 2007.

Halbert, H. S. Ball. *Creek War of 1813 and 1814.* Tuskaloosa: University of Alabama Press, 1995.

Haley, James L. *Sam Houston.* Norman: University of Oklahoma Press, 2002.

Hansen, Todd. *The Alamo Reader.* Mechanicsburg: Stackpole Books, 2003.

Hatch, Thom. *Encyclopedia of the Alamo.* Jefferson: McFarland & Co., 1999.

Haynes, Harry. *The Life and Writings of Rufus C. Burleson.* Waco: Georgia Burleson, 1901.

Heidler, Jeanna, and David Heidler. *Encyclopedia of the War of 1812.* Santa Barbara: ABC-CLIO, 1997.

Heiskell, S. G. *Andrew Jackson and Early Tennessee History.* Nashville: Ambrose Printing Co., 1918.

Herndon, Dallas T. *The High Lights of Arkansas History.* Whitefish: Kessinger Publishing, 2007.

Hodge, Carl, and Catthal Nolan. *U.S. Presidents and Foreign Policy, from 1786 to the Present.* Santa Barbara: ABC-CLIO, 2006.

Holloway, Laura C. *The Ladies of the White House.* Charleston: BiblioBazaar, 2009.

Huffines, Alan. *The Texas War of Independence, 1835–36.* Oxford: Osprey Publishing, 2005.

Irving, Washington. *A Tour on the Prairies.* Norman: University of Oklahoma Press, 1985.

Jackson, Andrew. *The Papers of Andrew Jackson. Vol. I, 1770–1803.* Sam B. Smith, and Harriet C. Chappell, eds. Knoxville: University of Tennessee Press, 1980.

_____. *The Papers of Andrew Jackson, Vol. IV, 1816–1820.* Harold D. Moser, ed. Knoxville: University of Tennessee Press, 1994.

_____. *The Papers of Andrew Jackson, Vol. VII, 1829.* Daniel Feller, and Harold D. Moser, and Laura-Eve Moss, and Thomas Coens, eds. Knoxville: University of Tennessee Press, 2009.

Jackson, Ron, and Lee White. *Joe, the Slave Who Became an Alamo Legend.* Norman: University of Oklahoma Press, 2015.

James, Charles. *A Collection of the Charges, Opinions and Sentences of General Courts Martial.* RareBooksClub.com, 2012.

James, Marquis. *The Raven: A Biography of Sam Houston.* Austin: University of Texas Press, 1988.

Jenkins, John H. *Recollections of Early Texas.* Austin: University of Texas Press, 1987.

Jones, Randell. *In the Footsteps of Davy Crockett.* Winston-Salem: John F Blair Publisher, 2006.

Kanon, Tom. *Tennesseans at War, 1812–1815.* Tuskaloosa: University of Alabama Press, 2015.

Lackey, Richard S. *Frontier Claims in the Lower South.* Boston: Polyanthus, 1977.

Latour, A. Lacarriere. *Historical Memoir of the War in West Florida and Louisiana in 1814–1815.* Whitefish: Kessinger Publishing, 2007.

Lester, C. Edwards. *Life of Sam Houston.* Charleston: Nabu Press, 2010.

Levy, Buddy. *American Legend: The Real-Life Adventures of David Crockett.* New York: G. P. Putnam's Sons, 2005.

Lindley, Thomas R. *Alamo Traces: New Evidence and New Conclusions.* Lanham: Republic of Texas Press, 2003.

Lord, Walter. *A Time to Stand: The Epic of the Alamo.* Lincoln: Bison Books, 1961.

Lubin, Robert, and Dan Massom. *Polar Remote Sensing.* Springer Berlin Heidelberg, 2006.

Maillard, N. Doran. *A History of the Republic of Texas.* New York: Gale, Sabin Americana, 2012.

McReynolds, Edwin C. *The Seminoles.* Norman: University of Oklahoma Press, 1957.

Meacham, Jon. *American Lion: Andrew Jackson in the White House.* New York: Random House, 2009

Meek, A. B. *The Red Eagle: A Poem of the South.* Lenox: Hard Press Publishing, 2013.

_____. *Romantic Passages in Southwestern History.* Whitefish: Kessinger Publishing, 2010.

Miller, David W. *The Taking of American Indian Lands in the Southeast.* Jefferson: McFarland & Co., 2011.

Montgomery, Horace. *Georgians in Profile: Historical Essays in Honor of Ellis Merton Coulter.* Athens: University of Georgia Press, 2010.

Moore, Stephen L. *Eighteen Minutes: The Battle of San Jacinto and the Texas Independence Campaign.* Boulder: Taylor Trade Publishing, 2003.

Morgan, Robert. *Lions of the West: Heroes and Villains of the Westward Expansion.* Chapel Hill: Shannon Ravenel Books, 2011.

Newton, David E. *Chemistry of Space.* New York: Facts on File, 2007.

Nolte, Vincente. *Fifty Years in Both Hemispheres.* Leeaf.com Classics, 2013.

O'Brien, Sean. *In Bitterness and in Tears: Andrew Jackson's Destruction of the Creeks and Seminoles.* Santa Barbara: Praeger, 2013.

Oliver, Willard M., and Nancy E. Marion. *Killing the President: Assassinations, Attempts and Rumored Attempts on U.S. Commanders-in-Chief.* Santa Barbara: Praeger, 2010.

Owsley, Frank L. *Struggle for the Gulf Borderlands, the Creek War and the Battle of New Orleans 1812–1815.* Tuscaloosa: University of Alabama Press, 1981.

Patterson, Benton R. *The Generals: Andrew Jackson, Sir Edward Packenham, and the Road to the Battle of New Orleans.* New York: NYU Press, 2005.

Peredes, Anthony, and Judith Knight. *Red Eagle's Children.* Tuscaloosa: University of Alabama Press, 2012.

Peterson, Dorothy B. *Patriot Ancestor Album: Daughters of the Republic of Texas.* Nashville: Turner Publishing, 1995.

Poore, Benjamin P. *Perley's Reminiscences of Sixty Years in the National Metropolis.* Charleston: Nabu Press, 2010.

Pope, Michael M. *Hidden History of Alexandria, D.C.* Stroud: The History Press, 2011.

Remini, Robert V. *Andrew Jackson*, New York: Harper Perennial, 1999.

Reynolds, David. *America, Empire of Liberty: A New History of the United States.* New York: Basic Books, 2011.

Roberts, Randy, and James S. Olsen. *A Line in the Sand: The Alamo in Blood and Memory.* New York: Free Press, 2002.

Shackford, James A. *David Crockett: The Man and the Legend.* Lincoln: University of Nebraska Press, 1994.

Smith, Gary S. *Religion in the Oval Office: The Religious Lives of American Presidents.* Oxford University Press, 2015.

Smithwick, Noah. *Evolution of a State, or Recollections of Old Texas Days.* Austin: University of Texas Press, 1983.

Starr, Emett. *History of the Cherokee Indians.* Clyde: Cherokee Publications, 2009.

Stiggins, George. *Creek Indian History: A Historical Narrative.* Tuskaloosa: University of Alabama Press, 2003.

Tegawa, Lynn B. *Sam Houston's Republic.* Camarillo: Xulon Press, 2012.

Thompson, Bob. *Born on a Mountaintop.* New York: Broadway Books, 2013.

Thompson, Frank. *The Alamo: a Cultural History.* Boulder: Taylor Trade Publishing, 2001.

Thrapp, Dan L. *Encyclopedia of Frontier Biography.* Lincoln: University of Nebraska Press, 1991.

Tucker, Phillip T. *Exodus from the Alamo.* Philadelphia: Casemate, 2010.

Wallis, Michael. *David Crockett: The Lion of the West.* New York, W.W. Norton & Co., 2011.

Ward, John W. *Andrew Jackson: Symbol for an Age.* Oxford University Press, 1962.

Index